D1071429

IMMIGRANT FAMILIES IN CONTEMPORARY SOCIETY

Duke Series in Child Development and Public Policy

Kenneth A. Dodge and Martha Putallaz, *Editors*

Aggression, Antisocial Behavior, and Violence among Girls:
A Developmental Perspective
Martha Putallaz and Karen L. Bierman, Editors

Enhancing Early Attachments:
Theory, Research, Intervention, and Policy
Lisa J. Berlin, Yair Ziv, Lisa Amaya-Jackson, and Mark T. Greenberg, Editors

African American Family Life:
Ecological and Cultural Diversity
Vonnie C. McLoyd, Nancy E. Hill, and Kenneth A. Dodge, Editors

Deviant Peer Influences in Programs for Youth:
Problems and Solutions
Kenneth A. Dodge, Thomas J. Dishion, and Jennifer E. Lansford, Editors

Immigrant Families in Contemporary Society
Jennifer E. Lansford, Kirby Deater-Deckard, and Marc H. Bornstein, Editors

Immigrant Families in Contemporary Society

Edited by

JENNIFER E. LANSFORD
KIRBY DEATER-DECKARD
MARC H. BORNSTEIN

THE GUILFORD PRESS
NEW YORK LONDON

A Division of Guilford Publications, Inc.
72 Spring Street, New York, NY 10012
www.guilford.com

Printed in the United States of America

This book is printed on acid-free paper.

Last digit is print number: 9 8 7 6 5 4 3 2 1

Library of Congress Cataloging-in-Publication Data

Immigrant families in contemporary society / edited by Jennifer E. Lansford, Kirby Deater-Deckard, Marc H. Bornstein.
p. cm. — (Duke series in child development and public policy)
Includes bibliographical references and index.
ISBN-10: 1-59385-403-X ISBN-13: 978-1-59385-403-4 (hardcover)
1. Emigration and immigration. 2. Acculturation. I. Lansford, Jennifer E. II. Deater-Deckard, Kirby D. III. Bornstein, Marc H.
JV6033.I46 2007
304.8—dc22

2006034075

About the Editors

Jennifer E. Lansford, PhD, is Research Scientist at the Duke University Center for Child and Family Policy. Her research focuses on the development of aggression and other behavior problems in youth, with an emphasis on how family and peer contexts contribute to or protect against these outcomes. Dr. Lansford examines how experiences with parents (e.g., discipline, physical abuse, divorce) and peers (e.g., rejection, friendships) affect the development of children's behavior problems, how influence operates in adolescent peer groups, and how cultural contexts moderate links between parents' discipline strategies and children's behavior problems.

Kirby Deater-Deckard, PhD, is Professor and Director of Graduate Programs in the Department of Psychology at the Virginia Polytechnic Institute and State University. In his research, he examines genetic and environmental influences on child and adolescent social-emotional and cognitive development, with particular emphasis on parenting and cultural influences. Dr. Deater-Deckard has written several papers and book chapters in the areas of developmental psychology and child development, as well as coedited *Gene–Environment Processes in Social Behaviors and Relationships* (2003, Haworth Press) and authored *Parenting Stress* (2004, Yale University Press). He is also Joint Editor of the *Journal of Child Psychology and Psychiatry.*

Marc H. Bornstein, PhD, is Senior Investigator and Head of Child and Family Research at the National Institute of Child Health and Human Development. He was a Guggenheim Foundation Fellow and has received awards from the National Institutes of Health and the American Psychological Association, among others. Dr. Bornstein is coauthor of *Development in Infancy,* now in its fifth edition, as well as numerous other volumes. He is Editor Emeritus of *Child Development* and Founding Editor of *Parenting: Science and Practice.*

Contributors

John W. Berry, PhD, Department of Psychology, Queen's University, Kingston, Ontario, Canada

Marc H. Bornstein, PhD, Child and Family Research, National Institute of Child Health and Human Development, National Institutes of Health, Bethesda, Maryland

Robert H. Bradley, PhD, Center for Applied Studies in Education, University of Arkansas, Little Rock, Arkansas

Anthony E. Burgos, MD, Department of Pediatrics, Stanford University School of Medicine, Palo Alto, California

Emily Cansler, BS, Department of Family and Human Development, Arizona State University, Tempe, Arizona

P. Lindsay Chase-Lansdale, PhD, Institute for Policy Research, Northwestern University, Evanston, Illinois

Doriane Lambelet Coleman, JD, Duke University Law School, Durham, North Carolina

Linda R. Cote, PhD, Child and Family Research, National Institute of Child Health and Human Development, National Institutes of Health, Bethesda, Maryland

Ann C. Crouter, PhD, Center for Work and Family Research, Pennsylvania State University, University Park, Pennsylvania

Angela Valdovinos D'Angelo, BA, Institute for Policy Research, Northwestern University, Evanston, Illinois

Kirby Deater-Deckard, PhD, Department of Psychology, Virginia Polytechnic Institute and State University, Blacksburg, Virginia

Nancy A. Denton, PhD, Department of Sociology, University at Albany, State University of New York, Albany, New York

Larry E. Dumka, PhD, School of Social and Family Dynamics, Arizona State University, Tempe, Arizona

Allison Sidle Fuligni, PhD, Center for Improving Child Care Quality, University of California, Los Angeles, California

Andrew J. Fuligni, PhD, Department of Psychiatry and Biobehavioral Sciences, University of California, Los Angeles, California

Miguelina Germán, MS, Department of Psychology, Arizona State University, Tempe, Arizona

Nancy A. Gonzales, PhD, Department of Psychology, Arizona State University, Tempe, Arizona

Donald J. Hernandez, PhD, Department of Sociology, University at Albany, State University of New York, Albany, New York

Joyce R. Javier, MD, Department of Pediatrics, Stanford University School of Medicine, Palo Alto, California

Neeraj Kaushal, PhD, School of Social Work, Columbia University, New York, New York

Claudia Lahaie, PhD, Institute for Health and Social Policy, McGill University, Montreal, Quebec, Canada

Jennifer E. Lansford, PhD, Center for Child and Family Policy, Duke University, Durham, North Carolina

Suzanne E. Macartney, MA, Department of Sociology, University at Albany, State University of New York, Albany, New York

Anne Marie Mauricio, PhD, Department of Psychology, Arizona State University, Tempe, Arizona

Lorraine McKelvey, PhD, Department of Pediatrics, University of Arkansas for Medical Sciences, Little Rock, Arkansas

Fernando S. Mendoza, MD, Department of Pediatrics, Stanford University School of Medicine, Palo Alto, California

Anthony D. Ong, PhD, Department of Psychology, University of Notre Dame, Notre Dame, Indiana

Natalia Palacios, BA, Institute for Policy Research, Northwestern University, Evanston, Illinois

Jean S. Phinney, PhD, Department of Psychology, California State University, Los Angeles, California

Cordelia Reimers, PhD, Department of Economics, Hunter College of the City University of New York, New York, New York

Fariyal Ross-Sheriff, PhD, School of Social Work, Howard University, Washington, DC

Carola Suárez-Orozco, PhD, Department of Applied Psychology, Steinhardt School of Education, New York University, New York, New York

M. Taqi Tirmazi, MSW, School of Social Work, Howard University, Washington, DC

Vappu Tyyskä, PhD, Department of Sociology, Ryerson University, Toronto, Ontario, Canada

Kimberly A. Updegraff, PhD, Department of Family and Human Development, Arizona State University, Tempe, Arizona

Adriana J. Umaña-Taylor, PhD, Department of Family and Human Development, Arizona State University, Tempe, Arizona

Jane Waldfogel, PhD, School of Social Work, Columbia University, New York, New York

Tasanee R. Walsh, MSW, School of Social Work, University of North Carolina, Chapel Hill, North Carolina

Bernard P. Wong, PhD, Department of Anthropology, San Francisco State University, San Francisco, California

Series Editors' Note

This volume is the fifth in the Duke Series in Child Development and Public Policy, an ongoing collection of edited volumes that addresses the translation of research in child development to contemporary issues in public policy. The goal of the series is to bring cutting-edge research and theory in the vibrant field of child development to bear on problems facing children and families in contemporary society. The success of the series depends on identifying important problems in public policy toward children and families at the time that researchers in child development have accumulated sufficient knowledge to contribute to a solution.

Each volume in the series has grown out of a national conference held at Duke University. These conferences have been lively occasions to absorb cutting-edge syntheses of empirical research while considering challenging public policy questions about current issues. The 125 participants in each conference have included an array of nationally renowned scholars from multiple disciplines, officials in public service who are charged with improving the lives of families and children, and students who are learning how to integrate scholarship with service. Each volume follows the model of an editorial partnership between scholars at Duke University and scholars at another university, and each brings together leading scholars with practitioners and policymakers to address timely issues.

The first volume addressed the growing problem of aggressive and delinquent behavior in girls. Although violent behavior rates have remained stable over the past decade, violence by girls has increased, to the dismay of public officials who are at a loss as to how to prevent these problems or respond through placement and treatment. The second volume examined emerging interventions and policies to promote secure attachment relationships between parents and infants. Developmental neuroscience, clinical therapies, and ecological analysis of family life all point toward the first several years of life as a crucial time for intervention to promote such relationships. The third volume addressed the state of African American families in the 21st century. A portrait of these families finds many strengths to celebrate but also challenges, ranging from the wealth gap to cultural uniqueness in parenting styles. The fourth volume assembled findings regarding the possibility that well-intentioned interventions and policies for deviant youth may actually bring harm by aggregating these youth in settings where they may adversely influence each other toward greater deviance. The volume reviewed the literature and generated alternatives to aggregation of deviant peers as well as ways to mitigate adverse effects through training and structure.

This fifth volume takes a new turn. No issue could be more timely and important to our society than the concerns of families immigrating to this country. Although we have always been a nation of immigrants, the number of immigrants living in U.S. households has risen by 16% over the past 5 years. One in five children in the United States (over 14 million children) is either an immigrant or the child of immigrants. Furthermore, the pattern of immigration has changed dramatically in recent years. The 35 million Latinos in this country represent over half of all foreign-born persons living here, and they are now the single largest minority group.

The challenges faced by immigrant families and society at large are formidable. Public policy issues range from how much to fund English as a second language (ESL) classes to whether social service agency officials should ask about a recipient's immigration status. Child development issues are well captured by the volume editors' questions: Why do some groups of foreign-born families—and particular individuals within those groups—show better "outcomes" than others? And what can we do, as social scientists, policymakers, practitioners, and engaged citizens, to use the answer to that question to improve the lives and communities of the children, parents, and grandparents for all families?

Like previous volumes, this report has benefited from financial support provided by the Duke Provost's Initiative in the Social Sciences. We are grateful to Duke Provost Peter Lange. Forthcoming volumes will address the prevention of depression in youth and the processes through which deviant peer influences operate.

KENNETH A. DODGE, PHD
MARTHA PUTALLAZ, PHD

Contents

Part II. Illustrations of Diversity in Family Processes

Part III. Immigrant Families in Social Contexts

Introduction

Immigrant Families in Contemporary Society

Marc H. Bornstein, Kirby Deater-Deckard,
and Jennifer E. Lansford

The world, it seems, is in motion. Locally, the United States continues to live up to its historical reputation as "a nation of immigrants," a country of immigrating and acculturating peoples, with the countries of origin and the numbers of its naturalizing citizens constantly in flux. Immigrants now make up 12.4% of the U.S. population. That amounts to an estimated 35.7 million people. During the past three decades, for instance, the Asian population in the United States grew from 1.5 million in 1970 to 11.9 million. Latinos are now the largest U.S. minority population (12.5% vs. 12.3% for African American); 35.3 million Latinos live in the United States (an increase of 58% since 1990); and Latinos are 52% of the foreign-born population in the United States (from 31% in 1980 to 42% in 1990). The number of immigrants living in U.S. households has risen 16% over the last 5 years. From 1990 to 2000, the total population showed a 57% increase in the foreign-born population, from 19.8 million to 31.3 million. Current U.S. Census statistics indicate that one out of every five children under the age of 18, or 14 million children, in the United States are either immigrants themselves or the children of immigrant parents.

In 2000, of the individuals residing in the United States who were at least 16 years old and in the workforce, 14% were foreign born (9% noncitizens and 5% naturalized citizens). From 1990 to 2002, overall growth in the size of the workforce was 17%. Of this growth, 76% is attributable to increases in the number of foreign-born workers. In 2002, about two-thirds of the population of foreign-born workers occupied jobs in service, retail, labor, manufacturing, and agriculture sectors of the economy. In contrast, about two-thirds of the population of native-born U.S. workers occupied positions in technical, sales, administration, management, and professional sectors (Migration Policy Institute, 2004a, 2004b).

There are many foreign-born workers who are undocumented or unauthorized. Although estimates vary widely, most center on 11–12 million currently in the United States, with two-thirds of all unauthorized immigrants residing (from the largest to smallest numbers) in California, Texas, Illinois, New York, and Florida. North Carolina witnessed one of the most explosive increases, on the order of nearly 700%, from 1990 to 2000 (up to an estimated 206,000—a number that has only continued to grow dramatically since 2000; Migration Policy Institute, 2003).

There are multiple mechanisms through which foreign-born individuals arrive in the United States. The largest pathway by far (accounting for about two-thirds of permanent immigration) is through family reunification. For citizens, there are few constraints for authorized immigration of immediate family members (e.g., spouses, unmarried children, and parents). There are annual caps and long waiting periods for family-sponsored applications for the immigration of citizens' adult children (single or married) and siblings, and for spouses of noncitizen permanent residents. Ninety-five percent of authorized immigration to the United States from Mexico occurs through family reunification, as it does from India (43%), Taiwan (59%), the Philippines (77%), and Vietnam (68%), the five nations that send the most immigrants to the United States. Other programs that account for the remaining one-third of immigrants each year include employment-based programs (i.e., temporary workers), diversity-based immigration (the "green card lottery"), and humanitarian programs for refugees and asylum seekers. There is a massive backlog of applications, which is in and of itself a disincentive for many families when it comes to authorized immigration (McKay, 2003).

Going beyond U.S. borders, immigration is a major transforming force worldwide. Migration has been a fact of the human condition ever since peoples of the African savannah began moving to new lands and did not stop until they had inhabited virtually all of the livable land on Earth. According to the International Organization for Migration and estimates from the United Nations, in 2000 approximately 160 million people were thought to be living outside their country of birth or citizenship, up from an estimated 120 million in 1990. Intercountry migration may be viewed as a natural and predictable response to differences in resources and jobs, differences in demographic growth and financial insecurity, and exploitation of human rights in immigrants' countries of origin and/or destination.

Despite all of this movement, immigration and acculturation as scientific phenomena are underresearched and still poorly understood. At the individual level, immigration and acculturation entail affective, behavioral, and cognitive components, as well as health and economic concerns that change over time. Immigrants face multiple challenges in acculturating within their new dominant or existing society. Migration is one of the most disorganizing individual experiences, entailing as it does thoroughgoing changes of social identity and self-image. Immigrants must learn to navigate different systems of speaking, listening, reading, and writing even to communicate effectively in their new communities. Indeed, they need to negotiate whole new cultures. Learning those systems requires gaining new knowledge, as well as adjusting responses of life scripts to compensate for cultural differences, language use, and disruption of familiar family roles. At the aggregate level, immigration and acculturation involve social change in demography, sociology, medicine, and economics, as well as the civic, educational, social service, and legal systems in the society. As a consequence, immigration and acculturation engage multiple perspectives and disciplines.

Our chief intention in issuing this volume is to open a dialogue on the interdisciplinary connections and social ramifications of immigration and acculturation in families. These are issues of pressing contemporary concern as extraordinary forces both push and pull on the emigration–immigration continuum. Peoples in both sending and receiving countries and cultures are affected by decisions to immigrate and by emigration and immigration alike. On one side, immigration is typically tragic for sending countries in terms of waning population and also in terms of loss of entrepreneurial spirit and talent, as normally émigrés are motivated and resourceful people who possess the élan to start a new life in a new context. On the other side, receiving countries benefit from the influx of resourceful and spirited individuals, but those individuals and their new societies must mutually accommodate. It is interesting to note that, while increasing numbers of individuals worldwide are today immigrating, receiving countries are usually democracies of one or another sort. That is, receiving cultures tend to be open (if not welcoming) societies to immigrating peoples. Even still, immigration is a source of cultural tension as single individuals bring their culture of origin into contact with a novel culture of destination. Are the most assimilated individuals the freest and most empowered among immigrants? Logic tells us that there are only a certain number of strategies immigrants may adopt. Immigrants may cast off the culture from which they came and embrace the culture of their new land, a strategy (once known and desired) called assimilation. As a direct alternative, immigrants may continue to cling to their culture of origin, isolating themselves from their new culture of settlement. These two whole-cloth options are complemented by two others. In one, immigrants do not maintain their culture of origin, but neither do they adopt the culture of settlement, and consequently find themselves in a position of social marginalization. Finally, immigrants can both maintain their original culture and integrate it with their new one, making the best of both worlds.

Our volume opens the important discussion of immigration and acculturation across disciplines. Until now, studies of immigration and acculturation have been reserved to one insulated field or another, each discipline conceiving of the topics and issues concerned with immigration and acculturation as its own and construing its challenges and benefits as specific to that discipline. However, it is clear to us, as it is to a growing body of experts in academia, government, and social policy, that immigration and acculturation are at base interdisciplinary problem spaces that need to be both addressed and understood through multidisciplinary approaches. In consequence of this belief, this volume organizes the contributions of individuals who are acknowledged leaders in their respective disciplines to represent their discipline, their work, and the intersection of their discipline and their work with significant issues in immigration/acculturation.

The volume is organized in three parts. In Part I, contributors from demography, medicine, psychology, sociology, and economics discuss how each discipline articulates with immigration and acculturation in immigrating families. The book opens with a chapter by Hernandez, Denton, and Macartney that provides a detailed demographic profile of immigrant families in the United States. Mendoza, Javier, and Burgos's chapter then describes the health status of immigrant children and recommends policies to improve their health. Next, Phinney and Ong review research on ethnic identity development in immigrant families. In the following chapter, Berry outlines four acculturation strategies (which we have already met) that vary in the extent to which immigrants continue to maintain connections with their heritage as well as the extent to which they embrace aspects of the culture to which they have immigrated. Tyyskä then writes from a sociological perspective on how immigrant families have been studied, suggesting that traditional sociological models may not fit well with immigrants' experiences. Part I concludes with a chapter by Kaushal and Reimers that offers a perspective on how economists have approached immigrant families.

Part II recounts case studies of immigrant families of diverse types at closer range. Contributors who have looked at more specific phenomena of immigration in specific groups of immigrants share what they have learned. The section is organized developmentally across the life course. In the first chapter, Bornstein and Cote describe Japanese immigrant, Korean immigrant, and South American immigrant mothers' knowledge of child development and how such knowledge is related to their parenting behavior. Chase-Lansdale, D'Angelo, and Palacios next present a multidisciplinary model that incorporates characteristics of parents and children as well as interactions within families and community contexts to account for the social and cognitive competencies of very young children of immigrants. Bradley and McKelvey then review early education programs such as Head Start and Even Start with particular emphasis on how effective such programs are for immigrant children and how early education may be improved to enhance benefits to immigrant children. Waldfogel and Lahaie continue the focus on education by examining the role that preschool and after-school programs have in promoting the school achievement of children of immigrants. Then, Ross-Sheriff, Tirmazi, and Walsh present a qualitative examination of how South Asian immigrant Muslim mothers in the United States socialize their adolescent daughters. Finally, Wong provides an anthropological perspective on an elite group of transnational Chinese migrants whose family structures have been transformed by the parents' extensive international travel for work. Taken together, these chapters provide an in-depth look at developmental issues that are salient at different points in the life span and for different immigrant groups.

Part III presents chapters that address the interface between immigrant families and a number of civic, economic, and social systems such as public education, the workplace, social services and intervention programs, and the law. This final part begins with a chapter by Fuligni and Fuligni who address the particular needs and impediments to fair access to public education for foreign-born children and their parents. Updegraff, Crouter, Umaña-Taylor, and Cansler discuss the stresses and strains of workforce participation for the parents of children and adolescents, with particular attention given to factors that may be specific to foreign-born workers and their families. Gonzales, Dumka, Mauricio, and Germán then provide an overview of community-based intervention programs that seek to promote optimal educational and psychological outcomes for immigrant youth and their families. Part III ends with Coleman's chapter on immigrant families and the legal system, with particular emphasis on clashes that occur between foreign-born parents and child protective services systems—conflicts that arise from cultural differences in beliefs about parenting practices that may be deemed neglectful or abusive by the predominant native culture and the law.

The volume closes with our thoughts and the reflections of Suárez-Orozco on the state of the science, policy, and practice regarding immigrant families. This includes a summary of the main findings and major implications from each part of the volume, some broad conclusions about what we know, and emphasis on lingering questions and concerns about the work that remains to be done.

In the 18th century, when the American colonies proclaimed independence from Great Britain, the colonists were *all* immigrants clinging to the narrow strip of land on the continent's Eastern Seaboard. Assembled in Philadelphia, the colonists' representatives charged Thomas Jefferson to write out their Declaration of Independence. That Declaration is divided into two main parts. The first is a brief theory of democratic government. In the second part, Jefferson enumerated 18 grievances the colonists held against the king of England. In Number 7 of the 18, the colonists, being immigrants and wanting to promote immigration, remonstrated King George for "endeavoring to prevent the population of the States; obstructing the Laws of Naturalization of Foreigners; refusing to pass others to encourage their migrations, and raising the conditions of new Appropriations of Lands." Immigration has been with us always, and will always be with us.

REFERENCES

McKay, R. (2003, May 1). *U.S. in focus: Family reunification.* Washington, DC: Migration Policy Institute.

Migration Policy Institute. (2003). *Unauthorized immigration to the United States* (Fact Sheet No. 3). Washington, DC: Author.

Migration Policy Institute. (2004a). *The foreign born in the U.S. labor force: Numbers and trends* (Fact Sheet No. 4). Washington, DC: Author.

Migration Policy Institute. (2004b). *What kind of work do immigrants do?: Occupation and industry of foreign-born workers in the United States* (Fact Sheet No. 5). Washington, DC: Author.

PART I

FOUNDATIONS AND PERSPECTIVES

CHAPTER 1

Family Circumstances of Children in Immigrant Families

Looking to the Future of America

Donald J. Hernandez, Nancy A. Denton, *and* Suzanne E. Macartney

Demography is the scientific study of human population change due to births, deaths, and migration, including changes in the size, distribution, composition, and characteristics of human populations. More broadly, demography studies the social, economic, cultural, and biological causes and consequences of population change. Thus, *immigration*—the movement of persons from one country to another with the purpose of permanently changing their place of residence—and the characteristics of immigrants are central to many demographic studies. This chapter presents a demographic portrait of children in immigrant families, that is, children who have at least one foreign-born parent.

The focus is on the family circumstances of children because families are important to society; they bear immediate and direct responsibility for rearing children, for creating and nurturing the next generation of parents, workers, and citizens. This is no less true for immigrant families than for others. The enormous rise in immigration since 1965 has brought corresponding growth in the proportion of U.S. children who live in immigrant families. Insofar as the circumstances and needs of children in immigrant and native-born families differ, it is important that educators, health providers, and policymakers be attuned to these differences as they make decisions that influence the current well-being and future prospects of the next generation. This requires an understanding of both the strengths of immigrant families and the challenges they confront to make the best use of available, but necessarily limited, public resources.

Results presented in this chapter pertain mainly to children ages 0–17 living with at least one parent, and are based on new analyses of data from Census 2000, using microdata files prepared by Ruggles and colleagues (2004). Following standard definitions in the field of demography, we define children in immigrant families as including both the first generation (foreign-born children) and the second generation (children born in the United States with at least one foreign-born parent), whereas children in native-born families are third and later generation (children and parents all born in the United States) (Hernandez & Charney, 1998). Most results discussed in this chapter, and additional indicators for many topics and additional country-of-origin and race–ethnic groups, are available at *mumford.albany.edu/children/index_sg.htm*, the website of the Center for Social and Demographic Analysis at the University at Albany, State University of New York.

IMMIGRATION IS LEADING TO A NEW U.S. MAJORITY

Historically, the vast majority of persons in the United States were European American, but we are in the midst of a profound transformation. Between 1960 and 2000, the percentages of all children accounted for by children in immigrant families more than tripled, from 6% to 20%, whereas the proportion of children in immigrant families with origins in Europe or Canada dropped from 71% to only 14% (Hernandez & Darke, 1999). Largely resulting from these changes, the proportion of all children who were European American dropped from near 80% in 1960 to 61% in 2000.

U.S. Census Bureau projections, based on the assumption that no major changes will occur in the magnitude and composition of immigration to the United States, indicate that most future population growth will occur due to immigration and births to immigrants and their descendants, and that the transformation of the race–ethnic composition will continue. By 2030, less than 25 years from now, the Census Bureau projects that the proportion of children who are European American will decline to about 50%, and still further during later decades (U.S. Census Bureau, 2004). The corresponding rise of the new U.S. majority will not, however, lead to the emergence of a single numerically dominant group, but instead to a mosaic of diverse race–ethnic groups from around the world. By 2030, the projections indicate that among all children, the proportions will rise to 26% Latin American, 16% African American, 5% Asian American, and 4% Native American or Hawaiian or other Pacific Islander. Insofar as children in race–ethnic minority and immigrant families are highly concentrated in a few states, but also spread widely across many states, this transformation will be felt throughout much of the United States.

IMMIGRANT FAMILIES HAVE VALUABLE STRENGTHS

Most children in immigrant families live with two parents, and they often also have grandparents, other relatives, or nonrelatives in the home who provide additional nurturance or economic resources to children and their families.

Two-Parent Families Are Quite Prevalent

Children living with two parents tend, on average, to be somewhat advantaged in their educational success, compared to children in one-parent families (Cherlin, 1999; McLanahan & Sandefur, 1994). Overall, children in immigrant families are more likely than children in native families to live with two parents (84% vs. 76%). Children in immigrant families from many regions are about as likely or more likely than European Americans in native families (85%) to have two parents in the home (including stepparents and the cohabiting partners of parents). The only exceptions are children with origins in the Caribbean at 64–70% (except Cuba) and children with origins in Cambodia (75%). Thus, large majorities of children in all immigrant and most native groups benefit from having two parents in the home, although significant portions of all groups (at least 5–20%) at any given time live with only one parent.

Many Children Have Many Siblings

Brothers and sisters can be a liability but also an asset. Insofar as the time and finances of parents are limited, they must be spread more thinly in larger families than in smaller ones. Hence, children in larger families tend, other things being equal, to experience less educational success and to complete fewer years of schooling than children with fewer siblings (Blake, 1985, 1989; Hernandez, 1986). Siblings also, however, can serve as childcare providers for younger siblings, as companions for siblings close in age, and as an important mutual support network throughout life. Dependent siblings living at home are most likely to share available resources. Children in various groups differ substantially in the proportion living in large families with many siblings ages 0–17 in the home.

Children in U.S. immigrant families are about one-third more likely than those in native families to live in homes with four or more siblings (19% vs. 14%). The proportion living in families with four or more siblings is two or three times the levels for European Americans and Asian Americans in native families (10–11%) among children in immigrant families from Mexico, Cambodia, Thailand, Afghanistan, Iraq, Israel/Palestine, and blacks from Africa (25–32%). This percentage jumps to 38% for children with origins in Laos and enormously to 75% for the Hmong. Thus, children with immigrant origins in these nine countries/regions are more likely than others to experience both the constraints and the benefits of having many siblings.

Children Also Often Live with Other Relatives or Nonrelatives

Grandparents, other relatives, and nonrelatives in the homes of children can provide essential childcare, nurturing, or economic resources. Children in most immigrant and race–ethnic minority native-born groups are two to four times more likely than European Americans in native families to have a grandparent in the home, 10–20% versus 5%.

Some groups also are likely to have other adult relatives age 18 or older, including siblings, in the home. The proportion is 25–37% for children in immigrant families who are from Mexico, Central America, the Caribbean (except Cuba), South America, the Philippines, Indochina, Pakistan/Bangladesh, Afghanistan, Iraq, and blacks from Africa. Nonrelatives in the home also are common (5–13%) among children in families from many of five regions (Mexico, Central America, the Caribbean [except Cuba], South America, and the Philippines).

Thus, many groups with large numbers of siblings also are especially likely to have grandparents, other relatives, or nonrelatives in the home who may be nurturing and providing childcare for, as well as sharing economic resources with, the immigrant children and their families. This is particularly likely to be the case for children in immigrant families from Mexico, Central America, the Dominican Republic, Haiti, Indochina, and Afghanistan.

Immigrant Families Have a Strong Commitment to Work

A strong work ethic characterizes both immigrant and native families. Among children living with a father, 93% in immigrant families and 95% in native families have fathers who worked for pay during the previous year. For most specific groups the proportion is 90% or more. Most children living with mothers also have mothers who work for pay to support the family. Other adult workers also live in the homes of many children.

Thus, children in both immigrant and native race–ethnic groups live in the United States with fathers and mothers who are strongly committed to working for pay to support their families, and many groups also are likely to have additional adult workers in the home. Especially noteworthy is that, among children in immigrant families from Mexico, the largest immigrant group, 92% have working fathers. In addition, although they are among the groups least likely to have a working mother (53%), they are substantially more likely than all other native and immigrant groups, except Central Americans, to have another adult worker in the home, at 29%, compared to the next highest proportions of 20–25%, and less than 20% for most groups. Clearly, children in immigrant families live in families with strong work ethics, regardless of their race–ethnicity or immigrant origins.

IMMIGRANTS CONFRONT EDUCATIONAL AND ECONOMIC CHALLENGES

Although most children in most immigrant and native race–ethnic groups live in strong families with two parents who are working to support their families, many have parents whose educational attainments are quite limited or who cannot find full-time year-round work. Many also live in poverty and experience other difficulties as a result.

Many Children Have Parents with Limited Education

Children in immigrant families are nearly as likely as those in native families to have a father who has graduated from college (24% vs. 28%), but they are more than three times as likely to have a father who has not graduated from high school (40% vs. 12%). The level is similar (21–24%) for native race–ethnic minorities who are African American, mainland-origin Puerto Rican, Mexican, other Hispanic, and Native

American, and for children in immigrant families from most Caribbean islands. However, 37% of island-origin Puerto Ricans have fathers who have not completed high school, similar to the level experienced by children in immigrant families (33–45%) who are from the Dominican Republic, Haiti, Laos, Thailand, Vietnam, and Iraq. Still higher, the proportion with a father not graduating from high school rises for children in immigrant families to 48% for Cambodia, 51% for the Hmong, 53% for Central America, and 69% for Mexico.

Especially striking is that fathers of children in many groups have not entered, let alone graduated from, high school. The proportion with fathers completing only 8 years of school or less is 12–20% for island-origin Puerto Ricans and for children in immigrant families from the Dominican Republic, China (not including Taiwan or Hong Kong), Thailand, Vietnam, and Iraq, and this rises to 24% for Thailand, 29% for Laos, 30% for Central America and Cambodia, 41% for the Hmong, and 45% for Mexico. Results for mothers are broadly similar to those for fathers.

It has long been known that children whose parents have completed fewer years of schooling tend, on average, to themselves complete fewer years of schooling and to obtain lower paying jobs when they reach adulthood (Blau & Duncan, 1967; Featherman & Hauser, 1978; Sewell & Hauser, 1975; Sewell, Hauser, & Wolf, 1980). Parents whose education does not extend beyond the elementary level may be especially limited in the knowledge and experience needed to help their children succeed in school. Immigrant parents often have high educational aspirations for their children (Hernandez & Charney, 1998; Kao, 1999; Rumbaut, 1999), but may know little about the U.S. educational system, particularly if they have completed only a few years of school.

Parents with little schooling may, as a consequence, be less comfortable with the education system, less able to help their children with schoolwork, and less able to effectively negotiate with teachers and education administrators. It may be especially important for educators to focus attention on the needs of island-origin Puerto Rican children, and on children in immigrant families from Mexico and Central America, the Dominican Republic and Haiti, China, Indochina, and Iraq, because these children are especially likely to have parents who have completed only a few years of school.

Many Children Have Parents Not Working Full Time Year-Round

Despite the strong work ethic of parents, many children in immigrant families live with fathers who cannot find full-time year-round work. The proportion is 30–37% for four native groups (African Americans, island-origin Puerto Ricans, Native Hawaiian and other Pacific Islanders, Native Americans), and for 15 immigrant groups from Latin America (Mexico, Central America), the Caribbean (the Dominican Republic, Haiti), Indochina (the Hmong, Cambodia, Laos, Thailand, Vietnam), and West Asia (Pakistan/Bangladesh, Afghanistan, Iraq), as well the former Soviet Union, and blacks from Africa. For these children the proportion with a father not working full time year-round approaches or exceeds twice the level experienced by European Americans in native families. Immigrant groups with high proportions of fathers not working full time year-round also tend to have fathers with low hourly wages.

Children are much more likely to have mothers than fathers who do not work full time year-round, no doubt in part because mothers often have greater responsibility for the day-to-day care of children than do fathers, but a large number of dependent siblings in the home is not necessarily a strong indication of the amount that mothers work.

Many Children Experience Poverty

Children with poverty-level incomes often lack resources for decent housing, food, clothing, books, other educational resources, childcare/early education, and health care. Children from low-income families also tend to experience a variety of negative developmental outcomes, including less success in school, lower educational attainments, and earning lower incomes during adulthood (Duncan & Brooks-Gunn, 1997; McLoyd, 1998; Sewell & Hauser, 1975). Poverty rates merit considerable attention because extensive research documents that poverty has greater negative consequences than either limited mother's education or living in a one-parent family (Duncan & Brooks-Gunn, 1997; McLoyd, 1998).

Children in various immigrant and race–ethnic groups differ enormously in their exposure to poverty in the United States. The official poverty rate is the measure most commonly used to assess economic need, but it has come under increasing criticism because it has not been updated since 1965 for increases in the real standard of living, and it does not account for the local cost of living (Citro & Michael, 1995; Hernandez, Denton, & Macartney, 2006). To provide a more complete picture of economic need for children, results are presented for two alternatives that take into account federal taxes and the local cost of various goods and services (Bernstein, Brocht, & Spade-Aguilar, 2000; Boushey, Brocht, Gundersen, & Bernstein, 2001; Hernandez et al., 2006).

The first alternative measure of economic need presented here is the "baseline" Basic Budget Poverty rate, which takes into account the local cost of food, housing, transportation for parents to commute to work, and "other necessities" such as clothing, personal care items, household supplies, telephone, television, school supplies, reading materials, music, and toys. The second, more comprehensive, Basic Budget Poverty rate takes into account, in addition, the local cost of childcare/early education and health care, although it may somewhat overestimate the effect of the cost of childcare/early education and underestimate the effect of health care costs (Hernandez et al., 2006).

The Baseline Basic Budget Poverty rate is only slightly higher than the official rate for children in native families who are European American (11% vs. 8%) or Asian American (14% vs. 8%), but the difference is much larger for the other immigrant and native groups with official poverty rates of 20% or more. For example, the Baseline Basic Budget Poverty rate for children in immigrant families from Mexico is 47%, compared to an official rate of 30%. Thus for the 11 immigrant country/region-of-origin groups and the six native race–ethnic groups with official poverty rates of 20% or more, the Baseline Basic Budget Poverty rates are between 30 and 54%, that is, about three to five times greater than for European Americans in native families.

The Baseline Basic Budget Poverty measure does not, however, take into account the cost of childcare/early childhood education, which is essential for many working parents, and which can have important beneficial consequences for the educational success of children in elementary school and beyond. It also does not take account of the cost of health insurance, which can assure timely access to preventive health care and to medical care for acute and chronic conditions, which in turn can affect the capacity of children to function effectively in school. A more comprehensive Basic Budget Poverty measure including these costs classifies about one-fourth (26–27%) of European American and Asian American children in native families as poor, compared to about one-half to four-fifths (45–82%) of children in other native race–ethnic groups, or in immigrant families from the former Soviet Union and "other" West Asia (45%); Vietnam and English-speaking Caribbean (48%); Africa (blacks only), Iraq, and Pakistan/Bangladesh (52–55%); Central America, Haiti, Cambodia, Laos, and Afghanistan (62–65%); Mexico and the Dominican Republic (73%); and the Hmong (82%).

In European countries, children have access to nearly universal preschool and national health insurance programs, but this is not the case in the United States. Comparable child poverty rates are 2–10% in the six European countries of Belgium, Denmark, Finland, France, Germany, and Sweden (Hernandez et al., 2006; UNICEF, 2005). Thus, taking into account the full range of needs of children and families, including childcare/early education and health care, no more than one in 10 children in several major European countries live in poverty, compared to one in four European American and Asian American children in native families, and between one-half and fourth-fifths of children in many immigrant and native race–ethnic groups.

Residential Stability and Homeownership

Immigrants are, by definition, distinguished by the fact that they were born in another country. Continuing relationships of immigrants with their origin countries, and the possibility of returning, lead some observers to question their commitment to the United States. Although temporary visits and permanent returns to the country of origin surely occur, 68% of children in immigrant families live with parents who have lived in the United States 10 years or more. In fact, among children in immigrant families, the proportion (28%) with a nonimmigrant parent who was born in the United States is nearly as high as the proportion (32%) with a parent who has lived in the United States fewer than 10 years.

Children in immigrant families also live in families with rates of homeownership and residential stability that are not greatly different from children in native families. The proportion living in homes owned by their parents or the householder is more than one-half, at 55% for children in immigrant families, compared to 70% for children in native families, a difference of only 15 percentage points. The homeownership gap is even smaller if similar subgroups are compared. Thus, many children in immigrant families have parents who are making strong financial investments in and commitments to their local communities by purchasing their own homes.

Children in immigrant and native families also have similar rates of 5-year residential mobility, 52% and 45%, respectively. There is little variation across groups. Thus, migration rates for children also indicate that immigrant and native families have broadly similar commitments to staying in (or moving from) their local communities. Children in various groups are broadly similar in the challenges and opportunities presented by changes in residence or by remaining in their communities for longer periods of time.

ENGLISH LANGUAGE PROFICIENCY IN IMMIGRANT FAMILIES

Because children in immigrant families live with at least one parent who was born in and moved from another country, many have parents whose first language is not English. As a consequence, many parents and children are limited in their English proficiency, whereas others are in the process of becoming bilingual, presenting both formidable challenges and valuable opportunities to schools, health providers, social service organizations, and other public and private agencies. Policies to implement family literacy programs and dual-language programs would be especially useful, as would outreach in the country-of-origin languages of immigrants by organizations serving immigrant populations.

Some Children Are Limited English Proficient, but Many Are Potentially Bilingual

Limited English proficiency among children in immigrant families may be a barrier to success in English-only schools. Overall, 26% of children ages 5–17 in immigrant families are limited English proficient. Of course, the proportions of limited English proficient are quite low for children in immigrant families from some countries, particularly if English is widely spoken in the origin country.

The percentages of limited English proficient is quite high, however, for children who are Hmong (51%) or in immigrant families from Mexico (38%); China, Cambodia, Laos, and Vietnam (33–37%); or Central America, the Dominican Republic, Thailand, or the former Soviet Union (27–29%). Proportions of limited English proficient are somewhat lower but substantial at 20–24% for children in immigrant families from Haiti, South America, Japan, Korea, Hong Kong, Taiwan, Pakistan/Bangladesh, Afghanistan, and Iraq.

Although many children in immigrant families are limited English proficient (26%), nearly twice as many (46%) speak a language other than English at home, but also speak English very well. These children are well positioned to become fluent bilingual speakers. The highest proportions (50–66%) are found for children in immigrant families from Mexico, Central America, Cuba, the Dominican Republic, Haiti, South America, China, Taiwan, Laos, India, Pakistan/Bangladesh, Afghanistan, Iran, Iraq, and other West Asia countries. Even among children in immigrant families from Mexico with the second highest proportion of limited English proficient (38%), a large 53% speak Spanish at home but also speak English very well. Thus, with appropriate support from schools for both languages, these children might become proficient in both languages. Bilingual speakers are a valuable economic resource for the United States in the global economy, and policies to make dual-language programs available to all U.S. children would enhance competitiveness in the global marketplace.

Many Children Have Parents with Limited English Proficiency

Parents with limited English skills are less likely to find well-paid full-time year-round employment than English-fluent parents, and they may be less able to help their children with school subjects taught in English. Insofar as early education, health, and social service institutions do not provide outreach to immigrants in the language of their country of origin, parents in immigrant families may be cut off from accessing programs important to their children and themselves. Immigrant groups with large proportions of limited English proficient parents also often are ones with limited parental education, high proportions not working full time year-round, and high proportions earning low wages.

For example, the highest proportions with a limited English proficient father are for children in immigrant families who are Hmong (80%), or from Mexico, Central America, the Dominican Republic, Cambodia, Laos, and Vietnam (60–70%). The percent with a limited English proficient father is also very high for children in immigrant families from China, Thailand, and the former Soviet Union (55–57%), and from Haiti, South America, Korea, Hong Kong, Taiwan, Thailand, Afghanistan, and Iraq (40–48%). Results for mothers are generally similar. Policies assuring outreach in country-of-origin languages by education, health, and social service organizations could help to ensure that children and families receive needed services.

Many Children Live in Linguistically Isolated Households

Many children with limited English proficient parents are themselves fluent in English or have an older sibling, another relative, or another adult in the home who is fluent in English. Linguistically isolated households are defined by the U.S. Census Bureau as households where no one over age 13 speaks English exclusively or very well. One-fourth (26%) of children in immigrant families live in linguistically isolated households, and the proportion is at least this high for children from a dozen countries/regions distinguished here.

Children in these families may be largely isolated from English-speaking society and institutions. Insofar as most or all family members in linguistically isolated households would benefit from learning English, not only for day-to-day interaction with the broader society but also as a means of improving education and work opportunities, two-generational family literacy programs offer an especially promising vehicle for public policies to facilitate the integration and foster the well-being of both children and parents in immigrant families.

POLICIES FOR EDUCATION, HEALTH, AND ECONOMIC SUPPORT

Beyond policies and programs that would foster English language proficiency and bilingualism, three additional policy arenas with important implications for the well-being, development, and future prospects of children in immigrant families focus on education, health, and economic resources. These are extremely complex topics that cannot be discussed in detail in this chapter. Data from Census 2000 do, however, provide a strong basis for a broad analysis of immigrant circumstances regarding the earliest years of education (pre-K/nursery school enrollment), and a key immigrant eligibility criterion for economic support programs (citizenship), whereas the Census Bureau's Current Population Survey provides the capacity for assessing health insurance coverage for a limited set of immigrant groups. These data provide the foundation for a discussion in this section of several key policy issues for children in immigrant families.

Pre-K/Nursery School Enrollment Rates Differ Greatly

Early education programs have been found to promote school readiness and educational success in elementary school and beyond (Gormley, Gayer, Phillips, & Dawson, 2005; Haskins & Rouse, 2005; Lynch, 2004). Research suggests that children with low family incomes and limited English proficiency may be most likely to benefit from early education programs (Gormley & Gayer, 2005; Takanishi, 2004), but children in several groups challenged by these circumstances are less likely than European Americans and the other groups noted above to be enrolled in early education programs. The overall difference in enrollment rates between children in immigrant and native families is accounted for mainly by five immigrant groups who experience high rates of poverty and limited English proficiency. The enrollment rates for these groups at age 3 are only 18–28% for children with origins in Mexico, Central America, Indochina, Iraq, and Pakistan/Bangladesh, compared to 37% for children in native families, and 43–49%, respectively at age 4, compared to 63% for children in native families. Children in native families who are Mexican also have low age-3 and age-4 enrollment rates, at 28% and 52%, respectively, as well as high poverty rates, and substantial proportions of limited English proficient parents.

What accounts for these very low enrollment rates? One reason sometimes cited, particularly for Latin American immigrants, is more familistic cultural values with parents desiring that their children be cared for at home, in preference to care by nonrelatives in formal educational settings (Liang, Fuller, & Singer, 2000; Takanishi, 2004; Uttal, 1999). But alternative explanations include the following socioeconomic or structural factors (Hernandez, Denton, & Macartney, 2007). First, early education programs are costly, but most low-income families eligible for childcare assistance receive none because of limited funding (Mezey, Greenberg, & Schumacher, 2002). Thus, cost can be an insurmountable barrier for poor families. Second, parents with extremely limited educational attainments may not be aware of the importance of early education programs or the fact that these programs are used by most highly educated parents to foster their children's educational success. Third, the number of openings available in immigrant neighborhoods with many non-English speakers may be too few to accommodate the demand (Hill-Scott, 2005). Fourth, even if spaces are available, such programs may not reach out to parents in their country-of-origin language, restricting access by limited English proficient parents (Matthews & Ewen, 2006). Fifth, parents may hesitate to enroll their children in programs that are not designed and implemented in a culturally competent manner, especially if teachers lack a minimal capacity to communicate with children in the country-of-origin language (Holloway, Fuller, Rambaud, & Eggers-Pierola, 1997; Shonkoff & Phillips, 2000).

Research indicates that socioeconomic or structural influences, especially family poverty, mother's education, and parental occupation, account for most or all of the enrollment gap separating children in immigrant and native Mexican families and children in immigrant families from Central America and Indochina from European American children in native families (Hernandez et al., in press). Depending on the age and the group, socioeconomic and structural factors account for at least one-half and perhaps all of the enrollment gap, but cultural influences account for no more than 14% of the gap for the Mexican groups, no more than 39% for the Central Americans, and no more than 17% for the Indochinese.

These results may be surprising, especially for the Latin Americans, but it is important to note that these estimates are consistent with the strong commitment to early education in contemporary Mexico, where universal enrollment at age 3 will become obligatory in 2008–2009 (Organization for Economic Cooperation and Development, 2006). In fact, in 2002–2003, 63% of children age 4 in Mexico were enrolled in preschool, precisely the proportion for European American children in native families in Census 2000 (Organization for Economic Cooperation and Development, 2006, p. 25 and Table 1). Insofar as preschool is less costly in Mexico than in the United States, and insofar as poverty for the Mexican immigrant group in the United States is quite high, it is not surprising that the proportion of children enrolled in school for the immigrant Mexican group at age 4 in the United States at 45% is substantially lower than the age-4 enrollment in Mexico at 63%.

In sum, familistic cultural values are sometimes cited as a plausible explanation for lower early education enrollment rates among children in immigrant families than among European American children in native families, but research indicates that socioeconomic and structural influences can account for at least 50% and for some groups essentially all the gap.

Health Insurance Coverage Rates Differ Greatly

Children and their families require good health to succeed in school and in work. Although Census 2000 does not measure health insurance coverage, health insurance coverage data for a more restricted set of race–ethnic and immigrant origin groups are presented here based on the U.S. Census Bureau's Current Population Survey data for 1998–2002. The proportion uninsured for children in immigrant families from the former Soviet Union and Yugoslavia is fairly low at 11%, but this jumps to 18–23% for those from Indochina, the Dominican Republic, and blacks from Africa; 30% for Central America; 35% for Mexico; and 44% for Haiti.

Thus, many children in immigrant families from countries of origin with high U.S. poverty rates are not covered by health insurance. Past research has found that substantial risk of not being insured remains even after controlling for parental education and duration of parental residence in the United States, as well as reported health status, number of parents in the home, and having a parent employed full time year-round (Brown, Wyn, Yu, Valenzuela, & Dong, 1999). This research also found the main reason reported by parents for lack of insurance coverage for children is the same for both immigrant and native groups: the lack of affordability of insurance coverage. The reason cited second most frequently related to employers not offering coverage at all, or not offering family coverage, or not offering coverage for part-time employees. These findings, and continuing high proportions not covered by health insurance, point to the need for public policies that increase access to health insurance for children in immigrant families, particularly those experiencing high poverty rates.

Family Citizenship Status Can Limit Access to Economic Supports

The vast majority of children in immigrant families (80%) are U.S. citizens because they were born in the United States. Although all children in immigrant families have at least one immigrant parent, according to Census 2000 a sizable minority of children in immigrant families (28%) have a parent who also was born in the United States. Despite the fact that most children in immigrant families are U.S. citizens, that many have parents born in the United States, and that adult immigrants are increasingly likely to become U.S. citizens the longer they live in this country, more than one-half of children in immigrant families (53%) live in mixed-citizenship-status families with at least one citizen and one noncitizen (often a parent and sometimes other siblings).

Eligibility requirements under the 1996 welfare reform drew, for the first time, a sharp distinction between noncitizen immigrants and citizens, with noncitizens becoming ineligible for important public benefits and services. As a result, many noncitizen parents who are ineligible for specific public benefits may not be aware that their children are eligible, or they hesitate to contact government authorities on behalf of their children for fear of jeopardizing their own future opportunities to become citizens (Capps, Kenney, & Fix, 2003; Fix & Passel, 1999; Fix & Zimmermann, 1995; Hernandez & Charney, 1998; Zimmermann & Tumlin, 1999). All together, 53% of children in immigrant families live in mixed-status nuclear families, with the proportions highest for children with origins in Mexico and Central America (65–66%), followed by the Dominican Republic, Haiti, Cambodia, Laos, and the Hmong (51–58%). Children with origins in these countries are not only most likely to live in mixed-citizenship-status nuclear families, they also are especially likely to experience high poverty rates, and therefore a need and eligibility for public benefits and services.

CONCLUSIONS

The strong families and vigorous work ethic of immigrants provide firm foundations for their children to succeed in the United States, but major challenges to successful integration include high poverty, limited access to full-time year-round work, and low levels of education and English fluency. Children with origins in the 17 countries or regions in Table 1.1 experience especially high Basic Budget Poverty Rates of 45% or more, compared to 26% for European American children in native-born families.

Among children of immigrants from the seven Western-hemisphere origins listed in Table 1.1, 40% or more have limited English proficient fathers, excepting only those from the English-speaking Caribbean, and 21% or more have fathers who have not graduated from high school, although many benefit from grandparents, other relatives, or nonrelatives

TABLE 1.1. Indicators of Well-Being for Children in Immigrant Families from 17 Countries/Regions with High Basic Budget Poverty Rates in the United States: 2000

	Number	Basic budget poverty (based on all costs)[a]	Father not H.S. grad	Father not working full time	Father limited English proficient (LEP)	Child limited English proficient (LEP)[b]	Child English-fluent and speaks other language at home[b]	Four or more siblings ages 0–17	Grand-parent in home	Other adult relative in home	Nonrelative in home	School enrollment age 3	School enrollment age 4
Native European American %		26%	10%	16%	1%	1%	2%	11%	5%	11%	3%	37%	63%
Immigrant %		45%+	21%+	30%+	40%+	10%+	40%+	21%+	10%+	26%+	6%+	<37%	<63%
Western hemisphere													
Mexico	5,165,982	×	×	×	×	×	×	×	×	×	×	×	×
Central America	939,082	×	×	×	×	×	×		×	×	×	×	×
South America	647,643	×	×		×	×	×		×	×	×		
Dominican Republic	350,101	×	×	×	×	×	×		×	×	×	×	×
Haiti	201,981	×	×	×	×	×	×	×	×	×	×		
Jamaica	230,808	×	×						×	×	×		
Other English-speaking Caribbean	226,786	×	×						×	×			
Southeast Asia													
Hmong	71,598	×	×	×	×	×	×	×	×	×		×	×
Cambodia	80,812	×	×	×	×	×	×	×	×	×	×	×	×
Laos	87,264	×	×	×	×	×	×	×	×	×	×	×	×
Thailand	60,487	×	×	×	×	×	×	×	×	×		×	×
Vietnam	386,645	×	×	×	×	×	×		×	×	×	×	×
West Asia													
Iraq	39,298	×	×	×	×	×	×	×	×	×		×	×
Afghanistan	17,897	×		×	×	×	×	×		×		—	—
Pakistan/Bangladesh	136,621	×		×		×	×		×	×		×	×
Europe													
Former Soviet Union	238,403	×		×	×	×	×		×				×
Africa													
Blacks from Africa	237,078	×		×	×			×		×			

Note. Calculated from Census 2000 5% microdata (IPUMS) by Donald J. Hernandez, Nancy A. Denton, and Suzanne E. Macartney, Center for Social and Demographic Analysis, University at Albany, State University of New York. ×, at or above threshold; —, sample size is too small to estimate.

[a] Basic budget poverty is based on all costs for a decent standard of living, including food, housing, other necessities, transportation for work, childcare, and health insurance.

[b] For children ages 5–17 years.

in the home. Children with Mexican, Central American, and Dominican origins also have lower pre-K/nursery school enrollment than European Americans in native-born families. Mexico alone accounts for 39% of all children in immigrant families, and together with the other Western-hemisphere origins in Table 1.1, they account for 58%.

Since at least the time of Theodore Roosevelt, the United States has, periodically, been involved economically, politically, and militarily with various Western-hemisphere countries, leading to the creation of pathways to immigration (Rumbaut, 1996). Mexico has long served as a source of agricultural labor needed by the U.S. economy. Since the 1960s the contributions of immigrants from Mexico to the U.S. economy have become much more diverse (Chavez, 1996). The U.S. military occupation of the Dominican Republic in 1965 opened the way to substantial Dominican immigration, while wars, deteriorating economic conditions, or both led many Central Americans from El Salvador, Guatemala, Honduras, and Nicaragua to flee to the United States during the 1980s, and many Haitians to seek a better life in the United States (Rumbaut, 1996).

Southeast Asia is another region with immigrants fleeing to the United States as a result of war, not only from Vietnam, but also from Cambodia, Laos, and Thailand, including the Hmong who were recruited to fight on behalf of the United States. Like those with origins in some, or all, of the Western-hemisphere countries/regions above, children in immigrant families with these Indochinese origins are likely to have fathers who are limited English proficient and/or who have not graduated from high school, to have grandparents, other relatives, or nonrelatives in the home, and if they are ages 3 or 4 not to be enrolled in pre-K/nursery school.

Children with parents from two West Asian nations where the United States has been involved for more than two decades, Iraq and Afghanistan, also have high poverty rates. Children with origins in Iraq have high proportions of fathers who are not high school graduates and limited English proficient; high proportions with grandparents, other relatives, or nonrelatives in the home; and low rates of pre-K/nursery school enrollment, whereas children with parents from Afghanistan share similar circumstances except fathers are more likely to be high school graduates, and sample size does not provide the basis for reliable estimates of pre-K/nursery school enrollment. These nations have suffered from wars and their sequelae since 1980. Children from Pakistan/Bangladesh also share these family and socioeconomic circumstances, except the proportion with limited English proficient fathers is lower. In the post-9/11 era, it is important to note that most Iraqis, Afghanistanis, Pakistanis, and Bangladeshis are Muslim and that their integration into U.S. society is of considerable importance.

The end of the cold war and the dissolution of the Soviet Union in 1991 opened the West, including the United States, to many refugees. Children with parents from the former Soviet Union are more likely than children from countries/regions above to have a father who graduated from high school, but have high proportions with limited English proficient fathers, and to have a grandparent in the home. Finally, blacks from Africa taken as a whole are more likely than children from the other countries/regions above to have a high school graduate father and less likely to have a limited English proficient father, but do, nevertheless, have a Basic Budget Poverty rate in excess of 45%.

Altogether, children with the origins included in Table 1.1 account for 68% of children in immigrant families, and children from these countries/regions, with the exceptions only of Iraq, Afghanistan, and the former Soviet Union, are Hispanic, Asian, or black. These immigrants arrive seeking economic opportunities in the United States, and many also were driven from their country of origin by war or by persecution because of their race, religion, nationality, or political opinion. It will be unfortunate for the future of these children and families, and for the United States as a whole, if the United States does not adopt education, language, health, and employment policies that will provide these children in immigrant families with the opportunity to overcome the challenges of limited education and English proficiency and high poverty to successfully integrate into U.S. society and achieve the aspirations for the American dream that brought them to this country.

REFERENCES

Bernstein, J., Brocht, C., & Spade-Aguilar, M. (2000). *How much is enough?: Basic family budgets for working families*. Washington, DC: Economic Policy Institute.

Blake, J. (1985). Number of siblings and educational mobility. *American Sociological Review, 50*(1), 84–94.

Blake, J. (1989). *Family size and achievement*. Berkeley: University of California Press.

Blau, P. M., & Duncan, O. D. (1967). *The American occupational structure*. New York: Wiley.

Boushey, H., Brocht, C., Gundersen, B., & Bernstein, J. (2001). *Hardships in America: The real story of working families*. Washington, DC: Economic Policy Institute.

Brown, E. R., Wyn, R., Yu, H., Valenzuela, A., & Dong, L. (1999). Access to health insurance and health care for children in immigrant families. In D. J. Hernandez (Ed.), *Children of immigrants: Health, adjustment, and public assistance* (pp. 126–186). Washington, DC: National Academy Press.

Capps, R., Kenney, G., & Fix, M. (2003). *Health insurance coverage of children in mixed-status immigrant families* (Snapshots of America's children, No. 12). Washington, DC: Urban Institute.

Chavez, L. R. (1996). Borders and bridges: Undocumented immigrants from Mexico and Central America. In S. Pedraza & R. G. Rumbaut (Eds.), *Origins and destinies: Immigration, race, and ethnicity in America* (pp. 250–262). Belmont, CA: Wadsworth.

Cherlin, A. J. (1999). Going to extremes: Family structure, children's well-being, and social sciences. *Demography, 36*(4), 421–428.

Citro, C. F., & Michael, R. T. (1995). *Measuring poverty: A new approach.* Washington, DC: National Academy Press.

Duncan, G. J., & Brooks-Gunn, J. (Eds.). (1997). *Consequences of growing up poor.* New York: Russell Sage Foundation.

Featherman, D. L., & Hauser, R. M. (1978). *Opportunity and change.* New York: Academic Press.

Fix, M., & Passel, J. (1999). *Trends in noncitizens' and citizens' use of public benefits following welfare reform: 1994–97.* Washington, DC: Urban Institute.

Fix, M., & Zimmerman, W. (1995). When should immigrants receive benefits? In I. V. Sawhill (Ed.), *Welfare reform: An analysis of the issues* (pp. 69–72). Washington, DC: Urban Institute.

Gormley, W. T., & Gayer, T. (2005). Promoting school readiness in Oklahoma: An evaluation of Tulsa's pre-K program. *Journal of Human Resources, 40*(3), 533–558.

Gormley, W. T., Jr., Gayer, T., Phillips, D., & Dawson B. (2005). The effects of universal pre-K on cognitive development. *Developmental Psychology, 41*(6), 872–884.

Haskins, R., & Rouse, C. (2005). *Closing achievement gaps. The future of children* (Policy Brief, Spring 2005). Princeton, NJ: Princeton University and Brookings Institute.

Hernandez, D. J. (1986). Childhood in sociodemographic perspective. In R. H. Turner & J. F. Short, Jr. (Eds.), *Annual review of sociology* (Vol. 12, pp. 159–180). Palo Alto, CA: Annual Reviews.

Hernandez, D. J., & Charney, E. (Eds.). (1998). *From generation to generation: The health and well-being of children in immigrant families.* Washington, DC: National Academy Press.

Hernandez, D. J., & Darke, K. (1999). Socioeconomic and demographic risk factors and resources among children in immigrant and native-born families: 1910, 1960, 1990. In D. J. Hernandez (Ed.), *Children of immigrants: Health, adjustment, and public assistance* (pp. 19–125). Washington, DC: National Academy Press.

Hernandez, D. J., Denton, N. A., & Macartney, S. E. (2006). Child poverty in the U.S.: A new family budget approach with comparison to European countries. In H. Wintersberger, L. Alanen, T. Olk, & J. Qvortrup (Eds.), *Children's economic and social welfare* (pp. 109–139). Odense: University Press of Southern Denmark.

Hernandez, D. J., Denton, N. A., & Macartney, S. E. (in press). Early education programs: Differential access among children in newcomer and native families. In

M. Waters & R. Alba (Eds.), *The next generation: Immigrant youth and families in comparative perspective* (pp.). Ithaca, NY: Cornell University Press.

Hill-Scott, K. (2005). *Facilities technical report.* Los Angeles: First 5 LA.

Holloway, S. D., & Fuller, B. (1999). *Through my own eyes: Single mothers and the cultures of poverty.* Cambridge, MA: Harvard University Press.

Holloway, S. D., Fuller, B., Rambaud, M. F., & Eggers-Pierola, C. (1997). *Through my own eyes: Single mothers and the cultures of poverty.* Cambridge, MA: Harvard University Press.

Kao, G. (1999). Psychological well-being and educational achievement among immigrant youth. In D. J. Hernandez (Ed.), *Children of immigrants: Health, adjustment, and public assistance* (pp. 410–477). Washington, DC: National Academy Press.

Liang, X., Fuller, B., & Singer, J. D. (2000). Ethnic differences in child care selection: The influence of family structure, parental practices, and country-of-origin language. *Early Childhood Research Quarterly, 15*(3), 357–384.

Lynch, R. G. (2004). *Exceptional returns: Economic, fiscal and social benefits of investment in early childhood development.* Washington, DC: Economic Policy Institute.

Matthews, H., & Ewen, D. (2006). *Reaching all children?: Understanding early care and education participation among immigrant families.* Washington, DC: Center for Law and Social Policy.

McLanahan, S., & Sandefur, G. (1994). *Growing up with a single parent: What hurts, what helps.* Cambridge, MA: Harvard University Press.

McLoyd, V. (1998). Socioeconomic disadvantage and child development. *American Psychologist, 53*(2), 185–204.

Mezey, J., Greenberg, M., & Schumacher R. (2002). *The vast majority of federally-eligible children did not receive child care assistance in FY2000.* Washington, DC: Center for Law and Social Policy. Retrieved March 16, 2005, from *www.clasp.org/publications/1in7full.pdf*

Organization for Economic Cooperation and Development (OECD). (2006). *Early childhood education and care policy: Country note for Mexico.* Organization for Economic Cooperation and Development Directorate of Education. Retrieved March 4, 2006, from *www.oecd.org/dataoecd/11/39/34429196.pdf*

Ruggles, S., Sobek, M., Alexander, T., Fitch, C. A., Goeken, R., Hall, P. K., et al. (2004). *Integrated public use microdata series: Version 3.0* [Machine-readable database]. Minneapolis: Minnesota Population Center [producer and distributor]. Retrieved January 2006 from *www.ipums.org*

Rumbaut, R. G. (1996). Origins and destinies: Immigration, race, and ethnicity in contemporary America. In S. Pedraza & R. G. Rumbaut (Eds.), *Origins and destinies: Immigration, race, and ethnicity in America* (pp. 21–42). Belmont, CA: Wadsworth.

Rumbaut, R. G. (1999). Passages to adulthood: The adaptation of children of immigrants in Southern California. In D. J. Hernandez (Ed.), *Children of immigrants: Health, adjustment, and public assistance* (pp. 478–545). Washington, DC: National Academy Press.

Sewell, W. H., & Hauser, R. M. (1975). *Education, occupation and earnings.* New York: Academic Press.

Sewell, W. H., Hauser, R. M., & Wolf, W. C. (1980). Sex, schooling, and occupational status. *American Journal of Sociology, 83*(3), 551–583.

Shonkoff, J. P., & Phillips, D. A. (2000). *From neurons to neighborhoods: The science of early child development.* Washington, DC: National Academy Press.

Takanishi, R. (2004). Leveling the playing field: Supporting immigrant children from birth to eight. *The Future of Children* [Special issue on children of immigrants], *14*(2), 61–79.

UNICEF. (2005). *Child poverty in rich countries, 2005* (Innocenti Report Card No. 6). Florence, Italy: UNICEF Innocenti Research Centre.

U.S. Census Bureau. (2004). *Population projections.* Released March 18, 2004.

Utall, L. (1999). Using kin for child care: Embedment in the socioeconomic networks of extended families. *Journal of Marriage and the Family, 61*(4), 845–857.

Zimmermann, W., & Tumlin, K. (1999) *Patchwork policies: State assistance for immigrants under welfare reform.* (Occasional Paper No. 24). Washington, DC: The Urban Institute.

CHAPTER 2

Health of Children in Immigrant Families

Fernando S. Mendoza, Joyce R. Javier, *and* Anthony E. Burgos

Child health research is contextualized around three premises. First, children are developing organisms with respect to the processes of physical and developmental growth. These processes can be significantly influenced by a child's early environment and may have lifelong consequences on a child's health. Second, children are dependent on their families and communities through childhood and adolescence. Thus, the well-being of children's families and communities can directly impact the health of children, for better or worse. Third, childhood is the preamble for adulthood, and as such it sets the level and character of success or failure in adulthood. The repetitiveness of adverse events and/or the chronicity of negative health factors can have a major impact on the subsequent health of adults.

In studying immigrant children, each of these premises needs to be examined with regard to how the experiences of immigrant children and their families differ from those of other children in the United States. Several factors may characterize these differences, including poverty, culture and acculturation, residential status, economic opportunity, community empowerment, and interface with the health care system. In many ways children are alike all over the world, but the ecology of health—factors in the environment that nurture, protect, and heal children—differs from country to country and from community to community. Immigrant children carry the burden of interfacing between two ecological spheres, that of their country of origin and that of their new country, the United States. How well children and their immigrant families transition from one sphere to the other can have a major impact on their health. The health of immigrant communities, in turn, determines the level of integration into the U.S. mainstream, and ultimately determines the degree to which immigrant communities add to society and to the country's national strength.

In order to contextualize the health status of children in immigrant families, one must recognize the existence of underlying health disparities for racial and ethnic minority groups in the United States. The Institute of Medicine's report *Unequal Treatment* documented multiple racial and ethnic health disparities and suggested that these disparities are the result of social and economic inequities and persistent ethnic and racial discrimination (Smedley, Stith, & Nelson, 2003). The report concluded that many sources contribute to disparities in health care—including the health care system, providers, managers, and the patients themselves. The report also clearly stated that bias, stereotyping, and prejudice contribute to disparities in health care for racial and ethnic populations. Therefore, since a large proportion of immigrant children live in similar communities, comparing them with the traditional U.S. minority groups can provide insight into the added burden children in immigrant families may experience beyond those of similar racial and ethnic backgrounds.

As described in Chapter 1 by Hernandez, Denton, and Macartney, Latin America and Asia are the predominant areas providing immigrants to the United States. Therefore, because of the predominance of their populations, and the availability of health information on these groups of immigrant children, this chapter reviews the health of children in immigrant families principally from Latin America and Asia. The chapter describes the primary data sources used to study children in immigrant families and important health determinants for immigrant children's health. A review of what is known about immigrant children's health status in multiple clinical areas, including health care services, is provided. These findings are used to propose a health model for better understanding the factors that may influence the health of immigrant children and lead to the "immigrant paradox." Finally, this chapter makes recommendations for research and policy aimed toward improving the health of children in immigrant families.

HOW CHILDREN IN IMMIGRANT FAMILIES ARE STUDIED IN HEALTH RESEARCH

Data Availability and Validity

A number of factors play a role in determining the amount and quality of research done on children in immigrant families. The key factor is the availability of data that identify generational status, race, ethnicity, and country of origin. A second factor is the availability (or lack thereof) of samples large enough to use to accurately assess prevalence and test hypotheses. A third important factor is the validity of measures used to assess immigrant subjects. Although measures may be appropriately translated, translation does not assure that measures have considered the appropriate conceptual models of health held by immigrant respondents. Thus, the response to a question may be invalid and not reflect the true situation of the respondent. Moreover, the process of acculturation also makes these beliefs changeable over time, emphasizing the need for longitudinal data, a fourth factor required for quality research in this area.

Review of the literature shows that studies of children in immigrant families in the United States have used both large survey data sets and smaller primary data sets. The former have been useful in determining prevalence rates, and the latter have been useful for exploring and assessing children's risk in greater depth. However, randomized clinical trials are rare in this field, although such research will be needed to eliminate the health disparities found among these children. The large secondary data sets available to study immigrant children in the United States include the National Health and Nutrition Examination Survey (NHANES), the National Health Interview Survey (NHIS), vital statistics (birth and mortality), and the National Longitudinal Study of Adolescent Health (ADD Health). The NHANES is a periodic survey of the nation's population conducted approximately every decade, and includes physical examination, laboratory, and questionnaire measures. The NHIS is a household survey conducted on a biannual basis with periodic supplements on children's health. The vital statistics provide annual data that can link births to deaths, and have been used to assess low birthweight, prematurity, and infant mortality. These federal surveys are conducted by the National Center for Health Statistics and are conducted in Spanish and English.

The ADD Health is a school-based survey of 90,000 adolescents at 132 schools across the country, and has data from an additional 5,000 adolescents sampled at home. Parent, teacher, and peer data are also collected. There are approximately 5,000 Mexican American adolescents in this survey. Unfortunately, the survey is not translated into other languages.

Few state-based surveys collect sufficient information on children in immigrant families to make accurate assessments of health status. One exception is the California Health Interview Survey (CHIS), a population-based, random-digit-dialing telephone survey of civilian households. CHIS is conducted in six languages: English, Spanish, Chinese,

Vietnamese, Korean, and Khmer (Cambodian) and is designed to produce reliable estimates for major racial categories as well as ethnic subgroups. Pertinent variables collected from each participant of CHIS include nativity status, citizenship/immigration status, and number of years in the United States. This survey has been conducted in 2001, 2003, and 2005. Among all of these surveys, the CHIS provides a model for assessing immigrant populations. It provides the survey questions in a number of languages, and attempts to assure validity for each language by reverse translating questions and assessing their cultural meaning.

Risk Factors for Poor Health: Poverty, Generational Status, and Language

The combination of poverty, generational status, and language adds up to greater risk for poor health for many immigrants, particularly those from Mexico. Around the world, poverty has been closely linked with poor health outcomes and increased mortality. In the United States, a sim ilar association was found in a review of the literature involving all causes of mortality, acute and chronic illness, injuries, and parental perceptions of children's health (Chen, Matthews, & Boyce, 2002). In characterizing this association, Chen et al. proposed three models of the relationship between poverty and health outcomes: (1) childhood limited model—effects depend on the developmental stage of the child; (2) childhood–adolescent persistent model—effect on early set point has lifelong affect; and (3) adolescent emergent model—negative effects are cumulative. Differences also can be seen based on who is reporting. In a five-site national study of 6- to 11-year-old children, Starfield, Robertson, and Riley (2002) compared self- and parental reports of health, and confirmed the presence of social class gradients. However, they were seen more in parental assessments of health than in those made by children, supporting the idea that differences may be more developmental and cumulative.

Poverty is a significant issue for immigrant families in the United States. The U.S. Census Bureau reports that African Americans, Latin Americans, and Native Americans have poverty rates three times that of European Americans, 24% versus 8% (DeNavas-Walt, Proctor, & Lee, 2005). However, poverty rates are much higher when examined for families with children, and when generational status is taken into account. Data from the NHANES III (Table 2.1) show that three-fourths of first-generation Mexican American children and their families live below the poverty line. This is approximately three times the percentage reported by the U.S. Census Bureau for Mexican Americans overall. Although

TABLE 2.1. Demographics and Health Parameters for Immigrant and Nonimmigrant Children in the United States: Data from NHANES III

	Mexican American (%)				
	First generation	Second generation	Third generation	African American (%)	European American (%)
Demographics, access, utilization					
Poverty index <1.0	76.1	53.3	34.1	47	14.9
Parental education < 9th grade	79.3	72.1	35	31.5	15.3
Language of family					
English	3.2	17.6	78.1	98.6	99.5
Spanish	93.8	71.9	7.6	1.1	0.4
Bilingual	3	10.4	14.3	0.3	0.1
Uninsured*	63.9	26.1	16.4	9.9	7.6
Usual source of care*	52.2	87.5	91.8	88.7	94.1
Specific provider*	48.1	72.4	80.2	78.1	86.2
Visit to MD in past year*	53.7	77.4	78.5	76.3	81.3
Asthma prevalence					
< 5 years	2.2 (1.20)	5.2 (0.88)	8.1 (1.72)	9.0 (0.75)	5.1 (0.55)
6–11 years	3.8 (2.74)	9.8 (2.71)	15.0 (4.09)	9.4 (1.00)	10.6 (1.41)
12–16 years	3.1 (1.77)	6.6 (1.91)	8.5 (1.92)	12.6 (1.63)	12.8 (1.67)
In fair or poor health					
< 5 years	23.9 (3.33)	16.8 (1.05)	6.3 (0.83)	4.9 (0.73)	1.8 (0.35)
6–11 years	27.6 (7.70)	20.0 (2.28)	6.6 (1.43)	6.9 (0.91)	2.0 (0.47)
12–16 years	28.7 (4.99)	15.4 (2.52)	6.8 (1.63)	7.4 (1.20)	3.5 (0.79)
Teeth in fair or poor condition					
< 5 years	39.3	26	21	13.7	6.9
6–11 years	60.1	42.6	23.5	22.7	12.2
12–16 years	50.8	36.3	16.4	20.2	11.5

* $p < .0001$.

levels of poverty decrease in the second generation, it is not until the third generation that Mexican Americans improve their economic and educational profiles to levels resembling those of African Americans. Thus, while poverty is a major issue for traditional minority groups in the United States, it can be an even greater problem for immigrants, as manifested by the plight of first-generation Mexican Americans. Linked with high poverty levels, low levels of educational attainment for parents may also add to the increased risk for poor health among children in immigrant families. Finally, while Mexican immigrants represent the largest group of immigrants, other immigrant groups may have different economic profiles, and therefore need to be assessed appropriately for their risk for poor health based on their socioeconomic status (SES).

Another major risk factor for poor health is not speaking the language of the health providers. For most immigrants this is a significant problem. For example, data from the 2000 California census indicated that 37.8% of households spoke a language other than English at home, and a quarter of this group was linguistically isolated, as no one over the age of 14 spoke English well (Lopez, 2003). Given that 31% of the population is Latino, the predominant foreign language spoken in California is Spanish. However, only 4% of physicians in California are Latino, and in a survey of Californian physicians only about one-quarter of primary care physicians and one-fifth of specialty care physicians reported that they spoke Spanish (Forte, McGinnis, Beaulieu, Hernandez, & Salsberg, 2004; Yoon, Grumbach, & Bindman, 2004). When stratified by physicians who care for publicly insured patients (Medi-Cal), the number of Spanish-speaking physicians decreased by an additional 60–70%. Consequently, those immigrants who do not speak English or are limited English proficient appear to be at greater risk for less access to health care, and thereby at risk for poorer health outcomes.

The Traditional Model of Health and Socioeconomic Status versus the Immigrant Paradox

In the above discussion, the traditional model of SES and health is represented. In this model (Figure 2.1), individuals contribute genetic and behavioral factors that affect their health outcomes. The environment, as

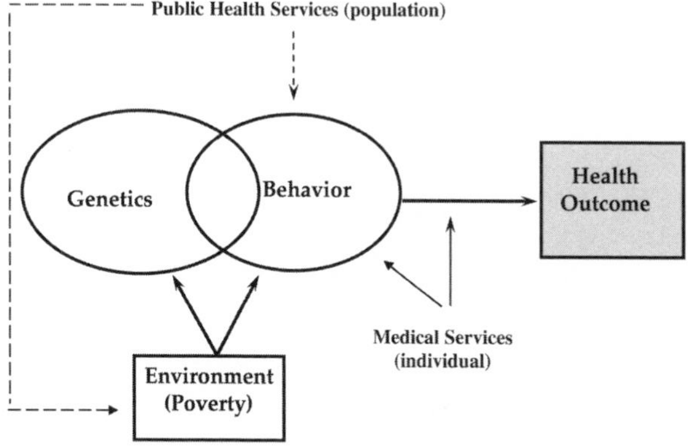

FIGURE 2.1. Traditional health.

determined by SES, interacts with an individual's genetic potential for illness and health behaviors to either increase or decrease their risk for poor health. For example, poverty increases the risk for external health risk factors, such as infectious diseases, which, given the individual's genetic propensity to combat infection and behaviors to avoid or manage them, leads to specific health outcomes. Although environmental factors influence the development of chronic illness by exposing a subject to external triggers, in general it is the individual's genetic predisposition for the illness that ultimately determines its presence. Asthma is one example of this type of chronic illness. Subjects must have the genetic predisposition for asthma, but the severity or exacerbation of symptoms can be the result of environmental factors, which are more often present in impoverished environments.

In addition to genetic and behavioral components, the model includes the factors of health care and public health that can influence the health outcomes of individuals. At an individual level, the health care system intercedes to improve health once a problem is identified and health care is accessed. In contrast, public health works to improve population health by changing the environmental elements or health behaviors of a certain population. Examples of such interventions include clean water, elimination of lead from gasoline, and antismoking campaigns.

Thus, in the traditional health model, even with public health interventions and access to health care, individuals living in poverty and/or with low educational attainment are presumed to be at high risk for poor health outcomes compared to those not in poverty. However, contradictory observations in immigrant populations raise questions about the robustness and generalizability of the traditional health model. For example, Table 2.1 shows that first- and second-generation Mexican American children have higher levels of poverty, lower levels of parental education, and more limited access to health care compared to European American children. Yet, as will be shown below, in some areas of health, first- and second-generation Mexican American children have equal or better health outcomes compared to European American children. This contradiction to the traditional health model has been named the "immigrant paradox."

The following section describes various health findings for children in immigrant families, from birth through adolescence. Some of these finding are supportive of the immigrant paradox while others are not. As a result of the availability of studies in the literature on children in immigrant families, most of the information presented is on Latin American children.

HEALTH PROFILES OF CHILDREN IN IMMIGRANT FAMILIES

Infant Mortality and Low Birthweight

Two commonly used measures of children's health are infant mortality and low birthweight (less than 2,500 grams). Birth and death certificates in the United States include a number of variables that may be associated with poor neonatal outcomes and/or infant death in the first year of life, including maternal race, ethnicity, and country of origin. Furthermore, the information from a birth certificate can also be linked to the death certificate for the same infant. For a number of years, birth and infant death data have been used to assess differences in these measures between immigrant and nonimmigrant mothers.

From studies using linked data, it is clear that infants of immigrant women have better outcomes in both infant mortality and low birthweight than nonimmigrant women (Landale, Oropeza, & Gorman, 1999). Although racial and ethnic differences have been shown in both infant mortality and low birthweight (e.g., African Americans and Filipino Americans have the highest rates in both parameters), children of immigrant mothers have better outcomes in all racial and ethnic groups. For example, children of immigrant Mexican American women had better infant mortality and lower prevalence of low birthweight than children of both United States–born Mexican American and European American women, despite much greater poverty and less access to prenatal care for immigrant Mexican American women. Similar differences were seen between United States–born and foreign-born African Americans. The unexpected differences in low birthweight and infant mortality between children of immigrants and United States–born mothers are the primary observations leading to the description of the "immigrant paradox." Similar findings have been confirmed repeatedly over the past two decades in multiple settings, suggesting that the phenomena is real and deserves deeper exploration.

Physical Growth and the History of Poverty

A child's physical growth is affected by poverty: greater poverty results in greater impairment of growth (Martorell, Mendoza, & Castillo, 1988). The two main mechanisms for this effect are (1) food insufficiency leading to lack of calories and micronutrients and (2) an environment that increases the risk of illness, usually in the form of recurrent infectious diseases (commonly diarrheal illness). Illness impairs growth either by increasing caloric needs or, in the case of diarrheal illness, by interfering with nutrient absorption. Anthropometrically, the resulting malnutrition can lead to underweight for age (wasting) or short stature for age (stunting).

As a result of malnutrition in the country of origin, poor immigrant children to the United States not infrequently have stunted and wasted growth, as well as micronutrient deficiencies that can lead to nutritional diseases, such as iron deficiency anemia. This is particularly true if the immigrant family has a history of long-term poverty in the country of origin. Clinical studies in medical clinics, public health centers, and public schools have documented both wasting and stunting among immigrant children, and have shown improvement with appropriate medical and nutritional services. In a study of predominately immigrant students in a school-based setting, Schumacher, Pawson, and Kretchmer (1987) showed that with appropriate medical and nutritional services, children could actually have "catch-up" growth, resulting in a higher velocity of growth. A review of growth studies and of current national data suggests that Mexican American immigrants are now more likely to suffer from obesity than from malnutrition (Malina, Martorell, & Mendoza, 1986; Ogden, Flegal, Carroll, & Johnson, 2002). This trend is believed to be the result of stunting without wasting, a phenomena that is commonly seen among Mexican Americans (Martorell, Mendoza, & Castillo, 1989; Pawson, Martorell, & Mendoza, 1991). The mismatch occurs because weight is more responsive to catch-up growth than height, when adequate calories and appropriate health care are received.

Interestingly, countries contributing immigrant children and families to the United States have also begun to report increased rates of obesity. In Mexico the prevalence of obesity has doubled (del-Rio Navarro et al., 2004), while at the same time the very impoverished part of the population continues to suffer from caloric malnutrition. Unlike in the United States, obesity in developing countries appears to be problematic for middle- and upper-SES groups. Thus, clinicians in the United States caring for immigrant children from developing countries are likely to see both ends of the nutritional spectrum, that is, both traditional malnutrition and obesity.

Unfortunately, immigrant families may not view obesity as a bad thing. Indeed, their perspective on the "healthy" body physique may be quite different than expected. Data from NHANES III showed that Mexican American children, when rated by their mothers, had higher body mass index values than European American children at every physique category (Klaudt, Schetzina, Mendoza, & Robinson, 2002). This suggests that immigrant families may perceive heavier children to be healthier.

Thus, the obesity epidemic in the United States is beginning to reach the children of immigrants, likely due to differences in caloric intake and maternal perception of the "healthy" body physique. The widespread penetration of this problem is showing itself in other groups—Asian and Pacific Islander children also have a growing rate of obesity—and programs are needed to prevent unhealthy acculturation-related changes in diet and physical activity and to promote the healthier aspects of traditional lifestyles (Harrison et al., 2005).

Overall, physical growth data indicates that immigrant children (from the first generation) may suffer from various levels of malnutrition, principally stunting, but they also now suffer from obesity. For children in immigrant families who are second generation, it is less clear whether stunting is a problem, but obesity is certainly a growing issue, as it is with other U.S. children. Lastly, since the physical growth data are mostly from Mexican American children, caution should be taken in generalizing to other groups. Nonetheless, the immigrant paradox in physical growth does not seem to hold, and physical growth of children in immigrant families is mostly dependent on the degree and duration of poverty.

Chronic Illness

Although chronic illness tends to be genetically determined, the identification or diagnosis and treatment of a chronic illness is often dependent on health care access. Early and effective treatment can improve quality of life and minimize morbidity and mortality. Asthma is the most common chronic illness of childhood and provides an effective model for illustrating these characteristics.

Lugogo and Kraft (2006) have reported lower asthma rates for Latin Americans compared to African and European Americans. Yet there is significant variability in asthma prevalence among Latin Americans. Puerto Rican children, though not considered immigrants, suffer much higher rates of asthma than the children of other Latino groups (Mendoza et al., 1991). Moreover, among U.S. children, Puerto Ricans have the highest asthma prevalence, morbidity, and mortality, while Mexican American are among the lowest in these areas. The variability in asthma rates in Latin American children is probably due to differences in genetic predisposition. In addition to differences in the prevalence of chronic illness, genetic differences among racial and ethnic groups may also manifest themselves physiologically. By utilizing genomic pharmacological techniques, Burchard and colleagues (2004) described ethnic-specific differences in the response to the drug albuterol, a mainstay in the treatment of asthma. These differences may contribute to differences in disease outcomes in asthma, and further underscore the need for additional research on racial–ethnic differences in chronic disease. These differences also emphasize the consequences of genetic variability, and the dangers of aggregating groups of children under one ethnic grouping (e.g., Latino or Asian).

For children, the prevalence and consequences of asthma and other chronic diseases are not only genetically determined, but also dependent on access to health care, which ensures identification and treatment of the chronic illness. Data from NHANES III (Table 2.1) showed that the reported prevalence of asthma increased by generation for Mexican American children. Third and later generations had the highest prevalence of any school-age group (Mendoza & Dixon, 1999). However, during adolescence, the prevalence of asthma was actually lower in Mexican American than in African American or European American children. These differences may be due to lack of access to a physician, which limits recognition of a child's asthma, and thereby also limits parents' knowledge of the presence of asthma in their children. In a follow-up study of the same data, the parental reported symptom of chronic cough in children was similar among first- and later generation Mexican Americans and equal to that of European American children, suggesting that the first-generation children may indeed have unrecognized asthma (Agredano, Schetzina, & Mendoza, 2004).

Thus, if the underdiagnosis of disease is prominent among children in immigrant families, then in the area of chronic illness and other reported conditions that require physician identification for validating their presence, the immigrant paradox of lower reported medical conditions may be erroneous, and a manifestation of lack of access to health care.

Health Behaviors, Health Perception, and Mental Health

Given that high-risk health behaviors can significantly impact children's health, it is important to examine the effects of race, ethnicity, SES, and immigrant status on such health behaviors. Analyses of the ADD Health by Harris (1999) showed that first-generation Mexican Americans had the lowest levels of risky health behaviors, but that these behaviors increased in every succeeding generation (see Table 2.2). Sexual activity was highest among African Americans and third- and later generation Mexican American adolescents. Acts of violence were lowest among first-generation Mexican American and European American adolescents, while tobacco and drug use were lowest among African American and first-generation Mexican American adolescents. These data seem to support the immigrant paradox, in that immigrant children exhibit better health behaviors, compared to later generations of similar ethnic children and other U.S. children. It also suggests that the U.S. lifestyle may increase the rates of risky health behaviors.

TABLE 2.2. Health Status and Risky Behaviors of Adolescents: Data from National Longitudinal Study of Adolescent Health

	Mexican American (%)				
Risk behavior	First generation	Second generation	Third + generation	African American (%)	European American (%)
Fair to poor health	13	15.5	13.4	11.5	8.1
Ever had sex	35.1	38.7	45.9	54.8	36.7
Acts of violence	16.6	24.9	32.9	27.2	19.4
Used tobacco or drugs	8.5	19.7	29.5	8.6	25.1

Note. Data from Harris (1999).

Harris's analysis also reported the proportion of adolescents who considered their health to be either fair or poor (Table 2.2). First-generation Mexican American adolescents had a rate comparable to subsequent generations of Mexican Americans and similar to the rate for African American adolescents. Yet all of these groups reported rates significantly higher than European American adolescents. In contrast, data from NHANES III showed that the proportion of adolescents reported to be in fair or poor health was highest among first-generation Mexican American children, and that the proportions decreased with each succeeding generation (Mendoza & Dixon, 1999, Table 1). This was true both for parental-reported (<12 yrs) and adolescent self-reported perceived health. Third- and later generation Mexican Americans and African Americans had similar responses (6–7%), which were twice as high as European Americans. However, these rates were still significantly lower than the first- and second-generation Mexican American children (29% and 15%). Thus, perceived health seems to be significantly affected by generational status. Whether this is a reflection of actual or perceived health requires further research, and should temper our characterization of immigrant children as healthier than nonimmigrant children.

Psychological health can also have a significant effect on perceived physical health. In this arena, immigrant families may have a number of stressors that can impact the psychological health of all family members. First, the reason for immigration may be a significant stressor, especially if physical or mental health threats were perceived or experienced by the family. Second, the process of immigration itself, particularly without documentation, can be stressful both during and after arrival in the United States. Third, the process of integration into U.S. society can be a major challenge. Children and adolescents must venture into a new world, and the entire family must adjust to changes in culture and values.

The best exploration of these issues is done with in-depth community and clinical studies, which allow the inclusion of a broader array of immigrant groups and the use of qualitative data. Such in-depth evaluation has revealed the complex effects of immigration on the mental health of children in immigrant families. For example, the examination of the phases of preflight, flight, and resettlement has shown that immigrant children and adolescents suffer from conflict-related exposure, which can have significant clinical implications (Lustig et al., 2004). Qualitative assessments of Bosnian war refugees have documented significant changes in family life after political violence, and these types of assessments have led to a better understanding of family needs. Improved understanding has in turn led to improved family-oriented mental health services (Weine et al., 2004). While immigrants face multiple challenges related to the process of immigration, similar stress is also experienced by those family members left behind, particularly children who are left fatherless when their fathers migrate. Indeed, adolescents with absent migrant fathers have been shown to be at higher risk for mental health problems compared to adolescents with fathers (Aguiler-Guzman, de Snyder, Romero, & Medina-Mora, 2004). Since the migration of the father before the rest of the family is not an unusual scenario, when children are finally brought to the United States they may have added risk for psychological problems as a result of having had an absent father for the period prior.

The complex impact that migration has on children's mental health emphasizes the need for mental health services for immigrant children. Data from the U.S. component of the 1997–1998 World Health Organization Study of Health Behavior in School Children showed that non-English-speaking adolescents experienced higher psychosocial and parental risks than European American adolescents. Environmental psychosocial risk factors for immigrant youth included alienation from classmates and being bullied, while in-home risk factors included the feeling that parents were not able or willing to help them (Yu, Huang, Schwalberg, Overpeck, & Kogan, 2003). These findings reinforce the need for culturally sensitive mental health services for immigrant children. For instance, Daley (2005) reported that United States–born Cambodian children in immigrant families, who were at risk for depression and gang involvement, showed improved utilization of health services when services were culturally sensitive.

Overall, there appears to be some degree of contradiction in the health behaviors and mental health status of children in immigrant families. While reports of less risky health behaviors among immigrant children imply good mental health status, there appears to be a high prevalence of poor perceived health and mental health problems. How these are related to each other needs further exploration, but again, these observations expose the flaws in the immigrant paradox.

Oral Health

While other physical health parameters appear to be better than expected, at least by parental report, dental problems are more frequently reported by the parents of immigrant children than by the parents of nonimmigrant children (Table 2.1). This may be explained by the severity of dental problems and the ease with which parents can identify them. Forty to 60% of first-generation Mexican American parents report their child's teeth to be in fair to poor condition. In contrast, less than 12% of parents of European American children report this same condition (Mendoza & Dixon, 1999). Similarly, data from HHANES in the early 1980s showed a higher prevalence of dental caries and of unmet restoration dental needs in Mexican American children and youth (Pollick, Pawson, Martorell, & Mendoza, 1991). Unfortunately, access to dental services is even more problematic for immigrant children than access to health care.

Environmental Health

Environmental health is another key factor in assessing the overall health status of poor immigrant children, as their housing and living circumstances frequently confer greater risk. The most concerning environmental toxin is lead, which even at low levels, 10 µg/dl or greater, can have significant impact on a child's health and development. In an analysis of NHANES III, children ages 1–5 years of age were assessed for lead levels greater than 10 µg/dl (Brody et al., 1994). The findings showed that African Americans in all SES and geographic conditions had the highest proportion of children with blood lead levels greater than 10 µg/dl compared to Mexican American and European American children. In contrast, among Mexican American children, only those in large inner-city areas had higher levels than European American children. Although these data were not examined with regard to children's immigrant status, the extrapolation of risk to poor immigrant children living in inner cities is clear, particularly when coupled with less access to health care, which would limit screening and monitoring of lead levels.

Infectious Diseases

Since many children immigrate to the United States from developing countries, it is not unusual to have children arrive in the United States with infections contracted in their country of origin. The most common infectious diseases reported are parasitic infections and tuberculosis. Immigrant children may harbor infectious diseases that U.S. physicians may be inexperienced in diagnosing and treating (Committee on Community Health Services, 2005). These include diseases such as malaria, amebiasis, schistosomiasis, and other helminthic infections; hepatitis A and hepatitis B; and tuberculosis. Tuberculosis and hepatitis B are especially relevant to children in immigrant families from Latin America and Asia who have not had access to health care (Armstrong, Mast, Wojczynski, & Margolis, 2001; Deuson, Brodovicz, Barker, Zhou, & Euler, 2001) .

Although the overall number of cases of tuberculosis in children is declining in the United States, foreign-born children remain at higher risk. Using national surveillance data from 1993–2001, Nelson, Schneider, Wells, and Moore (2004) reported that 24% of children with tuberculosis were foreign-born, with the largest numbers originating from Mexico (39.8%), the Philippines (8.6%), and Vietnam (5.7%). The diagnosis of active pulmonary tuberculosis in a child is considered a sentinel event, because such disease usually results from recent transmission from an adult with active disease. Access to appropriate health services for tuberculosis is imperative to ensure the health of the child, family, and community through adequate treatment and prevention.

Health Care Access and Utilization

Health care access for children in immigrant families is the most important health issue that needs to be addressed. Immigrant children and their parents have some of the lowest reported rates of health insurance, even though most parents in immigrant families are working. As seen in Table 2.1, first-generation Mexican American children have the highest rates of being uninsured and the lowest rates of having a regular source of care, a specific provider, and a visit to a physician in the past year (Burgos, Schetzina, Dixon, & Mendoza, 2005). Similarly, data from NHIS showed that immigrant Latino and Asian children had the highest rates of no physician visit in the past year (39% and 34%, respectively, compared to 17% for United States–born Latino and Asian children). Affordability and health insurance were shown to be the prime barriers to accessing health care (Brown, Wyn, Yu, Valenzuela, & Dong, 1998).

Immigration status also affects access to care for immigrant children. Data from the CHIS showed that almost half of children ages 0–17 years in California were either immigrants themselves or lived in families with at least one immigrant parent. In families of undocumented parents, both United States–born and undocumented children were more likely to have fair or poor perceived health, lack a usual source of care, and lack health insurance when compared to United States–born children of United States–born parents (Pourat, Lessard, Lulejian, Becerra, & Chakraborty, 2003). These findings suggest the need for culturally appropriate outreach programs to increase the enrollment of eligible children in health services. This finding also raises the question as to whether fear about immigration issues prevents parents from accessing programs and services for their eligible children. If this is the case, then more education of the immigrant community should be undertaken to increase enrollment in health access programs.

Role of Language and Cultural Competency in Access to Health Care

Even when access is granted to children in immigrant families, the health care system itself can affect utilization, treatment compliance, and patient satisfaction. Some investigators have begun to explore the role of the health care systems in the delivery of health care to immigrant populations. Using the CHIS 2001, Guendelman, Angulo, Wier, and Oman (2005) found that uninsured immigrant children had higher odds of perceiving discrimination and postponing emergency room (ER) and dental care visits. Furthermore, being undocumented and non-English-speaking contributed to missed physician and ER visits. Thus, in addition to insurance status, language, culture, and discrimination can all contribute to decreased access and utilization.

To further explore the effect of language on clinical care, Flores and colleagues (2003) examined language interpretation in clinical care and found that medical interpreters commonly made errors in interpreting, with an average of 31 errors per encounter. Of particular concern was that 63% of the errors had potential clinical consequences. These and other studies point to the need to explore the interaction between immigrant patients and the health care system. The health care system in every community will ultimately be challenged to become more culturally competent.

THE IMMIGRANT PARADOX AND THE FAMILY–COMMUNITY HEALTH PROMOTION MODEL

From the information presented above, one can conclude that the immigrant paradox is manifested in some health outcomes, such as low birthweight, infant mortality, and risky health behaviors in adolescents.

In other health areas, it is less evident. If the immigrant paradox is the result of cultural health behaviors, then these behaviors should be understood and promoted both in the immigrant community and in other communities. The Family–Community Health Promotion Model (Figure 2.2) was proposed to model factors that may contribute to the immigrant paradox. This model focuses on positive family health behaviors that are supported by the culture of the immigrant community and reinforced by improved functional health, a product of physical and mental health. It is functional health that directly affects the individual's perceived health status, and through that validates the belief in the positive cultural health behavior (Mendoza & Fuentes-Afflick, 1999). If the immigrant paradox is a product of culturally based health behaviors, then engaging in these behaviors would improve functional health and perceived health. Although SES is still a major factor in health outcomes, a buffer of positive health behaviors supported by the culture of the family and community could provide the counterbalance to an impoverished environment. This, however, is not to be mistaken as a replacement for adequate health care or good public health services. Indeed, the evidence presented above implies that the findings that contradict the immigrant paradox are the result of inadequate health care and public health services. Nonetheless, further research is needed to identify the behaviors that support the immigrant paradox and how to maintain and expand them.

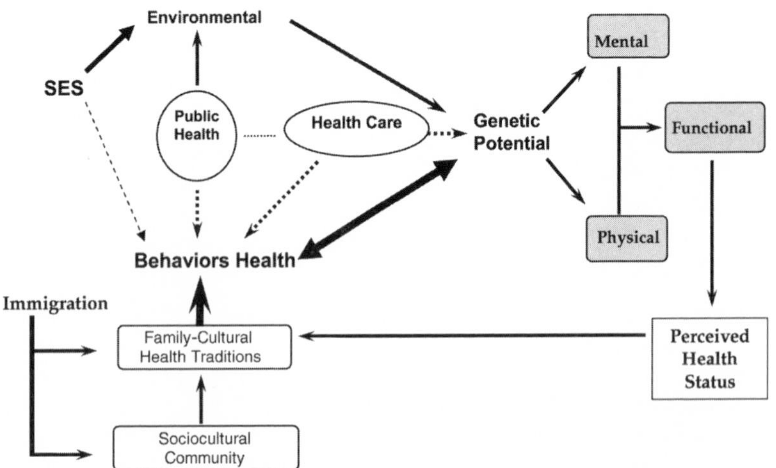

FIGURE 2.2. Family–Community Health Promotion model.

RESEARCH AND POLICY ISSUES FOR CHILDREN IN IMMIGRANT FAMILIES

The most important health policy issues for children in immigrant families fall into three areas. First, ongoing data collection is needed to monitor the health status of children in immigrant families, inclusive of mental health. Without such data, understanding both the problems and the changes in those problems will be impossible. This requires both federal and state data that can monitor the diversity of immigrant children and compare them with other U.S. children.

Second, children in immigrant families, whether U.S. citizens or not, need to have access to culturally competent health care. Without such care, there is risk of having a large group of children excluded from the American dream, and losing their potential as future citizens. This will require both financial resources and commitment from the heath care system to adapt to meet the needs of culturally diverse immigrant families.

Third, more research is needed to improve our knowledge about children in immigrant families, and about how to assist with their integration into this nation. This will require the collaboration of a number of disciplines, and similar to the approach taken in theses chapters, a view of the world of these children from a number of different perspectives.

REFERENCES

Agredano, Y., Schetzina, K., & Mendoza, F. (2004). Are immigrant Mexican American children at greater risk for asthma? *Pediatric Research*, *44*(4, Part 2 of 2), 234A.

Aguiler-Guzman, R. M., de Snyder, V. N., Romero, M., & Medina-Mora, M. E. (2004). Parental absence and international migration: Stressors and compensators associated with the mental health of Mexican teenagers of rural origin. *Adolescence*, *39*, 711–723.

Armstrong, G. L., Mast, E. E., Wojczynski, M. & Margolis, H. S. (2001). Childhood hepatitis B virus infections in the United States before Hepatitits B immunization. *Pediatrics*, *108*(5), 1123–1128.

Brody, D. J., Pirkle, J. L., Kramer, R. A., Flegal, K. M., Matte, T. D., Gunter, E. W., et al. (1994). Blood lead levels in the US population: Phase 1 of the Third National Health and Nutrition Examination Survey (NHANES III, 1988 to 1991). *Journal of the American Medical Association*, *272*(4), 277–283.

Brown, E. R., Wyn, R., Yu, H., Valenzuela, A., & Dong, L. (1999) Access to health insurance and health care for children in immigrant families. In D. J.

Hernandez (Ed.), *Children of immigrants: Health, adjustment, and public assistance* (pp. 126–186). Washington, DC: National Academy Press.

Burchard, E. G., Avila, P. C., Nazario, S., Casal, J., Torres, A., Rodriguez-Santana, J. R., et al. (2004). Lower bronchodilator responsiveness in Puerto Rican than in Mexican subjects with asthma. *American Journal of Respiratory and Critical Care Medicine, 169*(3), 386–392.

Burgos, A., Schetzina, K., Dixon, B., & Mendoza, F. (2005). Importance of generational status in examining access to and utilization of health care services by Mexican American children. *Pediatrics, 115*(3), e322–e330.

Chen, D., Matthews, K. A., & Boyce, W. T. (2002). Socioeconomic differences in children's health: How and why do these relationships change with age. *Psychological Bulletin, 128*(2), 295–329.

Committee on Community Health Services. (2005). Providing care for immigrant, homeless, and migrant children. *Pediatrics, 115*(4), 1095–1100.

Daley, T. C. (2005). Beliefs about treatment of mental health problems among Cambodian American children and parents. *Social Science and Medicine, 61*(11), 2384–2395.

del Rio-Navarro, B. E., Velazquez-Monroy, O., Sanchez-Castillo, C. P., Lara-Esqueda, A., Berber, A., Fanghanel, G., et al. (2004). The high prevalence of overweight and obesity in Mexican children. *Obesity, 12*(2), 215–223.

DeNavas-Walt, C., Proctor, B. D., & Lee, C. H. (2005). *Income, poverty, and health insurance coverage in the United States: 2004* (Current Population Reports, 60-229). Washington, DC: Bureau of the Census.

Deuson, R. R., Brodovicz, K. G., Barker, L., Zhou, F., & Euler, G. L. (2001). Economic analysis of a child vaccination project among Asian Americans in Philadelphia, PA. *Archives of Pediatric and Adolescent Medicine, 155*(8), 909–914.

Flores, G. L., Mayo, S. J., Zuckerman, B., Abreu, M., Medina, L., & Hardt, E. J. (2003). Errors in medical interpretation and their potential clinical consequences in pediatric encounters. *Pediatrics, 111*(1), 6–14.

Forte, G., McGinnis, S., Beaulieu, M., Hernandez, B., & Salsberg, E. (2004). *California physician workforce: Supply and demand through 2015.* Rensselaer, NY: Center for Health Workforce Studies, School of Public Health, University at Albany, State University of New York.

Guendelman, S., Angulo, V., Wier, M., & Oman, D. (2005). Overcoming the odds: Access to care for immigrant children in working poor families in California. *Maternal and Child Health Journal, 9*(4), 351–362.

Harris, K. M. (1999). The health status and risk behaviors of adolescents in immigrant families in children of immigrants. In D. Hernandez (Ed.), *Children of immigrants: Health, adjustment, and public assistance* (pp. 286–347). Washington, DC: National Academy Press.

Harrison, G. G., Kagawa-Singer, M., Foerster, S. B., Lee, H., Pham Kim, L., Nguyen, T. U., et al. (2005). Seizing the moment: California's opportunity to prevent nutrition-related health disparities in low-income Asian American population. *Cancer, 104*(12, Suppl.), 2962–2968.

Klaudt, M., Schetzina, K., Mendoza, F., & Robinson, T. (2002, February). *Racial/*

ethnic differences in maternal perception of children's weight. Paper delivered at the annual meeting of the Ambulatory Pediatric Association, Region IX and X, Carmel, CA.

Landale, N. S., Oropeza, R. S., & Gorman, B. K. (1999). Immigration and infant health: Birth outcomes of immigrant and native-born women. In D. Hernandez (Ed.), *Children of immigrants: Health, adjustment, and public assistance.* Washington, DC: National Research Council and Institute of Medicine, National Academy Press.

Lopez, A. (2003). *Californians' use of English and other languages: Census 2000 summary* (Race and ethnicity in California: Demographic report series No. 14). Stanford, CA: Center for Comparative Studies of Race and Ethnicity, Stanford University.

Lugogo, N. L., & Kraft, M. (2006). Epidemiology of asthma. *Clinics in Chest Medicine, 27*(1), 1–15.

Lustig, S. L., Kia-Keating, M., Knight, W. G., Geltman, P., Ellis, H., Kinzie, J. D., et al. (2004). Review of child and adolescent refugee mental health. *Journal of the American Academy of Child and Adolescent Psychiatry, 43*(1), 24–36.

Malina, R., Martorell, R., & Mendoza, F. (1986). Growth status of Mexican American children and youth: Historical trends and contemporary issues. *Yearbook of Physical Anthropology, 29*, 45–79.

Martorell, R., Mendoza, F., & Castillo, R. (1988). Poverty and stature in children. In J. C. Waterlow (Ed.), *Linear growth retardation in less developed countries* (Vol. 14 of the Nestle Nutrition Workshop Series, pp. 57–73). New York: Raven Press.

Martorell, R., Mendoza, F., & Castillo, R. (1989). Genetic and environmental determinants of growth in Mexican Americans. *Pediatrics, 84*(5), 864–871.

Mendoza, F., & Dixon, L. B. (1999). The health and nutritional status of immigrant Hispanic children: Analyses of the Hispanic Health and Nutrition Examination Survey. In D. Hernandez (Ed.), *Children of immigrants: Health, adjustment, and public assistance* (pp. 187–243). Washington, DC: National Academy Press.

Mendoza, F. S., & Fuentes-Afflick, E. (1999). Latino children's health and the family–community health promotion model. *Western Journal of Medicine, 170*(2), 85–92.

Mendoza, F. S., Ventura, S. J., Valdez, R. B., Castillo, R. O., Saldivar, L. E., Baisden, K., et al. (1991). Selected measures of health status for Mexican-American, Mainland Puerto Rican, and Cuban-American children. *Journal of the American Medical Association, 256*(2), 227–232.

Nelson, L. J., Schneider, E., Wells, C. D., & Moore, M. (2004). Epidemiology of childhood tuberculosis in the United States, 1993–2001: The need for continued vigilance. *Pediatrics, 114*(2), 333–341.

Ogden, C. L., Flegal, K. M., Carroll, M. D., & Johnson, C. L. (2002). Prevalence and trends in overweight among US children and adolescents, 1999–2000. *Journal of the American Medical Association, 288*(14), 1728–1732.

Pawson, I. G., Martorell, R., & Mendoza, F. (1991). Prevalence of overweight and obesity in US Hispanic populations. *American Journal of Clinical Nutrition, 53*, 1522S–1528S.

Pollick, H. F., Pawson, I. G., Martorell, R., & Mendoza, F. S. (1991). The estimated cost of treating unmet dental restorative needs of Mexican American children from Southwest US HHANES, 1982–83. *Journal of Public Health Dentistry, 51*(4), 195–204.

Pourat, N., Lessard, G., Lulejian, A., Becerra, L., & Chakraborty, R. (2003, March). *Demographics, health, and access to care of immigrant children in California: Identifying barriers to staying healthy.* Los Angeles: UCLA Center for Health Policy Research.

Schumacher, L. B., Pawson, I. G., & Kretchmer, N. (1987). Growth of immigrant children in the newcomer schools of San Francisco. *Pediatrics, 80*(6), 861–868.

Smedley, B. D., Stith, A. Y., & Nelson, A. R. (2003). *Unequal treatment: Confronting racial and ethnic disparities in healthcare.* Washington, DC: National Academy Press.

Starfield, B., Robertson, J., & Riley, A. (2002). Social class gradients and health in childhood. *Ambulatory Pediatrics, 2*(4), 238–246.

Weine, S. M. N., Kuauzovic, Y., Besic, S., Lezie, A., Mujagic, A., Muzurovic, J., et al. (2004). Family consequences of refugee trauma. *Family Process, 43*(2), 147–160.

Yoon, G., Grumbach, K., & Bindman, A. (2004). Access to Spanish-speaking physicians in California: Supply, insurance, or both. *Journal of the American Board of Family Practice, 17*(3), 165–172.

Yu, S. M., Huang, Z. J., Schwalberg, R. H., Overpeck, M., & Kogan, M. D. (2003). Acculturation and health and well-being of U.S. immigrant adolescents. *Journal of Adolescent Health, 33*(6), 479–488.

CHAPTER 3

Ethnic Identity Development in Immigrant Families

Jean S. Phinney *and* Anthony D. Ong

Identity, as Erikson (1968) noted, refers to "a process located in the core of the individual and yet also in the core of his communal culture" (p. 22). For immigrant families, both the individual and the communal culture are central to identity formation during acculturation. When immigrants leave one culture and settle in another, they are faced with fundamental questions regarding who they are and who they will become in their new country. Their ethnic identity, that is, their sense of belonging to their culture of origin, is a key factor in the way they adaptively respond to challenges in their new country. It is therefore important for researchers and practitioners to understand the multiple pathways that lead to the development of a secure ethnic identity, the way these pathways may change with time, and the factors that influence positive or negative identity outcomes. Such understanding can provide a base on which to build intervention programs to maintain and improve positive health and well-being in immigrant families.

In this chapter, we highlight the importance of taking a process approach to understanding ethnic identity development. Our goal is to review psychological research on ethnic identity development, discuss areas where further research is needed, and elaborate on the implications for process research in immigrant families. We begin by critically examining ethnic identity research in four areas. We consider the structure and measurement of ethnic identity and discuss factor analytic evidence, that is, research on the covariation patterns among measures designed to indicate the basic elements of ethnic identity. We next examine developmental research that suggests the ways in which ethnic identity develops with age, particularly in adolescence and young adulthood. Following this, we turn to the role of contextual factors, with a focus on immigrant families as the primary setting for ethnic identity development. We then review the role of ethnic identity in well-being and psychological adjustment among immigrants.

In the second half of the chapter we discuss directions for future research on ethnic identity development, with examples that illustrate how various approaches can be applied to questions concerning the temporal stability versus variability of ethnic identity. We conclude with a summary of the importance of ethnic identity for immigrant youth and families and some thoughts about the ways in which ethnic identity can be promoted and strengthened.

AN OVERVIEW OF ETHNIC IDENTITY RESEARCH

Constructs and Measurement

At its core, *ethnic identity* is a sense of belonging to one's ethnic group. Although ethnic identity is generally recognized as a complex and multidimensional construct, the attempt to synthesize studies of ethnic identity is plagued by the variation and ambiguity in how ethnic identity is defined and measured. The term is used in the literature with a wide range of meanings, from the specific label one uses to refer to oneself (Portes & Rumbaut, 2001) to the overall attitudes, knowledge, feelings, and behaviors related to one's ethnicity (Phinney, 1990). It is used both to refer to an enduring sense of one's ethnic self that develops over time (Phinney, 1993) and to the salience of one's ethnicity that may vary across contexts (Yip & Fuligni, 2002). It has been described in terms of individual differences in the strength of ethnic group affiliation (French, Seidman, Allen, & Aber, 2006) and in terms of specific categories and statuses (e.g., moratorium or achievement; Phinney, 1993). Furthermore, research has used a range of different measures for the assessment of ethnic identity. These different definitions and measurement approaches have hampered the study of ethnic identity and suggest the need for a theory-based review of factor analytic or measurement research on ethnic identity.

Factor analytic research is based on the logic of concomitant variation: if different operations of measurement yield measures that vary together and if such measures can be shown to be replicated in different samples of people, at different times, in different places, and, in general, under a variety of circumstances, it becomes increasingly plausible that a common factor is (or possibly several common factors are) indicated by the different measurement operations. This is the principle of concomitant variation. Most of the evidence on concomitant variation in the essential features of ethnic identity stems from use of the Multigroup Ethnic Identity Measure (MEIM) (Phinney, 1992; Roberts et al., 1999). The MEIM was developed to assess ethnic identity across diverse samples of adolescents and young adults. The measure, as presented by Roberts and colleagues (1999), has two subscales: (1) ethnic identity *exploration* (e.g., "I have spent time trying to find out more about my ethnic group, such as its history, traditions, and customs.") and (2) ethnic identity *commitment* (e.g., "I feel a strong attachment towards my own ethnic group").

Factor analytic evidence regarding the MEIM has varied across studies. In a number of studies, factor analyses of MEIM items have yielded a single-factor solution (Phinney, 1992; Ponterotto, Gretchen, Utsey, Stracuzzi, & Saya, 2003; Reese, Vera, & Pailkoff, 1998; Worrell, 2000). However, some researchers have identified a two-component structure (Roberts et al., 1999; Spencer, Icard, Harachi, Catalano, & Oxford, 2000; Yancey, Aneshensel, & Driscoll, 2001), whereas others have reported a three-factor structure (Lee & Yoo, 2004). The discrepancy in previous findings may stem from the fact that, to date, most factor analytic evidence for the MEIM comes from exploratory factor analyses and, to a much lesser extent, confirmatory factor analyses of the MEIM that have not tested and compared the relative fit of competing models (for a discussion, see Worrell, Conyers, Mpofu, & Vandiver, 2006).

To address these inconsistencies, Phinney and Ong (in press) tested competing models of the structure of ethnic identity. Results from surveys carried out with ethnically diverse college students provided evidence that ethnic identity, as assessed by a revised version of the MEIM, can best be viewed as consisting of two correlated factors: exploration and commitment. A confirmatory factor analysis revealed that, compared to the single-factor model which assumes that the measures of ethnic identity reflect a common source of variance, a two-factor correlated model provided a vastly improved fit to the data ($\chi^2/df = 1.91$, $p < .001$, RMSEA = .04, CFI = .98).

Ethnic Identity Development

Although factor analytic research provides a basis for studying individual differences in ethnic identity and gives some indications of how ethnic identity is organized across individuals, it does not indicate how ethnic identity develops, how individual differences in ethnic identity come about, or how ethnic identity relates to important attitudes, adaptations, and achievements. From a developmental perspective, ethnic identity is assumed to exist in childhood in only rudimentary form, as a self-label together with basic information about ethnicity and attitudes about one's group derived largely from one's parents (Bernal, Knight, Ocampo, Garza, & Cota, 1993). A true ethnic identity is conceptualized as developing during adolescence and early adulthood through a process of exploring one's ethnicity and attaining a clear understanding of the meaning of one's group membership for oneself (Phinney, 1993). However, research attempting to document exactly how ethnic identity changes with development is limited.

Existing research generally suggests that adolescents and college students report stronger or more mature ethnic identity with increasing age. A 3-year longitudinal study surveyed early and middle adolescents from African American, Latin American, and European American backgrounds (French et al., 2006) using two scales: ethnic identity exploration and group esteem (similar to ethnic identity commitment). The results showed that group esteem rose in both early and middle adolescence, whereas exploration rose only in middle adolescence. Increases in group esteem were larger for the two minority groups than for the European Americans. Similar results were reported for a sample of adolescents in Canada (Perron, Vondracek, Skorikov, Tremblay, & Corbiere, 1998). Minority youth, primarily immigrants, and majority (Canadian) adolescents were surveyed using the 14-item MEIM (Phinney, 1992). The minority youth, but not the majority youth, showed an increase in ethnic identity over 15 months. A 3-year longitudinal study of 18 ethnic minority high school students (Phinney & Chavira, 1992) used interviews to assess ethnic identity statuses: *unexamined* (the least mature level of ethnic identity), *moratorium* (an intermediate level, characterized by exploration), and *achieved* (a mature ethnic identity based on both exploration and commitment). At age 16, nearly half of the adolescents were classified as being in the unexamined status, and less than a fourth were in the achieved status. Three years later, only 20% were in the unexamined status and over 80% were ethnic identity achieved.

Several short-term longitudinal studies have been carried out with college students. A longitudinal study of minority students at a predominantly European American college (Saylor & Aries, 1999) found that strength of ethnic identity increased in minority students across the first year of college, although those with lower precollege ethnic identity showed the greatest increase. A longitudinal study of college students at two large, relatively diverse, universities (Syed, Azmitia, & Phinney, 2006) found no changes in mean levels of ethnic identity exploration and commitment over the freshman year at the university. However, when students were assigned to ethnic identity statuses (unexamined, moratorium, and achieved) using cluster analysis, shifts were found that are consistent with past longitudinal research (Phinney & Chavira, 1992). In a sample of 19- to 30-year-old university students (Ontai-Grzebik & Raffaelli, 2004), age was not related to ethnic identity exploration, suggesting that exploration of ethnic identity does not extend beyond adolescence. However, Phinney (2006) points out that there is wide variability in the extent to which exploration continues beyond adolescence, depending on individual and contextual factors. As a result, many individuals from minority and immigrant backgrounds continue to explore and reexamine their ethnicity well into adulthood. In sum, there is some evidence that the strength of ethnic identity increases over time, but the results are difficult to compare and integrate because of the many different ways in which ethnic identity has been measured, the different ethnic groups and age cohorts that have been studied, and the limited number of longitudinal studies that have been conducted.

Contexts of Ethnic Identity Development: The Family and Beyond

Any exploration of ethnic identity and its processes must eventually turn its attention to the family. More than any other social institution, the family provides the basic foundation for ethnic identity development. It is the institution that unites people to both preceding and succeeding generations, and provides much of the meaning and many of the markers of positive developmental adaptation. Moreover, for immigrants, the family can be the setting from which stressors emerge, the arena in which conflicts are negotiated, and the place where many immigrants may find the strength and the means to move forward in their lives.

The family environment provides the foundation for the development of knowledge and understanding of one's ethnic background. The work of Knight, Bernal, and colleagues (Knight, Bernal, Garza, Cota, & Ocampo, 1993; Knight, Cota, & Bernal, 1993) provides strong evidence for the important role of the family in ethnic identity development during childhood. In addition, the parents' role remains important to ethnic identity outcomes during adolescence. In a study of immigrant adolescents and their parents from three cultural backgrounds (Mexican, Armenian, and Vietnamese), parents reported the extent to which they attempted to maintain and transmit their culture to their adolescent children, through teaching about their culture, discussing the group's history, encouraging children to learn about cultural traditions and to learn the ethnic language, and instilling ethnic pride (Phinney, Romero, Nava, & Huang, 2001). Adolescents reported their ethnic identity using the MEIM (Phinney, 1992). Results showed that parental cultural maintenance predicted ethnic identity in all groups, although there were variations across groups. For all three groups, the impact of cultural maintenance was mediated in part by the adolescents' ethnic language proficiency; that is, cultural maintenance contributed to greater ethnic language proficiency, which in turn predicted strong ethnic identity. Furthermore, for Armenian families, cultural maintenance had a direct effect on ethnic identity.

The importance of the family was shown as well in a study in which Mexican American adolescents were surveyed regarding their perceptions of their families' ethnic socialization and their ethnic identity (Umaña-Taylor & Fine, 2004). Results indicated that both explicit forms of socialization (e.g., parental teaching about the family ethnic background) and implicit forms (e.g., ethnic objects in the home) were strongly related to adolescents' ethnic identity.

The impact of socialization in the family on ethnic identity has also been shown with college students. For example, Spanish use in the family was found to correlate with ethnic identity in college students (Ontai-Grzebik & Raffaelli, 2004). However, the effect appears to decline over time. Saylor and Aries (1999) reported that at the beginning of college, students' reports of family participation in cultural practices predicted ethnic identity, but at the end of students' freshman year family participation was no longer a predictor of ethnic identity.

The fact that some young people maintain their ethnic ties more strongly than others as they get older may be due to variation in the family environment. A study of Chinese American and Chinese Australian high school students (Rosenthal & Feldman, 1992) showed that when adolescents describe their family environments as being warm, controlling, and autonomy promoting, their ethnic pride was higher. The results suggest that if immigrant parents provide a warm family environment with clear structure but some allowance for adolescent autonomy, then adolescents will continue to feel good about their cultural heritage as they grow older.

Nevertheless, the family is not a static entity. Rather, its structure and function are in a constant state of change as its members move across the life course. To construct a mature, integrated ethnic identity, immigrant adolescents must typically resolve the conflicting needs to maintain their identification with an ethnic group that values family interdependence while at the same time functioning within a larger society that values autonomy and self-assertion. The way in which adolescents and young adults manage cultural conflicts is illustrated in a study of ethnic minority youth ages 14–22 (Phinney, Kim, Osorio, & Vilhjalmsdottir, 2005). Adolescents and emerging adults from immigrant (Mexican, Korean, and Armenian) and nonimmigrant (European American) backgrounds were asked to report what they would do in response to hypothetical situations of conflict with parents. Open-ended responses were coded in terms of compliance (going along with parental wishes), self-assertion (doing what they wanted), or negotiation (finding a mutual resolution). Adolescents also completed a measure of the extent to which they valued family interdependence (e.g., putting family needs before their own and consulting with parents before making decisions).

As expected, immigrant youth, compared to European American adolescents, gave stronger endorsement to family interdependence values and reported more often that they would comply with parental wishes even when parents' wishes conflicted with their own. However, among the immigrant youth, older participants (19–22) were more assertive than younger ones (14–15). The reasons for being assertive that were given by older immigrant youth show that these young people were thinking about their family even as they reported doing what they wanted to do. For example, they made comments such as "I respect my parents, but at the same time I'm an adult, and I make my own decisions" and "I'm not trying to disrespect them, just make my own life." Thus, immigrant youth, in forming their ethnic identity, continue to maintain their cultural values and relationship to their parents while at the same time developing their own individuality.

Although one's family provides the initial basis for one's sense of ethnic group belonging, ethnic identity evolves and changes throughout life in relation to school, community, and work contexts, as well as broader contextual factors such as the density, status, and history of one's ethnic group. Beyond the family, more cohesive and well-structured communities contribute to stronger ethnic identity (Rosenthal & Hrynevich, 1985). The larger environmental context, particularly the ethnic density of schools and communities, is also assumed to be important, although the existing evidence is inconclusive. Umaña-Taylor (2004), in a study of Latino adolescents in three high schools that varied in the ethnic group density, found that the strength of ethnic identity differed by context. Latino adolescents attending a primarily non-Latino high school reported higher levels of ethnic identity than adolescents at both mostly Latino and ethnically balanced schools. In contrast, Syed and colleagues (in press) found no differences in ethnic identity between Latino students at a predominantly ethnic minority university with a Latino majority student body and a predominantly white university with a small percentage of Latinos. More complex results are reported by Juang, Nguyen, and Lin (2006), who found no differences in strength of ethnic identity among Asian American college students from two social contexts that differed in terms of ethnic group density, institutional completeness, and ethnic group political power and status. However, the relations among variables differed by context; ethnic identity was linked to more positive functioning (in lower depression scores and higher ratings of connectedness to parents) only in the ethnically enriched environments.

Ethnic Identity and Well-Being

In the last 10 years a substantial body of research has emerged showing the importance of ethnic identity to the psychological health of individuals across a wide range of ages and backgrounds. Both social psychological and developmental approaches support the view of a positive relations between ethnic identity and well-being. Social identity theory (Tajfel & Turner, 1986) suggests strong links between group identification and self-concept. People are assumed to strive to achieve and maintain a positive identification with social groups to which they belong, thereby bolstering their self-esteem. Developmental models of ethnic identity likewise suggest that a secure or achieved ethnic identity is associated with good mental health (Phinney & Kohatsu, 1997). Maintenance of a strong ethnic identity has been shown to be related to psychological well-being among immigrants in various countries (Liebkind, 1996; Nesdale, Rooney, & Smith, 1997). Among immigrant groups in the United States, the relation of ethnic identity to measures of well-being has been well documented. For example, in a large sample of early adolescents in the United States from a wide variety of immigrant backgrounds (e.g., Mexican, Central American, Vietnamese, Chinese, Indian, and Pakistani), Roberts and colleagues (1999) reported positive correlations of ethnic identity with self-esteem, coping, mastery, and optimism, and negative correlations with depression and loneliness.

Despite evidence of a link between ethnic identity and well-being, empirical studies indicate that the relation is modest. Correlations of ethnic identity and self-esteem are generally in the range of .20 to .30 (see Phinney, Cantu, & Kurtz, 1997; Roberts et al., 1999). Such findings suggest that the link between ethnic identity and well-being is likely to be stronger for some immigrants under some conditions, as results based on heterogeneous groups may mask subgroup differences in the impact of ethnic identity. For example, in a sample of 472 immigrant adolescents in the United States from a larger international study of immigrant youth (Berry, Phinney, Sam, & Vedder, 2006), the relation between ethnic identity and measures of adaptation (i.e., self-esteem, life satisfaction, school adjustment, and psychological problems) was found to be stronger among second-generation immigrant adolescents than among their first-generation peers. Ethnic identity and self-esteem were correlated .25 for first-generation youth (i.e., immigrant adolescents born in their country of origin), whereas among second-generation youth, born in the United States, the correlation was .58. Similar results were evident for life satisfaction; for first-generation youth, ethnic identity was unrelated to life satisfaction, whereas among the second generation, it was significantly related to life satisfaction, .28. Ethnic identity also predicted school adjustment more strongly for second- (.13) compared with first-generation youth (.03). Finally, ethnic identity was unrelated to psychological problems (depression and anxiety) in the first generation, but was a negative predictor in the second (–.14). Although the coefficients from this research are modest, they are in a consistent direction, suggesting that the importance of ethnic identity as a factor in well-being becomes stronger with longer residence in the country of settlement.

DIRECTIONS FOR FUTURE RESEARCH

In this section, we highlight theoretical areas of research on ethnic identity that have received relatively little attention in previous work. We identify unresolved methodological challenges associated with the measurement and analysis of within-person phenomena and elaborate on the implications of these challenges for process research in ethnic minority populations. We conclude with a discussion of issues that might profitably be considered in future research, with an emphasis on research directions to promote resilience and well-being in immigrant families.

Measurement Invariance

Implicit in the comparison of groups and individuals is the assumption of equivalence of measurement. This assumption, however, is rarely tested directly in ethnic identity research. Yet the interpretation of either interindividual or intraindividual results, based on nonequivalent measurements, is riddled with ambiguity (Horn & McArdle, 1992). Measurement invariance is fundamentally important for evaluating factor analytic, developmental, and well-being evidence. In each case, before any construct validation results can be sensibly interpreted, there must be assurances that the scales measure the same attributes in the same way in different groups and circumstances. If scales do not measure (1) the same factors in the same way in different groupings of people or (2) in the same people measured in different places and times, there is no logical basis for interpreting the results of analyses of differences between means or variances or correlations (Meredith & Horn, 2001).

Do people interpret the items of the MEIM in comparable ways? The finding that ethnic identity increases with age (Phinney & Chavira, 1992) may reflect valid developmental changes in ethnic identity, but it is also possible that certain MEIM items capture aspects of ethnic identity that are likely to be differentially endorsed by early, middle, or late adolescents. Establishing that an instrument is factorally invariant, therefore, provides evidence not only that respondents from different groups can be legitimately compared, but also that observed group mean differences in raw scores reflect valid and meaningful group differences at the level of the latent variable assumed to underlie those scores. Thus, there is need for evidence of measurement invariance, as a necessary prerequisite for understanding other research pertaining to the structural and developmental validity of ethnic identity (Meredith & Horn, 2001).

Longitudinal Studies of Ethnic Identity Development

From a lifespan perspective (e.g., Baltes, 1987), development is conceptualized as a dynamic and continuous interplay between growth and decline. This perspective suggests the fluid and developmental nature of ethnic identity. The application of this framework to the study of adaptational processes results in a complex conceptualization of intraindividual change. We thus highlight the need for more studies of ethnic identity as a dynamic process. For certain immigrants, trajectories of ethnic identity and well-being may be anchored in conditions that may precede the decades in which these trajectories take shape. For example, does early life advantage, in the form of ethnic pride and affirmation, serve to modify the potent effects of later life adversity? Does the development of an achieved ethnic identity in later life serve to avert or forestall trajectories of negative outcomes that otherwise would result from early life challenges? The inclusion of longitudinal assessments of ethnic identity would significantly strengthen understanding of the long-term sequelae, as well as developmental significance, of early resources and intervening processes among immigrant groups.

Longitudinal research is also important in identifying the distinct but often confounded effects of developmental changes and changes related to acculturation (Schonpflug, 1997). As ethnic identity issues become salient during adolescence, young people can understand ethnicity in more complex ways as a result of their growing cognitive abilities (Quintana, Castaneda-English, & Ybarra, 1999). At the same time, immigrant adolescents are increasingly exposed to a wide range of cultural factors that influence their sense of self. Thus, changes in ethnic identity may be considered as part of the acculturation process. Untangling the interactive effects of development and acculturation on ethnic identity presents methodological challenges for researchers. In addition to longitudinal methods, comparisons of immigrants with native or nonimmigrant individuals can help distinguish phenomena that are common to both groups (and hence more likely to be developmental) from phenomena that are unique to acculturating individuals (see Berry et al., 2006).

Person-Centered Approaches

In addition to methods that model change in developmental trajectories over time, person-centered approaches to studying ethnic identity are receiving increasing attention in the literature. In comparison to variable-centered approaches, person-centered approaches, such as cluster analysis and latent class analysis, allow researchers to capture the subgroup heterogeneity that may be reflected in qualitatively distinct subtype patterns or subpopulations (Nagin, 1999). Such methods allow for the consideration of whether hidden categorical variables (classes) explain the trajectories of individuals over time.

For example, Phinney, Berry, Vedder, and Liebkind (2006), using cluster analysis, reported evidence of four distinct profiles of immigrant youth based on their varying levels of acculturation attitudes, ethnic and national identities, language proficiency and usage, peer contacts, family relationship values, and perceived discrimination. The four profiles (i.e., integration, ethnic, national, and diffuse) highlight different ways in which immigrants handle the challenges of acculturation. Furthermore, the study revealed the differing impact of ethnic identity on well-being across the profiles. For U.S. immigrant youth with an integration profile (those with a strong ethnic identity together with a strong national identity), the correlation of ethnic identity and self-esteem was .65, accounting for over 40% of the variance. For those with an ethnic profile, that is, a strong ethnic identity but little identification or involvement in the larger society, the correlation of ethnic identity with self-esteem was .26, about 7% of the variance. For youth with a national (or assimilated) profile, who were oriented toward the larger society and had little involvement in their ethnic culture, ethnic identity was negatively related to self-esteem, –.10. For the diffuse group, who lacked a clear sense of identity, the correlation was .11. The results demonstrate that ethnic identity is of greatest importance to the well-being of those who are integrated, that is, identify with both their ethnic group and the larger society, and to a somewhat less degree for those who identify primarily with their own ethnic group. For youth who are assimilated, ethnic identity has little or no impact on well-being.

Thus, a person-oriented approach can provide a more nuanced understanding of variation in the role of ethnic identity depending on its association with other variables. Importantly, the results of this work illustrate that the intercultural variables central to the acculturation process do not simply involve overlapping distributions, but rather these variables interact with one another to lead to characterizations of genuinely distinct forms of ethnic identity. This work paves the way for future inquiries, wherein a major aim is to describe how different profiles of ethnic identity interrelate through time. Recognizing the complex, dynamic relations between ethnic identity and other key acculturation constructs may yield a more complete understanding of the nature and etiology of intraindividual change in ethnic identity development.

Integrating Qualitative Assessments with Quantitative Process Measures

Ontogenetic development or intraindividual change occurs in the context of social, cultural, historical, and familial changes (Baltes, 1987). Qualitative approaches can provide information on how individuals ascribe meaning to, and communicate about, their own life experiences, both of which are difficult to capture through traditional research techniques (Hendricks, 1996). Qualitative research encompasses a number of different approaches, including ethnographies and participant observation, open-ended interviews and focus groups, oral histories and life stories, and content analysis. Across these approaches, the goal is to gather in-depth information and to understand the meaning of events and behavior in context.

For example, in a study of ethnic and American identity (Phinney & Devich Navarro, 1997), adolescents completed both survey and interview questions. Interview responses provided insight into variation among adolescents in the way they viewed their ethnic identity. For some, their sense of belonging to their group appeared rather impersonal, emphasizing the history and past accomplishments of their group; for others, their identity was an intense, often joyful, feeling of being part of something very immediate to them. Qualitative methods also enhanced the study described earlier (Phinney et al., 2005), in which immigrant adolescents gave open-ended explanations for their reasons for disagreeing with their parents. The responses provide an understanding of the ways young people make sense of their sense of closeness to their family and ethnic group values in combination with their need for autonomy.

In the context of ethnic minority research, qualitative assessments can provide an invaluable means to understand the core themes in the lives of racial and ethnic minority groups; how such themes are grounded in social, cultural, historical, and familial contexts; and the extent to which events and behaviors in context shape the varying life history pathways through adversity and to resilience. How do we begin to probe the emotional depths that may embody the chronic, repetitive nature of ethnic discrimination and racism? What are the turning points that change the development of ethnic identity? To answer these questions, there is a need for incorporating mixed-methods approaches (Hanson, Creswell, Plano Clark, Petska, & Creswell, 2005) to explore the farther reaches of human resilience.

Extending Research on Contexts of Ethnic Identity Formation

Even though ethnic identity is a social identity, rooted in the context of a particular ethnic group and ethnic community, it has been conceptualized and studied largely at the individual level, as being constructed by individuals through the processes of exploration and commitment (Phinney, 1993). The limited research on the role of context in ethnic identity is primarily correlational and provides little understanding of the complex ways in which context influences the formation of an ethnic identity and of how contextual factors interact with individual factors such as age, attitudes, and other personal characteristics. Ecological models (Bronfenbrenner, 1986) can be useful in thinking about ethnic identity in the context of acculturation. Contexts that may affect ethnic identity extend from the family, to the immediate neighborhood, school, community, city or town, the media, the national scene, and, increasingly, the world, via the Internet and other media. To address the complexity of these interacting factors, both large-scale surveys and in-depth qualitative studies are needed. Even case studies can be useful in showing how personal, social, and historical factors influence cultural identity formation for a migrating individual (Phinney, 2000).

Daily Process Approaches to Studying Ethnic Identity

Unlike long-term longitudinal investigations, daily process studies allow researchers to capture proximal events and outcomes closer to their actual daily occurrence. In addition, process approaches have methodological advantages that are well suited for idiographic research. First, daily process designs allow individuals to report their behavior and experiences over the range of situational circumstances experienced in everyday life. Second, they allow for statistical modeling of behavior over time. Third and most important, daily process designs allow for the test, rather than assumption, of validity of the nomothetic approach. This assumption can be tested by summarizing experience or behavior within an individual over time (and across situations), and by testing whether the pattern generalizes across individuals in a sample.

Although daily process designs have been applied successfully to study an array of psychological phenomena (for reviews, see Tennen & Affleck, 2002), relatively less work has been directed at using daily process designs to track the adaptational processes of minority populations as they unfold over fairly short time intervals. An exception is research by Fuligni and colleagues. Yip and Fuligni (2002), for example, asked 96 first- and second-generation Chinese American high school students to complete daily diaries for 2 weeks. The authors found that participants who were high on ethnic identity felt better on days when their awareness of their ethnicity was particularly high. In a subsequent experience sampling study, Yip (2005) found that stable ethnic pride, defined as "esteem based on being Chinese" (p. 1607), moderated the momentary association between ethnic salience and positive mood. Taken together, this research illustrates how person or trait data (i.e., stable ethnic pride) may become especially powerful explanatory constructs when viewed in connection with dynamic processes (i.e., momentary ethnic salience and positive emotional states). We underscore the need for more research that examines how the dynamic interplay between trait and state processes (see Fleeson, 2004) provide substantive insight into positive adaptations in ethnic minority populations.

CONCLUSION

We have sought in this chapter to provide some sense of the role of ethnic identity across the range of experiences to which immigrant families may be exposed and how one's ethnic identity can be a resource in the face of stressful experiences. The study of ethnic identity is a complex undertaking, partly because it depends on an amalgamation of constructs from several different perspectives. There is much still to be learned about ethnic identity, but there is no question that that it is a highly salient and critically important issue for immigrant families. Most immigrant parents are deeply involved in their ethnic culture and strive to maintain it while living in a culture that is typically quite different from their own and may be hostile to their values. Immigrant children and youth adapt more quickly than their parents to the culture of the larger society, but they nevertheless retain a clear and positive sense of belonging to their ethnic group over time (Berry et al., 2006). Cross-sectional research shows that ethnic identity remains strong among second- and even third-generation immigrants (Phinney, 2003). For both immigrant parents and their children, a secure sense of who they are in ethnic terms underlies psychological well-being and adjustment. Individuals who are secure in their sense of belonging to their ethnic group also hold more positive attitudes toward members of other ethnic groups (Phinney, Jacoby, & Silva, in press). A strong ethnic identity can be a resource that contributes to the resilience of individuals facing the challenges of adapting to a new society.

Because of the important role of ethnic identity in the lives of immigrants and in their contacts with those outside their own group, it is essential for institutions and community leaders to recognize the needs of immigrant parents and their children to have their ethnicity acknowledged and valued. Immigrant families thrive when they can practice and express their culture in their lives. Schools and community programs can help by giving recognition to diverse cultures and encouraging young people to explore and learn about their own and others' ethnicity. The development and maintenance of secure ethnic identities in immigrant families benefits immigrants, their communities, and the society.

REFERENCES

Baltes, P. B. (1987). Theoretical propositions of life-span developmental psychology: On the dynamics between growth and decline. *Developmental Psychology, 23*, 611–626.

Bernal, M., Knight, G., Ocampo, K., Garza, C., & Cota, M. (1993). Development of Mexican American identity. In M. Bernal & G. Knight (Eds.), *Ethnic identity: Formation and transmission among Hispanics and other minorities* (pp. 31–46). Albany: State University of New York Press.

Berry, J., Phinney, J., Sam, D., & Vedder, P. (2006). *Immigrant youth in cultural transition: Acculturation, identity, and adaptation across national contexts.* Mahwah, NJ: Erlbaum.

Bronfenbrenner, U. (1986). Ecology of the family as a context for human development: Research perspectives. *Developmental Psychology, 22*, 723–742.

Erickson, E. (1968). *Identity: Youth and crisis.* New York: Norton.

Fleeson, W. (2004). Moving personality beyond the person–situation debate: The challenge and the opportunity of within-person variability. *Current Directions in Psychological Science, 13*, 83–87.

French, S., Seidman, E., Allen, L., & Aber, J. L. (2006). The development of ethnic identity during adolescence. *Developmental Psychology, 42*, 1–10.

Hanson, W. E., Creswell, J. W., Plano Clark, V. L., Petska, K. S., & Creswell, J. D. (2005). Mixed methods research designs in counseling psychology. *Journal of Counseling Psychology, 52*, 224–235.

Hendricks, J. (1996). Qualitative research: Contributions and advances. In R. H. Binstock & L. K. George (Eds.), *Handbook of aging and the social sciences* (4th ed., pp. 52–72). San Diego, CA: Academic Press.

Horn, J. L., & McArdle, J. J. (1992). A practical and theoretical guide to measurement invariance in aging research. *Experimental Aging Research, 18*(3–4), 117–144.

Juang, L., Nguyen, H., & Lin, Y. (2006). The ethnic identity, other-group attitudes, and psychosocial functioning of Asian-American emerging adults from two contexts. *Journal of Adolescent Research, 21*, 542–568.

Knight, G., Bernal, M., Garza, C., Cota, M., & Ocampo, K. (1993). Family socialization and the ethnic identity of Mexican-American children. *Journal of Cross-Cultural Psychology, 24*, 99–114.

Knight, G., Cota, M., & Bernal, M. (1993). The socialization of cooperative, competitive, and individualistic preferences among Mexican American children: The mediating role of ethnic identity. *Hispanic Journal of Behavioral Sciences, 15*, 291–309.

Lee, R. M., & Yoo, H. C. (2004). Structure and measurement of ethnic identity for Asian American college students. *Journal of Counseling Psychology, 51*, 263–269.

Liebkind, K. (1996). Acculturation and stress—Vietnamese refugees in Finland. *Journal of Cross-Cultural Psychology, 27*, 161–180.

Meredith, W., & Horn, J. L. (2001). The role of factorial invariance in modeling growth and change. In L. M. Collins & A. G. Sayer (Eds.), *New methods for the analysis of change* (pp. 203–240). Washington, DC: American Psychological Association.

Nagin, D. S. (1999). Analyzing developmental trajectories: A semiparametric, group-based approach. *Psychological Methods, 4*, 139–157.

Nesdale, D., Rooney, R., & Smith, L. (1997). Migrant ethnic identity and psychological distress. *Journal of Cross Cultural Psychology, 28*, 569–588.

Ontai-Grzebik, L. L., & Raffaelli, M. (2004). Individual and social influences on ethnic identity among Latino young adults. *Journal of Adolescent Research, 19*, 559–575.

Perron, J., Vondracek, F., Skorikov, V., Tremblay, C., & Corbiere, M. (1998). A longitudinal study of vocational maturity and ethnic identity development. *Journal of Vocational Behavior, 52*, 409–424.

Phinney, J. S. (1990). Ethnic identity in adolescents and adults: Review of research. *Psychological Bulletin, 108*(3), 499–514.

Phinney, J. S. (1992). The Multigroup Ethnic Identity Measure: A new scale for use with diverse groups. *Journal of Adolescent Research, 7*, 156–176.

Phinney, J. S. (1993). A three-stage model of ethnic identity development in adolescence. In G. P. Knight & M. E. Bernal (Eds.), *Ethnic identity: Formation and transmission among Hispanics and other minorities* (pp. 61–79). Albany: State University of New York Press.

Phinney, J. S. (2000). Identity formation across cultures: The interaction of personal, societal, and historical change. *Human Development, 43*, 27–31.

Phinney, J. S. (2003). Ethnic identity and acculturation. In K. Chun, P. Organista, & G. Marin (Eds.), *Acculturation: Advances in theory, measurements, and applied research* (pp. 63–81). Washington, DC: American Psychological Association.

Phinney, J. S. (2006). Ethnic identity exploration in emerging adulthood. In J. J. Arnett & J. L. Tanner (Eds.), *Emerging adults in America: Coming of age in the 21st century* (pp. 117–134). Washington, DC: American Psychological Association.

Phinney, J. S., Berry, J. W., Vedder, P., & Liebkind, K. (2006). The acculturation experience: Attitudes, identities, and behaviors of immigrant youth. In J. W. Berry, J. S. Phinney, D. L. Sam, & P. Vedder (Eds.), *Immigrant youth in cultural transition: Acculturation, identity, and adaptation across national contexts* (pp. 71–116). Mahwah, NJ: Erlbaum.

Phinney, J. S., Cantu, C. L., & Kurtz, D. A. (1997). Ethnic and American identity as predictors of self-esteem among African American, Latino, and white adolescents. *Journal of Youth and Adolescence, 26*, 165–185.

Phinney, J. S., & Chavira, V. (1992). Ethnic identity and self-esteem: An exploratory longitudinal study. *Journal of Adolescence, 15*(3), 271–281.

Phinney, J. S., & Devich Navarro, M. (1997). Variations in bicultural identification among African American and Mexican American adolescents. *Journal of Research on Adolescence, 7*, 3–32.

Phinney, J. S., Jacoby, B., & Silva, C. (in press). Positive intergroup attitudes: The role of ethnic identity. *International Journal of Behavioral Development.*

Phinney, J. S., Kim, T., Osorio, S., & Vilhjalmsdottir, P. (2005). Autonomy and relatedness in adolescent-parent disagreements: Ethnic and developmental factors. *Journal of Adolescent Research, 20*, 8–39.

Phinney, J. S., & Kohatsu, E. L. (1997). Ethnic and racial identity development and mental health. In J. L. Maggs & J. Schulenberg (Eds.), *Health risks and developmental transitions during adolescence* (pp. 420–443). New York: Cambridge University Press.

Phinney, J., & Ong, A. (in press). Conceptualization and measurement of ethnic identity: Current status and future directions. *Journal of Counseling Psychology.*

Phinney, J. S., Romero, I., Nava, M., & Huang, D. (2001). The role of language, parents, and peers in ethnic identity among adolescents in immigrant families. *Journal of Youth and Adolescence, 30*(2), 135–153.

Ponterotto, J. G., Gretchen, D., Utsey, S. O., Stracuzzi, T., & Saya, R., Jr. (2003). The Multigroup Ethnic Identity Measure (MEIM): Psychometric review and further validity testing. *Educational and Psychological Measurement, 63*, 502–515.

Portes, A., & Rumbaut, R. (2001). *Legacies: The story of the immigrant second generation.* Berkeley: University of California Press.

Quintana, S., Castaneda-English, P., & Ybarra, V. (1999). Role of perspective-taking abilities and ethnic socialization in development of adolescent ethnic identity. *Journal of Research on Adolescence, 9*, 161–184.

Reese, L. R., Vera, E. M., & Pailkoff, R. L. (1998). Ethnic identity assessment among inner-city African American children: Evaluating the applicability of the Multigroup Ethnic Identity Measure. *Journal of Black Psychology, 24*, 289–304.

Roberts, R. E., Phinney, J. S., Masse, L. C., Chen, Y., Roberts, C. R., & Romero, A. (1999). The structure of ethnic identity of young adolescents from diverse ethnocultural groups. *Journal of Early Adolescence, 19*, 301–322.

Rosenthal, D., & Feldman, S. (1992). The relationship between parenting behaviour and ethnic identity in Chinese-American and Chinese-Australian adolescents. *International Journal of Psychology, 27*, 19–31.

Rosenthal, D., & Hrynevich, C. (1985). Ethnicity and ethnic identity: A comparative study of Greek-, Italian-, and Anglo-Australian adolescents. *International Journal of Psychology, 20*, 723–742.

Saylor, E. S., & Aries, E. (1999). Ethnic identity and change in social context. *Journal of Social Psychology, 139*, 549–566.

Schonpflug, U. (1997). Acculturation: Adaptation or development? *Applied Psychology: An International Review, 46*, 52–55.

Spencer, M. S., Icard, L. D., Harachi, T. W., Catalano, R. F., & Oxford, M. (2000). Ethnic identity among monoracial and multiracial early adolescents. *Journal of Early Adolescence, 20*, 365–387.

Syed, M., Azmitia, M., & Phinney, J. S. (in press). Stability and change in ethnic identity among Latino emerging adults in two contexts. *Identity: An International Journal of Theory and Research.*

Tajfel, H., & Turner, J. (1986). The social identity theory of intergroup behavior. In S. Worchel & W. Austin (Eds.), *Psychology of intergroup relations* (pp. 7–24). Chicago: Nelson-Hall.

Tennen, H., & Affleck, G. (2002). The challenge of capturing daily processes at the interface of social and clinical psychology. *Journal of Social and Clinical Psychology, 21*, 610–627.

Umaña-Taylor, A. J. (2004). Ethnic identity and self-esteem: Examining the role of social context. *Journal of Adolescence, 27*, 139–146.

Umaña-Taylor, A. J., & Fine, M. A. (2004). Examining ethnic identity among Mexican-origin adolescents living in the United States. *Hispanic Journal of Behavioral Sciences, 26*, 36–59.

Worrell, F. C. (2000). A validity study of scores on the Multigroup Ethnic Identity Measure based on a sample of academically talented adolescents. *Educational and Psychological Measurement, 60*, 439–447.

Worrell, F. C., Conyers, L., Mpofu, E., & Vandiver, B. (2006). Multigroup Ethnic Identity Measure scores in a sample of adolescents from Zimbabwe. *Identity: An International Journal of Theory and Research, 6*, 35–59.

Yancey, A. K., Aneshensel, C. S., & Driscoll, A. K. (2001). The assessment of ethnic identity in a diverse urban youth population. *Journal of Black Psychology, 27*(2), 190–208.

Yip, T. (2005). Sources of situational variation in ethnic identity and psychological well-being: A Palm Pilot study of Chinese American students. *Personality and Social Psychology Bulletin, 31*, 1603–1616.

Yip, T., & Fuligni, A. (2002). Daily variation in ethnic identity, ethnic behaviors, and psychological well-being among American adolescents of Chinese descent. *Child Development, 73*, 1557–1572.

CHAPTER 4

Acculturation Strategies and Adaptation

John W. Berry

Acculturation is a process of cultural and psychological change in cultural groups, families, and individuals following intercultural contact. The processes and outcomes are highly variable, with large-group, generational, and individual differences. Three questions will guide the presentation: How do individuals and groups seek to acculturate? How well do they succeed? Are there any relationships between how they go about acculturation and their psychological and social success? The chapter begins with a description of these acculturation processes, the strategies people use to deal with them, and the adaptations that result. A study addressing these questions is then reviewed, with particular emphasis on the experience of immigrant youth and their parents. Evidence indicates that the most common strategy is *integration* (defined as preferring to maintain one's cultural heritage while seeking to participate in the life of the larger society), rather than assimilation, separation, or marginalization. In most cases, this integration strategy is also the most adaptive, both psychologically and socioculturally. Finally, some policy implications are proposed for the promotion of the integration strategy, at the societal, family, and individual levels.

CULTURAL, FAMILIAL, AND INDIVIDUAL ACCULTURATION

Acculturation is the process of cultural and psychological change that takes place as a result of contact between cultural groups and their individual members (Redfield, Linton, & Herskovits, 1936). Such contact and change occurs during colonization, military invasion, migration, and sojourning (such as tourism, international study, and overseas posting); it continues after initial contact in culturally plural societies, where ethnocultural communities maintain features of their heritage cultures. Adaptation to living in culture-contact settings takes place over time; occasionally it is stressful, but often it results in some form of mutual accommodation. Although much research has examined the cultural and individual levels of acculturation phenomena (Berry, 2001), many immigrant-receiving societies now emphasize "family reunification" as a positive way to receive newcomers. In this kind of program, whole families, rather than individuals, come simultaneously, or in some cases, one adult comes first followed by the rest of his or her family. So, in addition to working at the cultural and the individual levels, it is imperative that acculturation research should focus also on the social unit that is the family.

The initial research interest in acculturation grew out of a concern for the effects of European domination of colonial and indigenous peoples. Later, it focused on how immigrants (both voluntary and involuntary) changed following their entry and settlement into receiving societies. More recently, much of the work has been involved with how ethnocultural groups and individuals relate to each other, and change, as a result of their attempts to live together in culturally plural societies. Nowadays, all three foci are important, as globalization results in ever-larger trading and political relations; indigenous national populations experience neocolonization; new waves of immigrants, sojourners, and refugees flow from these economic and political changes; and large ethnocultural populations become established in most countries.

Graves (1967) introduced the concept of *psychological acculturation*, which refers to changes in an individual who is a participant in a culture-contact situation, being influenced both directly by the external (usually dominant) culture and by the changing culture (usually nondominant) of which the individual is a member. There are two reasons for keeping the cultural and psychological levels distinct. The first is that in cross-cultural psychology, we view individual human behavior as interacting with the cultural context within which it occurs; hence separate conceptions and measurements are required at the two levels (Berry, Poortinga, Segall, & Dasen, 2002). The second is that not every individual enters into, and participates in, the new context, or changes in the same way; there are vast individual differences in psychological acculturation, even among individuals who live in the same acculturative arena (Sam & Berry, 2006).

A framework that outlines and links cultural and psychological acculturation, and identifies the two (or more) groups in contact (Berry, 2003), provides a map of those phenomena that I believe need to be conceptualized and measured during acculturation research. At the cultural level, we need to understand key features of the two original cultural groups prior to their major contact. In particular, there is now substantial evidence that families around the world vary in their cultural and psychological attributes (Georgas et al., 2006). Hence it is essential to understand this precontact variation among the groups that are now attempting to live together following migration. It is also important to understand the nature of their contact relationships and the resulting dynamic cultural changes in both groups and in the ethnocultural groups that emerge during the process of acculturation. The gathering of this information requires extensive ethnographic, community-level work. These changes can be minor or substantial, and range from being easily accomplished to being a source of major cultural disruption.

At the individual level, we need to consider the psychological changes that individuals in all groups undergo, and their eventual adaptation to their new situations. Identifying these changes requires sampling a population and studying individuals who are variably involved in the process of acculturation. These changes can be a set of rather easily accomplished behavioral shifts (e.g., in ways of speaking, dressing, and eating) or they can be more problematic, producing acculturative stress (Berry, 1976; Berry, Kim, Minde, & Mok, 1997) as manifested by uncertainty, anxiety, and depression. Adaptations can be primarily internal or psychological (e.g., sense of well-being, or self-esteem) or sociocultural (Ward, 1996), linking the individual to others in the new society as manifested, for example, in degree of competence in the activities of daily intercultural living.

ACCULTURATION STRATEGIES

The concept of *acculturation strategies* refers to the various ways that groups and individuals seek to acculturate. Knowledge of these variations has increased substantially in recent years (see Berry, 2003), challenging the assumption that everyone would assimilate and become absorbed into the dominant group (Gordon, 1964). At the cultural level, the two groups in contact (whether dominant or nondominant) usually have some notion about what they are attempting to do (e.g., colonial policies). For families, knowledge of their motives for migration is essential for understanding how their acculturation will take place. And, at the individual level, persons will vary within their cultural group (e.g., on the basis of their educational or occupational background). Within their families, persons will vary according to their gender or position (e.g., mother, son). The more immediate outcomes of the acculturation process (including the behavior changes and acculturative stress phenomena) are known to be a function, at least to some extent, of what people try to do during their acculturation; and the longer term outcomes (both psychological and sociocultural adaptations) often correspond to the strategic goals set by the groups of which they are members (Berry, 1997).

Four acculturation strategies have been derived from two basic issues facing all acculturating peoples. These issues are based on the distinction between orientations toward one's own group and those toward other groups (Berry, 1980). This distinction is rendered as (1) a relative preference for maintaining one's heritage culture and identity and (2) a relative preference for having contact with and participating in the larger society along with other ethnocultural groups. It has now been well demonstrated that these two dimensions are empirically, as well as conceptually, independent from each other (Ryder, Alden, & Paulhus, 2000). This two-dimensional formulation is presented in Figure 4.1.

These two issues can be responded to on attitudinal dimensions, shown as varying along bipolar dimensions, rather than as bald (positive or negative) alternatives. Orientations to these issues intersect to define four acculturation strategies. These strategies carry different names, depending on which ethnocultural group (the dominant or nondominant) is being considered. From the point of view of nondominant ethnocultural groups (on the left of Figure 4.1), when individuals do not wish to maintain their cultural identity and seek daily interaction with other cultures, the assimilation strategy is defined. In contrast, when individuals place a value on holding on to their original culture, and at the same time wish to avoid interaction with others, then the separation alternative is defined. When there is an interest in maintaining one's original culture, while having daily interactions with other groups, integration is the option. In this case, some degree of cultural integrity is maintained, while at the same time seeking, as a member of an ethnocultural group, to participate as an integral part of the larger social network. Finally, when there is little possibility or interest in cultural maintenance (often for reasons of enforced cultural loss), and little interest in having relations with others (often for reasons of exclusion or discrimination), then marginalization is defined.

This presentation was based on the assumption that nondominant groups and their individual members have the freedom to choose how they want to acculturate. This, of course, is not always the case. When the dominant group enforces certain forms of acculturation, or con-

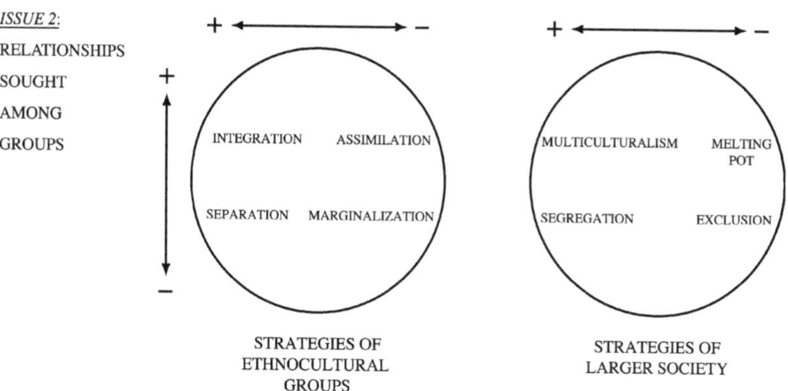

FIGURE 4.1. Acculturation strategies framework.

strains the choices of nondominant groups or individuals, then other terms need to be used. Thus, integration can only be "freely" chosen and successfully pursued by nondominant groups when the dominant society is open and inclusive in its orientation toward cultural diversity. Thus a mutual accommodation is required for integration to be attained, involving the acceptance by both groups of the right of all groups to live as culturally different peoples. This strategy requires nondominant groups to adopt the basic values of the larger society, while at the same time the dominant group must be prepared to adapt national institutions (e.g., education, health, labor) to better meet the needs of all groups now living together in the plural society.

These two basic issues were initially approached from the point of view of the nondominant ethnocultural groups. However, the original anthropological definition clearly established that *both* groups in contact would change and become acculturated. Hence, a third dimension was added: that of the powerful role played by the dominant group in influencing the way in which mutual acculturation would take place (Berry, 1974). The addition of this third dimension produces the right side of Figure 4.1. Assimilation, when sought by the dominant group, is termed the "melting pot." When separation is forced by the dominant group, it is segregation. Marginalization, when imposed by the dominant group, is exclusion. Finally, integration, when diversity is a widely accepted feature of the society as a whole, including all the various ethnocultural groups, is called multiculturalism.

With the use of this framework, comparisons can be made between individuals and their groups, and between nondominant peoples and the larger society within which they are acculturating. The acculturation ideologies and policies of the dominant group constitute an important element of intercultural research (see Berry, Kalin, & Taylor, 1977; Bourhis, Moise, Perreault, & Senecal, 1997), while the preferences of nondominant peoples are a core feature in acculturation research (Berry, Kim, Power, Young, & Bujaki, 1989). Inconsistencies and conflicts between these various acculturation preferences are common sources of difficulty for those experiencing acculturation. For example, this can occur when individuals do not accept the main ideology of their society (when individuals oppose immigrant cultural maintenance in a society where multiculturalism is official policy), or when immigrant children challenge the way of acculturating set out by their parents. Generally, when acculturation experiences cause problems for acculturating individuals, we observe the phenomenon of acculturative stress, with variations in levels of adaptation.

THREE MAIN ACCULTURATION QUESTIONS IN CROSS-CULTURAL PSYCHOLOGY

Three questions have guided much of the recent research on acculturation at all levels: societies, families, and individuals. These questions have existed in various forms for many years, but have become formalized in a recent book (Berry, Phinney, Sam, & Vedder, 2006a, 2006b) that make them explicit. Although these questions have a long history, they have been clarified by recent research, partly in response to critical comments and debate in the acculturation literature (e.g., Berry & Sam, 2003; Rudmin & Ahmadzadeh, 2001).

The three questions are the following:

1. *How do people acculturate?* Are there variations in the goals that societies, families, and individuals seek to achieve? Are there variations in the process that people experience or in the end result that people attain? As noted above, for many years this question seemed to be settled: the goal, the process, and the end result of acculturation was thought to be the inevitable absorption of nondominant groups and individuals into the dominant society, leading to a culturally homogeneous society. However, there is now some agreement that there are variations. Despite this agreement, there is no consensus on how many there are, on how distinct they are one from another, and how best to assess them.

2. *How well do people adapt?* For many years it was thought that people inevitably encounter problems, and that these experiences result in poor adaptation, mainly of a psychological nature. Much of this generalization came from reports prepared by those professionals (mainly psychiatrists, social workers, counselors, and other clinicians) who were working with immigrants who were in fact experiencing, and seeking help for, their problems.

3. *What is the relationship between how they acculturate and how well they adapt?* If there are variations in how people acculturate, and variation in how well they adapt, this third question inevitably arises. If there are systematic relationships, the possibility exists for some "best practices" in how to acculturate in order to achieve better, rather than worse, adaptations.

Following is a brief overview of an empirical study that allows us to gain partial answers to these three questions.

ACCULTURATION RESEARCH ON IMMIGRANT YOUTH AND PARENTS

To illustrate these concepts and questions, I offer an overview of a study of the acculturation and adaptation of immigrant youth (Berry et al., 2006a, 2006b). Samples included immigrant youth (ages 13–18 years) settled in 13 societies (N = 5,298), a sample of their parents (N = 2,350), as well as samples of national youth (N = 2,631) and parents (N = 967). The study was guided by the three core questions identified above: How do they acculturate? How well do they adapt? and Are there important relationships between how they acculturate and how well they adapt?

To address the first question of how immigrant youth live during their acculturation, a number of acculturation variables were measured in the study (such as the four acculturation attitudes, ethnic and national identities, language use, and peer relations). These variables were included in a cluster analysis. Four clusters resulted: integration (36.4% of the sample), ethnic (22.5%), national (18.7%), and diffuse (22.4%). In the integration cluster, youth were oriented toward both their heritage culture and the national society, they preferred an integration strategy, and rejected assimilation, separation, and marginalization; they had positive ethnic and national identities, used both their heritage and national languages, and had friends from both groups. In the ethnic cluster, they were primarily oriented toward their heritage culture: they preferred the separation strategy and rejected the integration, assimilation, and marginalization strategies; they had a positive ethnic identity and a negative national identity; they used their heritage language, but not the national language; and they had friends from their own ethnocultural group, but not from the national group. In the national cluster, youth preferred the assimilation strategy, and rejected the integration, separation, and marginalization strategies; they had a positive national identity and a negative ethnic identity; they used the national language, but not their heritage language; and they had friends from the national society, but not from their own ethnocultural group. In the diffuse cluster, youth appeared confused, exhibiting ambivalence and uncertainty: they had a preference for marginalization, but also for assimilation and (to a lesser extent) separation, while rejecting the integration strategy; they had negative ethnic and national identities; they used their heritage language, but not the national language; and they had some friends from their ethnocultural group, but not from the national society. This pattern resembles the "diffuse" period during identity formation (Marcia, 1994), where young people seem to lack commitment to a direction or purpose in their lives. It also resembles the classic description of the marginal person (Stonequist, 1937), characterized as being poised in psychological uncertainty between two cultural worlds, uncertain which way to turn.

In addition to these acculturation variables, two family relationship values (family obligations and adolescent rights; see below) were included in this cluster analysis. In the integration cluster, both obligations and rights were moderately supported; in the ethnic cluster, obligations were more supported; in the national cluster, obligations were much less supported; in the diffuse cluster, both values were minimally supported.

The study also addressed the second question: How well are immigrant youth adapting to living in their new society? Previous research has indicated that there are two distinct forms of adaptation: psychological and sociocultural (Ward, 1996). Two factors were indeed found: the first factor included life satisfaction, self-esteem, and lack of psychological problems (such as anxiety, depression, and psychosomatic symptoms). The second factor (sociocultural adaptation) included school adjustment and lack of behavior problems (e.g., truancy, petty theft). Adaptation was weakly but significantly related to gender, with immigrant boys having a slightly better psychological adaptation score than immigrant girls, while immigrant boys scored lower on sociocultural adaptation.

With respect to our third question, is it the case that how an adolescent acculturates relates to how well he or she adapts? The pattern in our findings is very clear: those in the integration profile had the best psychological and sociocultural adaptation outcomes, while those in the a diffuse profile had the worst. In between, those with an ethnic profile had moderately good psychological adaptation but poorer sociocultural adaptation, while those with a national profile had moderately poor psychological adaptation, and slightly negative sociocultural adaptation. This pattern of results was largely replicated using structural equation modeling with the same data set (see Berry et al., 2006b).

In addition to these acculturation and adaptation variables examined, we included a scale of family relationship values (Georgas, Berry, Shaw, Christakopoulou, & Mylonas, 1996). Factor analysis yielded two factors, one of which we termed *family obligations* (10 items), and the other *adolescent rights* (four items; see Table 4.1).

Mean scores on these two family relationship values varied over immigrant and national youth, and over immigrant and national parents (see Figure 4.2). These family values are known to vary across cultures, and hence differ between the society of origin of immigrants and the society of settlement (Georgas, Van de Vijver, & Berry, 2004; Georgas et al., 2006). Discrepancies are common in immigrant families because the primary socialization of parents is in the country of origin, while, depending on the age of arrival, their children receive at least some of their primary socialization in the society of settlement. Moreover, immigrant children are usually more exposed to the values of the new society, contributing to their acceptance of the values held by their national peers.

TABLE 4.1. Family Relationship Values (Family Obligations and Adolescent Rights): Factor Analysis in 13 Societies of Settlement

Family obligations	
Item	Factor 1 loading
Authority at home	.39
Obedience to parents	.64
Parental training	.54
Speaking back to parents	.58
Children's responsibility to parents	.49
Working at home—girls	.60
Parents know best	.60
Working at home—boys	.46
Living at home until marriage—girls	.63
Living at home until marriage—boys	.57
Adolescent rights	
Item	Factor 2 loading
Boy's right to choose marriage partner	.72
Boy's right to date	.79
Girl's right to choose marriage partner	.80
Girl's right to date	.79

Note. Data from Berry, Phinney, Sam, and Vedder (2006b).

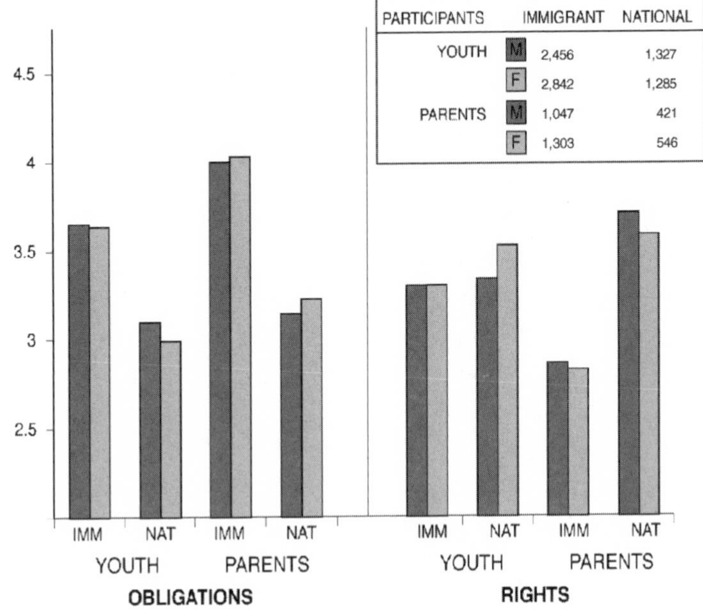

FIGURE 4.2. Family relationship values of immigrant parents and youth in 13 societies of settlement. Data from Berry, Phinney, Sam, and Vedder (2006b).

However, generational discrepancies in these values are also common in nonimmigrant families, as well as in immigrant families. This may well be due to age difference or to social change phenomena.

Immigrant adolescents had higher scores on family obligations than did national adolescents. They also valued adolescents' rights somewhat less than their peers from the national society. Overall, for immigrant youth, the family obligations score was higher than the adolescent rights score, but, for national youth, the mean scores for rights were higher than their mean obligation scores. Surprisingly, there were no overall gender differences among immigrants in the endorsement of obligations or rights.

Adolescents' scores for obligations were higher with shorter residence: adolescents with less than 6 years of residence endorsed family obligations more strongly than adolescents who had lived in their new society longer. Gender also made a difference: girls showed lower obligations score with longer residence, but boys did not.

Immigrant parents had higher scores on obligations than national parents, but they scored lower on rights than national parents. Parents' scores differed from those of their offspring, but in different ways according to their immigrant status. Immigrant parents had higher obligation scores than their children, while national parents and adolescents did not differ. In contrast, immigrant youth had higher scores on rights than their parents, while surprisingly national parents had slightly higher scores than their children. In general, mothers and fathers did not differ on either value, nor in either the immigrant or the national samples.

An important question is whether immigrant families experience greater intergenerational discrepancies than do national families. For family obligations, the discrepancy score was significantly higher for immigrant families than for national families, but there were no differences between immigrant and national families on their discrepancy scores on rights.

The relationship between intergenerational value discrepancies and adolescents' adaptation differs among adolescents with differing acculturation profiles. Across all four profiles, the obligations discrepancy had a negative impact on adaptation, but the effect varied depending on the profile and the type of adaptation. The strongest effect was for adolescents with an integrated profile; for these adolescents, a discrepancy in obligations had a negative effect on sociocultural adaptation, but not on psychological adaptation. For adolescents with a national profile, a discrepancy in obligation scores had a significant negative impact on both psychological and sociocultural adaptation, such that adolescents who are oriented toward the national society were impacted by differences with their parents over obligations. For those with a diffuse orientation, differences with their parents over obligations again impacted both psychological and sociological adaptation.

Higher intergenerational discrepancies in family obligations were associated with poorer psychological and sociocultural adaptation for both immigrant and national adolescents. Discrepancies in adolescents' rights did not relate to adaptation.

IMPLICATIONS

Given the evidence available from the previous literature and from the study reviewed here, it is possible to venture some implications for policy and practice.

First, there are indeed variations in the ways that youth seek to acculturate. The fourfold conceptual framework was supported empirically, suggesting that it is a valid way to understand the options facing acculturating people. The presence of these variations in how people acculturate alerts us to the need to ask what individuals and families are trying to achieve during their acculturation. It is not sensible to assume that they are seeking assimilation, or indeed any other particular way of acculturating. When working with families, and their individual members, it is essential to develop ways of assessing these differential preferences, and to discover any discrepancies that may be present among family members.

Second, there are substantial variations in how well people are adapting to their acculturation experiences. In the youth study, these variations had links to gender and to length of residence. Moreover, levels of adaptation were generally on a par with the comparison national samples. These variations need to be explored further, both in research and when working with youth and families. It is not possible to assume that all immigrants have poor adaptation; however, some do, and these persons need to be identified and cared for.

Third, the relationship between how people acculturate and how well they adapt has implications for all three levels of application. At the cultural-group level, the general pattern is one that alerts both policymakers in the larger society and ethnocultural groups to the adaptive value of seeking to combine cultural maintenance with equitable participation (i.e., multiculturalism; see Berry, 1991). There is also evidence that cultural maintenance alone (i.e., a preference for separation) is sometimes beneficial, while assimilation and marginalization are rarely helpful ways to acculturate. At the family level, there are similar implications: the joint search for maintaining one's heritage culture and identity (possibly emphasizing this aspect within the family and in the cultural community) and participation in the day-to-day life of the larger society outside the family are suggested as the most adaptive way to carry out family life during acculturation. At the individual level, the adaptive value of the integration path is indicated in the youth study. This relationship appears to be sufficiently robust to employ it as a kind of "best practice" when advising and assisting acculturating individuals, especially when individuals within families have discrepant acculturation strategies; in such cases, counseling, based on sharing this evidence with family members, may bring about consensus in working toward achieving a common integration strategy.

REFERENCES

Berry, J. W. (1974). Psychological aspects of cultural pluralism: Unity and identity reconsidered. *Topics in Culture Learning*, 2, 17–22.

Berry, J. W. (1976). *Human ecology and cognitive style: Comparative studies in cultural and psychological adaptation.* New York: Sage/Halsted.

Berry, J. W. (1980). Acculturation as varieties of adaptation. In A. Padilla (Ed.), *Acculturation: Theory, models and findings* (pp. 9–25). Boulder, CO: Westview Press.

Berry, J. W. (1991). Understanding and managing multiculturalism. *Journal of Psychology and Developing Societies*, *3*, 17–49.

Berry, J. W. (1997). Immigration, acculturation and adaptation. *Applied Psychology: An International Review*, *46*, 5–68.

Berry, J. W. (2001). A psychology of immigration. *Journal of Social Issues*, *57*, 615–631.

Berry, J. W. (2003). Conceptual approaches to acculturation. In K. Chun, P. Balls-Organista, & G. Marin (Eds.), *Acculturation* (pp. 3–37). Washington, DC: American Psychological Association.

Berry, J. W., Kalin, R., & Taylor, D. (1977). *Multiculturalism and ethnic attitudes in Canada*. Ottawa: Supply & Services.

Berry, J. W., Kim, U., Minde, T., & Mok, D. (1987). Comparative studies of acculturative stress. *International Migration Review*, *21*, 491–511.

Berry, J. W., Kim, U., Power, S., Young, M., & Bujaki, M. (1989). Acculturation attitudes in plural societies. *Applied Psychology: An International Review*, *38*, 185–206.

Berry, J. W., & Sam, D. L. (2003). Accuracy in scientific discourse. *Scandinavian Journal of Psychology*, *44*, 65–68.

Berry, J. W., Phinney, J. S., Sam, D. L., & Vedder, P. (2006a). Immigrant youth: Acculturation, identity and adaptation *Applied Psychology: An International Review*, *55*, 303–332.

Berry, J. W., Phinney, J. S., Sam, D. L., & Vedder, P. (Eds.). (2006b). *Immigrant youth in cultural transition: Acculturation, identity and adaptation across nations. Mawah, NJ: Erlbaum.*

Berry, J. W., Poortinga, Y. H., Segall, M. H., & Dasen, P. R. (2002). *Cross-cultural psychology: Research and applications* (2nd ed.). New York: Cambridge University Press.

Bourhis, R., Moise, C., Perreault, S., & Senecal, S. (1997). Towards an interactive acculturation model: A social psychological approach. *International Journal of Psychology*, *32*, 369–386.

Georgas, J., Berry, J. W., Shaw, A., Christakopoulou, S., & Mylonas, S. (1996). Acculturation of Greek family values. *Journal of Cross-Cultural Psychology*, *27*, 329–338.

Georgas, J., Berry, J. W., Van de Vijver, F., Kagitcibasi, C., & Poortinga, Y. H. (2006). *Family across cultures: A 30 nation psychological study*. Cambridge, UK: Cambridge University Press.

Georgas, J., Van de Vijver, F. J. R., & Berry, J. W. (2004). The ecocultural framework, ecosocial indicators and psychological variables in cross-cultural research. *Journal of Cross-Cultural Psychology*, *35*, 74–96.

Graves, T. (1967). Psychological acculturation in a tri-ethnic community. *South-Western Journal of Anthropology*, *23*, 337–350.

Gordon, M. (1964). *Assimilation in American life*. New York: Oxford University Press.

Marcia, J. (1994). The empirical study of ego identity. In H. Bosma, T. Graafsma, H. Grotevant, & D. De Levita (Eds.), *Identity and development: An interdisciplinary approach* (pp. 67–80. Thousand Oaks, CA: Sage.

Redfield, R., Linton, R., & Herskovits, M. (1936). Memorandum on the study of acculturation. *American Anthropologist, 38*, 149–152.

Rudmin, F. W., & Ahmadzadeh, V. (2001). Psychometric critique of acculturation psychology: The case of Iranian migrants in Norway. *Scandinavian Journal of Psychology, 42*, 41–56.

Ryder, A., Alden, L., & Paulhus, D. (2000). Is acculturation unidimensional or bidimensional? *Journal of Personality and Social Psychology, 79*, 49–65.

Sam, D. L., & Berry, J. W. (Eds.). (2006). *Cambridge handbook of acculturation psychology.* Cambridge, UK: Cambridge University Press.

Stonequist, E. V. (1937). *The marginal man.* New York: Scribners.

Ward, C. (1996). Acculturation. In D. Landis & R. Bhagat (Eds.), *Handbook of intercultural training* (2nd ed., pp. 124–147). Newbury Park, CA: Sage.

CHAPTER 5

Immigrant Families in Sociology

Vappu Tyyskä

SOCIOLOGY AND THE MONOLITHIC MODEL OF THE FAMILY

As a subdiscipline, the sociology of the family has a long history of structural-functionalist theorizing (Baker, 2001; Eichler, 1997; Riedmann, Lamanna, & Nelson, 2003). This approach holds, as normative, the model of a traditional nuclear family with a breadwinner husband/father and a dependent wife/mother and children. The socialization of children is a parental responsibility, with an emphasis on the primary responsibility of the mother (Ambert, 2006). Eichler (1988, 1997; also see Baker, 2001) used the term "monolithic" to describe this type of idealized family that excludes and stigmatizes large segments of the population who do not fit into its male-dominated, Western, white, middle-class, heterosexual norm. Over time, the monolithic bias in family sociology has been challenged by a number of critical and feminist family sociologists (Bernard, 1972; Li, 1980; Mandell & Duffy, 1995; Veevers, 1991).

In an early study, Li (1980) demonstrated the inapplicability of the traditional nuclear family model to Chinese Canadian immigrants' experiences. He showed that their stigmatized "broken families" were not a reflection of a "deficient" cultural trait, but resulted from discriminatory immigration policies that prevented the immigration of Chinese women and children in the early 20th century. Other immigrant communities have experienced similar difficulties both historically (Albanese, 2005;

Makabe, 2005) and in the present. For example, immigrant domestic workers cannot sponsor their families until 3 years after arriving in Canada (Calliste, 2003; Cohen, 2000). Thus, family relationships among spouses, parents, and children and extended families change and challenge the monolithic model, as families stretch beyond the nuclear family and beyond the borders of nation-states (Ambert, 2006; Hernandez, Denton, & Macartney, Chapter 1, this volume; Panagakos, 2004; Waters, 2002). Similarly, the gender-based and intergenerational power differences that are ignored in the monolithic model have been subjected to increasing analysis, with attention to the different experiences of family members with regard to education, work, and home life (Ambert, 2006; Creese, Dyck, & McLaren, 1999; Tyyskä, 2001, 2003a, 2003b).

The following selective review of the sociological literature on immigrant families addresses some of the themes arising from the critique of the monolithic model of the family. First, I outline some of the economic and immigration policy conditions surrounding immigrant families. Second, I address questions related to gender and intergenerational relations in immigrant families. Third, I touch on globalization and transnational families. I highlight some of the main policy issues while giving voice to selected immigrants through examples from my research.

STRUCTURAL CONDITIONS

> They are working. They just say that this is not a country to chill with your family and everything. They think work, money is a big problem. So basically that's the main issue. Basically money problems. You are working 24/7. There's no time for family.
>
> —TAMIL, MALE, AGE 19 (in Tyyskä, 2006, p. 21)

Both the United States and Canada are immigrant-receiving nations. As of 2001, the former boasts a foreign-born population of 11.1%, while the latter has a foreign-born population of 18.4% (Liu & Kerr, 2003). There has been a shift in source countries of immigration over the last century. Whereas in the 19th century and most of the 20th century, British and other European immigrants were preferred, the last quarter of the 20th century has seen an influx of immigrants from non-European countries who now make up over three-quarters of all immigrants entering Canada (Ambert, 2006; Momirov & Kilbride, 2005). In contrast to the white immigrants of the past, recent immigrants to Canada tend to be from racialized minorities: over half are Asian, with three of the largest groups being Chinese, South Asians, and blacks (Ambert, 2006). This diversity of the immigrant population is also reflected in the presence of over 90 ethnic groups in Canada, each with 15,000 members or more (Albanese, 2005). Similarly, immigration to the United States is leading to a "new U.S. majority" (Hernandez et al., Chapter 1, in this volume).

By the 1990s, 73% of newcomer immigrant families in Canada lived in large metropolitan centers (Statistics Canada, 2004a, 2004c, 2005b), attracted by better job opportunities and by access to family, friends, and services (Statistics Canada, 2005c). Immigrants have the promise of a good start, as the Canadian immigration system favors those with higher education (Shields, 2004). In fact, at 40%, almost twice as many immigrants ages 25–54 hold university degrees, relative to the Canadian-born population (Frenette & Morissette, 2005; Momirov & Kilbride, 2005).

The promise of a prosperous life in the new land is often unfulfilled because even highly educated immigrants often struggle to find employment. Both U.S. and Canadian research has shown that immigrant newcomers experience economic difficulties for several years after immigration, in part due to discrimination (Ambert, 2006; Hernandez et al., Chapter 1, this volume; Kaushal & Reimers, Chapter 6, this volume; Li, 1988; Liu & Kerr, 2003; Momirov & Kilbride, 2005). Liu and Kerr (2003) summarize research showing that those of European ancestry are located in better jobs, whereas those from Africa, Asia, and Latin America are less successful, even if they are educated. They report a "substantial decline" in the "average levels of well-being" of immigrant families within the last 10 years. Low earnings among immigrants correlate with poverty, poor health, and poor housing conditions (Anisef & Kilbride, 2000; Beiser, Hou, Hyrnan, & Tousignant, 2002; Statistics Canada, 2004a, 2004b, 2004d, 2005a, 2005c; Shields, 2004), which in turn create stresses on internal family dynamics, to be discussed below.

The policy and program solutions in this area obviously have to do with increasing immigrants' access to gainful employment while reducing their welfare dependency. However, improvements in this area would require nearly a full reversal of the trends that began over two decades ago. Particularly since the 1990s, social and economic restructuring have eroded the ability of the welfare state to provide for the needs of immigrant populations. The logic behind changing Canadian immigrant entry requirements in the early 1990s was to create a highly flexible, adaptable immigrant mass who had transferable skills (Arat-Koc, 1993; Shields, 2004). Instead, underemployment, unemployment (Arat-Koc, 1993), and poverty (Frenette & Morissette, 2005) have increased among immigrants. The problems are compounded by cuts in funding to social services and settlement services aimed at immigrants in Canada (Shields, 2004).

Similarly, the 1996 welfare reforms in the United States made noncitizens "ineligible for important public benefits and services" (Hernandez et al., Chapter 1, this volume). All of this has created additional barriers for immigrants who also have to combat racism and anti-immigrant attitudes in many aspects of their lives.

GENDER RELATIONS

> Navigating life over here is brutal for a lot of cultures. First of all, many times, it's easier for a woman to pick up a low paying job than a man to pick up a low paying job. It changes the roles dramatically. But it changes the roles sometimes only physically, like I mean, in that she is earning a pay check, it doesn't necessarily mean that the guy can make that kind of adjustment and pick up where she left off, you know, in parenting and that type of stuff. So sometimes we find that the moms are carrying kind of a double burden there because they are earning an income and they also have to go home and deal with issues.
>
> —IMMIGRANT SERVICE PROVIDER (in Tyyskä, 2002b)

The vast majority (77%) of the principal immigration applicants to Canada are men (Momirov & Kilbride, 2005). This overrepresentation means that there tends to be a corresponding practice of "essentializing," that is, representing the lives of immigrant families based on the experiences of men in the public (economic and political) sphere (Pizanias, 1996), in keeping with the monolithic family model. This has begun to shift since the 1980s, with more attention to differences brought on by the intersection of race, gender, and immigrant status, particularly by black and antiracist feminists (Abbott & Wallace, 1997).

Some researchers suggest that there is a trend toward more gender-egalitarian arrangements on immigration to North America (Anisef, Kilbride, Ochoka, & Janzen, 2001; Haddad & Lam, 1988; Jain & Belsky, 1997), particularly as women may find full-time employment faster than men (Ali & Kilbride, 2004; Creese et al., 1999; Grewal, Bottroff, & Hilton, 2005; Momirov & Kilbride, 2005). These studies suggest that, while women are employed, men's lives are changed fundamentally through their unemployment and taking on more domestic responsibilities. Some men may experience lowered self-esteem over the loss of their traditional male breadwinner role, as it is still the case in many families—whether immigrants or not—because the husband/father typically holds more power (Tyyskä, 2002a, 2002b, 2003a). Even so, we need to move away from the assumption that immigrants are "traditional" and the West is "modern" with regard to employment and family patterns (Tyyskä, 2003b; Walton-Roberts & Pratt, 2003). In fact, studies show that the consequences of immigration are varied for gender relations, depending on the country of origin, culture, social class, and urban versus rural origins (Shahidian, 1999; Tyyskä, 2003b; Walton-Roberts & Pratt, 2003). These combine with conditions of entry. Although immigration systems favor educated professionals, most immigrant women arrive in Canada as dependents of their husbands, in the "family class" of immigrants. For example, Man (2003) demonstrated that many of the women who emigrated from China to Canada after the points system was instituted are educated female professionals. However, they most often enter as dependents and stay-at-home mothers. Some of these women, as well as the South Asian women in Grewal and colleagues' (2005) study, feel trapped by their financial dependence on their husbands and their secondary and submissive roles in their families.

However, contrary to general Western feminist expectations (Moghissi, 1999), and highlighting the need to consider social class and cultural differences among women, not all immigrant women want to escape the nuclear family. Thus, Man (2003) reports that some Chinese middle- and upper-class women enjoy the high status acquired through the newly found economic success of their husbands. Indeed, some women see the family as a refuge from the oppressions they face in the public realm, and want to protect their right to have a family (Momirov & Kilbride, 2005, p. 104). This may be the case despite the arguably contradictory combination of acquiescing to patriarchy while fighting racism (Moghissi, 1999).

Nevertheless, the forced dependency of immigrant women through the family class immigrant category gives them initially a poorer starting point compared to immigrant men. As emphasized earlier, this is yet another illustration of the forcible changes that state policies impose on immigrant family structure (Albanese, 2005; Calliste, 2003; Cohen, 2000; Li, 1980; Makabe, 2005). Policy changes required include improvements in all settlement services aimed at women, including employment re/training and provision of better childcare services. Insofar as English language proficiency is an issue of concern for all adult immigrants (Fuligni & Fuligni, Chapter 13, this volume; Hernandez et al., Chapter 1, this volume), women face challenges different from men, due to their familial responsibilities and different, more limited sets of opportunities to learn English (Kilbride, 2006). Breaking this cycle requires—among other things—creating language programs that correspond to immigrant women's circumstances.

INTERGENERATIONAL RELATIONS

> They were raised 40 or 50 years ago in Sri Lanka and I was raised ten years ago in Canada. . . . Some parts of them, they still hold on to some values they learned when they were a child. Things like what girls should do and what boys should do and what they should wear. But for us, everything is changed. It's not the same—what girls should do here is not the same as what girls should do there. So, I think [. . .] the generation gap—how we are raised.
>
> —FEMALE, AGE 18 (in Tyyskä, 2006, p. 23)

A number of studies have documented changes in newcomer parents' roles and relationships with their children in North America (Ambert, 1992; Anisef et al., 2001; Dhruvarajan, 2003; Foner, 1997; Kilbride, Anisef, Baidman-Anisef, & Khattar, 2001; Tyyskä, 2003a, 2005, 2006). Many immigrant parents feel that their parenting ability is under serious stress in a number of ways (Fuligni & Yoshikawa, 2003; Noivo, 1993; Tyyskä, 2005, 2006). Poverty alone creates situational and systemic obstacles that undermine attentive and nurturing parental behaviors (Beiser, Hou, Kasper, & Who, 2000). As immigrant parents struggle with unemployment, underemployment, multiple job holding, and shifts in gender-based economic roles, their children may not get the attention they deserve, while parents also put added pressures on them in areas of education and future employment (Creese et al., 1999; Tyyskä, 2005, 2006). Because their families are likely to face economic hardship, youth poverty is a big issue (Beiser et al., 2000). For some immigrant groups, there is a danger in both Canada and the United States (Hernandez et al., Chapter 1, this volume) alike that the economic hardships experienced by parents will leave a legacy of intergenerational pauperization, despite the promise of upward mobility through education.

Children often learn the official language faster than their parents, due to the influence of schools and peers (Hernandez et al., Chapter 1, this volume). This can lead to two types of intergenerational problems. First, language differences can create conflict in intergenerational communication and transmission of culture and identity (Anisef et al., 2001; Bernhard, Lefebvre, Chud, & Lange, 1996). Second, role reversals and shifts in parental authority may result, as parents rely on their children as mediators of official language, social institutions (schools, hospitals, social services), and culture (Ali & Kilbride, 2004; Creese et al., 1999; Momirov & Kilbride, 2005; Tyyskä, 2005, 2006). However, while immigrant children may claim new roles and responsibilities in their families, parents often expect to retain the same degree of authority over their children (Creese et al., 1999).

Added factors in the realignment of parental authority are shifts in maternal and paternal work and family roles and authority patterns that change parents' relationships with one another and their children (Ali & Kilbride, 2004; Anisef et al., 2001; Creese et al., 1999; Grewal et al., 2005; Haddad & Lam, 1988; Jain & Belsky, 1997; Momirov & Kilbride, 2005; Shimoni, Este, & Clark, 2003; Tyyskä, 2005). The resulting tensions also contribute to the onset or increase in severity of family violence against women and children (Creese et al., 1999; MacLeod & Shin, 1993; Smith, 2004; Tyyskä, 2005; Wiebe, 1991).

Much of the research into intergenerational relations in immigrant families tends to focus on intergenerational conflict ("the generation gap") in terms of expectations of "Old World" parents and their "New World" children (Tyyskä, 2005, 2006), including issues such as peer relationships and social behavior (Wade & Brannigan, 1998; Wong, 1999), dating and spouse selection patterns (Dhruvarajan, 2003; Mitchell, 2001; Morrison, Guruge, & Snarr, 1999; Zaidi & Shuraydi, 2002), educational and career choices (Dhruvarajan, 2003; Fuligni, 1997; Li, 1988; Noivo, 1993), and retention of culture (James, 1999).

Immigrant youth often feel torn between their desire to fit in with their peers and their desire to meet their parents' expectations (Tyyskä, 2003b, 2006). Particularly stark differences emerge among some immigrant communities with regard to parental expectations of male and female children (Tyyskä, 2003b). Adolescent girls in some immigrant families have much less freedom of movement and decision-making power than their brothers (Anisef & Kilbride, 2000; Anisef et al., 2001; Dhruvarajan, 2003; Handa, 1997; Shahidian, 1999; Tyyskä, 2001, 2006). Parental fears for daughters relate predominantly to dating, which is equated with premarital sexuality, whereas fears for sons center on drugs and violence (Anisef et al., 2001; Shahidian, 1999; Tyyskä, 2006).

The main policy and program recommendations are clearly linked to employment. Policies need to ease the economic pressures on immigrant parents, in order for them to fully participate in the lives of their children and to create for them a good starting point in life. Another area requiring attention is better integration of training in official languages for parents, to bridge the language and cultural gap between generations. In the education system, children and youth need the respect of educators for their culture and language through a wider provision of heritage language classes and cultural activities. Improved cultural sensitivity, including training of educators about different immigrant groups, is required to alleviate the isolation and racism experienced by immigrant children and youth in the education system and among their peers (Ali & Kilbride, 2004; Bradley & McKelvey, Chapter 9, this volume;

Waldfogel & Lahaie, Chapter 10, this volume). Research in both Canada and the United States shows that many immigrant parents want and seek out opportunities for more effective parenting which could be provided in the context of schools and community organizations (Hernandez et al., Chapter 1, this volume; Tyyskä & Colavecchia, 2001).

Although employment and education are clearly in the public realm, some policy solutions fall outside this comfort zone. Family policy in general belongs in the uneasy realm that seems to cross the boundaries between the public and the private. This is the case with parental control over girl children. Girls hold a special place as "cultural vessels" in many immigrant communities, and their conduct is seen to reflect the family and the whole community. Nevertheless, families with girls and young women may need interventions to prevent the escalation of family conflict and possible violence, and the alienation of girls from their families (Handa, 1997; Tyyskä, 2006).

Family violence is difficult to approach through policy measures. Many immigrant communities react defensively at the suggestion of family violence, afraid of public stigmatization. Solutions in this area require sensitivity and the full involvement of the communities in question which can offer the best ways of alleviating the problem among people they know (Bui & Morash, 1999; Maiter, Trocme, & George, 2003; Martin & Mosher, 1995; Menjivar & Salcido, 2002; Pratt, 1995; Preston, 2001; Wiebe, 1991).

TRANSNATIONAL FAMILIES

> I came from a culture where we had extended family that participated in raising children who gave the mother the help and relief that she needed. On the contrary here I find parents with less children going through so much stress—especially those working parents.
>
> —SOMALI MOTHER (in Tyyskä & Colavecchia, 2001, p. 105)

As stressed from the beginning, the definition of families among many immigrant groups is not limited to the traditional nuclear family. At the same time, the distinction between nuclear and extended families does not adequately capture the richness of local, national, and international/transnational networks that immigrants rely on (Creese et al., 1999). The impact of globalization is evident in the multiple border crossings across the boundaries of nation-states. Transnational families (or "astronaut families") are a result of migrations related to the search for work for adults and education for children, and are characterized by separation and reunification of different members of the family unit over time

(Ambert, 2006; Panagakos, 2004; Waters, 2002; Wong, Chapter 12, this volume).

Although some families arrive as multigenerational units (Noivo, 1993), others experience fracturing due to a combination of restrictive definitions of "family" in immigration policies and the circumstances of their departure from their countries of origin. Some families undergo continuous transnational shifts over generations (Gordon, 1999; Panagakos, 2004; Shahidian, 1999), creating intergenerational ruptures and complex family dynamics over distance. One major change in some immigrant communities is that the loss of extended family in helping rear children may lead to new parenting arrangements and parenting support networks (Anisef et al., 2001; Tyyskä, 2002a, 2003b).

Transnational family arrangements stress spousal and parent–child relationships. In some cases, spouses may remain separated for several years. These lengthy separations often result in extramarital affairs (Cohen, 2000; Shahidian, 1999), spouses growing apart, and a host of negative emotions including jealousy, hostility, depression, and indifference (Cohen, 2000; Man, 2003). Parent–child relationships are particularly stress-ridden in these circumstances. One type of transnational family in Canada centers on women who are brought here under the Foreign Immigrant Domestic Program, from developing countries such as the Philippines and the Caribbean nations (Arat-Koc, 1997; Bakan & Stasiulis, 1996). These women leave their children behind to come and work as low-wage domestics and nannies to escape the poverty created in their home countries by the legacy of colonialism and expanding global economic exploitation (Ambert, 2006; Arat-Koc, 1997; Bakan & Stasiulis, 1996).

Regardless of the circumstances of their immigration, mothers are commonly held responsible for their children, and face stigma and social disapproval if they leave them behind as they search for better opportunities abroad (Ambert, 2006; Bernhard, Landolt, & Goldring, 2005). Immigration policies do not make it easy for families to reunite, as the process takes a long time. This means that by the time children are reunited with their parents, families face many adjustment issues, including fear of abandonment, or anger toward and jealousy of siblings who accompanied the immigrating parent. Parental authority may be undermined as a number of children grow up separated from their parents and without anyone to step into the role of parents. At the same time, there is a double loss for children who first were separated from their parents, and now face another separation from a caregiver they have grown attached to (Ambert, 2006; Bernhard et al., 2005; Cohen, 2000; Wong, Chapter 12, this volume). Newly reunited children can also become overly dependent on their mothers, preventing the latter from connecting with their communities (Creese et al., 1999).

The shifting frames of reference for immigrant families have resulted in an increasing attention to issues of identity and belonging among sociologists (Driedger, 2001; Kalbach & Kalbach, 1999). Fuelled by postmodernist theory, an increasing number of studies focus on the different interpretations of national and ethnic identity among immigrants, stamped by gender and age differences (Handa, 1997; Karakayali, 2005; Tyyskä, 2003b). These analyses move the debate beyond the traditional "acculturation thesis" which measures degrees to which immigrants adapt to the host society. According to this thesis, acculturation is seen as a natural progression in which each successive immigrant generation adopts more of the "behaviours, rules, values, and norms of the host society" (Boyd, 2000, cited in Tyyskä, 2001, p. 138; see also Berry, Chapter 4, this volume). Instead, the focus in more recent sociological literature is on multiple and "hybrid" identities (Gordon, 1999; Berry, Chapter 4, this volume) that may result in conflicting interpretations within families (Karakayali, 2005; Tyyskä, 2003). In other words, the premise of recent studies is that identities are flexible, subject to multiple influences and interpretations of equal validity. Acculturation as adaptation to the host society is no longer seen as the only foreseeable and/or desired end result (Berry, Chapter 4, this volume; Tyyskä, 2006). Additionally, there is a renewed appreciation in the sociology of identity development being a two-way street, that is, immigrants also influence the development of "national" identities in the host society (Kalbach & Kalbach, 1999).

In terms of nation-specific policies, governments can make transnational family lives easier through changing residency and citizenship requirements. However, individual nations' policies and programs can only go so far. Economic and political globalization and associated population movements raise multiple issues that can only be partly addressed by individual immigrant and emigrant states. This is where reliance on multinational and international bodies is required. In short, the problems are a matter for international law and human rights organizations through the development of measures that protect the human rights of people, including the right to mobility and family life, while safeguarding the conditions under which such movement and settlement take place.

CONCLUSIONS

Sociological debates on immigrant families continue to be framed in relation to conservative or structural-functionalist ideology. This is manifested in the multiple ways in which immigrant families are approached as "the other" in relation to the presumably normative "monolithic" North American nuclear families. This tendency prevails, even as North American critical and feminist family sociologists have charted the many significant changes in families that have taken place in the last century, including shifts in both patriarchal and intergenerational power arrangements. The term "immigrant families" continues to carry negative associations with extreme patriarchy, abuse of parental power, and holding onto "Old World" ideas. Some of this characterization applies to specific immigrant groups that may have lower levels of education, lack English language skills, and consequently are slower off the mark in terms of their settlement conditions and success in economic and political integration. However, what is notable is that immigration policies, such as the Canadian points system of entry, favor immigrants with language proficiency, education, and training. Thus, the lack of settlement success that particularly non-European and racialized immigrants are shown to suffer is less explainable by presumed inherent properties of immigrants, and more by structural conditions—including systemic racism—on arrival that set immigrants up for a life of menial employment, poverty, and struggle. As outlined above, it is not coincidental that the increase in non-European immigration is combined with deterioration in the employment and economic chances of immigrants.

In sociology, particular attention is paid to the ways in which multiple structural conditions influence group dynamics, including family lives. Changes brought about by immigration put pressure on the whole family unit through unemployment, underemployment, lack of financial resources, and changing roles and power relations of spouses. Even if women and men in some immigrant communities continue the wage-earning patterns they were accustomed to in their countries of origin, the North American gender-divided and racist labor market has often little to offer to them even if they have the requisite English language skills, education, and training. Additional problems are created as children learn to navigate their new surroundings faster, resulting in a role reversal in parent–child relationships. Intergenerational conflicts among im migrants are not inevitable, but their likelihood increases as young people are exposed to the influence of their peers as their parents struggle amidst multiple challenges. If barriers to family separation and reunification in the migration experience are added into this mix, it can become truly toxic for some non-European racialized immigrant groups, with increased chances of alienation of family members from one another.

It has also been noted that the policy solutions to the many problems that immigrants face are becoming more complex. In the conflict-ridden global atmosphere, the post-9/11 political climate, and the legacy of neoconservatism of the 1990s, comprehensive solutions bear the stamp of increased prohibitions against immigration and minority rights. Ideally, the piecemeal policies that make a loose patchwork quilt of "immigration policy" should be comprehensive and coherent, linking immigration policies more consciously and systematically to education, training, employment, language, and family policy, to allow immigrants to fulfill the promise of prosperity their host countries offer globally. The global corollary of this approach would be an integrated multinational effort to safeguard migrating families' human rights, including their access to economic opportunity, a dignified family life, and right to cultural practices. However, this seems relatively utopian in the present climate of fear and racism in North America. It is equally unlikely that under these conditions the conservative cloak will be fully shed from sociological studies of immigrant families.

REFERENCES

Abbott, P., & Wallace, C. (1997). *An introduction to sociology: Feminist perspectives* (2nd ed.). New York: Routledge.

Albanese, P. (2005). Ethnic families. In M. Baker (Ed.), *Families: Changing trends in Canada* (pp. 121–142). Toronto: McGraw-Hill.

Ali, M., & Kilbride, K. (2004). *Forging new ties: Improving parenting and family support services for new Canadians with young children.* Ottawa: Human Resources and Skill Development Canada.

Ambert, A. (1992). *The effect of children on parents.* Binghamton, NY: Haworth Press.

Ambert, A. (2006). *Changing families: Relationships in context* (Canadian edition). Toronto: Pearson.

Anisef, P., & Kilbride, K. M. (2000). *The needs of newcomer youth and emerging "best practices" to meet those needs.* Toronto: Joint Centre of Excellence for Research on Immigration and Settlement.

Anisef, P., Kilbride, K. M., Ochocka, J., & Janzen, R. (2001). *Parenting issues of newcomer families in Ontario.* Kitchener, Ontario: Center for Research and Education in Human Services and Center of Excellence for Research on Immigration and Settlement.

Arat-Koc, S. (1993). Neo-liberalism, state restructuring and immigration: Changes in Canadian policies in the 1990s. *Journal of Canadian Studies, 34*(2), 31–56.

Arat-Koc, S. (1997). From "mothers of the nation" to migrant workers. In A. B. Bakan & D. Stasiulis (Eds.), *Not one of the family: Foreign domestic workers in Canada* (pp. 53–79). Toronto: University of Toronto Press.

Bakan, A. D., & Stasiulis, D. (1996). Structural adjustment, citizenship, and foreign domestic labour: The Canadian case. In I. Bakker (Ed.), *Rethinking restructuring: Gender and change in Canada* (pp. 217–242). Toronto: University of Toronto Press.

Baker, M. (2001). *Families, labour and love: Family diversity in a changing world.* Vancouver: University of British Columbia Press.

Beiser, M., Hou, F., Hyrnan, I., & Tousignant, M. (2002). Poverty, family process and the mental health of immigrant children in Canada. *American Journal of Public Health*, *92*(2), 220–228.

Beiser, M., Hou, F., Kasper, V., & Who, S. (2000). *Changes in poverty status and developmental behaviour: A comparison of immigrant and non immigrant children in Canada.* Hull, Quebec: Applied Research Branch, Strategic Policy Division, Human Resources Development Canada.

Bernard, J. (1972). *The future of marriage.* New York: World Publishing.

Bernhard, J. K., Landolt, P., & Goldring, L. (2005). *Transnational, multi-local motherhood: Experiences of separation and reunification among Latin American families in Canada* (Working Paper No. 40). Toronto: Joint Centre of Excellence for Research on Immigration and Settlement.

Bernhard, J. K., Lefebvre, M. L., Chud, G., & Lange, R. (1996). Linguistic match between children and caregivers in Canadian early childhood education. *Canadian Journal of Research in Early Childhood Education*, *5*(2), 202–222.

Bui, H., & Morash, M. (1999). Domestic violence in the Vietnamese immigrant community: An exploratory study. *Violence against Women*, *5*(6), 769–795.

Calliste, A. (2003). Black families in Canada: Exploring the interconnections of race, class, and gender. In M. Lynn (Ed.), *Voices: Essays on Canadian families* (2nd ed.). Toronto: Nelson Canada.

Cohen, R. (2000). "Mom is a stranger": The negative impact of immigration policies on the family life of Philipina domestic workers. *Canadian Ethnic Studies*, *32*(3), 76–88.

Creese, G., Dyck, I., & McLaren, A. (1999). *Reconstituting the family: Negotiating immigration and settlement* (Working Paper No. 99-10). Vancouver, British Columbia: Research on Immigration and Integration in the Metropolis.

Dhuravarajan, V. (2003). Hindu Indo-Canadian families. In M. Lynn (Ed.), *Voices: Essays on Canadian families* (2nd ed.). Toronto: Nelson Canada.

Driedger, L. (2001). Changing visions in ethnic relations. *Canadian Journal of Sociology*, *26*(3), 421–442.

Eichler, M. (1988). *Families in Canada today* (2nd ed.). Toronto: Gage.

Eichler, M. (1997). *Family shifts: Families, policies, and gender equality.* Toronto: Oxford University Press.

Foner, N. (1997). The immigrant family: Cultural legacies and cultural changes. *International Migration Review*, *31*(4), 961–974.

Frenette, M., & Morissette, R. (2005). Will they ever converge?: Earnings of immigrant and Canadian-born workers over the last two decades. *International Migration Review*, *39*(1), 228–258.

Fuligni, A. J. (1997). The academic achievement of adolescents from immigrant families: The roles of family background, attitudes, and behavior. *Child Development*, *68*(2), 351–363.

Fuligni, A. J., & Yoshikawa, K. (2003). Socioeconomic resources, parenting, and the child development among immigrant families. In M. Bornstein & R. Bradley (Eds.), *Socioeconomic status, parenting, and child development* (pp. 107–124). Mahwah, NJ: Erlbaum.

Gordon, E. (1999). *Separation, reunification and the hybridization of culture: A study of Caribbean immigrant families in Toronto.* Unpublished master's thesis, York University, Toronto.

Grewal, S., Bottroff, J., & Hilton, A. (2005). The influence of family on immigrant South Asian women's health. *Journal of Family Nursing, 11*(3), 242–263.

Haddad, T., & Lam, L. (1988). Canadian families—Men's involvement in family work: A case study of immigrant men in Toronto. *International Journal of Comparative Sociology, 29*(3–4), 269–281.

Handa, A. (1997). *Caught between omissions: Exploring "culture conflict" among second generation South Asian women in Canada.* Unpublished doctoral dissertation, University of Toronto.

Jain, A., & Belsky, J. (1997). Fathering and acculturation: Immigrant Indian families with young children. *Journal of Marriage and Family, 59*, 873–883.

James, C. E. (1999). *Seeing ourselves: Exploring race, ethnicity and culture* (2nd ed.). Toronto: Thompson Educational.

Kalbach, M. A., & Kalbach, W. E. (1999). Becoming Canadian: Problems of an emerging identity. *Canadian Ethnic Studies, 31*(2), 1–16.

Karakayali, N. (2005). Duality and diversity in the lives of immigrant children: Rethinking the "problem of the second generation" in light of immigrant autobiographies. *Canadian Review of Sociology and Anthropology, 42*(3), 325–344.

Kilbride, K.M. (2006). *Facilitating the acquisition of proficiency in English among adult immigrant women: Filling the gaps.* Ottawa: Canadian Council on Learning.

Kilbride, K. M., Anisef, P., Baichman-Anisef, E., & Khattar, R. (2001). *Between two worlds: The experiences and concerns of immigrant youth in Ontario.* Toronto: Joint Centre of Excellence for Research on Immigration and Settlement.

Li, P. (1980). Immigration laws and family patterns: Some demographic changes among Chinese families in Canada, 1883–1971. *Canadian Ethnic Studies, 12*(1), 58–73.

Li, P. (1988). *Ethnic inequality in class society.* Toronto: Thompson Educational.

Liu, J., & Kerr, D. (2003). Family change and economic well-being in Canada: The case of recent immigrant families with children. *International Migration, 41*(4), 113–140.

MacLeod, L., & Shin, M. (1993). *"Like a wingless bird . . . ": A tribute to the survival and courage of women who are abused and who speak neither English nor French.* Ottawa: National Clearinghouse on Family Violence.

Maiter, S., Trocme, N., & George, U. (2003). Building bridges: The collaborative development of culturally appropriate definitions of child abuse and neglect for the South Asian community. *Affilia: Journal of Women and Social Work, 18*(4), 411–420.

Makabe, T. (2005). Intermarriage: Dream becomes reality for a visible minority? *Canadian Ethnic Studies, 37*(1), 121–126.

Man, G. (2003). The experience of middle class women in recent Hong Kong Chinese immigrant families in Canada. In M. Lynn (Ed.), *Voices: Essays on Canadian families* (2nd ed., pp. 271–300). Toronto: Thomson Nelson.

Mandell, N., & Duffy, A. (Eds.). (1995). *Canadian families: Diversity, conflict and change*. Toronto: Harcourt Brace.

Martin, D., & Mosher, J. (1995). Unkept promises: Experiences of immigrant women with the neo-criminalization of wife abuse. *Canadian Journal of Women and the Law, 8*, 3–44.

Menjivar, C., & Salcido, O. (2002). Immigrant women and domestic violence: Common experiences in different countries. *Gender and Society, 16*(6), 898–920.

Mitchell, B. (2001). Ethnocultural reproduction and attitudes toward cohabiting relationships. *Canadian Review of Sociology and Anthropology, 38*(4), 391–414.

Moghissi, H. (1999). Away from home: Iranian women, displacement, cultural resistance and change. *Journal of Comparative Family Studies, 30*(2), 207–218.

Momirov, J., & Kilbride, K. (2005). Family lives of native peoples, immigrants and visible minorities. In N. Mandel & A. Duffy (Eds.), *Canadian families: Diversity, conflict and change* (pp. 87–110). Toronto: Thomson Nelson.

Morrison, L., Guruge, S., & Snarr, K. A. (1999). Sri Lankan Tamil immigrants in Toronto: Gender, marriage patterns, and sexuality. In G. Kelson & D. DeLaet (Eds.), *Gender and immigration* (pp. 144–162). New York: New York University Press.

Noivo, E. (1993). Ethnic families and the social injuries of class, migration, gender, generation and minority status. *Canadian Ethnic Studies, 23*(3), 66–76.

Panagakos, A. (2004). Recycled odyssey: Creating transnational families in the Greek diaspora. *Global Networks, 4*(3), 299–311.

Pizanias, C. (1996). Greek families in Canada: Fragile truths, fragmented stories. In M. Lynn (Ed.), *Voices: Essays on Canadian families* (pp. 329–360). Toronto: Nelson Canada.

Pratt, A. (1995). New immigrant and refugee battered women: The intersection of immigration and criminal justice policy. In Centre for Criminology, University of Toronto (Ed.), *Wife assault and the Canadian criminal justice system: Issues and policies* (pp. 84–103). Toronto: Centre for Criminology, University of Toronto.

Preston, B. (2001). *A booklet for service providers who work with immigrant families on issues relating to child discipline, child abuse and child neglect*. Ottawa: National Clearinghouse on Family Violence.

Riedmann, A., Lamanna, M. A., & Nelson, A. (2003). *Marriages and families*. Toronto: Thomson Nelson.

Shahidian, H. (1999). Gender and sexuality among immigrant Iranians in Canada. *Sexualities, 2*(2), 189–222.

Shields, J. (2004). *No safe haven: Markets, welfare and migrants* (CERIS Working Paper No. 22). Toronto: Joint Centre of Excellence for Research on Immigration and Settlement.

Shimoni, E., Este, D., & Clark, D. (2003). Paternal engagement in immigrant and refugee families. *Journal of Comparative Family Studies, 34*(4), 555–571.

Smith, E. (2004). *Nowhere to turn?: Responding to partner violence against immi-*

grant and visible minority women. Ottawa: Department of Justice Canada, Sectoral Involvement in Departmental Policy Development.

Statistics Canada. (2004a, August 18). Immigrants in Canada's urban centres. *The Daily*.

Statistics Canada. (2004b, June 23). Immigrants settling for less? *The Daily*.

Statistics Canada. (2004c, April 7). Low income in Census Metropolitan Areas. *The Daily*.

Statistics Canada. (2004d, May 17). Why the earnings of new immigrants to Canada have deteriorated over time. *The Daily*.

Statistics Canada. (2005a, February 3). Decline in home ownership rates among immigrant families. *The Daily*.

Statistics Canada. (2005b, June 29). Initial destination and redistribution of major immigrant groups in Canada. *The Daily*.

Statistics Canada. (2005c). *Longitudinal survey of immigrants to Canada: A portrait of early settlement experiences* (Cat. No. 89-614-XIE). Ottawa: Statistics Canada.

Tyyskä, V. (2001). *Long and winding road: Adolescents and youth in Canada today*. Toronto: Canadian Scholars Press.

Tyyskä, V. (2002a). *Report of individual interviews with parents—Toronto: Toronto: Improving parenting and family supports for new Canadians with young children: Focus on resources for service providers*. Ottawa, ON: Human Resources Development Canada.

Tyyskä, V. (2002b). *Report of key informant interviews—Toronto: Improving parenting and family supports for new Canadians with young children: Focus on resources for service providers*. Ottawa, ON: Human Resources Development Canada.

Tyyskä, V. (2003a). *Report of focus groups with newcomer parents—Toronto: Toronto: Improving parenting and family supports for new Canadians with young children: Focus on resources for service providers*. Ottawa, ON: Human Resources Development Canada.

Tyyskä, V. (2003b). Solidarity and conflict: Teen–parent relationships in Iranian immigrant families in Toronto. In M. Lynn (Ed.), *Voices: Essays on Canadian families* (2nd ed., pp. 411–431). Toronto: Nelson Canada.

Tyyskä, V. (2005). Immigrant adjustment and parenting of teens: A study of newcomer groups in Toronto, Canada. In V. Puuronen, J. Soilevuo-Grønnerød, & J. Herranen (Eds.), *Youth—similarities, differences, inequalities* (Reports of the Karelian Institute, No. 1/2005.) (pp. 139–149). Joensuu, Finland: Joensuu University.

Tyyskä, V. (2006). *Teen perspectives on family relations in the Toronto Tamil community* (CERIS Working Paper No. 45). Toronto: Joint Centre of Excellent for Research on Immigration and Settlement.

Tyyskä, V., & Colavecchia, S. (2001). *Report on individual interviews in Toronto: Study of parenting issues of newcomer families in Ontario* (Report for the Centre for Research and Education in Human Services [CREHS], Joint Centre of Excellence for Research on Immigration and Settlement [CERIS]). Kitchener-Waterloo, Ontario: CREHS/CERIS.

Veevers, J. E. (Ed.). (1991). *Continuity and change in marriage and family.* Toronto: Holt, Rinehart and Winston of Canada.

Wade, T. J., & Brannigan, A. (1998). The genesis of adolescent risk-taking: Pathways through family, school and peers. *Canadian Journal of Sociology*, *23*(1), 1–20.

Walton-Roberts, M., & Pratt, G. (2003). *Mobile modernities: One South Asian family negotiates immigration, gender and class* (RIIM Working Paper No. 03-13). Vancouver, British Columbia: Research on Immigration and Integration in the Metropolis.

Waters, J. L. (2002). Flexible families?: "Astronaut" households and the experiences of lone mothers in Vancouver, British Columbia. *Social and Cultural Geography*, *3*(2), 117–134.

Wiebe, K. (1991). *Violence against immigrant women and children: An overview of community workers* (2nd ed.). Vancouver, British Columbia: Women Against Violence Against Women/Rape Crisis Centre.

Wong, S. K. (1999). Acculturation, peer relations, and delinquent behaviour of Chinese-Canadian youth. *Adolescence*, *34*, 107–119.

Zaidi, A., & Shuraydi, M. (2002). Perceptions of arranged marriages by young Pakistani Muslim women living in Western society. *Journal of Comparative Family Studies*, *33*(4), 37–57.

CHAPTER 6

How Economists Have Studied the Immigrant Family

Neeraj Kaushal *and* Cordelia Reimers

> Political economy or economics is a study of mankind in the ordinary business of life.
>
> —ALFRED MARSHALL

Demand and supply, cost minimization, profit, and utility maximization may seem rather dry and unsuitable tools for studying the family. For a long time economists, the creators of these tools, left research on the family to the other social science disciplines such as sociology, psychology, and anthropology. Family did not enter the "study of mankind in the ordinary business of life," to use the words of Alfred Marshall, the 19th-century British economist, until Gary Becker started applying the principles of economics to study human behavior outside the traditional realm of economics. Becker's great contribution, for which he won the Nobel Prize, was to see how the theories that economists had developed for studying the market and people's behavior in the market could be applied to the family and other nonmarket activities. His theories of household production, human capital, and the marriage market (Becker 1975, 1976, 1991) revolutionized labor economics and spawned the "new home economics."

Becker's theory of the allocation of time—the ultimate scarce resource—gave rise to his theory of household production, in which desired things (such as children) are produced using time and purchased goods and services (Becker, 1976). According to this theory, as wages rise, time becomes more valuable and individuals limit their time at home to its most valuable uses; to conserve time they substitute purchased goods and services where possible, and produce less of things that take a lot of time—such as children. This theory predicts that husbands and wives spend their time earning money or caring for children according to their comparative advantage—an idea taken from the theory of international trade—and thus can explain the traditional division of labor in the household. Mincer (1962) applied the theory of household production to explain how married women's participation in the paid labor force depends on their and their husband's wages and other income. Even declining fertility rates can be explained as a trade-off between the quantity and quality of children, with rising wages inducing a shift to smaller families and higher quality children (Becker, 1976). These theories were later applied to explain parental investments in children and joint family decisions about the migration behavior of married couples (Becker, 1991; Leibowitz, 1974; Mincer, 1978).

In this chapter we show how economists have applied these theories to increase our understanding of the immigrant family. We limit this review to studies by economists of immigrant families and children in the United States. We exclude the large body of work in the economics of immigration that deals with the economic progress of immigrants themselves or the impact of immigration on the labor market and other U.S. institutions, and confine ourselves to studies of immigrants in a family context or immigrants' children. A limitation of most empirical research relating to immigrants is that it fails to distinguish among legal immigrants, foreign-born nonimmigrants, and undocumented immigrants because most data sets do not provide any information on a noncitizen's visa status. For the purpose of this chapter, we define "immigrants" as persons living in the United States who were born abroad.

We first discuss studies by economists of the role of the family in the migration and assimilation process, then intergenerational mobility, receipt of welfare and other public benefits by immigrant families, and immigrant families' access to health insurance and health care and health outcomes of immigrant children.

STUDIES OF IMMIGRANT FAMILIES AND IMMIGRANTS' CHILDREN

The Role of the Family in Economic Assimilation

With some exceptions, economists have viewed immigrants as independent individuals whose immigration experiences, including the initial decision to migrate, economic progress in the destination country, and decisions pertaining to return migration, are based on their net gains as individuals. This disregard for family involvement is ironic, as over 70% of U.S. immigration is based on family unification and most immigrants follow family members to the United States. The significance of family ties and family well-being in immigrant decision making is obvious from a purely economic point of view as well; for example, every year immigrants remit large amounts of money to family members in their country of origin.

The few economists who have sought to understand the role of the family have primarily focused on immigrants' assimilation process. Their research can be divided into two parts: research relating to the so-called family investment model and research concerning the role of family members who arrive earlier in the integration of those who arrive later.

The family investment model postulates that immigrant families strategize to maximize household income. In the initial phase of immigration, husbands devote more time to enhancing their United States–specific labor market skills, and wives increase their labor force participation to offset their husbands' low earnings. Later, however, as men acquire United States–specific skills and their earnings rise, wives reallocate their time to nonmarket activities and their earnings are reduced. Long (1980), in one of the initial papers in this area, found that the earnings of married European immigrant women declined with their stay in the United States. He explained this phenomenon by postulating the family investment model.

The evidence from empirical studies designed to test the family investment model is mixed. MacPherson and Stewart (1989) and Duleep and Sanders (1993) used cross-sectional data to probe the association between married women's decision to work and their husband's investment in United States–specific human capital. Using 1980 census data, they found evidence that married women's labor force participation increases if their husbands are attending school. However, given the cross-sectional nature of the data used, these findings may be biased if the unobserved characteristics of immigrant entry cohorts changed over time, as has been the case in the United States. Indeed, Blau and colleagues (2003), who use repeated cross-sectional data (1980 and 1990 censuses) to control for these cohort effects, find evidence against the family investment hypothesis. They find that on arrival both husbands and wives work less than comparable natives; both increase their labor supply with time in the United States, eventually overtaking comparable natives. The magnitude of assimilation is similar for both husbands and wives. These findings suggest that, in contrast to the family investment model, both spouses seem to invest in their own human capital, rather than their spouse's, and that married women's employment decisions appear to be more responsive to their own labor market opportunities than to their husbands' earnings.

How family members who migrated earlier influence the economic opportunities and earnings of subsequent arrivals is Borjas and Bronars's (1991) focus. They construct "migration histories" to characterize the composition of households at the time of immigration and the presence of chain migration in the family. They find that family wage structure reflects intrafamily migration history. The skills and earnings of individuals who form the earlier links in the immigration chain are lower than the skills and earnings of individuals who arrive subsequently, and the skills and earnings of immigrants who are part of a family immigration chain are higher than those of single immigrants.

Intergenerational Mobility

Studies of intergenerational mobility by economists have aimed at learning whether the descendants of the post-1965 wave of immigrants from Latin America and Asia have progressed economically as quickly as the Europeans who arrived at the turn of the 20th century. The most common outcomes investigated by economists are measures of human capital, such as earnings and educational attainment, although some have also examined labor supply, marriage rates, and fertility (Blau & Kahn, 2006), or even marital endogamy (Card, DiNardo, & Estes, 2000).

Cross-Sectional Comparison of "Generations"

Many studies have used a single cross section of data to compare the first, second, and subsequent generations. These comparisons are usually made by national origin, with third- and higher generation European Americans often used as a reference group. Multivariate regression methods are used to adjust for differences in age, state or region of residence, education, English fluency, and other factors to sort out the reasons for differences across generations and national origin groups.

These cross-sectional studies indicate whether the children and further descendants of Latin American and Asian immigrants seem to be successfully integrating economically, in the sense that their education and earnings levels are converging with those of European Americans of native parentage. However, these studies face two major problems. First, one cannot identify the true third generation in census or Current Population Survey (CPS) data because there is no information about grandparents' birthplaces. The so-called third generation is actually a conglomerate of everyone whose parents were both born in the United States, no matter how long ago their ancestors arrived. Furthermore, the national origin of this "third" generation must be inferred from answers to the race and Hispanic origin questions. Second, these studies do not actually trace intergenerational progress because the immigrants in the data set are not the parents of the second generation, much less the grandparents of the third. In a single cross section, generation effects are confounded with cohort effects. Because the characteristics of immigrant entry cohorts have changed over time, a comparison with today's first generation doesn't reveal how the current second generation compares with their actual parents' generation 25 or 30 years ago.

Cross-sectional studies on the economic progress of immigrants, also referred to as "assimilation" in the economics literature, began in 1977 with Chiswick's short article, "Sons of Immigrants." He found that the earnings of second-generation European-origin men in the 1970 census (including Latin Americans who identified their race as "white") were higher than those of the third (or higher) generation, even after controlling for education and other demographic characteristics—a result corroborated by Carliner (1980) and Card and colleagues (2000). Chiswick attributed this to sons' inheriting some of their immigrant fathers' above-average ability, which gradually reverts toward the average across generations. He also found that Mexicans had lower earnings than European ethnic groups in both the second and "third" generations.

Card and colleagues (2000) found that the gap between the second and third generations decreased between 1940 and 1970 and then increased in 1995, owing to the decline and subsequent rise in overall wage inequality. Card (2005) found that the relatively higher wages of the second generation as compared to the third (or higher) generation in the 1995–2002 CPS can be explained by differences in education and location of residence.

Several economists have focused on the economic progress of Mexicans or Latin Americans (Blau & Kahn, 2006; Duncan, Hotz, & Trejo, 2006; Duncan & Trejo, 2006; Grogger & Trejo, 2002; Trejo, 2003). A common finding of this research is that even third- and higher generation Mexican Americans earn less than other groups, largely because they have less education and also because they are younger. Educational attainment and earnings jump between the first and second generation, but there is little improvement in later generations. However, the apparent lack of improvement may be illusory, a result of cohort effects rather than a true lack of progress, because today's second-generation Mexicans grew up in a more favorable environment than the parents of today's third generation. Indeed, as discussed in the next section, Smith (2006) found that true intergenerational progress in education has been *greater* for Mexicans than for Europeans or Asians.

Grogger and Trejo (2002) and Trejo (2003) also suggested that attrition from the Mexican ethnic category may contribute to the apparent lack of progress in the third generation. If intermarriage and upward mobility lead the more successful descendants of immigrants to lose their ancestral identities, estimates of intergenerational improvement would be biased downward. Duncan and Trejo (2006) find evidence that such attrition occurs among Mexicans.

Economists' studies of intergenerational progress have often been limited to men. Blau and Kahn (2006) include women as well, and add marriage and fertility rates to the commonly studied outcomes: educational attainment, labor supply, and wages. They find that Mexican men's labor supply drops after the first generation but women's labor supply rises, so that the difference from European Americans in gender specialization disappears by the second generation. Mexican immigrants are more likely to be married than Europeans, but by the second and third generations Mexicans are less likely to be married than European Americans. This is explained by the education gap: less-educated individuals are less likely to be married, and Mexicans are as likely to be married as others at the same level of education. Mexicans have higher fertility than European Americans. The fertility gap shrinks across generations, but is not eliminated by the third generation.

Comparisons of Children with "Parents" 25–30 Years Earlier

As noted above, comparing generations at a point in time is not the correct way to measure intergenerational mobility. It implicitly assumes that immigrant cohorts are similar over time, when in all likelihood the actual immigrant parents or grandparents of today's second or third generation had very different characteristics from today's immigrants. A number of economists have dealt with cohort effects by using cross sections from censuses and CPS 25–30 years apart to compare generations. Another strategy for dealing with cohort effects in a single cross section is to study outcomes that change little during adulthood, such as education, and compare young second-generation individuals with first-generation individuals who are 25–30 years older (Reed, Hill, Jepsen, & Johnson, 2005).

Studies that have used the first strategy group the data by national origin and generation. The group means of an outcome (usually earnings or educational attainment) for the "children" generation are regressed on the group means for the "parents" generation 25–30 years earlier. One minus the regression coefficient measures the rate of regression toward the overall population mean, or the "assimilation rate."

Studies of this type can tell us how much the children of yesterday's immigrants have converged economically with the general population, but they confound "period" effects—such as the civil rights movement or widening overall wage inequality—with the underlying transmission rate of human capital from parents to children. Another problem is that, because the true third generation cannot be identified in Census or CPS data, this type of study does a better job of estimating the transmission parameter between immigrants and their children than between the second and third generations.

Reed and colleagues (2005, Chap. 3) used 1996–2004 CPS data to investigate intergenerational progress in educational attainment. They compare 30- to 39-year-old third- and higher generation Asians and Latin Americans nationwide with their second-generation counterparts who were 27 years older in that year (their "parents"), and they similarly compare the second and first generations. They found dramatic progress between the first and second generations for all groups; and some progress continues from the second to the third generation, even among Mexicans. Nevertheless, because Mexican immigration has long been dominated by extremely low-skilled workers, their grandchildren have not yet caught up with the European American majority, despite the Mexicans' greater intergenerational progress in education as compared with other groups. In contrast, even by the second generation Asians have more education than European Americans.

Borjas (1993) used each generation's earnings *relative to* third- and higher generation Americans (an effort to control for period effects) as a measure of intergenerational progress. Controlling for education, age, marital status, and metropolitan residence, and grouping by national origin, he found that the correlation of (relative) earnings between the second generation in 1970 and the first generation in 1940 is .40–.60, and source country characteristics are strong determinants of earnings of both generations. The second generation's relative earnings are 7% higher than the earnings of their "parents," on average. These results tell us whether a group is converging with third- and higher generation Americans, but not how each generation compares with its own parents, because the reference group is a moving target. The attempt to control for period effects by measuring outcomes relative to third- and higher generation Americans doesn't work when the period effects—civil rights, changing wage inequality—are specific to less-skilled minorities. Borjas (1994) used the 1910, 1940, and 1980 censuses to compare generations, and found that a 20% wage difference between groups in the first generation results in a 12% wage difference in the second and a 5% difference in the third (and higher).

Card and colleagues (2000), on the other hand, used data grouped by national origin from the 1940 and 1970 censuses and the 1994–1996 CPS and regressed the second generation's ("children") mean education and wages on the first generation's ("fathers") 25 or 30 years earlier. Their estimates of the regression coefficient (.40–.60) are consistent with other studies. They find that rates of intergenerational transmission of both education and wages have been stable over time, apart from the effect of changes in overall wage inequality, and are the same for both sons and daughters. Card (2005) further refined the comparison of "children" with their "fathers." Grouping the data by country of origin, he regressed the mean education of the second generation ages 21–40 in the 1995–2002 CPS against the mean education of the fathers of children age 0–15 in the 1980 census. He found the transmission coefficient is .30, somewhat smaller than the other estimates that used a cruder definition of "fathers." Even among Mexicans the second generation closes 80% of the education gap between their fathers and all United States–born fathers.

Smith (2003, 2006) traced the intergenerational progress in education and earnings of Latin American, Mexican, Asian, and European immigrants, their children, and grandchildren during the 20th century. To do this, he first grouped all the available census and CPS data into 5-year birth cohorts by generation (e.g., Mexican immigrants born in 1910–1914). He next averaged education and age-standardized earnings across all the data files in which a given cohort appeared. He then aligned each immigrant birth cohort with the second-generation cohort born 25 years later and with the third (and higher) generation cohort born 50 years later. Third-generation Mexicans born in the 1970s averaged almost 7 years more schooling than their grandparents and almost a year more than their parents, so that they are less than 1 year behind native European American men and earn 17% less (Smith, 2003). In contrast, his cross-sectional comparison of generations shows only a 2.4-year advance in education between first- and second-generation men and an actual decline between the second and third generations. Smith (2003) also found that the schooling and earnings gaps between third-generation Mexican and native European American men decreased in each successive birth cohort during the 20th century. Moreover, in every cohort the gains between generations are greater for Mexicans than for Europeans and Asians.

The intergenerational transmission parameter estimated by regressions on group means is generally considerably larger than estimates of intergenerational transmission from parent to child within a single family. As Card and colleagues (2000) pointed out, one reason is that the use of group means includes the effects of any omitted variables that are correlated with the group mean and eliminates the bias due to measurement error when the father's current wage is used as a proxy for the parents' human capital. Another possible reason is the influence of "ethnic capital" (what sociologists would call "social" or "cultural" capital). Borjas (1992) used General Social Survey (GSS) and National Longitudinal Survey of Youth (NLSY) microdata, in which children can be matched to their own parents, to disaggregate the intergenerational transmission parameter into the influence of the child's own parents and that of the national origin group's ethnic capital, as measured by the group's average skills in the parents' generation. Borjas (1994) extended this analysis to three generations by using the 1910 census and the GSS. He estimated the intergenerational transmission parameter for group mean education or wages, including the ethnic capital effect, to be .40–.50 and constant across generations. About half of that is the parental effect, and about half is due to ethnic capital.

But Leon (2005) pointed out that these estimates may be biased by measurement error and omitted variables. Using 1910 and 1920 census data, he regressed children's school enrollment on father's literacy in English and the nationality group's average literacy rate. Estimates using instrumental variables for both parental skills and ethnic capital show a much larger parental effect than OLS estimates. But the estimates of the effect of the ethnic capital are similar, whichever method is used.

Benefits Receipt by Immigrant Families

A large body of research in economics has addressed the issue of immigrant dependence on state-sponsored welfare programs and intergenerational transmission of welfare dependency. This research is handicapped by the lack of information on visa status in most data sets. This flaw is particularly serious in policy research because the policies that are examined only affect legal immigrants, and often just a subset of this population such as low-income families headed by single mothers.

Economists have focused on the following four questions in their research concerning welfare and immigrant families: Do immigrant families make a greater use of welfare than natives? Do differences in welfare use between native and immigrant families "die out" across generations over time, or is welfare dependency transmitted from generation to generation? Does welfare generosity attract low-skilled immigrants who are prone to becoming a state liability? And finally, how does welfare, or lack of it, affect immigrant behavior and well-being?

Earlier research (Blau, 1984; Simon, 1984) analyzed cross-sectional data from the 1976 Survey of Income and Education and concluded that immigrants were less likely to depend on welfare, broadly defined to include payments from the Aid to Families with Dependent Children (AFDC) program, Supplemental Security Income, and other forms of public assistance. The probability that an immigrant family would become dependent on welfare, however, has changed over time as the composition of immigrants has changed. Borjas and Trejo (1991) and Borjas (1995) used census data and found that later waves of immigrants are more likely to receive welfare as compared with natives, and among immigrants belonging to a particular entry cohort, use of means-tested programs increases with the duration of their stay in the United States.

One criticism of this body of research is that it does not control for immigrant characteristics, such as education. Butcher and Hu (2001), who do adjust for individual characteristics, found that immigrant families are less likely to use welfare programs than natives with similar characteristics. They attribute this difference in welfare use between natives and immigrants to four possible factors: unobserved immigrant characteristics that make them ineligible for benefits, other resources or savings that also make immigrants ineligible for benefits, greater sensitivity to "stigma" from welfare dependency among immigrants than natives, and simply lack of information about welfare programs among immigrants.

Butcher and Hu (2001) also investigated the intergenerational association in welfare use between immigrants in the 1970s and their children in 1994–1996. After controlling for characteristics, on average the second generation is always less likely than the third (or higher) generation to use transfer programs. The first generation's receipt of welfare is positively correlated with the second generation's receipt. The estimated coefficient of association, however, is less than 1, indicating that the difference between the immigrant generation and natives should die out across generations over time. On a related issue, Borjas and Hilton (1996) found that the types of benefits received by earlier immigrants from the same country influences the types of benefits received by new arrivals. This finding leads them to speculate that ethnic networks might transmit information about particular benefits to new immigrants.

Do such networks exist? More specifically, has the U.S. welfare state been instrumental in attracting low-skilled immigrants who are likely to become a state liability? This "welfare magnet hypothesis" has generated a good deal of research by economists (Borjas, 1999; Buckley, 1996; Dodson, 2001; Kaushal, 2005; Zavodny, 1999). The empirical evidence is mixed. Buckley (1996), Borjas (1999), and Dodson (2001) find that immigrant residential choices in the United States are affected by state generosity, Zavodny (1999) and Kaushal (2005) do not find any evidence to this effect.

Research that finds evidence in support of the welfare magnet hypothesis has been subject to criticism on two main counts. One, it applies time-series or cross-state variation in welfare benefits under AFDC to identify the effect of welfare policy on location choices of immigrants

(Borjas, 1999; Buckley, 1996; Dodson, 2001). Because macroeconomic variables or differences in state characteristics may be confounded with benefit generosity, these estimates may be biased. Two, most of the papers are based on census data that do not distinguish between legal permanent residents, who are eligible for benefits under AFDC, and temporary residents or illegal residents, who are ineligible for benefits. Zavodny (1999) and Kaushal (2005) used data on all newly arrived permanent legal residents from the Bureau of Citizenship and Immigration Services. Kaushal exploited changes in welfare eligibility for new immigrants under the 1996 Personal Responsibility and Work Opportunity Act (PRWORA) and state responses to federal policy to set up a natural experiment research design that controls for state and year effects. She found no evidence that in the post-PRWORA period, newly arrived immigrants preferred to settle in states that reinstated benefits for immigrants (e.g., California and Maine) over states that did not (e.g., Texas and Florida).

Most of the other research on how welfare, or its denial, affects the behavior and well-being of immigrants has been done in the context of changes in welfare policy during the mid-1990s (Borjas, 2001, 2003, 2004; Davies & Greenwood, 2004; Haider, Scheni, Bao, & Danielson, 2004; Kaestner & Kaushal, 2005, in press; Kaushal & Kaestner, 2005). As expected, most researchers find that the 1996 welfare reform, which restricted immigrant eligibility for several means-tested programs, resulted in a decline in immigrant participation in these programs. Haider and colleagues (2004), however, argued that macroeconomic factors explain most of the pre- versus postwelfare reform differences in receipt of means-tested programs between immigrants and natives. Other researchers, who have used specific aspects of the 1996 welfare law, have reached different conclusions. For instance, Borjas (2004) found that denial of food stamps under the 1996 welfare law increased food insecurity among immigrant families, Davies and Greenwood (2004) found that welfare reform is associated with a decline in SSI receipt among immigrants, and Borjas (2003) and Kaushal and Kaestner (2005) concluded that the policy change lowered Medicaid use in immigrant families.

A source of confusion about this body of research is that investigators have identified the target population of welfare reform differently, and consequently have reached different conclusions about the policy's effect. An example is the articles by Borjas (2003) and Kaushal and Kaestner (2005), who investigate the effect of the 1996 welfare reform on the health insurance of immigrants, using the March Current Population Surveys. Borjas found that welfare reform was associated with a decrease in Medicaid coverage, but this decline was completely offset by an increase in private insurance coverage. Thus there was no change in the proportion uninsured. In contrast, Kaushal and Kaestner find that PRWORA was associated with a decline in Medicaid coverage among low-educated single mothers without a corresponding increase in private insurance, resulting in a 23% increase in the proportion of low-educated single mothers who were uninsured and a 68% increase in the proportion of uninsured children in low-educated, foreign-born, single-mother-headed families.

Most of the difference between the findings of Borjas (2003) and Kaushal and Kaestner (2005) can be explained by the differences in samples used and research methods. Borjas used all immigrant households, whereas Kaushal and Kaestner restricted their analysis to low-educated single women and their children. Borjas used natives as a comparison group for immigrants, and Kaushal and Kaestner used married low-educated immigrant women and their children as the comparison. Borjas assumed that, in the absence of PRWORA, changes in immigrant and native health insurance status pre- and post-PRWORA would have been the same, which is inconsistent with the fact that mean levels of health insurance differ significantly between immigrants and natives. Borjas also assumed that determinants of health insurance are the same for all subpopulations of immigrants. However, the determinants of employer-sponsored health insurance may be quite different for young unmarried single mothers than for older married men. Thus, the estimates obtained by Borjas are likely to be biased.

Health Insurance, Medical Care Utilization, and Health of Immigrant Families

Beyond the effects of welfare reform, economists have studied disparities in health insurance, medical care utilization, and health outcomes between immigrant and native families. Economists have not been the pioneers, but have often followed researchers in public health and medical sciences, using tools most commonly applied in economics and larger, nationally representative datasets.

This research has produced a large number of papers documenting the inequalities among groups (see Escarce, Morales, & Rumbaut, 2006, and Escarce & Kapur, 2006, for a survey of this research; see also Hernandez & Charney, 1998, for literature on health and well-being of children in immigrant families.). In general, immigrants have better health, are less likely to have health insurance, and make relatively less use of medical care than natives. Jasso, Massey, Rosenzweig, and Smith (2004) argued that individuals self-select as migrants or nonmigrants, and their current and expected future health profiles influence the decision to migrate. Therefore, immigrants may be positively selected, as only people with relatively good health decide to move to another country. Once they are in the United States, however, immigrants' health is influenced by a complex set of factors. Because immigrants experience an increase in income subsequent to their arrival in the United States, their health outcomes should improve because income is positively associated with health. However, adoption of U.S. consumption habits and sedentary lifestyles may have an adverse effect on health. Besides, if the immigration experience increases their stress level, it may negatively affect the health of immigrants.

Economists have used age at arrival and duration of stay in the United States as proxies for immigrant acculturation to examine the association between health outcomes and acculturation. Using the National Health Interview Survey (NHIS) for 1990 to 2004, Kaushal (2006) examined the effect of age at arrival and duration of stay in the United States on the prevalence of obesity among adult immigrants and finds that among those without a BA degree, obesity increases with the length of their stay. The increase is greater during the first 5 years of residence than later and greater for those who arrived at a relatively young age.

An important determinant of immigrant health and that of their children is the parents' visa status in the United States, which may influence access to medical care. Unfortunately, as mentioned above, most national data sets do not provide any information on whether an individual is residing in the United States legally or illegally. A number of researchers have used the Los Angeles Family and Neighborhood Survey (LAFNS), which does provide this information, and have found that visa status affects both access to insurance and health outcomes in immigrant families (Bitler, 2005; Goldman, Smith, & Sood, 2005). Goldman and colleagues (2005) found that, except for undocumented aliens, most of the insurance disparities between natives and foreign-born persons can be explained by "traditional" socioeconomic factors such as education, assets, income, and industry of employment. They find that country of birth is not associated with differences in health insurance between natives and immigrants.

Bitler (2005) studied racial and ethnic disparities in health outcomes using the LAFNS and found that naturalized adults are less likely to have hypertension than the United States–born and both documented and undocumented immigrants are less likely to have asthma than the United States–born. Children of foreign-born parents are also less likely to have asthma or an asthma attack during the last year. However, after controlling for immigration status, Latin American children are more likely to have asthma than European American or African American children.

The children of immigrants are less likely to have health insurance than the children of natives. Using the 1989 and 1992 waves of the NHIS, Currie (1999) found that children of immigrants are less likely than children of the native-born to have private insurance and more likely to be eligible for Medicaid but less likely to use Medicaid, even when eligible. The disparities are widest for the children of the immigrants who arrived most recently. This is the group that was most adversely affected by the 1996 welfare reform. However, there is no evidence that welfare reform adversely affected the health of immigrant children.

Kaushal and Kaestner (in press) studied the effect of welfare reform on health care use and health outcomes of immigrants. The decline in welfare caseload since 1996 was associated with foreign-born, low-educated single mothers reporting delays in receiving care or reporting no care due to cost and a decline in visits to a health professional in the past 12 months. They found no consistent evidence that welfare reform affected the health insurance, medical care utilization, and health of children living with single mothers. Similarly, Joyce, Bauer, Minkoff, and Kaestner (2001) found that the 1996 welfare reform had no substantive impact on the perinatal health and health care utilization of foreign-born Latin American women relative to United States–born Latin American women.

CONCLUSION

In this chapter, we have provided a literature review to show how economists have studied the immigrant family. A major limitation of this research is the lack of a longitudinal data set on the family, or the extended family. As a result, several research questions have remained unanswered. The extensive economic literature on intergenerational mobility illustrates this omission. Neither cross-sectional studies nor studies that compare generations 25–30 years apart provide a precise answer to how immigrant parents' economic progress in the United States affects the educational achievement and economic progress of their children.

Research on later waves of immigrant families is further complicated by the fact that an increasingly large proportion of them are without legal documents. No nationally representative data set provides information on the visa status of noncitizens. But we do know that a large number of children, United States–born as well as foreign-born, live in households containing members who lack legal status. How living in such a household affects the health and developmental outcomes of children is unknown, but is a critical issue from a policy perspective.

We end this chapter by noting that there are many theoretical and empirical issues with regard to immigrant families that economists have not yet addressed. In several areas, economists have taken only a first step toward understanding decision making in immigrant families. For example, we do not know how their parents' immigration experience or economic progress affects the health and developmental outcomes of immigrants' children. Moreover, many immigrant children live in extended households with relatives or others beyond their nuclear family. The family investment model could be applied to extended households to study, for example, whether the employment and human capital investment of extended family members are linked or jointly determined, and how the extended family facilitates immigrant integration. Our understanding of the economic integration of immigrants would be greatly improved if it were studied jointly for the members of a family instead of treating each person as an isolated individual.

REFERENCES

Becker, G. S. (1975). *Human capital* (2nd ed.). New York: Columbia University Press for National Bureau of Economic Research.

Becker, G. S. (1976). *The economic approach to human behavior.* Chicago: University of Chicago Press.

Becker, G. S. (1991). *A treatise on the family* (Enlarged ed.). Cambridge, MA: Harvard University Press.

Bitler, M. (2005, September 23). *Racial and ethnic health disparities in Los Angeles: The role of immigration status and neighborhoods.* Unpublished paper, Public Policy Institute of California.

Blau, F. D. (1984). The use of transfer payments by immigrants. *Industrial and Labor Relations Review, 37*(2), 222–239.

Blau, F. D., & Kahn, L. M. (2006). Gender and assimilation among Mexican Americans. In G. J. Borjas (Ed.), *Mexican immigration.* Cambridge, MA: National Bureau of Economic Research.

Blau, F. D., Kahn, L. M., Moriarty, J. Y., & Souza, A. P. (2003). The role of the family in immigrants' labor market activity: An evaluation of alternative explanations: Comment. *American Economic Review, 93*(1), 429–447.

Borjas, G. J. (1992). Ethnic capital and intergenerational mobility. *Quarterly Journal of Economics, 107*(1), 123–150.

Borjas, G. J. (1993). The intergenerational mobility of immigrants. *Journal of Labor Economics, 11*(1), 113–135.

Borjas, G. J. (1994). Long-run convergence of ethnic skill differentials: The children and grandchildren of the Great Migration. *Industrial and Labor Relations Review, 47*(4), 553–573.

Borjas, G. J. (1995). Immigration and welfare, 1970–1990. *Research in Labor Economics*, *14*, 253–282.

Borjas, G. J. (1999). Immigration and welfare magnets. *Journal of Labor Economics*, *17*(4, Part 1), 607–637.

Borjas G. J. (2001). Welfare reform and immigration. In R. M. Blank & R. Haskins (Eds.), *The new world of welfare* (pp. 369–390). Washington, DC: Brookings Institution.

Borjas, G. J. (2003). Welfare reform, labor supply and health insurance in the immigrant population. *Journal of Health Economics*, *22*(6), 933–958.

Borjas, G. J. (2004). Food insecurity and public assistance. *Journal of Public Economics*, *88*(7–8), 1421–1443.

Borjas, G. J., & Bronars, S. G. (1991). Immigration and the family. *Journal of Labor Economics*, *9*(2), 123–148.

Borjas, G. J., & Hilton, L. (1996). Immigration and the welfare state: Immigrant participation in means-tested entitlement programs. *Quarterly Journal of Economics*, *111*(2), 575–604.

Borjas, G. J., & Trejo, S. J. (1991). Immigrant participation in the welfare system. *Industrial and Labor Relations Review*, *44*(2), 195–211.

Buckley, F. H. (1996). The political economy of immigration policies. *International Review of Law and Economics*, *16*(1), 81–99.

Butcher, K. F., & Hu, L. (2001). Use of means-tested transfer programs by immigrants, their children, and their children's children. In D. Card & R. M. Blank (Eds.), *Finding jobs: Work and welfare reform* (pp. 465–506). New York: Russell Sage Foundation.

Card, D. (2005). *Is the new immigration really so bad?* (NBER Working Paper No. 11547). Cambridge, MA: National Bureau of Economic Research.

Card, D., DiNardo, J., & Estes, E. (2000). The more things change: Immigrants and the children of immigrants in the 1940s, the 1970s, and the 1990s. In G. J. Borjas (Ed.), *Issues in the economics of immigration* (pp. 227–269). Chicago: University of Chicago Press for National Bureau of Economic Research.

Carliner, G. (1980). Wages, earnings and hours of first, second and third generation American males. *Economic Inquiry*, *18*(1), 87–102.

Chiswick, B. (1977). Sons of immigrants: Are they at an earnings disadvantage? *American Economic Review*, *67*(1), 376–380.

Currie, J. (1999). Do children of immigrants make differential use of public health insurance? In G. J. Borjas (Ed.), *Issues in the economics of immigration* (pp. 271–307). Chicago: University of Chicago Press for National Bureau of Economic Research.

Davies, P. S., & Greenwood, M. J. (2004, September). *Welfare reform and immigrant participation in the supplemental security income program* (Working Paper WP 2004-087). Ann Arbor: Michigan Retirement Research Center, University of Michigan.

Dodson, M. E., III. (2001). Welfare generosity and location choices among new United States immigrants. *International Review of Law and Economics*, *21*(1), 47–67.

Duleep, H. O., & Sanders, S. (1993). The decision to work by married immigrant women. *Industrial and Labor Relations Review*, *46*(4), 677–690.

Duncan, B., Hotz, V. J., & Trejo, S. J. (2006). Hispanics in the U.S. labor market. In M. Tienda & F. Mitchell (Eds.), *Hispanics and the future of America* (pp. 228–290). Washington, DC: National Academies Press.

Duncan, B., & Trejo, S. J. (2006). Ethnic identification, intermarriage, and unmeasured progress by Mexican Americans. In G. J. Borjas (Ed.), *Mexican immigration*. Cambridge, MA: National Bureau of Economic Research.

Escarce, J. J., & Kapur, K. (2006). Access to and quality of health care. In M. Tienda & F. Mitchell (Eds.), *Hispanics and the future of America* (pp. 410–446). Washington, DC: National Academies Press.

Escarce, J. J., Morales, L. S., & Rumbaut, R. G. (2006). The health status and health behaviors of Hispanics. In M. Tienda & F. Mitchell (Eds.), *Hispanics and the future of America* (pp. 362–409). Washington, DC: National Academies Press.

Goldman, D. P., Smith, J. P., & Sood, N. (2005). Legal status and health insurance among immigrants. *Health Affairs*, *24*(6), 1640–1653.

Grogger, J., & Trejo, S. J. (2002). *Falling behind or moving up?: The inter-generational progress of Mexican Americans*. San Francisco: Public Policy Institute of California.

Haider, S. J., Schoeni, R., Bao, Y., & Danielson, C. (2004). Immigrants, welfare reform, and the economy. *Journal of Policy Analysis and Management*, *23*(4), 745–764.

Hernandez, D. J., & Charney, E. (Eds.). (1998). *From generation to generation: The health and well-being of children in immigrant families*. Washington, DC: National Academies Press.

Jasso, G., Massey, D. S., Rosenzweig, M. R., & Smith, J. P. (2004). Immigrant health-selectivity and acculturation. In N. B. Anderson, R. A. Bulatao, & B. Cohen (Eds.), *Critical perspectives on racial and ethnic differences in health in late life* (pp. 227–266). Washington, DC: National Academies Press.

Joyce, T., Bauer, T., Minkoff, H., & Kaestner, R. (2001). Welfare reform and the perinatal health and health care use of Latino women in California, New York City, and Texas. *American Journal of Public Health*, *91*(11), 1857–1864.

Kaestner, R., & Kaushal, N. (2005). Immigrant and native responses to welfare reform. *Journal of Population Economics*, *18*(1), 69–92.

Kaestner, R., & Kaushal, N. (in press). Welfare reform and immigrants: Does the five year ban matter? *Research in Labor Economics*.

Kaushal, N. (2005). New immigrants' location choices: Magnets without welfare. *Journal of Labor Economics*, *23*(1), 59–80.

Kaushal, N. (2006). *Super size aliens: Adversities of acculturation?* Unpublished paper, Columbia University, School of Social Work.

Kaushal, N., & Kaestner, R. (2005). Welfare reform and health insurance of immigrants. *Health Services Research*, *40*(3), 697–722.

Kaushal, N., & Kaestner, R. (in press). Welfare reform and the health of immigrant children. *Journal of Immigrant and Minority Health*. Heidelberg, Germany: Springer.

Leibowitz, A. (1974). Home investments in children. *Journal of Political Economy, 82*(2, Part II), S111–S131.

Leon, A. (2005). *Does "ethnic capital" matter?: Identifying peer effects in the intergenerational transmission of ethnic differentials*. Unpublished paper, University of Pittsburgh, Department of Economics.

Long, J. E. (1980). The effect of Americanization on earnings: Some evidence for women. *Journal of Political Economy, 88*(3), 620–29.

MacPherson, D. A., & Stewart, J. B. (1989). The labor force participation and earnings profiles of married female immigrants. *Quarterly Review of Economics and Business*, *29*(3), 57–73.

Mincer, J. (1962). Labor force participation of married women. In H. G. Lewis (Ed.), *Aspects of labor economics* (pp. 63–105). Princeton, NJ: Princeton University Press/National Bureau of Economic Research.

Mincer, J. (1978). Family migration decisions. *Journal of Political Economy, 86*(5), 749–773.

Reed, D., Hill, L. E., Jepsen, C., & Johnson, H. P. (2005). *Educational progress across immigrant generations in California*. San Francisco: Public Policy Institute of California.

Simon, J. L. (1984). Immigrants, taxes, and welfare in the United States. *Population and Development Review, 10*(1), 55–69.

Smith, J. P. (2003). Assimilation across the Latino generations. *American Economic Review, 93*(2), 315–319.

Smith, J. P. (2006). Immigrants and the labor market. *Journal of Labor Economics*, *24*(2), 203–233.

Trejo, S. J. (2003). Intergenerational progress of Mexican-origin workers in the U.S. labor market. *Journal of Human Resources*, *38*(3), 467–489.

Zavodny, M. (1999). Determinants of recent immigrants' locational choices. *International Migration Review, 33*(4), 1014–1030.

PART II

ILLUSTRATIONS OF DIVERSITY IN FAMILY PROCESSES

CHAPTER 7

Knowledge of Child Development and Family Interactions among Immigrants to America

Perspectives from Developmental Science

Marc H. Bornstein *and* Linda R. Cote

Developmental science has been occupied historically with the ways in which biological ("nature") and environmental/experiential ("nurture") forces codetermine development. The specific research goals of developmental science are to (1) describe what human beings are like at different ages and the ways in which they stay the same or change from age to age in relation to their experiences (including immigration); (2) explain influences on development (including culture); (3) predict what individuals will be like at later points in development based on what is known about their past and present characteristics; and (4) intervene to enhance development and prevent or remediate problem development. Developmental science is concerned with individual variation as well as group differences; with stability and continuity over time; with the nature of change (gradual, incremental, and quantitative or saltatory, stage-like, and qualitative); with motives and mechanisms of change; with which domains of development are plastic and which refractory to experience; and with which interventions are effective in promoting positive development and which in preventing atypical or problematic development. To meet this multifaceted charge, developmental science strives to integrate multiage, multivariate, multidomain (e.g., physical, cognitive, and social), and multicontext (e.g., interpersonal, institutional, social, cultural) empirical investigations. After more than 100 years as a formal field of inquiry, during which all areas of human functioning have been observed, recorded, and analyzed, the research base of developmental science is now positioned to inform health, education, and public policy.

IMMIGRANT FAMILIES

Immigration to the United States is on the rise. Data from the 2000 U.S. Census indicate that approximately one in five children under the age of 18 in the United States is either an immigrant or a child of immigrants (Federal Interagency Forum on Child and Family Statistics, 2002). In addition, first- and second-generation immigrant children are the fastest growing sectors of the child population (see Hernandez, Denton, & Macartney, Chapter 1, this volume). Despite this circumstance, immigrant families, particularly those with infants and young children, have received comparatively little empirical attention (see Chase-Lansdale, D'Angelo, & Palacios, Chapter 8, this volume), and generally the nature of children's development and parenting in acculturating populations is underresearched. Like other modern societies, the United States is not culturally homogeneous and is experiencing sociopolitical changes associated with immigration (see Introduction, this volume). It is now widely recognized that immigrants to the United States do not "assimilate" in the sense that they reject the ideas, values, and behaviors of their cultures of origin and wholeheartedly adopt those of U.S. society; rather, immigrants retain beliefs and practices of their cultures of origin in varying degree, integrate some traditional beliefs and practices with those of the new majority culture, and adopt some majority group norms (e.g., Foner, 2005). Early acculturation research (e.g., of Japanese American family interactions) suggested that family interactions, and socialization in particular, tend to resist change (Masuda, Matsumoto, & Meredith, 1970), especially among Asian families (Foner, 2005). On this account, it is particularly important to study whether and how child development and parenting change among immigrant families during acculturation (García-Coll & Pachter, 2002).

In psychology, immigrant families are typically studied with respect to the "acculturation gap" and overcoming traumas in their country of origin that may have precipitated migration (more common with refugees than with immigrants). In developmental science, immigrant families are typically studied with respect to language barriers and bilingualism, school achievement, and delinquency. Most of this research focuses on school-age children or adolescents (see Chase-Lansdale et al., Chapter 8, this volume). Our longitudinal research concerns infant and child development and parenting in different acculturating groups over time. We investigate many aspects of family life. Here we discuss the degree to which immigrant mothers' knowledge of child development conforms to U.S. norms and how their knowledge relates to their interactions with their young children.

IMPORTANCE OF MOTHERS' KNOWLEDGE OF CHILD DEVELOPMENT

Knowledge of child development covers many domains (see Goodnow & Collins, 1990; Sigel & McGillicuddy-De Lisi, 2002) including understanding how to care for children, how children develop, and the role of parents in children's lives. Parents rely on this knowledge to make everyday decisions about their children's care and upbringing (e.g., Conrad, Gross, Fogg, & Ruchala, 1992). Knowledgeable parents have more realistic expectations of their children and are more likely to behave in developmentally appropriate ways with their children than parents who harbor unrealistic developmental expectations (Grusec & Goodnow, 1994). Thus, judgments and expectations that underestimate or overestimate children's development vis-à-vis norms help to shape parents' caregiving beliefs and behaviors, which in turn affect children's development (Benasich & Brooks-Gunn, 1996; Conrad et al., 1992).

Furthermore, parents' descriptions and adjudications of their children's behavior can influence the decision making of others who come into contact with the child, such as teachers, health care professionals, and physicians. Pediatricians routinely draw on mothers' expectations, concerns, and opinions about their children's health and development (Pachter & Dworkin, 1997). Moreover, more than 80% of pediatricians are European American (see Mendoza, Javier, & Burgos, Chapter 2, this volume), and they expect the parents in their practice to share their ideas about normative child development.

However, cross-cultural comparisons show that virtually all aspects of parenting—beliefs as well as practices—are informed by their cultural framework (Bornstein, 1991, 2006). Some expert knowledge of child development may be universal, but some is clearly culturally constructed, and parents' knowledge varies among groups with diverse cultural values and practices. For example, Pachter and Dworkin (1997) enlisted mothers from minority (Puerto Rican, African American, West Indian/Caribbean) and majority cultural groups and asked them about normal ages of attainment of typical developmental milestones during the first 3 years of life: although all responses fit within a normative developmental range, significant differences emerged among ethnic groups for more than one-third of the developmental milestones tested. Mothers in rural Thailand do not believe their newborns can see (only 1.7% believe their babies can see at 1 week, 14.7% at 1 month), and often during the day they swaddle infants on their backs or in a fabric hammock in such a way that allows the baby only a narrow slit view of the ceiling or sky (Kotchabhakdi, Winichagoon, Smitasiri, Dhanamitta, & Valyasevi, 1987). Gusii and Samoan caregivers believe that it is nonsensical to talk to infants before they are capable of speech (Ochs, 1988; Richman, Miller, & LeVine, 1992).

These considerations of the significance of parents' knowledge of child development to competence in parenting, children's healthy and successful growth and development, and clinical decision making gave rise to the questions that motivated the research we discuss here. Our empirical studies have concerned how accurate immigrant parents' knowledge of child development is, what kinds of knowledge parents have, how parents acquire their knowledge, and what factors are related to differences in parents' knowledge level. Because mothers are the main caregivers of young children, investigating the amount and types of knowledge they possess about child development and childcare is a necessary step to increasing the dissemination and improving the utilization of the knowledge base of developmental science and thereby augmenting children's well-being.

RESEARCH IN IMMIGRANT MOTHERS' KNOWLEDGE OF CHILD DEVELOPMENT

We are engaged in a longitudinal study of child development, parenting, and family life among three groups of immigrant families to the United States. We observe mother–child interactions in the home when the children are 5, 13, 20, and 48 months of age, and ask mothers to complete a series of questionnaires to provide information about their demographic background, cultural beliefs, and ideas about parenting and child development. Our research has shown that Japanese and South American immigrant (first- and second-generation) mothers of young children score significantly (more than 10%) lower on an evaluation of their knowledge of child development when their children were 20 months old than do otherwise comparable European American mothers whose ancestors have been in the United States for at least four generations (Bornstein & Cote, 2004). Here, we report new analyses of mothers' knowledge of child development, obtained when the children were 5 months of age; we compare three immigrant samples (Japanese, Korean, and South

American); and we report relations between mothers' knowledge and some significant parenting behaviors.

Research Participants

We studied immigrant mothers from both Asia and Latin America for several theoretical and practical reasons. First, from a practical point of view, most immigrants to the United States today come from Asia or Latin America, yet they have received comparatively little attention in psychological research (e.g., Chao & Tseng, 2002; García-Coll & Pachter, 2002; see Hernandez et al., Chapter 1, this volume). Because Asian and Latin American cultures are themselves diverse, and research suggests that there are childrearing differences among Asians and Latinos (Field & Widmayer, 1981; Uba, 1994), we selected specific subgroups of each. Our choices are not meant to represent "Asians" or "Latinos" at large; indeed, no one cultural group could. Second, we recruited three immigrant groups into our longitudinal studies so that we could observe, contrast, and compare how parenting and child development adapt in different groups. This strategy allows us to identify culturally common as well as culture-specific patterns of acculturation. In the same way, recruiting two East Asian groups allows similar comparisons between groups emigrating from neighboring regions of the world. Finally, most immigrants to the United States today come from collectivist cultures, yet they are emigrating to one of the most individualistic cultures in the world. Of course, no culture is uniformly collectivist or individualist; collectivism and individualism vary within cultures (Oyserman, Coon, & Kemmelmeier, 2002). However, consistent with earlier research (e.g., Hofstede, 1991), each group of mothers considered themselves to be more collectivist than individualist (see Table 7.1 for descriptive statistics). This is noteworthy because there are differences in parenting beliefs and practices between individualist and collectivist cultures (e.g., Greenfield & Suzuki, 1998).

One hundred Japanese, Korean, and South American immigrant families living in the Washington, DC, metropolitan area have so far participated in our research. Mothers completed acculturation and demographic questionnaires when their infants were 5 months old (see Tables 7.1 and 7.2, respectively). All mothers in our study either immigrated to the United States themselves (first-generation Americans) or were the children of immigrants (second-generation Americans) (see Hernandez et al., Chapter 1, this volume). Most were born outside the United States (Table 7.1). On average, mothers were bicultural, meaning that they identified themselves as belonging to both their native and to U.S. culture. Significantly, all mothers *self-identified* as Japanese American, Korean American, or South American, an important methodological issue for research with ethnic minorities

TABLE 7.1. Cultural Characteristics of the Immigrant Mothers

	Japanese immigrant (n = 34)	Korean immigrant (n = 26)	South American immigrant (n = 40)
Generation (first:second)[a]	31:3	21:5	33:7
Age at immigration[b]	27.92 (3.66)	16.21 (11.22)	23.84 (7.90)
Years lived in United States[b]	5.52 (3.11)	14.45 (11.36)	10.56 (6.51)
Acculturation level[c]	2.17 (0.63)	2.68 (0.67)	2.38 (0.53)
Individualism score[d]	5.81 (0.95)	5.25 (1.48)	5.87 (1.14)
Collectivism score[d]	6.53 (0.92)	6.50 (1.24)	7.15 (0.82)

Note. M (SD) unless otherwise specified. For ratio and interval data, ANOVAs followed by Tukey HSD ($p < .05$) tested differences among immigrant samples; for categorical data, chi-square tests examined differences among immigrant samples.

[a] First-generation participants were not born in the United States and immigrated to the United States during their lifetimes, and second-generation participants were born in the United States but their parents were not. Mothers' generation level did not differ across groups, χ^2 (2, N = 100) = 1.58, *ns*.

[b] Only participants who were not born in the United States were included. Japanese and South American immigrant mothers were older at the time they immigrated to the United States than Korean immigrant mothers, F (2, 69) = 12.28, $p < .001$, $\eta^2_p = .26$. Korean and South American immigrant mothers had lived in the United States longer than Japanese immigrant mothers at the time of the study, F (2, 70) = 8.27, $p = .001$, $\eta^2_p = .19$.

[c] The Korean American (KAAS-I), Japanese American (JAAS), and South American (SAAS) Acculturation Scales were used (Cote & Bornstein, 2003); scores ranged from 1 to 5, with higher scores indicating a stronger identification with U.S. culture (relative to the culture of origin); reliability scores were excellent and ranged from a = .91 to .96 across cultural groups. Korean immigrant mothers were more acculturated than Japanese immigrant mothers, F (2, 97) = 5.29, $p < .01$, $\eta^2_p = .10$.

[d] Scores on Triandis's (1995) Individualism–Collectivism Scale (INDCOL) ranged from 1 to 9 for both Individualism and Collectivism (measured separately), with higher scores indicating a higher degree of individualism or collectivism. In order to increase subscale reliability as suggested by Triandis (1995), five items from the Collectivism subscale were omitted. Subscale reliabilities for Individualism ranged from α = .73 to .87 and for Collectivism ranged from α = .63 to .81 across cultural groups. No differences in mothers' levels of individualism emerged, F (2, 97) = 2.46, *ns*, $\eta^2_p = .05$. South American immigrant mothers were more collectivist than either Korean or Japanese immigrant mothers, F (2, 97) = 5.06, p .01, $\eta^2_p = .09$. Korean, $t(25) = 3.04$, $p < .01$, Japanese, $t(33) = 2.97$, $p < .01$, and South American, $t(39) = 5.76$, $p < .001$, immigrant mothers each rated themselves as significantly more collectivist than individualist.

(Marín & Marín, 1991). Our participants were immigrants and not refugees, and so were not subject to the psychological difficulties known to affect people who emigrate from their country as refugees (Berry & Sam, 1997). South American mothers were from metropolitan areas primarily in Argentina, Peru, and Colombia, and did not differ on any of the demographic or dependent variables.

Acculturating mothers were not only demographically similar to each other but representative of Japanese, Korean, and South American

TABLE 7.2. Sociodemographic Characteristics of the Immigrant Families

	Japanese immigrant (n = 34)	Korean immigrant (n = 26)	South American immigrant (n = 40)
Mothers' age[a]	31.67 (3.60)	31.15 (3.12)	31.84 (4.74)
Mothers' education level[b]	5.74 (0.79)	6.15 (1.35)	5.90 (0.84)
Hours per week mother works[c]	28.27 (17.18)	30.76 (13.28)	28.95 (11.39)
Nuclear family (yes:no)[d]	31:3	18:8	30:10
Infant age (in months)[e]	5.66 (0.44)	5.63 (0.51)	5.55 (0.42)
Infant gender (girl:boy)[f]	17:17	16:10	17:23

Note. M (SD) unless otherwise specified. For ratio and interval data, ANOVAs followed by Tukey HSD ($p < .05$) tested differences among immigrant samples; for categorical data, chi-square tests examined differences among immigrant samples.

[a] Mothers' age did not differ across immigrant groups, F (2, 97) = 0.24, *ns*, $\eta^2_p = .01$.

[b] Because differences exist between countries in the duration, quality, and content of schooling, bicultural researchers adjusted mothers' years of schooling so that the scales were equivalent to the 7-point Hollingshead (1975) index. On this scale, a 4 indicates that the mother's highest level of educational attainment was a high school degree or equivalent, a 5 indicates some college, and a 6 indicates a college degree. Immigrant mothers' education level did not differ, F (2, 97) = 1.34, *ns*, η^2_p = .03.

[c] Only employed mothers were included. The number of hours per week mothers worked did not differ across immigrant groups, F (2, 47) = 0.14, *ns*, $\eta^2_p = .01$.

[d] Family composition did not differ across immigrant groups, χ^2 (2, N = 100) = 4.92, *ns*.

[e] Infants' age did not differ across immigrant groups, F (2, 97) = 0.55, *ns*, $\eta^2_p = .01$.

[f] Infants' gender distribution did not differ across immigrant groups, χ^2 (2, N = 100) = 2.28, *ns*.

immigrants in the Washington, DC, metropolitan area, whose immigrant population is increasing and ethnically diverse (Whoriskey & Cohen, 2001; Wilson & Pan, 2000). All mothers had only one child at the time of the study; were urban, middle class, similar in age, and had comparable work schedules; and were married to the baby's father. More specific demographic information about our participants appears in Table 7.2.

Research Methods

To evaluate mothers' knowledge about parenting and child development, mothers completed the Knowledge of Infant Development Inventory (KIDI; MacPhee, 1981) when their infants were 5 months of age. This measure has good test–retest stability, construct validity, and reliability with culturally diverse samples of U.S. mothers (Cote & Bornstein, 2003; MacPhee, 1981). An example item from the KIDI is, "The newborn can see a face 6 feet away as well as an adult can." Mothers are asked either to indicate whether a statement is true or false or to choose the correct response among several options. The dependent variable for this measure is the percentage of items the mother answered correctly, although we also look more closely at individual items. As is standard, measures were first translated into Japanese, Korean, and Spanish and then independently back-translated into English by bilingual, bicultural researchers. Mothers were allowed to choose the language in which they completed the questionnaires.

Immigrant Mothers' Knowledge of Child Development and Childcare

Immigrant mothers answered about 70% of the items on the KIDI correctly. An analysis of covariance (controlling for mothers' acculturation and education levels) showed no differences among Japanese, Korean, or South American immigrant mothers' levels of parenting knowledge, $F(2, 95) = 0.02$, *ns*, $\eta^2_p = .01$: Japanese immigrant, $M = .71$, $SD = .09$; Korean immigrant, $M = .74$, $SD = .09$; South American immigrant, $M = .72$, $SD = .11$, respectively. Although in our previous research we found significant improvement in mothers' total knowledge over a 15-month period for Japanese and South American immigrant mothers, it was a small (2%) increase; moreover, mothers' knowledge of child development is individually stable over time (Cote & Bornstein, 2003).

Although three distinct groups of immigrant mothers were sampled, their overall knowledge of child development scores were similar. Moreover, immigrant mothers answered the same kinds of questions correctly and incorrectly. Which items did immigrant mothers answer correctly? They had little problem answering questions about children's physical health and safety. This finding is certainly good news, although not entirely surprising, because some research has reported that children of immigrants have lower injury rates than low-income children of United States–born parents (Schwebel, Brezausek, Ramey, & Ramey, 2005). For example, we found that approximately three in four immigrant mothers were aware that a frequent cause of accidents among 1-year-olds is pulling an object (e.g., a lamp) down on top of themselves. Also, nearly all immigrant mothers (nine in 10) knew that they should not put soft pillows in their infants' crib, which is reassuring because this practice has been associated with a higher incidence of sudden infant death syndrome (SIDS; American Academy of Pediatrics, 2005). It also suggests that the National Institute of Child Health and Human Development's Back to Sleep campaign has been successful in educating new parents about one of the causes of SIDS.

In what areas could mothers' knowledge improve? Immigrant mothers had difficulty answering questions about normative infant development. Table 7.3 contains the items that half or more of immigrant mothers did not answer correctly. One area about which immigrant mothers need more information concerns children's physiological and perceptual development. For example, most immigrant mothers are not aware of developmental milestones for the onset of infant babbling. Mothers who are knowledgeable about this developmental mile-

TABLE 7.3. KIDI Items the Majority of Immigrant Mothers Had Difficulty Answering

	% mothers who answered correctly			
KIDI item	All immigrant mothers	Japanese immigrants	Korean immigrants	South American immigrants
Development: Physical and physiological				
A 4-month-old lying on his (her) stomach can lift his (her) head.	13	24	8	8
A newborn's toes fan out when you stroke the bottom of its foot.	45	53	31	48
Altogether, the average newborn cries about: 1–2 hours out of every 24.	48	53	58	38
Babbling ("a-bah-bah" or "bup-bup") begins around 5 months.	36	29	42	38
Development: Cognitive and perceptual				
Infants have depth perception by 6 months of age (can tell that they are on a high place).	26	44	23	13
Two-month-olds can tell some speech sounds apart.	29	15	39	35
Development: Emotional				
A baby of 6 months will respond to someone differently depending on whether the person is happy, sad, or upset.	47	41	58	45
Development: Temperament and personality				
Some normal babies do not enjoy being cuddled.	36	21	58	35
A baby's personality (individuality) is set by 6 months of age.	48	41	77	35
Parent–infant relationships				
Some mothers do not get really involved with their infants until the baby starts to smile and look at them.	28	35	31	20
The way the parent responds to the baby in the first few months of life determines whether the child will grow up to be happy and well-adjusted, or moody and a misfit.	29	29	42	20

stone are more likely to identify potential hearing problems and bring them to the attention of their pediatrician. As a second example, fewer than half of immigrant mothers know that the average newborn cries 1–2 hours out of every 24 hours, and one in three immigrant mothers thinks it is normal for an infant to cry for longer periods of time. Crying is one of the primary ways newborn infants communicate their needs, and if parents think that several hours of crying per day is normal, they may be less likely to respond to infant distress. In turn, as is known from the work of Bowlby, Ainsworth, and other attachment researchers, maternal sensitivity and responsiveness are vital to a number of positive child mental and socioemotional outcomes. As a final example, a majority of mothers are not aware that 6-month-olds respond differently to people based on the person's emotional expression. Mothers without this knowledge might tend to argue in front of their infant, or fail to seek help for postpartum depression, not realizing that their infant too will be affected by their behavior. Thus, such information has practical implications.

Knowledge of Child Development and Parenting Behavior

Knowledge of normative child development can impact a mother's sense of competence and her investment in parenting (Bornstein & Cote, 2003) and influence the mother–infant relationship (Benasich & Brooks-Gunn, 1996; Conrad et al., 1992; Grusec & Goodnow, 1994). We have also found this to be true for our immigrant mothers. For example, correlational analysis of items from the KIDI with observational data from a visit to the home at 5 months suggests that those immigrant mothers who know that newborn infants cry about 1–2 hours out of every 24 express negative affect less frequently when they are with their baby than mothers who overestimate the amount of time newborns cry or report they do not know. As a second example, immigrant mothers who understand that a baby of 6 months responds differently to people based on their emotions display less negative affect when with their infants than immigrant mothers who are not aware that infants are sensitive to the emotions of those around them. As a final example, mothers who score higher on the KIDI overall are more likely to engage in activities that enhance their children's development (specifically, they talk to their babies more frequently). Thus, mothers' knowledge of parenting and child development matters; it matters to the mothers themselves and their sense of competence in the parenting role, and it matters to infants and young children because it affects mothers' investment in parenting and the character and quality of mother–child interactions.

Origins of Maternal Knowledge

Immigrant mothers hold some ideas about child development that differ from U.S. scientific knowledge. What predicts mothers' knowledge of child development? European American mothers report that they tend to rely on expert advice about children, particularly in the form of published childrearing materials (Clarke-Stewart, 1998; Young, 1991), perhaps because pediatrician visits tend to be brief and medically oriented, rather than developmentally oriented. However, despite their availability, and despite the fact that the immigrant mothers in our study were literate, well educated, and middle class by U.S. standards, written materials are not a primary source of information about child development for them. For example, Shwalb, Kawai, Shoji, and Tsunetsugu's (1995) survey of 1,147 mothers and 1,150 fathers in Japan revealed that Japanese mothers (and fathers) reported that their spouse was the main source of information about young children, even though U.S. childrearing books have been translated into Japanese, Japanese childrearing books incorporate Western ideas, and every pregnant woman receives the *Mother and Child Health Handbook* (Shwalb et al., 1995). Furthermore, in Japan and South America, community services that provide information about child development are routinely available to parents.

In Japan, mothers visit clinics for regular developmental screening, and not simply assessment of physical health (N. Okazaki, personal communication, April 14, 2000). In Korea, parents traditionally rely on relatives, especially their mothers or mothers-in-law, for information about child development. It is now becoming more common for young mothers to obtain information from the Internet (J. Kim, personal communication, May 2, 2006). In Argentina, nurses visit new mothers at home to assist them with all aspects of infant care, including administering vaccinations to infants and providing mothers with information and support (K. Schulthess, personal communication, April 13, 2000). Thus, unlike European American mothers in the United States, parents in these other cultures are not primarily responsible for monitoring their young children's development; instead it is a community activity. These distributed sources of information and responsibility may explain why European American mothers know more about child development than some immigrant mothers (Bornstein & Cote, 2004). It is noteworthy that Japanese American mothers' acculturation level, when their infants were 5 months old, predicted their parenting knowledge when their children were 20 months old, suggesting that mothers who are more acculturated to U.S. society are more likely to learn about child development (Bornstein & Cote, 2003).

Knowledge of developmental milestones is important because early intervention is key to preventing long-term problems in children. If parents are unaware of what developmental milestones are, they will be less likely to recognize and bring problems to the attention of health care professionals. So what can be done?

POLICY IMPLICATIONS

Mothers' knowledge of child development and childcare is especially relevant to child health care and pediatric practice (Pachter & Dworkin, 1997) because during child health visits clinicians must ask about and interpret parents' (usually mothers') expectations, concerns, and opinions about their children's health and development. As physicians routinely draw on parents' knowledge, they need to be aware that parents' replies to their questions are moderated by parents' cultural knowledge about children's development and parents' own childrearing experiences. In other words, when interpreting the information parents provide, physicians must take the sources and contexts of parents' cognitions into serious consideration.

However, research suggests that physicians' knowledge of other cultures is lacking. For example, a survey of resident physicians revealed that one in four felt ill-prepared to care for new immigrants, one in four professed insecurity about caring for patients who hold beliefs at odds with Western medicine, and one in four felt that they lacked skills to identify cultural customs that impact medical care (Weissman et al., 2005). Thus, U.S. physicians do not fully understand immigrant family life, and our research suggests that immigrant parents may not be able to adequately identify developmental problems in their children. It is important to discover developmental problems as soon as possible, however, because those that are have the best chance to be remedied by early intervention. Thus, our first recommendation is to broaden physician education to include information about and interactions with culturally diverse populations. Because of the large influx of new immigrants to the United States, physicians are increasingly likely to see immigrant families in their practices (Levine, 2006), but more than 80% of pediatricians themselves are European American (see Mendoza et al., Chapter 2, this volume).

Based on our finding that immigrant mothers from collectivist cultures are accustomed to having assistance with child development issues and childcare questions, our second recommendation is to offer more informed support to immigrant parents. For example, a pilot program in which developmental specialists were added to pediatric practices in the Washington, DC, area proved helpful to both parents and medical staff

(Eggbeen, Littman, & Jones, 1997). Pediatricians reported that they came to rely on the developmental specialists' understanding of developmental issues. Parents reported that developmental specialists helped them to better understand their child's development. Outreach programs of this kind could especially benefit immigrant parents, particularly those with limited literacy skills.

Finally, a number of good and free resources on child development and childcare have been created for parents by the federal government, most of which are available in Spanish and English. For example, the U.S. Department of Health and Human Services offers one-page pamphlets listing normative developmental milestones and signs of problems (*www.cdc.gov/ncbddd/autism/actearly/downloads.html*). These pamphlets highlight important milestones in physical, cognitive, and social development for children ages 3 months, 7 months, and each year from 1 to 5 years. The U.S. Department of Health and Human Services (in cooperation with the U.S. Departments of Education and Agriculture) also publishes magazines from the White House's "Healthy Start, Grow Smart" initiative that summarize infants' behaviors and needs in a variety of developmental areas each month for the first year of life and discuss how parents can best foster their infants' healthy development (*www.whitehouse.gov/firstlady/initiatives/healthystart.html*). The National Institute of Child Health and Human Development's *Adventures in Parenting* brochure describes developmentally appropriate parenting practices for children of different ages (*www.nichd.nih.gov/publications/pubs.cfm*). This brochure teaches parents, through the use of vignettes, how to respond to their child appropriately, prevent risky behavior, monitor their child's environment, and mentor and model desired behaviors. The Department of Health and Human Services also offers pamphlets on positive parenting techniques for children of different ages (*www.cdc.gov/ncbddd/child/default.htm*). Some are distributed to mothers participating in the WIC program, and some are offered for free to all health care providers; these pamphlets are downloadable for those with computer access. The availability of these free materials should be widely publicized, and translations into additional languages should be disseminated.

CONCLUSION

In sum, increasing parents' knowledge of child development and increasing physician's knowledge of parents' cultural beliefs seem key to creating parent–physician partnerships that will foster the growth and well-being of all children, the burgeoning population of immigrant children not the least.

ACKNOWLEDGMENTS

This chapter summarizes selected aspects of our research. Portions of the text have appeared in previous scientific publications, and preparation of this chapter was supported by the Intramural Research Program of the National Institutes of Health, National Institute of Child Health and Human Development.

REFERENCES

American Academy of Pediatrics. (2005). Policy statement: The changing concept of sudden infant death syndrome: Diagnostic coding shifts, controversies regarding the sleeping environment, and new variables to consider in reducing risk. *Pediatrics*, *116*, 1245–1255.

Benasich, A. A., & Brooks-Gunn, J. (1996). Maternal attitudes and knowledge of child-rearing: Associations with family and child outcomes. *Child Development*, *67*, 1186–1205.

Berry, J. W., & Sam, D. L. (1997). Acculturation and adaptation. In J. W. Berry, M. H. Segall, & C. Kagitcibasi (Eds.), *Handbook of cross-cultural psychology: Vol. 3. Social behavior and applications* (2nd ed., pp. 291–326). Boston: Allyn & Bacon.

Bornstein, M. H. (1991). *Cultural approaches to parenting*. Hillsdale, NJ: Erlbaum.

Bornstein, M. H. (2006). Parenting science and practice. In I. E. Sigel & K. A. Renninger (Eds.), W. Damon & R. M. Lerner (Series Eds.), *Handbook of child psychology: Vol. 4. Child psychology and practice* (6th ed., pp. 893–949). New York: Wiley.

Bornstein, M. H., & Cote, L. R. (2003). Cultural and parenting cognitions in acculturating cultures: II. Patterns of prediction and structural coherence. *Journal of Cross-Cultural Psychology*, *34*, 350–373.

Bornstein, M. H., & Cote, L. R. (2004). "Who is sitting across from me?": Immigrant mothers' knowledge of parenting and children's development. *Pediatrics*, *114*, e557–e564.

Chao, R., & Tseng, V. (2002). Parenting in Asians. In M. H. Bornstein (Ed.), *Handbook of parenting: Vol. 4. Applied parenting* (2nd ed., pp. 59–93). Mahwah, NJ: Erlbaum.

Clarke-Stewart, K. A. (1998). Historical shifts and underlying themes in ideas about rearing young children in the United States: Where have we been? Where are we going? *Early Development and Parenting*, *7*, 101–117.

Conrad, B., Gross, D., Fogg, L., & Ruchala, P. (1992). Maternal confidence, knowledge, and quality of mother–toddler interactions: A preliminary study. *Infant Mental Health Journal*, *13*, 353–362.

Cote, L. R., & Bornstein, M. H. (2003). Cultural and parenting cognitions in acculturating cultures: I. Cultural comparisons and developmental continuity and stability. *Journal of Cross-Cultural Psychology*, *34*, 323–249.

Eggbeen, L., Littman, C. L., & Jones, M. (1997). Zero to Three's developmental specialist in pediatric practice report: An important support for parents and young children. *Zero to Three*, *17*, 3–8.

Federal Interagency Forum on Child and Family Statistics. (2002). *America's children: Key national indicators of well-being*. Washington, DC: U.S. Government Printing Office.

Field, T. M., & Widmayer, S. M. (1981). Mother–infant interactions among lower SES black, Cuban, Puerto Rican and South American immigrants. In D. S. Palermo (Series Ed.), T. M. Field, A. M. Sostek, P. Vietze, & P. H. Leiderman (Vol. Eds.), *Child psychology: Cultural and early interactions* (pp. 41–62). Hillsdale, NJ: Erlbaum.

Foner, N. (2005). The immigrant family: Cultural legacies and cultural changes. In M. M. Suárez-Orozco, C. Suárez-Orozco, & D. Baolian Qin (Eds.), *The new immigration: An interdisciplinary reader* (pp. 157–166). New York: Routledge.

García-Coll, C. T., & Pachter, L. M. (2002). Ethnic and minority parenting. In M. H. Bornstein (Ed.), *Handbook of parenting: Vol. 4. Applied parenting* (2nd ed., pp. 1–20). Mahwah, NJ: Erlbaum.

Goodnow, J. J., & Collins, W. A. (1990). *Development according to parents: The nature, sources, and consequences of parents' ideas*. Hillsdale, NJ: Erlbaum.

Greenfield, P. M., & Suzuki, L. K. (1998). Culture and human development: Implications for parenting, education, pediatrics, and mental health. In W. Damon (Series Ed.), I. E. Sigel & K. A. Renninger (Vol. Eds.), *Handbook of child psychology: Vol. 4. Child psychology in practice* (5th ed., pp. 1059–1109). New York: Wiley.

Grusec, J. E., & Goodnow, J. J. (1994). Impact of parental discipline methods on the child's internalization of values: A reconceptualization of current points of view. *Developmental Psychology*, *30*, 4–19.

Hofstede, G. (1991). *Cultures and organizations: Software of the mind*. London: McGraw-Hill.

Hollingshead, A. B. (1975). *The four-factor index of social status*. Unpublished manuscript, Department of Sociology, Yale University.

Kotchabhakdi, N. J., Winichagoon, P., Smitasiri, S., Dhanamitta, S., & Valyasevi, A. (1987). The integration of psychosocial components in nutrition education in northeastern Thai villages. *Asia-Pacific Journal of Public Health*, *1*, 16–25.

Levine, S. (2006, February 26). Reshaping bedside manner in a diverse world. *Washington Post*, p. A01.

MacPhee, D. (1981). *Manual: Knowledge of Infant Development Inventory*. Unpublished manuscript, Department of Psychology, University of North Carolina at Chapel Hill.

Marín, G., & Marín, B. V. (1991). *Applied social research methods series: Vol. 23. Research with Hispanic populations*. Newbury Park, CA: Sage.

Masuda, M., Matsumoto, G. H., & Meredith, G. M. (1970). Ethnic identity in three generations of Japanese Americans. *Journal of Social Psychology*, *81*, 199–207.

Ochs, E. (1988). *Culture and language development*. Cambridge, UK: Cambridge University Press.

Oyserman, D., Coon, H., & Kemmelmeier, M. (2002). Rethinking individualism and collectivism: Evaluation of theoretical assumptions and meta-analyses. *Psychological Bulletin, 128*, 3–72.

Pachter, L. M., & Dworkin, P. H. (1997). Maternal expectations about normal child development in 4 cultural groups. *Archives of Pediatric and Adolescent Medicine, 151*, 1144–1150.

Richman, A. L., Miller, P. M., & LeVine, R. A. (1992). Cultural and educational variations in maternal responsiveness. *Developmental Psychology, 28*, 614–621.

Schwebel, D. C., Brezausek, C. M., Ramey, C. T., & Ramey, S. L. (2005). Injury risk among children of low-income U.S.-born and immigrant mothers. *Health Psychology, 24*, 501–507.

Shwalb, D. W., Kawai, H., Shoji, J., & Tsunetsugu, K. (1995). The place of advice: Japanese parents' sources of information about childrearing and child health. *Journal of Applied Developmental Psychology, 16*, 629–644.

Sigel, I. E., & McGillicuddy-De Lisi, A. V. (2002). Parent beliefs are cognitions: The dynamic belief systems model. In M. H. Bornstein (Ed.), *Handbook of parenting: Vol. 3. Being and becoming a parent* (2nd ed., pp. 485–508). Mahwah, NJ: Erlbaum.

Triandis, H. C. (1995). *Individualism and collectivism*. Boulder, CO: Westview Press.

Uba, L. (1994). *Asian Americans: Personality patterns, identity, and mental health*. New York: Guilford Press.

Weissman, J. S., Betancourt, J., Campbell, E. G., Park, E. R., Kim, M., Clarridge, B., et al. (2005). Resident physicians' preparedness to provide cross-cultural care. *Journal of the American Medical Association, 294*, 1058–1067.

Whoriskey, P., & Cohen, S. (2001, November 23). Immigrants arrive from far and wide: Suburbs see surge from range of areas. *Washington Post*, p. B01.

Wilson, S., & Pan, P. P. (2000, January 23). A diverse, growing population. *Washington Post*, p. A18.

Young, K. T. (1991). What parents and experts think about infants. In F. S. Kessel, M. H. Bornstein, & A. J. Sameroff (Eds.), *Contemporary constructions of the child* (pp. 79–90). Hillsdale, NJ: Erlbaum.

CHAPTER 8

A Multidisciplinary Perspective on the Development of Young Children in Immigrant Families

P. Lindsay Chase-Lansdale,
Angela Valdovinos D'Angelo, *and* Natalia Palacios

As of 2000, one in five children in the United States is living in an immigrant family, and this subgroup is expanding more rapidly than any other group of children (Hernandez, 2004; Hirschman, 2005; Van Hook, Brown, & Kwenda, 2004). Against this backdrop of rapid demographic change, we focus our attention on the immigrant family and very young children.

How families function and raise their children are key determinants of healthy child development (Chase-Lansdale & Pittman, 2002). Extensive research in developmental science documents the lasting impact of early experience, such that positive experiences during early childhood increase the likelihood of successful trajectories over the life course (e.g., Chase-Lansdale & Votruba-Drzal, 2004; Shonkoff & Phillips, 2000). For children to become healthy, educated, and productive members of society, interventions during early childhood are more effective than those at later ages (Heckman, 2006). Thus, our goal is to stimulate new research that will lay a stronger foundation for the prevention of risky development and the enhancement of strengths in immigrant children.

A number of scholars (e.g., García-Coll & Magnuson, 1997; Spencer, 2006; Suárez-Orozco & Suárez-Orozco, 2001) have been instrumental in fostering a developmental perspective on immigrant families. However, the current empirical literature primarily addresses immigrant adolescents, and to a lesser extent school-age children (e.g., Fuligni & Hardway, 2004; Gonzalez, Umaña-Taylor, & Bamaca, 2006; Harris, 1999; Phinney, Romero, Nava, & Huang, 2001). In the 1980s, the mean age of children when their families emigrated to the United States was 9.8 years (D. Dixon & M. Fix, personal communication, May 2, 2006); this has since declined to approximately 5 years of age, based on recent analyses of the 2002 round of the National Survey of American Families (K. Fortuny & R. Capps, personal communication, May 3, 2006) and the 2000 U.S. Census (D. Hernandez, personal communication, May 2, 2006). Moreover, the majority of young children in immigrant families are born in the United States (Tienda & Mitchell, 2006b). These data support our call for more research on very young children in immigrant families.

PLAN FOR THE CHAPTER

Our plan for the chapter is as follows: (1) We present a multidisciplinary model of immigration and young child development with a brief overview. (2) We then synthesize literatures that are relevant to certain aspects of the model, in particular family contexts and family processes. It is beyond the scope of this chapter to cover every element of the model, but we believe that the full model serves a heuristic purpose in outlining the numerous factors affecting early child development in immigrant families. While our model applies to all young immigrant children, more studies are needed by country of origin, and by ethnic and racial subgroups. Where possible, we will draw on research on Latinos and give specific examples regarding Mexican American children and families as an illustration. (3) Throughout the chapter we suggest recommendations for future research.

A MULTIDISCIPLINARY MODEL OF IMMIGRATION AND CHILD DEVELOPMENT

Figure 8.1 displays our multidisciplinary model of the role of immigration in the development of young children. Our approach draws heavily on the phenomenological variant of ecological systems theory by Spencer (1995, 2006), the integrative model for the study of developmental competencies in minority children by García-Coll, Crnic, Lamberty, Wasik, and Vazquez (1996), the cultural ecological stress process model for ethnic minority children by Gonzales and Kim (1997), the model of ethnic

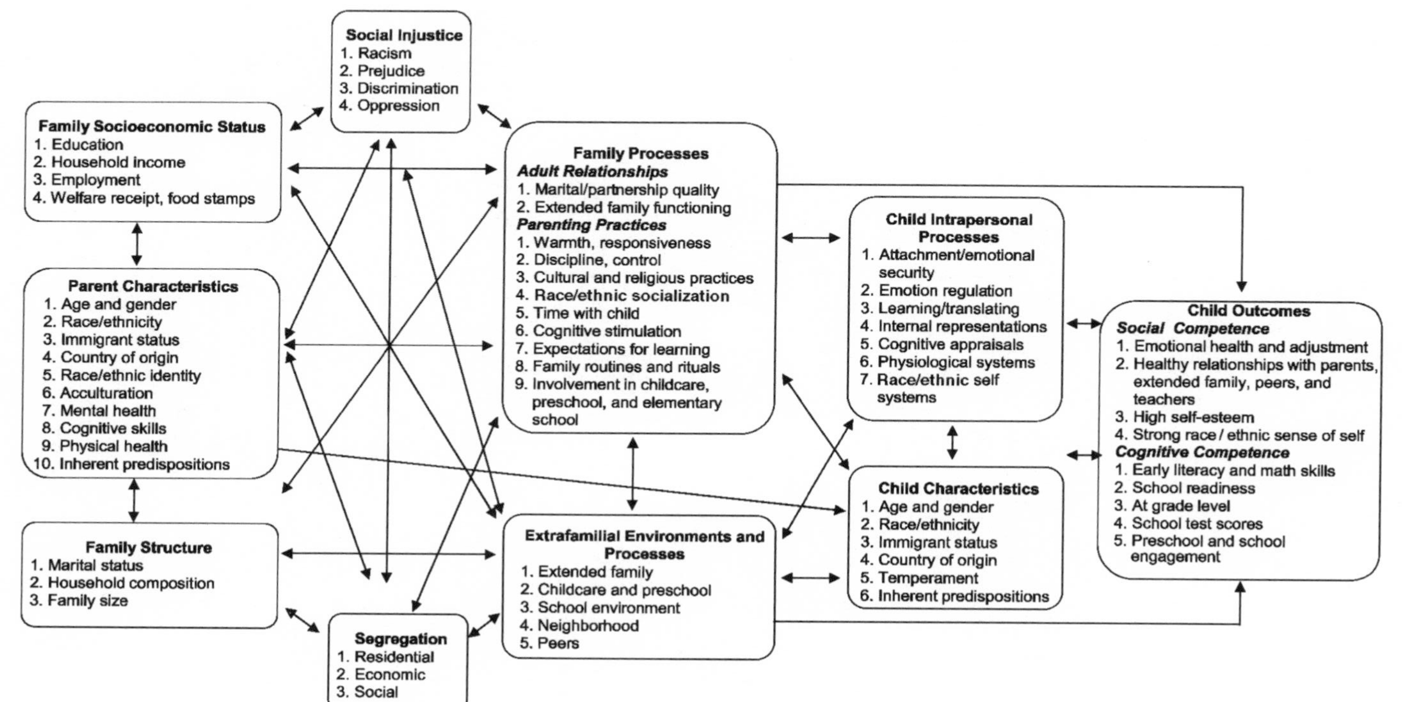

FIGURE 8.1. A multidisciplinary model of immigration and the development of young children.

identity development among adolescents by Umaña-Taylor and Fine (2004), and the theoretical model of Latino youth development by Raffaelli, Carlo, Carranza, and Gonzalez-Kruger (2005). These important theoretical models have expanded and reframed basic ecological and transactional theories that view child development as the result of reciprocal interactions between children and the many environments in which they live (Bronfenbrenner, 1979; Sameroff, 1975).

Psychological researchers on immigrant and minority children (e.g., Cauce & Domenech-Rodríguez, 2002; García-Coll et al., 1996; Gonzales & Kim, 1997; Spencer, 1990; Spencer et al., 2006) have convincingly argued that models of immigrant and minority child development should be balanced, addressing both risk and resilience. We share this perspective (Friedman & Chase-Lansdale, 2002). Immigration can be associated with risks, such as poverty, racial and ethnic discrimination, neighborhood segregation, low levels of education, limited English proficiency, and blocked or lost opportunities to reach one's full potential (Gonzales & Kim, 1997). Immigration can also be associated with strengths, such as the courage and determination to leave home and come to the United States, strong cultural and ethnic identities and traditions, high expectations for achievement, and close, cohesive family functioning.

Child Outcomes

Our model of young child development emphasizes the hopes of immigrant parents and the potential positive developmental outcomes for young children from infancy through the transition to elementary school. As can be seen in the far right box of Figure 8.1, social competence includes emotional health and adjustment; healthy relationships with parents, extended family members, peers, and teachers; high self-esteem; and a strong race/ethnic sense of self. Cognitive competence includes early literacy and mathematics skills, school readiness, being at grade level, good grades and test scores, and positive engagement with childcare settings, preschool, and elementary school. It is beyond the scope of this chapter to review the role of these extrafamilial settings, but see Crosnoe (2005), Magnuson, Lahaie, and Waldfogel (2006), Palacios, Guttmannova, and Chase-Lansdale (2006), Palacios and Stephan (2006), and Waldfogel and Lahaie (Chapter 10, this volume), for new empirical work on preschool attendance, elementary school achievement, and state policies regarding immigrant children.

Very little is known about socioemotional outcomes in young immigrant children. While some important small-scale studies have been conducted on infant–mother attachment in Latino families (Carlson & Harwood, 2003; Fracasso, Busch-Rossnagel, & Fisher, 1994), to date, we have virtually no large-scale reports of immigrant children's attachment patterns to mothers and fathers, prevalence of behavior problems, early peer relations, or mental health (Flores et al., 2002). More importantly, very few studies examine the processes of risk and resilience for young immigrant children, the developmental patterns that may be linked to generational status and acculturation, and the various factors that may promote socioemotional competence. Thus, echoing Flores and colleagues (2002), our first recommendation for future research is an epidemiological approach that can describe the social, cognitive, and physical health of young immigrant children by country of origin and generational status.

Culture and Acculturation

Our model assumes that culture is multifaceted, composed of many intersecting constructs, and cannot be represented by only one variable (Carlson & Harwood, 2003). Moreover, as outlined by Szapocznick and Kurtines (1993), families operate within highly varied cultural frameworks. García-Coll (2004) has argued that even though most developmental scientists believe that culture is central to human development, few theoretical models of human development examine the way developmental and biological processes intertwine over time. Swanson and colleagues (2003) propose that "we need to think of culture in a process-oriented manner: to focus on cultural socialization and the learning of these practices, along with their meaning to the individual. . . . People live culturally rather than live in cultures" (p. 747). Similarly, *acculturation*—the experience of the interchange and bidirectional influence between two cultures—is presumed to be an ongoing process for families and young children in our model (Berry, Chapter 4, this volume). Following García-Coll and Magnuson (1997), our model assumes that infants and young children are primarily influenced indirectly by their parents' acculturation processes, and in turn, that children's biological endowments and internal psychological structures influence their parents' acculturation. During the preschool years, young children's acculturation is also directly affected by their experiences in extrafamilial settings, such as childcare, prekindergarten, and other early childhood education programs. In general, the limited available research suggests that the family systems and parenting patterns reflecting the culture of foreign-born immigrant parents are protective and health promoting (García-Coll, Meyer, & Brillion, 1995; Harwood, Leyendecker, Carlson, Asencio, & Miller, 2002), but more work remains to be done.

Child Characteristics

An important component of normative development for all children involves the role of child characteristics. Young children influence their parents and other adults through such characteristics as age, gender, race–ethnicity, temperament, and inherent predispositions. Children's characteristics may shape their exposure to particular environments (e.g., a toddler with developmental delay may need special services) and may also affect their interactions with others. For example, if a child has a sunny and easygoing temperament, then parents or teachers are more likely to respond positively and provide more engaging interactions and opportunities for learning than if a child has a difficult temperament and is moody or easily upset (Chase-Lansdale & Pittman, 2002; García-Coll, 2004). Similarly, children who have higher cognitive skills and enthusiasm for learning will enhance and encourage the efforts of parents, childcare providers, and teachers to facilitate learning. Few of these child characteristics and their influences on the key adults in their lives have been examined in young immigrant children. However, an important new longitudinal study of 2,500 low-income toddlers and preschoolers finds some support for the transactional patterns described above, where in English-speaking but not Spanish-speaking Latino families mothers' book reading and children's vocabulary at 14 months both predict increases in maternal book reading and children's language development at 24 months (Raikes et al., 2006).

Inherent Predispositions

Parents and children share genes, and thus parenting and children's development will have a genetic component (García-Coll, 2004). Children's genetic or inherent dispositions, however, do not set in stone how children will develop (Dickens, 2005). Developmental science is now moving forward in new, more cutting-edge directions, studying specific environmental contexts that lead to gene expression, or, conversely, environmental conditions that deter gene expression (e.g., Caspi et al., 2002). Current research shows that children's development is shaped by a complex interaction of genetic and environment influences or *nature through nurture* (Shonkoff & Phillips, 2000). In the postgenomic era, studies of gene–environment interactions among immigrant children are essential.

Parent Characteristics

Parent characteristics encompass a number of dimensions including age and gender, immigrant status, race–ethnicity, racial and ethnic identity, acculturation, mental health, cognitive skills, physical health, and inherent predispositions. We emphasize that parental characteristics are important determinants of the environments that adults choose and create for children within prevailing environmental constraints. For example, the mental health of the parents is linked to the quality of their parenting and is understudied among immigrant parents. To our knowledge, the only available epidemiological information on Mexican American parents comes from a groundbreaking population study of 3,012 individuals of Mexican descent from Fresno County, California, in the Mexican American Prevalence and Services Survey (MAPSS; Vega, Sribney, Aguilar-Gaxiola, & Kolody, 2004). Foreign-born Mexican American adults have significantly lower 12-month levels of psychiatric disorders than United States–born Mexican Americans or the U.S. national population, signifying a potential buffer for children of first-generation parents. The rates are 9.2% for Mexican American adults who have been in the United States less than 13 years and 18.4% for those in the United States more than 13 years, compared to 24.7% for United States–born Mexican Americans and 28.5% for the U.S. national population. National population-based studies of mental health among immigrant adults, analyzed separately by parenthood and fertility, represent essential new research directions.

Family Socioeconomic Status

In national data sets such as the National Longitudinal Survey of Youth (e.g., McLeod & Shanahan, 1993) and large-scale psychological studies of primarily European American families and African American families (e.g., Conger et al., 2002), family economic resources are linked to parents' mental health, family structure, and parenting. Economic hardship in particular is related to single parenthood, higher rates of parental psychological distress and marital conflict, and less effective parenting (Chase-Lansdale & Pittman, 2002; McLoyd, 1998). These links have been largely unexplored among immigrant families with very young children. We take a first step in this chapter by providing a snapshot of key demographic statistics for first-generation Mexican Americans, drawing on new reports from the National Academy of Sciences (Tienda & Mitchell, 2006a, 2006c).

Despite high levels of men's employment—88.5%—first-generation Mexican Americans face many socioeconomic challenges (Tienda & Mitchell, 2006a). Almost 70% do not have a high school degree, and only 4.4% have obtained or exceeded a college degree (Schneider, Martinez, & Owens, 2006). The mean household income for first-generation families is $29,799, compared with $54,752 and $31,775 for United States–born European Americans and United States–born African Americans. More than 42% of children in these first-generation Mexican American families live in poverty (Reimers, 2006). The early child development literature shows that economic hardship is a significant risk to young children (Duncan & Brooks-Gunn, 1997), but virtually no studies have examined how economic hardship is related to family functioning and the development of young immigrant children, nor how immigrant families can protect their children from the ravages of poverty.

Family Structure

A large body of research links family structure with parenting processes (e.g., Hetherington, Bridges, & Insabella, 1998; McLanahan & Sandefur, 1994). For example, married parents tend to provide more responsive parenting with appropriate levels of firmness and discipline than do single parents (Chase-Lansdale & Pittman, 2002). Reasons for this differential indicate that single mothers have higher levels of psychological distress, lower levels of economic resources, and greater residential mobility than married parents (McLanahan & Sandefur, 1994). Again, investigations of the important links between these structural dimensions of family contexts and the family processes in immigrant families with young children are undeveloped.

One important research direction along these lines involves Mexican American families and "familism," which denotes a deep commitment to family life (Buriel, 1993; Cauce & Domenech-Rodríguez, 2002; García-Coll & Garrido, 2000; Umaña-Taylor & Fine, 2004; Zambrana, Silva-Palacios, & Powell, 1992). Evidence of familism can be seen in the structural or demographic characteristics of Mexican American families, such as high rates of marriage, high rates of fertility, and larger family size (Durand, Telles, & Flashman, 2006; Landale, Oropesa, & Bradatan, 2006), in addition to various family traditions, values, and parenting styles. For example, the majority of first- and second-generation Mexican American immigrants are married, with lower rates for second-generation individuals (72.4% vs. 64.7%; Landale et al., 2006). The comparable figures for marriage among European Americans and African Americans are 79.3% and 45.8%, respectively. Moreover, the percentage of children living in single-mother families is lower among first-generation Mexican Americans than among European Americans: 13.8% versus 16%. The higher rate of single motherhood in second-generation families (20.1%) is seen as a probable negative consequence of acculturation and thus the incorporation of family patterns from mainstream America (Landale et al., 2006). Similarly, the proportion of Mexican American immigrant households with extended family members is 9.6% and 7.8% for first- and second-generation households, respectively, compared to 2.7% for European Americans and 7% for African Americans. Given the severed ties often related to immigration, it is noteworthy that almost 10% of first-generation Mexican American households include extended family members. Thus, we have a snapshot of Mexican American immigrant family structure, but virtually no studies of any immigrant group have been conducted on family formation and dissolution over time nor on the implications of family structure changes for child development. This is a significant new direction for future research.

Family Processes

Our model combines distal contexts of family structure and socioeconomic status with key family processes. These include the quality of marriages, cohabitations, or partnerships; the quality of relationships with extended family members; and the parenting practices of mothers and fathers. Marital or couple relationship quality typically refers to high levels of warmth, closeness, and expression of "we-ness," and low levels of criticism, stonewalling, hostility, and contempt (Gottman, 1994; Stanley, Markman, & Whitton, 2002). Moreover, measures of relationship quality have not been widely validated on immigrant populations (but see Negy & Snyder, 1997, for an exception). In European American families, high-quality marital relationships are related to better mothering and fathering, and in some studies fathering is more affected than mothering (Coiro & Emery, 1998). Virtually none of these processes has been examined in immigrant families with young children, although a recent study by Parke and colleagues (2004) largely replicated the economic stress model developed by Conger and colleagues (2002) in a sample of 280 Mexican American and European American families with 11-year-old children. Studies of positive dimensions of family processes during children's early years would also be an essential part of a new knowledge base underlying possible family interventions.

How immigrant parents of young children relate to their own parents and other adult relatives is highly likely to affect their marital or couple relationship and their patterns of mothering and fathering. The quality and influence of relationships with the older generation have been examined in some middle-class European American studies (e.g., Cowan & Cowan, 1992) and to some extent in low-income African American families (e.g., Chase-Lansdale, Gordon, Coley, Wakschlag, & Brooks-Gunn, 1999). This focus would be a fruitful area for family process research among immigrant families, especially if qualitative and observational methodology were combined with survey and interview methods. The mother–father relationship can have direct effects on child outcomes as well as indirect effects through parenting. Yet we have much to learn about culturally meaningful ways in which husbands and wives in immigrant families relate to one another.

Mother–Child Relationship

There is a small but growing literature on mothering of infants, toddlers, and preschoolers in Latino families. Most of the research has focused on warmth and responsiveness as well as on intrusiveness and control. The latter dimensions, often referred to as "authoritarian parenting," are viewed as negative for European American families but not for African American or Latino families (Carlson & Harwood, 2003; Ispa et al., 2004). For example, compared to European American mothers, Latino mothers place a higher value on obedience and politeness, exercise discipline more often, emphasize connectedness over autonomy development, and frequently use commands to structure their toddlers' activities (Harwood, Schoelmerich, Schulze, & Gonzalez, 1999; Ispa et al., 2004). This parenting style is linked to some positive socioemotional outcomes for toddlers of first-generation Mexican American families, but negative outcomes for children in European American families. Ispa and colleagues (2004) propose that in collectivistic cultures, such as those from which Latino parents descend, authoritarian parenting is practiced intentionally and with less negativity compared to authoritarian parents in mainstream America where individualism dominates the culture. This study also suggests that as Mexican American parents become more acculturated, they take on "characteristically European American child-rearing values and practices" (Ispa et al., 2004, p. 1617).

Another compelling illustration of culturally different parenting practices involves the link between maternal intrusiveness and insecure infant attachments. Carlson and Harwood (2003) propose that European Americans view maternal control and intrusiveness as negative, but that this is not the case for minority and immigrant mothers. In fact, Carlson and Harwood show that high ratings of physical control were related to secure attachments among Puerto Rican infants, but to insecure attachments in European American infants. Similarly, Fracasso and colleagues (1994) found that contrary to middle-class samples, mothers' physical interventions during interactions with their infants were associated with secure infant–mother attachments among Puerto Ricans and Dominicans. These findings highlight the critical need for "culturally specific definitions of sensitive caregiving" (Carlson & Harwood, 2003, p. 66).

Research on other dimensions of mothering in our model is largely undeveloped. There are very few studies of cultural and religious practices or family routines and rituals. Racial socialization and a focus on Afrocentric culture are related to positive social and cognitive development among African American preschoolers (Caughy, O'Campo, Randolph, & Nickerson, 2002), but the study of racial and ethnic socialization is undeveloped for immigrant youngsters. We would expect that first- and second-generation parents' emphasis on their own racial and ethnic identities and cultural heritage, their protection of their young children from racism and discrimination, and their efforts to teach their children about these insults would predict positive social and cognitive development among their preschoolers. Additional parenting practices in our model—time with children, cognitive stimulation, and expectations for learning—all deserve more research attention. For example, about 39% of first-generation Mexican American mothers are not employed (Duncan, Hotz, & Trejo, 2006), so investigations of how they spend their time and how their parenting compares with employed Mexican American first-generation mothers would be welcome.

Several empirical studies of cognitive stimulation have taken immigrant status or acculturation into account. One study indicates that poverty status is a stronger correlate of lower levels of opportunities and expectations for learning than race or ethnicity (Bradley, Corwyn, McAdoo, & García-Coll, 2001). However, a recent large-scale investigation finds that in a sample of 6- to 16-year-olds, Mexican American immigrants had slower verbal growth than all other immigrant and nonimmigrant groups, patterns that stress the importance of considering immigrant status in tandem with race and ethnicity (Leventhal, Xue, & Brooks-Gunn, 2006). Two recent studies use language as a proxy for immigrant status. Raikes and colleagues (2006) find that among low-income families, when Spanish-speaking mothers engaged in daily reading with their preschoolers at 36 months, their children showed better language and cognitive outcomes, compared to Spanish-speaking mothers who read a few times a week. Similarly, Cabrera, Shannon, West, and Brooks-Gunn (2006) use English proficiency as a proxy for acculturation and find that higher English proficiency among Latino mothers is associated with more positive interactions with their infants and with increased father involvement in literacy-related activities. Palacios and colleagues (2006), using the Early Childhood Longitudinal Study—Kindergarten, report higher levels of reading achievement in kindergarten and greater rates of growth in reading achievement through third grade among first-generation students compared to third-generation students, controlling for English proficiency and a host of background factors. Additional studies are needed that further examine immigrant differences in child cognitive outcomes and in parental involvement in learning activities and expectations.

Father–Child Relationship

Research on father involvement in ethnically and racially diverse families has only recently emerged (Carlson & McLanahan, 2004; Coley &

Morris, 2002; Tamis-LeMonda, 2004). While there is considerable consensus on the idea that fathers contribute positively to the healthy development of children, debate ensues regarding the dimensions and measurement of father involvement, including who is the most valid reporter: the mother, the father, or the child (Coley, 2001; Lamb, 2000; Palkovitz, 1997; Pleck, 1997).

Our model suggests that the numerous parenting practices apply to both mothers and fathers. For example, the traditional view of Latino fathers as uninvolved with their infants has been criticized as inaccurate. In fact, recent work shows that Latino fathers are actively involved with their children in play and caretaking, are willing to negotiate parenting responsibilities with their partner, and can adapt to more egalitarian roles in the family (Cabrera et al., 2006; Caldera, Fitzpatrick, & Wampler, 2002). In the first longitudinal, large-scale observational study of low-income mothers, fathers, and preschoolers in an ethnically diverse sample, Tamis-LeMonda, Shannon, Cabrera, and Lamb (2004) show that mothers and fathers interact similarly with their young children. In particular, mothers' and fathers' responsiveness, positive interaction, and cognitive stimulation predicted 3-year-olds' verbal abilities, problem solving, early number concepts, language, and social skills. Although this latter study did not examine immigrant status, it too serves as a model for designs of future investigations of father involvement in young immigrant families.

A recent paper on immigrant fathers in the Fragile Families and Child Wellbeing Study suggests that there are significant differences between native- and foreign-born fathers, where immigrant fathers are less involved with their 12-month old infants, especially in the dimensions of cognitive stimulation (e.g., reading to the child) and basic care activities (e.g., diapering and feeding) than United States–born fathers. However, immigrant and United States–born fathers report just as much warmth toward their infants (Valdovinos D'Angelo, Guttmannova, & Chase-Lansdale, 2006). Valdovinos D'Angelo and colleagues (2006) found that immigrant fathers participate about one-third to two-fifths of a day per week less in cognitive stimulation or basic care than do nonimmigrant fathers, even after controlling for an extensive set of factors, including demographic information, child and human capital characteristics, traditional attitudes, and couple relationship quality. Further research is needed to understand why this is the case and whether this matters for healthy child development.

In general, the field of father involvement in immigrant families would benefit from new conceptual work that links cultural dimensions of family life to fathers' behavior (Parke et al., 2004) and to mothers' behavior as well. This would include the role of familism, traditionality, collectivism, obligation to the family, and other key cultural constructs. Observational and qualitative studies are especially needed.

Child Intrapersonal Processes

The final component of our multidisciplinary model of immigration and the development of young children is child intrapersonal processes. We believe that these may comprise the most important dimension for understanding why some immigrant children are resilient while others are at risk. Spencer (1990) has long emphasized the significance of intrapersonal processes in the healthy development of minority children and youth, indicating that "there are normative developmental processes and experiences common to all [children and] youth" (Swanson et al., 2003, p. 747). The intrapersonal processes in our model are especially relevant for early child development, and they represent various ways in which young children "make meaning" (Swanson et al., 2003, p. 348) or interpret their worlds as they participate in family life and extrafamilial settings (Friedman & Chase-Lansdale, 2002).

As shown in our model, attachment and emotional security reflect the child's internalized views of key family members as trustworthy, available, and loving (Friedman & Chase-Lansdale, 2002). Emotion regulation indicates the processes through which emotional arousal is managed and modulated (e.g., Li-Grining, Votruba-Drzal, Bachman, & Chase-Lansdale, 2006). Self-regulation is central to a child's ability to delay gratification and to interact in challenging situations and is influenced in part by the development and functioning of physiological systems, such as the hypothalamic–pituitary–adrenal axis (Adam, Klimes-Dougan, & Gunnar, 2006). In early childhood, children develop internal working models of social interaction to appraise and understand the behavior of others; these models are essential to healthy social and cognitive development. Young children who are able to perceive and interpret cues accurately during diverse social interactions show positive developmental trajectories (Dodge & Crick, 1990).

To date, the major theorists of development among ethnic and minority children have highlighted the importance of intrapersonal processes for healthy development. Yet most of the literature has addressed the self systems of adolescents or elementary school children. We need to understand the ways in which parents in immigrant families facilitate adaptive, healthy intrapersonal processes in their very young children. It is the child's early interpretation of his or her own psychological experiences that can be central to the development of a secure attachment, close relationships, a sense of efficacy, enthusiasm for learning, and a strong sense of race/ethnic sense of self. We strongly recommend that the relevant fields strengthen research on this aspect of development among young children in immigrant families.

CONCLUSION

This chapter was designed to issue a clarion call for multidisciplinary research on young children in immigrant families, a significantly understudied group. We hope that our multidisciplinary model will stimulate future research on the diverse and growing population of young immigrant children in the United States. We have drawn extensively on the pioneering work of many other scholars to integrate a model that emphasizes multiple levels and types of contexts for families combined with internal family processes. Much work remains to be done, especially along the lines of integrating population- or community-based samples with extensive demographic data as well as in-depth psychological measurement of family interaction, mental health, intrapersonal processes, and biological systems. Unfortunately, many large nationally representative data sets include only small percentages of immigrant children and families, thus limiting analyses by country of origin. Moreover, these and other population- and community-based data sets are hindered by the absence of high-fidelity measurement of family processes and culturally relevant constructs. Smaller scale psychological studies and qualitative investigations are essential for the development of new constructs and measurement that are steeped in cultural expertise and knowledge. We hope that, over the next several decades scholars will create many multidisciplinary opportunities to expand our understanding of young immigrant children and to promote their healthy development.

ACKNOWLEDGMENT

We wish to thank Ruby Takanishi for her helpful comments.

REFERENCES

Adam, E. K., Klimes-Dougan, B., & Gunnar, M. R. (2007). Social regulation of the adrenocortical response to stress in infants, children and adolescents: Implications for psychopathology health and education. In D. Coch, G. Dawson, & K. W. Fischer (Eds.), *Human behavior, learning, and the developing brain: Atypical development* (pp. 264–304). New York: Guilford Press.

Bradley, R. H., Corwyn, R. F., McAdoo, H. P., & García-Coll, C. (2001). The home environments of children in the United States: Part I. Variations by age, ethnicity, and poverty status. *Child Development*, *72*, 1844–1867.

Bronfenbrenner, U. (1979). *The ecology of human development: Experiments by nature and design*. Cambridge, MA: Harvard University Press.

Buriel, R. (1993). Childrearing orientations in Mexican American families: The influence of generation and sociocultural factors. *Journal of Marriage and the Family*, *55*, 987–1000.

Cabrera, N. J., Shannon, J. D., West, J., & Brooks-Gunn, J. (2006). Paternal interactions with Latino infants: Variation by country of origin and English proficiency. *Child Development*, *77*(5), 1190–1207.

Caldera, Y. M., Fitzpatrick, J., & Wampler, K. S. (2002). Coparenting in intact Mexican American families: Mothers' and fathers' perceptions. In J. M. Contreras, K. A. Kerns, & A. M. Neal-Barnett (Eds.), *Latino children and families in the United States: Current research and future directions* (pp. 107–132). Westport, CT: Praeger.

Carlson, M. J., & McLanahan, S. S. (2004). Early father involvement and the diversity of family context. In R. D. Day & M. E. Lamb (Eds.), *Conceptualizing and measuring father involvement* (pp. 241–272). Mahwah, NJ: Erlbaum.

Carlson, V. J., & Harwood, R. L. (2003). Attachment, culture, and the caregiving system: The cultural patterning of everyday experiences among Anglo and Puerto Rican mother–infant pairs. *Infant Mental Health Journal*, *24*, 53–73.

Caspi, A., McClay, J., Moffitt, T. E., Mill, J., Martin, J., Craig, I. W., et al. (2002). Role of genotype in the cycle of violence in maltreated children. *Science*, *297*, 851–854.

Cauce, A. M., & Domenech-Rodríguez, M. (2002). Latino families: Myths and realities. In J. M. Contreras, K. A. Kerns, & A. M. Neal-Barnett (Eds.), *Latino children and families in the United States* (pp. 3–26). Newbury Park, CA: Sage.

Caughy, M. O. B., O'Campo, P. J., Randolph, S. M., & Nickerson, K. (2002). The influence of racial socialization practices on the cognitive and behavioral competence of African American preschoolers. *Child Development*, *73*, 1611–1625.

Chase-Lansdale, P. L., Gordon, R. A., Coley, R. L., Wakschlag, L. S., & Brooks-Gunn, J. (1999). Young African-American multigenerational families in poverty: The contexts, exchanges, and processes of their lives. In E. M. Hetherington (Ed.), *Coping with divorce, single parenting, and remarriage: A risk and resiliency perspective* (pp. 165–191). Mahwah, NJ: Erlbaum.

Chase-Lansdale, P. L., & Pittman, L. D. (2002). Welfare reform and parenting: Reasonable expectations. *Future of Children*, *12*, 167–183.

Chase-Lansdale, P. L., & Votruba-Drzal, E. (2004). Human development and the potential for change from the perspective of multiple disciplines: What have we learned? In P. L. Chase-Lansdale, K. Kiernan, & R. J. Friedman (Eds.), *Human development across lives and generations: The potential for change* (pp. 343–366). New York: Cambridge University Press.

Coiro, M. J., & Emery, R. E. (1998). Do marriage problems affect fathering more than mothering?: A quantitative and qualitative review. *Clinical Child and Family Psychology Review*, *1*, 23–40.

Coley, R. L. (2001). (In)visible men: Emerging research on low-income, unmarried, and minority fathers. *American Psychologist*, *56*, 743–753.

Coley, R. L., & Morris, J. E. (2002). Comparing father and mother reports of father involvement among low-income minority families. *Journal of Marriage and the Family*, *64*, 982–997.

Conger, R. D., Wallace, L. E., Sun, Y., Simons, R. L., McLoyd, V., & Brody, G. H. (2002). Economic pressure in African American families: A replication and extension of the family stress model. *Developmental Psychology*, *38*, 179–193.

Cowan, C. P., & Cowan, P. A. (1992). *When partners become parents: The big life change for couples*. New York: Basic Books.

Crosnoe, R. (2005). Double disadvantage or signs of resilience?: The elementary school contexts of children from Mexican immigrant families. *American Educational Research Journal*, *42*, 269–303.

Dickens, W. T. (2005). Genetic differences and school readiness. *The Future of Children*, *15*, 55–69.

Dodge, K. A., & Crick, N. R. (1990). The social information processing bases of aggressive behavior in children. *Personality and Social Psychology Bulletin*, *16*, 8–22.

Duncan, B., Hotz, V. J., & Trejo, S. J. (2006). Hispanics in the U.S. labor market. In M. Tienda & F. Mitchell (Eds.), *Hispanics and the future of America* (pp. 228–290). Washington, DC: National Academy Press.

Duncan, G. J., & Brooks-Gunn, J. (1997). *Consequences of growing up poor*. New York: Russell Sage Foundation.

Durand, J., Telles, E., & Flashman, J. (2006). The demographic foundations of the Latino population. In M. Tienda & F. Mitchell (Eds.), *Hispanics and the future of America* (pp. 66–99). Washington, DC: National Academy Press.

Flores, G., Fuentes-Afflick, E., Barbot, O., Carter-Pokras, O., Claudio, L., Lara, M., et al. (2002). The health of Latino children: Urgent priorities, unanswered questions, and a research agenda. *Journal of the American Medical Association*, *288*, 82–90.

Fracasso, M. P., Busch-Rossnagel, N. A., & Fisher, C. B. (1994). The relationship of maternal behavior and acculturation to the quality of attachment in Hispanic infants living in New York City. *Hispanic Journal of Behavioral Sciences*, *16*, 143–154.

Friedman, R. J., & Chase-Lansdale, P. L. (2002). Chronic adversities. In M. Rutter & E. Taylor (Eds.), *Child and adolescent psychiatry* (4th ed., pp. 261–276). London: Blackwell.

Fuligni, A. J., & Hardway, C. (2004). Preparing diverse adolescents for the transition to adulthood. *The Future of Children*, *14*, 99–119.

García-Coll, C. (2004). The interpenetration of culture and biology in human development. *Research in Human Development*, *1*, 145–159.

García-Coll, C., Crnic, K., Lamberty, G., Wasik, B. H., & Vazquez, G. H. (1996). An integrative model for the study of developmental competencies in minority children. *Child Development*, *67*, 1891–1914.

García-Coll, C., & Garrido, M. (2000). Minorities in the United States: Sociocultural context for mental health and developmental psychopathology. In A.

J. Sameroff, M. Lewis, & S. M. Miller (Eds.), *Handbook of developmental psychopathology* (pp. 177–196). New York: Kluwer Academic/Plenum Press.

García-Coll, C., & Magnuson, K. (1997). The psychological experience of immigration: A developmental perspective. In A. Booth (Ed.), *Immigration and the family: Research and policy on U.S. immigrants* (pp. 91–131). Hillsdale, NJ: Erlbaum.

García-Coll, C., Meyer, E. C., & Brillion, L. (1995). Ethnic and minority parenting. In M. Bornstein (Ed.), *Handbook of parenting: Biology and ecology of parenting* (Vol. 2, pp. 189–209). Mahwah, NJ: Erlbaum.

Gonzales, N. A., & Kim, L. (1997). Stress and coping in an ethnic minority context: Children's cultural ecologies. In S. A. Wolchik & I. N. Sandler (Eds.), *Handbook of children's coping: Linking theory and intervention* (pp. 481–511). New York: Plenum Press.

Gonzalez, A. G., Umaña-Taylor, A. J., & Bamaca, M. Y. (2006). Familial ethnic socialization among adolescents of Latino and European descent: Do Latina mothers exert the most influence? *Journal of Family Issues, 27*, 184–207.

Gottman, J. M. (Ed.). (1994). *What predicts divorce?* Mahwah, NJ: Erlbaum.

Harris, K. M. (1999). The health status and risk behavior of adolescents in immigrant families. In D. J. Hernandez (Ed.), *Children of immigrants: Health, adjustment, and public assistance* (pp. 286–347). Washington, DC: National Academy Press.

Harwood, R. L., Leyendecker, B., Carlson, V., Asencio, M., & Miller, A. (2002). Parenting among Latino families in the U.S. In M. H. Bornstein (Ed.), *Handbook of parenting: Social conditions and applied parenting* (2nd ed., Vol. 4, pp. 21–46). Mahwah, NJ: Erlbaum.

Harwood, R. L., Schoelmerich, A., Schulze, P. A., & Gonzalez, Z. (1999). Cultural differences in maternal beliefs and behaviors: A study of middle-class Anglo and Puerto Rican mother–infant pairs in four everyday situations. *Child Development, 70*, 1005–1016.

Heckman, J. J. (2006). Skill formation and the economics of investing in disadvantaged children. *Science, 312*, 1900–1902.

Hernandez, D. J. (2004). Demographic change and the life circumstances of immigrant families. *The Future of Children, 14*, 17–47.

Hetherington, E., Bridges, M., & Insabella, G. M. (1998). What matters? What does not? Five perspectives on the association between marital transitions and children's adjustment. *American Psychologist, 53*, 167–184.

Hirschman, C. (2005). Immigration and the American century. *Demography, 42*, 595–620.

Ispa, J. M., Fine, M. A., Halgunseth, L. C., Harper, S., Robinson, J., Boyce, L., et al. (2004). Maternal intrusiveness, maternal warmth, and mother–toddler relationship outcomes: Variations across low-income ethnic and acculturation groups. *Child Development, 75*, 1613–1631.

Lamb, M. E. (2000). The history of research on father involvement: An overview. *Marriage and Family Review, 29*, 23–42.

Landale, N. S., Oropesa, R. S., & Bradatan, C. (2006). Hispanic families in the United States: Family structure and process in an era of family change. In M.

Tienda & F. Mitchell (Eds.), *Hispanics and the future of America* (pp. 138–178). Washington, DC: National Academy Press.

Leventhal, T., Xue, Y., & Brooks-Gunn, J. (2006). Immigrant differences in school-age children's verbal trajectories: A look at four racial/ethnic groups. *Child Development*, *77*(5), 1359–1374.

Li-Grining, C. P., Votruba-Drzal, E., Bachman, H. J., & Chase-Lansdale, P. L. (2006). Are certain preschoolers at risk in the era of welfare reform?: The moderating role of children's temperament. *Children and Youth Services Review*, *28*, 1102–1123.

Magnuson, K. A., Lahaie, C., & Waldfogel, J. (2006). Preschool and school readiness of children of immigrants. *Social Science Quarterly*, *87*(5), 1241–1262.

McLanahan, S., & Sandefur, G. (1994). *Growing up with a single parent: What hurts, what helps*. Cambridge, MA: Harvard University Press.

McLeod, J. D., & Shanahan, M. (1993). Poverty, parenting and children's mental health. *American Sociological Review*, *58*, 351–366.

McLoyd, V. (1998). Socioeconomic disadvantage and child development. *American Psychologist*, *53*, 185–204.

Negy, C., & Snyder, D. K. (1997). Ethnicity and acculturation: Assessing Mexican American couples' relationships using the Marital Satisfaction Inventory—Revised. *Psychological Assessment*, *9*, 414–421.

Palacios, N., Guttmannova, K., & Chase-Lansdale, P. L. (2006, June). *Immigrant differences in early reading achievement: Evidence from the ECLS-K*. Poster presented at the Institute for Education Sciences Research Conference, Washington, DC.

Palacios, N., & Stephan, J. (2006). *State pre-K policies: Classification and alignment with access*. Unpublished manuscript, School of Education and Social Policy, Northwestern University.

Palkovitz, R. (1997). Reconstructing "involvement": Expanding conceptualizations of men's caring in contemporary families. In A. J. Hawkins & D. C. Dollahite (Eds.), *Generative fathering: Beyond deficit perspectives* (pp. 200–216). Thousand Oaks, CA: Sage.

Parke, R. D., Coltrane, S., Borthwick-Duffy, S., Powers, J., Adams, M., Fabricius, W., et al. (2004). Assessing father involvement in Mexican-American families. In R. D. Day & M. E. Lamb (Eds.), *Conceptualizing and measuring father involvement* (pp. 17–38). Mahwah, NJ: Erlbaum.

Parke, R. D., Coltrane, S., Duffy, S., Buriel, R., Dennis, J., Powers, J., et al. (2004). Economic stress, parenting, and child adjustment in Mexican American and European American families. *Child Development*, *75*, 1632–1656.

Phinney, J., Romero, I., Nava, M., & Huang, D. (2001). The role of language, parents, and peers in ethnic identity among adolescents in immigrant families. *Journal of Youth and Adolescence*, *30*, 135–153.

Pleck, J. H. (1997). Paternal involvement: Levels, sources, and consequences. In M. E. Lamb (Ed.), *The role of the father in child development* (3rd ed., pp. 66–103). Hoboken, NJ: Wiley.

Raffaelli, M., Carlo, G., Carranza, M. A., & Gonzalez-Kruger, G. E. (2005). Understanding Latino children and adolescents in the mainstream: Placing culture at the center of developmental models. *New Directions for Child and Adolescent Development*, *109*, 23–32.

Raikes, H., Pan, B. A., Luze, G., Tamis-LeMonda, C. S., Brooks-Gunn, J., Constantine, J., et al. (2006). Mother–child bookreading in low-income families: Correlates and outcomes during the first three years of life. *Child Development*, *77*, 924–953.

Reimers, C. (2006). Economic well-being. In M. Tienda & F. Mitchell (Eds.), *Hispanics and the future of America* (pp. 291–361). Washington, DC: National Academy Press.

Sameroff, A. J. (1975). Transactional models in early social relations. *Human Development*, *18*, 65–79.

Schneider, B., Martinez, S., & Owens, A. (2006). Barriers to educational opportunities for Hispanics in the United States. In M. Tienda & F. Mitchell (Eds.), *Hispanics and the future of America* (pp. 179–227). Washington, DC: National Academy Press.

Shonkoff, J., & Phillips, D. A. (Eds.). (2000). *From neurons to neighborhoods*. Washington, DC: National Academy of Sciences.

Spencer, M. B. (1990). Development of minority children: An introduction. *Child Development*, *61*, 267–269.

Spencer, M. B. (1995). Old issues and new theorizing about African American youth: A phenomenological variant of ecological systems theory. In R. L. Taylor (Ed.), *Black youth: Perspectives on their status in the United States* (pp. 37–70). Westport, CT: Praeger.

Spencer, M. B. (2006). Phenomeonology and ecological systems theory: Development of diverse groups. In W. Damon & R. Lerner (Eds.), *Handbook of child psychology: Theoretical models of human development* (6th ed., Vol. 1, pp. 828–893). New York: Wiley.

Spencer, M. B., Harpalani, V., Cassidy, E., Jacobs, C. Y., Donde, S., Goss, T. N., et al. (2006). Understanding vulnerability and resilience from a normative developmental perspective: Implications for racially and ethnically diverse youth. In D. Cicchetti & D. J. Cohen (Eds.), *Developmenal psychopathology* (pp. 627–672). Hoboken, NJ: Wiley.

Stanley, S. M., Markman, H. J., & Whitton, S. (2002). Communication, conflict, and commitment: Insights on the foundations of relationship success from a national survey. *Family Process*, *41*, 659–675.

Suárez-Orozco, C., & Suárez-Orozco, M. (2001). *Children of immigration*. Cambridge, MA: Harvard University Press.

Swanson, D. P., Spencer, M. B., Harpalani, V., Dupree, D., Noll, E., Ginzburg, S., et al. (2003). Psychosocial development in racially and ethnically diverse youth: Conceptual and methodological challenges in the 21st century. *Development and Psychopathology*, *15*, 743–771.

Szapocznik, J., & Kurtines, W. M. (1993). Family psychology and cultural diversity: Opportunities for theory, research and application. *American Psychologist*, *48*, 400–407.

Tamis-LeMonda, C. S. (2004). Conceptualizing fathers' roles: Playmates and more. *Human Development*, *47*, 220–227.

Tamis-LeMonda, C. S., Shannon, J. D., Cabrera, N. J., & Lamb, M. E. (2004). Fathers and mothers at play with their 2- and 3-year-olds: Contributions to language and cognitive development. *Child Development*, *75*, 1806–1820.

Tienda, M., & Mitchell, F. (Eds.). (2006a). *Hispanics and the future of America*. Washington, DC: National Academy Press.

Tienda, M., & Mitchell, F. (2006b). Introduction: E pluribus plures or E pluribus unum. In M. Tienda & F. Mitchell (Eds.), *Hispanics and the future of America* (pp. 1–15). Washington, DC: National Academy Press.

Tienda, M., & Mitchell, F. (Eds.). (2006c). *Multiple origins, uncertain destinies: Hispanics and the American future*. Washington, DC: National Academy Press.

Umaña-Taylor, A. J., & Fine, M. A. (2004). Examining ethnic identity among Mexican-origin adolescents living in the United States. *Hispanic Journal of Behavioral Sciences*, *26*, 36–59.

Valdovinos D'Angelo, A., Guttmannova, K., & Chase-Lansdale, P. L. (2006). *The role of immigration in father involvement with infants*. Unpublished manuscript, School of Education and Social Policy, Northwestern University.

Van Hook, J., Brown, S. L., & Kwenda, M. (2004). A decomposition of trends in poverty among children of immigrants. *Demography*, *41*, 648–670.

Vega, W. A., Sribney, W. M., Aguilar-Gaxiola, S., & Kolody, B. (2004). 12-month prevalence of DSM-III-R psychiatric disorders among Mexican Americans: Nativity, social assimilation, and age determinants. *Journal of Nervous and Mental Disease*, *192*, 532–541.

Zambrana, R. E., Silva-Palacios, V., & Powell, D. (1992). Parenting concerns, family support systems, and life problems in Mexican-origin women: A comparison by nativity. *Journal of Community Psychology*, *20*, 276–288.

CHAPTER 9

Managing the Differences Within

Immigration and Early Education in the United States

Robert H. Bradley *and* Lorraine McKelvey

As new waves of immigrants come to inhabit the social, political, geographical, and cultural landscape of a society, there is both a tension and a challenge: how to assimilate the recent arrivals, yet accommodate life to their presence. Typically, the process of accommodation lags behind the process of assimilation. It is easier to treat newcomers as similar (with all that demands of the newcomers) than different—this explains our tendency to talk louder and more slowly in the first language rather than work to bridge the language divide in a fundamentally more meaningful way. Gradually, and sometimes grudgingly, deeper, more substantive, and more productive changes are made—often stumbling against romanticized notions of what life was like before the new arrivals. In this process, education is often viewed as a means to enable full participation in society. The truth is, however, education (aka. early intervention) is not always a refreshing oasis on the landscape of assimilation for immigrants. Why is that? Because, as an institution, education is often slow to accommodate to the unique needs and styles of the newcomers. The changes made to serve the newcomer are too often fashion over function, cosmetic changes rather than substantive adjustments in approach.

As we move into the 21st century, there is a mismatch between early education programs offered to young immigrant children and what those children bring to the experience of formal education in the United States. Consequently, for educational and developmental psychologists, there is a need to examine the context of education for immigrant children, the capacities and proclivities immigrant children bring to their first formal educational experiences, and the practices used by early childhood educators to inculcate learning. That task requires a consideration of how the principles of learning and development apply to early childhood curricula as well as an analysis of how the various components of family and school context help determine the success of particular curricular approaches. Accordingly, the goals of this chapter are to (1) describe the policy context of governmental efforts to provide early education programs for low-income families and the general nature of those programmatic efforts; (2) discuss what is known about the success of these efforts for young immigrant children and their families; and (3) offer recommendations regarding educational practice that might increase the likelihood that programs will show positive benefits for such children.

THE CONTEXT OF EARLY EDUCATION FOR IMMIGRANT CHILDREN

The fact is there is neither a comprehensive nor a coherent set of policies and programs aimed at getting the children of immigrants ready for school. This gap in policy is not surprising given the lack of comprehensive and coherent policies for young children more generally. The education of children is partly a local, partly a state, partly a federal, partly even a private matter. Since World War II, as the proportion of working women has increased, there has been an upsurge in programs aimed at children under age 6. States have gradually moved toward universal, mostly all-day, kindergarten and more recently to providing wider access to prekindergarten (pre-K) programs on a universal or demographically selected basis. However, none of those state efforts has been specifically targeted to immigrant children, nor have the programs implemented at the federal level. Most federal programs (Head Start, Even Start, Comprehensive Child Development Programs, New Hope, IDEA: Part C) have targeted low-income families or children with disabilities, sometimes with the understanding that the programs would be serving substantial numbers of poor immigrant children in certain locales.

Programs such as Head Start were always intended to be comprehensive as well as sensitive to family and community needs. Even so, access has been limited, as have been the means and the methods for turning the goal of school readiness into reality. In the 1960s and 1970s actual program models were built on white middle-class templates of what children needed to be successful in school. In 1997, Lubeck, DeVries, Nicholson, and Post published an article entitled "Head Start in Transition." The point of their article was that parent involvement had always been a goal of Head Start. Despite the fact that parents have always been members of the policy advisory councils for local Head Start provider agencies, the levels of parent participation and the influence of parents on local practice had generally been quite low. In response to disappointing early results from Head Start, Bronfenbrenner (1975) remarked that there was too much "discontinuity" between the program and the child's family and home experience. Head Start has always been a program in transition, seeking the means and the methods to realize its goals. In 1972, the Education of All Handicapped Children Act required Head Start to serve children with disabilities, and the Child Development Associate training and credentialing program was implemented to improve the quality of teaching for preschool children. When Head Start was reauthorized in 1974, new standards and practices guidelines were mandated. Regional and state technical assistance programs were also established. In 1984 services to Native Americans and migrants were spun off into separate departments within Head Start. In 1988 Congress authorized the Comprehensive Child Development Program so as to provide more intensive and integrated support services to low-income children and families. They also established 66 Family Service Center projects and the Head Start School Transition Project. The latter was done with the hope of better aligning preschool services with services in public schools. In the reauthorization of Head Start, new program performance standards were established and more attention was given to assessing children and monitoring local programs. The Early Head Start program (serving children from birth to age 3) was established, followed quickly (in 1996) by more rigorous curriculum standards, requirements for personnel training, and partnerships with local agencies and groups. The Head Start Bureau developed cooperative agreements with the Center for Family Literacy and undertook a series of national evaluation studies of its programs (e.g., the Head Start Impact Study and FACES [Family and Child Experiences Survey]).

The field of early education has long struggled with meeting the needs of children from diverse cultures. In the 1970s limited success and emerging sensitivities regarding culture moved the field toward a model that was better designed to accommodate America's largest ethnic minority, African Americans. Accordingly, something of an African American template was superimposed on the white, middle-class template. Both targets and strategies were adjusted. Perhaps because of these adjustments, recent evaluations of Head Start have shown particularly strong impacts on African American children and families. In the 1980s, and especially the 1990s, as the flood of immigrants began to impact the early education service sector, a second reevaluation of program priorities took place. This one was centered on language and cultural issues pertaining to Latin American immigrants. Garcia (1997) argued that, for the most part, Latin American children had been "shortchanged" by the early education community because of the failure of most providers to tailor programs so as to take advantage of the ways of knowing and behaving of people from Latin America (e.g., the use of contextualized learning, a cooperative approach to goal attainment, and compliance with adult directives). There have, of course, been important exceptions to this general pattern such as the AVANCE program, which heavily emphasizes partnership with the Latin American community (Johnson, Walker, & Rodriguez, 1996). Sadly, large-scale survey studies (e.g., the Survey of Income and Program Participation, the Early Childhood Longitudinal Study–Birth Cohort Current Population Survey) have consistently shown that Latin American children (20–24%) are only about half as likely to be enrolled in center-based preschool programs as African American (44–49%) or European American (42–43%) children (Magnusson & Waldfogel, 2005; Takanishi, 2004).

Just as providers of early education have typically not adapted to the strengths, needs, and proclivities of immigrant communities, so academicians have generally failed to build a relevant information base to guide education practice for children and families from those communities. A review of major early education journals is revealing in what it says about the education of immigrant children. Few articles on the topic of immigration can be found prior to 2000; and even now articles dealing with topics other than English as a second language are relatively scarce. Only in the 21st century has an appreciation of immigration begun to have impact on program targets and strategies and only gradually are frameworks expanding to consider immigrants other than Latinos (Takanishi, 2004). For example, a *Head Start Bulletin* produced in 2005 was devoted to English language learners, and the Head Start Bureau has sponsored several recent institutes aimed at exploring the needs of immigrants. That said, most shifts in program frameworks around the United States are anchored to notions of cultural sensitivity rather than the unique problems of immigration per se.

Illustrative of the lag in attention to the issues surrounding immigrant children are analyses of program impacts. Only recently have large-scale evaluations looked at ethnic group differences in outcomes, and there has been almost no effort to consider immigration status or acculturation per se. There has been no systematic effort to determine how program models have differentially affected specific groups of immigrants. Neither has there been a significant shift in the outcomes examined (i.e., the targets). Accordingly, the literature speaks with limited authority and precision regarding the kinds of programs needed to support immigrant children and their families.

EVIDENCE FOR POSITIVE IMPACTS OF EARLY CHILDHOOD PROGRAMS ON IMMIGRANT CHILDREN

There are few published evaluation studies of early education programs specifically focused on children of immigrants. In this section, information from evaluations of several large-scale studies are reviewed. None of the programs has specifically targeted immigrant families, so there has been little effort to examine the impacts on immigrant children as a specific subgroup. However, some federally sponsored programs have served significant numbers of Latin American families, many of whom are first- or second-generation immigrants. Evaluators have occasionally looked at impacts on Latin American, Spanish-speaking or non-English-speaking participants, so that information is provided as a proxy for impacts on immigrants.

Head Start Impact Study

The congressionally mandated Head Start Impact Study is being conducted across eight nationally representative grantee agencies. It involves about 5,000 3- and 4-year-old children randomly assigned to either a Head Start program or to available community non–Head Start services selected by their parents. Data collection began in the fall of 2002 and will continue through 2006. A wide array of measures is being used to assess program impacts on children and families. First-year findings indicated significant improvements for English-speaking children in the areas of prereading, prewriting, and vocabulary but only in vocabulary for Spanish-speaking children (U.S. Department of Health and Human Services, 2005). Significant impacts were also found on total problem behavior for English-speaking children but not Spanish-speaking children, although there was a reduction in hyperactive behavior for Spanish-speaking children. Native English-speaking parents who received Head Start services were less likely to use spanking than those who did not receive the services. They were also more likely to read to their children. The same impacts were not observed in parents with limited English proficiency.

These findings comport with findings from the Head Start FACES 2000 study (Zill et al., 2003). Language-minority children improved in the PPVT-III (Dunn & Dunn, 1997) standard scores from 59.7 in the fall to 66.7 in the spring but this was still 20 points lower than the mean vocabulary score for language-majority Head Start children (89.1). However, the language-minority children actually showed declines in vocabulary in Spanish (from 84.9 to 84.4), and letter identification in both Spanish (from 89.6 to 86.2) and English (from 84.9 to 84.4).

The Head Start Impact Study findings also comport with an earlier study of Latin American children involved in Head Start (Currie & Thomas, 1996). Currie and Thomas (1996) analyzed data from the National Longitudinal Survey of Youth. For children of native-born mothers, participation in Head Start (controlling for a variety of demographic confounders) was associated with superior performance on the PPVT and the PIAT Reading and Math scores compared to children who did not attend preschool. However, there was no such advantage for children of foreign-born mothers.

New Chance

The New Chance program targeted young welfare mothers who were high school dropouts (Quint, Bos, & Polit, 1997). It offered participants basic academic instruction, GED (general equivalent diploma) preparation, employability skills training, work experience, job placement assistance, health and family planning services, and parenting workshops. It also offered childcare services to participants. A randomized design was used, with 1,401 mothers assigned to the experimental group and 678 to the control group. Participants were from 16 program sites in 10 states. New Chance did result in greater likelihood of receiving a GED but there were few positive impacts on parenting except for 16- to 17-year-old participants. There were no positive impacts on children's development either. In fact, treatment group children were actually perceived as having more problem behaviors than control group children. In addition, treatment group Latin American children scored lower on the Bracken Basic Concept Scale than control group Latin American children.

Even Start

Even Start addresses the basic educational needs of low-income families including parents and children from birth through age 7 by providing a unified program of family literacy services (St. Pierre, Riccuitti, & Rimdzius, 2005; St. Pierre et al., 2003). These include interactive literacy activities for parent and child, training for parents in how to be the primary teacher of their children, parent literacy training (including GED preparation and ESL [English as a second language] training if needed) and early childhood education (often in conjunction with Head Start or Early Head Start agencies). There is no set model for delivering services across Even Start sites. Each program site selects its own models for each component. In all cases, however, parents must make a substantial commitment of their time so as to take advantage of all four components. Even Start has been reauthorized several times, most recently through the Literacy Involves Families Act of 2000 and the No Child Left Behind Act of 2001. In general Even Start serves a very high-risk, low-income population, with most below the poverty threshold, about 80% without a high school diploma, and the majority on welfare.

A total of 463 families from 18 program sites in 14 states were randomly assigned to Even Start treatment (N = 309) and control (N = 154) groups. Seventy-five percent of the participants were classified as Hispanic or Latino, and 45% were ESL. In 65% of the homes, Spanish was spoken. Even Start children and parents made marginal gains on literacy measures and continued to score low on national norms when they left the program. Treatment group children gained about 4 points on the Peabody Picture Vocabulary Test, but so did the control group children. The children also scored low on the Woodcock–Johnson subtests Letter–Word Identification, Dictation, Applied Problems, Incomplete Words, and Sound Blending. One reason for limited progress in Even Start is that families did not take full advantage of the services offered by programs, that is, only about one-third of families participated in the services for at least 12 months and about one-third did not even participate long enough to be involved in the full evaluation. On average, families were active for about 10 months, but received services during only seven of those 10 months. By the end of 24 months, only 11% remained active in the program. Parents from Latin America were the most likely to remain more than 12 months (45%), African Americans the least (18%). The amount of time spent in adult education increased over time, but the amount of time spent in parenting education decreased. Children from birth to age 2 averaged only about 6 hours per week of early childhood education and children ages 3 to 5 averaged only about 8 hours per week. Because of the limited levels of participation by many Even Start children and families, the data were reanalyzed; specifically, only those Even Start children who actually received early childhood services were included and they were compared to control group children who received no early education services. The results of this more restrictive analysis produced no evidence for positive impacts of program participation. That said, when further analyses were done looking not just at whether children participated but the amount of their participation, the results were more promising. Specifically, the more hours children participated in the early childhood education component, the better their language scores. Likewise, the more intensively parents participated in the parent education component, the better children did on language and achievement measures. However, the level of parent participation in the adult literacy component bore no relation to children's performance.

Early Head Start

In 1995 and 1996, the U.S. Department of Health and Human Services funded 143 Early Head Start (EHS) programs across the United States. EHS was conceived as a downward extension of Head Start, covering the period from birth to age 3. It was designed as a two-generation program for low-income families. From the original 143 sites, 17 were selected for participation in the national evaluation study, Early Head Start Research and Evaluation (EHSRE) of 3,001 families. The service models used at individual sites varied, the only requirement being that they had to conform to EHS performance standards. Seven sites utilized a home-based approach, four were center-based, and the remaining six used a combination of home- and center-based approaches. However, even the center-based programs were required to make at least two home visits annually to participating families. A major advance of the EHS national evaluation strategy was its intensive data collections on program implementation, thereby giving evaluators a way of determining the extent to which observed impacts reflected the degree to which program plans were actually implemented for families (Love et al., 2002).

Overall, the program had small, but statistically significant, impacts on children's cognitive and language development. There were also some small, scattered positive impacts on socioemotional development. These positive impacts on children appeared to be connected to some favorable impacts on parents. Treatment group parents read more often to their children, were less negative and detached, spanked their children less, used a broader repertoire of discipline techniques, and scored higher on the HOME (Home Observation for Measurement of the Environment; Caldwell & Bradley, 1984).

As part of the EHSRE national evaluation study, subgroup differences in program impact were also examined. Two sets of analyses provide windows on the likely degree of impact on immigrant children and families: (1) ethnic group comparisons, and (2) comparisons of English-speaking and non-English-speaking families. As regards the ethnic group comparisons, the most consistent positive impacts occurred for African

American children. Significant differences favoring the treatment group occurred for both language and socioemotional outcomes. For Hispanic children, there appeared to be positive impacts in the area of language, but no impacts in the area of general cognitive functioning or socioemotional behavior. The improvements in language appear to have tracked improvements in the amount of reading treatment group parents did with their children. Treatment group Latin American parents also scored better in the quality of assistance provided to their children in a puzzle task compared to control group parents. Results from the analyses of English-speaking versus non-English-speaking families largely mirror the ethnic group comparison. There were small, positive impacts on child cognitive and language measures among English-speaking families. However, the only positive impacts on cognitive performance for non-English-speaking families involved a reduction in low-functioning children (< 85 on the Bayley Mental Development Index; Bayley, 1993). There was no evidence of improved child language competence in non-English-speaking families.

We reanalyzed data from the EHSRE, this time comparing treatment and control participants in families where the parents had immigrated to the United States. A total of 441 parents were born outside the United States (283 in Mexico). Preliminary analyses using analysis of covariance, with controls for type of program (home-based, center-based, mixed), family demographic risk, age at parent immigration, and observer rating of the quality of English spoken in the home, show few impacts on either parenting or child well-being. Table 9.1 displays results for outcomes at 36 months. One of the few exceptions involved children who were tested using the Spanish-language version of the Peabody Picture Vocabulary Test (Test de Vocabuilario en Imágenes Peabody; TVIP; Dunn, Lugo, Padilla, & Dunn, 1986). Perhaps because the number of treatment group children using the English-language version of the PPVT was small, they did not score significantly higher than control group children. (Note: The treatment group scored higher at both age 3 years and pre-K but the observed differences were not statistically different.) Treatment group immigrant parents showed lower levels of negative regard for their children during a semistructured play task and marginally lower levels of parenting stress as measured by the Parenting Stress Index—Short Form (Abidin, 1990). Just prior to entry into kindergarten, treatment group children were rated by their parents as having fewer behavior problems and were observed to have a more positive approach to learning (see Table 9.2). As was shown at 36 months, treatment group children tested with the TVIP scored higher in vocabulary than their control group counterparts. In all other respects they were no

TABLE 9.1. Estimated Marginal Means of Treatment and Control Groups for Parent and Child Outcomes (36 Months)

Outcome measure	Control group mean (*SE*)	Treatment group mean (*SE*)	Significance
Child			
Bayley Behavior Rating Scale (Engagement)	3.54 (.07)	3.52 (.06)	NS
Bayley Behavior Rating Scale (Emotion Regulation)	3.99 (.07)	3.90 (.07)	NS
Bayley MDI	88.92 (1.18)	89.44 (1.06)	NS
PPVT-III (receptive language, English)	79.98 (2.58)	82.38 (2.51)	NS
TVIP (receptive language, Spanish)	93.25 (0.87)	96.53 (0.78)	<.01
Child Behavior Checklist (Aggression)	10.18 (0.56)	10.94 (0.51)	NS
Parent			
Parenting Stress Index (Distress)	28.07 (0.91)	25.80 (0.82)	<.07
Parenting Stress Index (Dysfunctional Interaction)	19.01 (0.75)	18.91 (0.67)	NS
HOME Inventory	26.67 (0.36)	25.80 (0.34)	NS
Parent–child interaction			
Parent supportiveness	3.72 (.09)	3.81 (.08)	NS
Parent intrusiveness	1.62 (.08)	1.59 (.07)	NS
Parent negative regard	1.16 (.03)	1.08 (.03)	<.05
Parent detachment	1.27 (.06)	1.27 (.06)	NS
Child engagement	4.60 (10)	4.57 (.09)	NS
Child negativity toward parent	1.30 (.05)	1.20 (.04)	NS
Child sustained attention	4.80 (.10)	4.79 (.09)	NS

different from control group children. There were no group differences in parental behavior or attitudes.

Almost no studies of early education programs have specifically examined program impacts on immigrant children or their families. In a small number of instances, separate analyses were done by ethnic group or by primary language spoken at home, which serve as proxies for immigrant group status. Across all the studies reviewed, there were few instances where significant positive impacts on either children or parents were observed. Moreover, when positive impacts were observed on parents or parenting, there were few connected impacts on children's development (Johnson et al., 1996). One study that provides suggestive evidence of possible impacts on one group of immigrants, Latin Americans, is the evaluation of the Oklahoma pre-K program (Gormley, Gayer, Phillips, & Dawson, 2005). The researchers used a regression discontinuity design to

TABLE 9.2. Estimated Marginal Means of Treatment and Control Groups for Parent and Child Outcomes (Prekindergarten)

Outcome measure	Control group mean (*SE*)	Treatment group mean (*SE*)	Significance
Child			
Positive Approach to Learning	10.83 (.21)	11.71 (.20)	<.01
Behavior Problem Index	6.40 (.31)	5.46 (.29)	<.05
Leiter-R (Sustained Attention)	11.36 (.28)	11.04 (.26)	NS
Leiter-R (Emotion Regulation)	90.98 (1.05)	90.76 (0.97)	NS
PPVT-III	87.31 (2.21)	92.10 (2.07)	NS
TVIP (Vocabulary)	72.44 (4.15)	87.78 (2.93)	<.01)
WJ-III (Letter–Word Identification)	87.13 (1.41)	85.90 (1.34)	NS
WJ-III (Applied Problems)	83.32 (1.71)	86.22 (1.63)	NS
Parent			
Depressive Symptoms (CES-D)	5.78 (.55)	4.67 (.53)	NS
Parent–child interaction			
Parent supportiveness	3.95 (.10)	3.95 (.12)	NS
Parent intrusiveness	1.73 (.09)	1.73 (.08)	NS
Parent negative regard	1.11 (.04)	1.14 (.03)	NS
Parent detachment	1.19 (.06)	1.22 (.05)	NS
Child engagement	4.45 (.08)	4.58 (.08)	NS
Child quality of play	4.15 (.08)	4.27 (.07)	NS
Child negativity	1.17 (.05)	1.23 (.05)	NS

examine impacts of the Oklahoma pre-K program on achievement on entry into kindergarten. The analyses indicated that Latin American children who participated in the program had higher scores on three scales from the Woodcock–Johnson achievement test battery (Letter–Word Identification, Spelling, and Applied Problems) than comparable children who did not. The greatest difference was on Letter–Word Identification. This difference was not surprising in view of the fact that the Oklahoma pre-K program stressed prereading skills. Although the results suggest the possibility of positive impacts on immigrant children from Latin America, two cautions must be raised regarding the findings. First, the evaluators did not perform separate analyses on first-generation immigrants (as contrasted to children whose parents were born in the United States). Second, the study was done on families who selected to place their children in pre-K (i.e., there is a likely selection bias in the findings).

Our reanalysis of data on immigrant families participating in the EHSRE likewise produced only limited evidence of positive impacts on child adaptive functioning (i.e., only one significant difference emerged from analyses of nine measures at age 3 and only three out of 11 at pre-K). However, one of the strengths of the EHSRE design is that information was gathered concerning the degree to which individual programs were implemented as planned. Thus, it allowed us to investigate the question: Do early education programs have positive impacts on immigrant children and families if they are implemented in accordance with guidelines established for the programs? About two-thirds of the programs studied were considered fully implemented based on careful observation by evaluators from Mathematica Policy Research, Inc. From these, we selected programs that used home-based models, based on the assumption that program impacts on children would likely be greater if their parents were also heavily involved in the intervention. Reanalysis, based on 150 immigrant children from sites that had fully implemented programs with home-based programs, revealed a somewhat more positive picture. At age 3, treatment group Spanish-speaking children scored higher on the TVIP (Vocabulary), and marginally higher on the Bayley scales. There was also a trend in parental reported dysfunctional interactions. At pre-K, Spanish-speaking children scored higher in Vocabulary and Applied Problems (with trends on book comprehension). Parents rated them higher on social skills and approaches to learning and lower on behavior problems and hyperactivity. Children were also observed to be more highly engaged during a learning task with their parents. In sum, although there was suggestive evidence that well-implemented home-based programs might have significant benefits for immigrant children, these findings have to be judged against two critical standards: (1) the total number of significant findings favoring treatment group children was quite modest compared to the total number of tests performed, and (2) the restriction to well-implemented programs.

CONSTRUCTING WORKABLE PROGRAMS FOR IMMIGRANT CHILDREN IN THE UNITED STATES

Why has there been so little positive impact of government-sponsored early childhood programs on poor immigrant children and their parents? Historically, there has been a mismatch between the hopes, needs, styles, and resources of U.S. immigrants and the approach used by governmental institutions to prepare young children for productive citizenship (Perez Carreon, Drake, & Barton, 2005; McLaughlin, Liljestrom, Lim, & Meyers, 2002). On the part of governmental agencies, there has been a lack of integrative planning that fosters a step-by-step movement toward competence and full integration into society; on the part of immigrant families, there has been a lack of sufficient connection and engagement with existing programs and services (Takanishi, 2004). In defense of each, it may be less a lack of will than a lack of "way." For example, Perez Carreon and colleagues (2005) conducted a qualitative study of immigrant parents' involvement in their children's schooling. Parents consistently pointed to their unfamiliarity with the U.S. school system and their uncertainty as to "how to" be effectively involved in the child's education. Language was identified as a major barrier to effective communication with school personnel, as was the feeling that their views were not respected. Many parents found it difficult to form trusting relationships with the child's teacher or to act as an effective advocate for the child. A study of Latin American parents and students with limited English proficiency and their teachers identified many of the same problems (McLaughlin et al., 2002). All three groups described struggles with communication as well as frustrations that came as a result of uncertainties about how best to connect with each other in their joint pursuit of education for the students. Finally, all three groups acknowledged worries about the unwelcoming, sometimes hostile, attitudes of some teachers and administrators.

One of the major dilemmas facing early childhood educators is how to address the need for English-language proficiency. Gutierrez and Garcia (1989) characterize the debate on the instructional use of English versus a child's native language "myopic" in that it fails to fully appreciate the complex interplay between life at home and in the community and life at school and in the envisioned society beyond (see also Padilla et al., 1991). They make the critical point that learning is inherently sociocultural and that learning is enhanced when it is infused with socioculturally and linguistically meaningful experiences—a point in keeping with views espoused decades ago by Vygotsky. Each learning environment (e.g., home, neighborhood, school) has a specialized code that confers meaning on activity. For young immigrant children there is often a mismatch between home/community codes and the codes of school. The key to successful learning in preschool and the primary grades is not to force a child to abandon the language and ways of understanding that permeate home or to remain outside the language and ways of understanding characteristic of schools. The key is to find ways of bridging the two. Accordingly, neither a native language only nor an immersion approach to early education would seem to fit the bill. Slavin and Cheung (2005) recently conducted a review and meta-analysis comparing bilingual and English-only reading programs for English-language learners. The evidence, although mixed, favors a bilingual approach—that is, reading is taught in the native language and English is used throughout the day as part of other instructional activities (see Berry, Chapter 4, this volume).

An additional reason to use a bilingual approach is to take advantage of the human and social capital immigrant parents can bring to their children's formal education. Enshrined in Head Start's code of operations is the notion that parents are "the child's first teacher"—hence, the long-standing mission of involving parents in the child's educational program. Requiring that instruction be in English serves to sever this desired connection and support from parents (Perez Carreon et al., 2005). Portes and Rumbaut (2001) argue that the success of immigrants in assimilating to life in a new country depends both on what they bring by way of skills, experiences, and resources (human and social capital) and on what is afforded by the environment that receives them—what they refer to as "modes of incorporation." The quality of reception offered by native individuals and institutions can facilitate, alter, or prevent the deployment of the capital parents bring to the new country. Insistence on English-language-only and on the styles, values, beliefs, and ways of knowing characteristic of mainstream culture can undermine parental authority, create dissonance between home and school, and reduce the likelihood of productive parental involvement in the child's formal educational experience (Quintero, 1999).

According to García-Coll and Szalacha (2004), segregation in its many forms—residential, economic, linguistic, social, psychological—places children at risk and contributes to mistrust among populations of diverse cultural backgrounds. There is evidence that interventions targeted to children and families of diverse cultural backgrounds are successful only to the extent that they incorporate culturally relevant resources. Communication and interaction styles common to a culture affect not only the trajectory of development in children but also the ways parents understand and utilize the inputs from social and educational agencies. If there are conflicts (or just mismatches), the likelihood of maximum positive impacts is low. Accordingly, there is need for the approaches used by schools to be compatible with parental values and approaches to learning and interaction. Then the inputs provided by schools can be transformed into assets for children. Studies are beginning to show that balanced bilingualism may promote cognitive growth by contributing to metalinguistic awareness and language proficiency (Slavin & Cheung, 2005).

Finding ways to bridge the divide between home and school can be especially important for young children in that they generally find it easier to learn new information if it contains elements similar to information previously learned (West, 2001). As well, preschool-age children can find it difficult to "decenter," making the daily transition from the world of home to the world of school a constant threat to undermine learning in either arena. Gutierrez and Garcia (1989) recommend greater use of collaborative "authentic" learning activities, that is, activities where the learning of certain specific knowledge and skills is gained in group-based problem-focused exercises that allow students to bring their own experiences and ways of knowing to the task of solving the problem. The teacher functions as director of the task, keeps children focused on the specific learning goals at issue in the task, but engages each learner (and the whole group) so that individual learners can utilize existing knowledge and skills. It is more dialogic than individual seat work or whole-class presentations, and it allows children to interpret questions and approach learning from their own frameworks of meaning. It would also facilitate discussions about classroom activities between child and parent. This practice is consistent with the language and literacy practices observed in some immigrant families (Rodriguez, 2006). It is interesting that one of the findings of the Even Start evaluation, which showed few positive impacts on children's development, was that teachers generally did not engage children in dialogic learning or expand on children's comments (St. Pierre et al., 2005).

In like vein, Ramirez (1989) argues for approaches to teaching that are more "culturally democratic," that move from matching teaching behaviors to the child's predominant learning style and ways of knowing toward a "gradual mismatch" that incorporates the styles and ways of knowing more common to the dominant culture. This is based on the belief that different learning communities (i.e., societies) tend to socialize children into their preferred learning styles and ways of understanding. These more sensitive, democratic, and authentic approaches to learning are consistent with the National Association for the Education of Young Children's (NAEYC) recommendations on curriculum—specifically, that children should be active and engaged; that valued content is learned through investigation, play, and focused intentional teaching; and that instruction for new learning should build on prior learning and experiences (NAEYC, 2003). That said, there have been few strong tests of this approach and it is not clear whether it might conflict in some ways with the No Child Left Behind Act directives.

If educational programs for young children move in the direction of bilingual approaches to instruction and instruction that brings styles of learning and ways of knowing characteristic of the country of origin for students, it will represent something of a departure for U.S. education. In their analysis of public education in the United States, Rong and Preissle (1998) found a strong emphasis on socializing immigrant children into the dominant culture. They conclude, "U.S. public education . . . has strongly rejected conserving and maintaining native language and cultural values"

(p. 12). Their conclusion is consistent with views expressed by the League of United Latin American Citizens (2002) who observed that limited English proficient learners are often stigmatized and judged to have developmental problems due to lack of progress in the early years of school. They recommend that government-sponsored programs take into account the specific needs of immigrant children and do more to encourage parent involvement in ways that are "culturally sensitive and non-threatening." This recommendation is consistent with findings showing that many immigrant parents are intimidated and uncertain as they attempt to be involved in their children's schooling (Perez Carreon et al., 2005).

There is overwhelming evidence that poor immigrant children are coming to kindergarten lacking the skills to do well in school and that this lack of readiness initiates a pattern of long-term underachievement (see Waldfogel & Lahaie, Chapter 10, this volume). Perhaps that is sufficient evidence to agree with Garcia (1997) that the "Americanization solution has not worked" (p. 11). That said, there is not complete consensus on what local, state, and federal governments should do to improve the achievement of immigrant children (Haskins, Greenberg, & Fremstad, 2004). It is not as if there have been no efforts to increase the skills and knowledge of immigrant children; but as has been discussed earlier, fewer than the expected number of immigrant children are enrolled in preschool programs and those that enroll do not seem to be benefiting to the degree hoped for. There has been an upsurge in recent attention to the needs of immigrant children by agencies such as Head Start and organizations such as the NAEYC. As well, new frameworks for addressing some of the shortcomings of prior efforts to educate young children have been articulated. An excellent, quite comprehensive resource for "how to" plan and implement culturally and linguistically competent services for young immigrant children and their families was published by Hepburn in 2004. This toolkit goes a long way in the direction of identifying the full array of materials and procedures needed by classroom teachers and administrators of early childhood programs. It remains to be seen whether these new efforts will connect with immigrant children and their families as well as work within the current political climate; but they would appear to be a move in the direction of the kind of coherence, comprehensiveness, and credibility needed for quality programs.

EPILOGUE

Every child born needs a life path that enables him or her to thrive and to function productively in the families, communities, and societies in which he or she lives. At present young immigrant children, especially those being reared in conditions of poverty, are being offered early educational opportunities to a greater extent than at any time in history. However, they are being challenged to engage the early education system with insufficient support to assure their success. On the positive side, there has been a history in programs such as Head Start of making adaptations to practices and policies so that the program more fully accomplishes its mission of serving children and families. As well, there are concerted efforts in many states to establish effective pre-K programs for children, with many states engaged in ongoing evaluations of their new programmatic efforts. One additional development at the federal level may well increase the likelihood of implementing programs that fulfill the promise of early education for immigrant children, namely, the Preschool Evaluation Research Program of the Institute for Education Sciences at the U.S. Department of Education. That said, it is incumbent upon both researchers and the education community to carefully examine the impact of early education programs on immigrant children and their families and to devise ways of more adequately serving them. As well, it remains critical for politicians and child advocates to keep focus on the issue of early education to make certain that a generation is not lost in the longer term process of integrating fully into U.S. society.

REFERENCES

Abidin, R. (1990). *Parenting Stress Index/Short form*. Charlottesville, VA: Pediatric Psychology Press.

Achenbach, T. M., & Rescorla, L. A. (2000). *Manual of ASEBA preschool forms and profiles*. Burlington: University of Vermont, Research Center for Children, Youth, and Families.

Administration for Children and Families. (2002). *Making a difference in the lives of children and families: The impacts of Early Head Start programs on infants and toddlers and their families*. Washington, DC: U.S. Department of Health and Human Services.

Bayley, N. (1993). *Bayley Scales of Infant Development, second edition: Manual*. New York: Psychological Corporation/Harcourt Brace & Company.

Bronfenbrenner, U. (1975). Is early intervention effective? In S. Friedlander, S. Sterritt, & G. Kirk (Eds.), *Exceptional infant* (Vol. 3, pp. 183–198). New York: Brunner/Mazel.

Caldwell, B. M., & Bradley, R. H. (1984). *Home Observation for Measurement of the Environment: Administration manual, revised edition*. Unpublished manuscript, University of Arkansas at Little Rock.

Currie, J., & Thomas, D. (1996). *Does Head Start help Hispanic children?*

(Working Paper Series 96-17). Santa Monica, CA: Rand Corporation, Labor and Population Program. (*ERIC Document* 404-008)

Dunn, L. M., & Dunn, L. M. (1997). *Examiner's manual for the Peabody Picture Vocabulary Test—Third Edition (PPVT-III)*. Circle Pines, MN: AM Guidance Service.

Dunn, L. M., Lugo, D. E., Padilla, E. R., & Dunn, L. M. (1986) *Test de Vocabulario en Imágenes Peabody 1986*. Circle Pines, MN: American Guidance Service.

Garcia, E. E. (1997). The education of Hispanics in early childhood: Of roots and wings. *Young Children*, *52*, 5–14.

García-Coll, C., & Szalacha, L. A. (2004). The multiple contexts of middle childhood. *The Future of Children*, *14*, 81–97.

Gormley, W. T., Gayer, T., Phillips, D., & Dawson, B. (2005). The effects of universal pre-K on cognitive development. *Developmental Psychology*, *41*, 872–884.

Gormley, W. T., & Phillips, D. (2003). *The effects of universal pre-K in Oklahoma: Research highlights and policy implications* (CROCUS Working Paper No. 2). Washington, DC: Georgetown University, Institute for Public Policy.

Gutierrez, K. D., & Garcia, E. E. (1989). Academic literacy in linguistic minority children: The connections between language, cognition and culture. *Early Child Development and Care*, *51*, 109–126.

Haskins, R., Greenberg, M., & Fremstad, S. (2004). *Federal policy for immigrant children: Room for common ground?* (Future of Children Policy Brief). Washington, DC: The Brookings Institution.

Hepburn, K. S. (2004). *Building culturally and linguistically competent services to support young children, their families, and school readiness*. Baltimore: Annie E. Casey Foundation.

Johnson, D., Walker, T., & Rodriquez, G. (1996). Teaching low-income mothers to teach their children. *Early Childhood Research Quarterly*, *11*, 101–114.

League of United Latin American Citizens. (2002). *LULAC national education agenda: Challenges and policy recommendations 2002–2003*. Washington, DC: Author.

Love, J., Kisker, E., Ross, C., Schochet, P., Brooks-Gunn, J., Boller, K., et al. (2002). *Making a difference in the lives of infants and toddlers and their families: The impacts of Early Head Start: Vol. 1. Final technical report*. Washington, DC: U.S. Department of Health and Human Services, Administration on Children and Families, Office of Planning Research and Evaluation.

Lubeck, S., DeVries, J., Nicholson, J., & Post, J. (1997). Head Start in transition. *Early Education and Development*, *8*, 219–244.

Magnusson, K. A., & Waldfogel, J. (2001). Early childhood care and education: Effects on ethnic and racial gaps in school readiness. *The Future of Children*, *15*, 169–196.

McLaughlin, H. J., Liljestrom, A., Lim, J. H., & Meyers, D. (2002). LEARN: A community study about Latino immigrants and education. *Education and Urban Society*, *34*, 212–232.

National Association for the Education of Young Children. (2003). *Early child-*

hood curriculum, assessment, and program evaluation. Available online at *pubaff@naeyc.org*.

Padilla, A. M., Lindholm, K. J., Chen, A., Duran, R., Hakuta, K., Lambert, W., et al. (1991). The English-only movement: Myths, reality, and implications for psychology. *American Psychologist*, *46*, 120–130

Perez Carreon, G., Drake, C., & Barton, A. C. (2005). The importance of presence: Immigrant parents' school engagement experiences. *American Educational Research Journal*, *42*, 465–498.

Portes, A., & Rumbaut, R. G. (2001). The forging of a new America: Lessons for theory and policy. In R. G. Rumbaut & A. Portes (Eds.), *Ethnicities: Children of immigrants in America* (pp. 301–317). Berkeley: University of California Press.

Quint, J. C., Bos, J. M., & Polit, D. F. (1997). *New Chance: Final report on a comprehensive program for young mothers in poverty and their children*. New York: Manpower Demonstration Research Corporation

Quintero, E. (1999). The new faces of Head Start: Learning from culturally diverse families. *Early Education and Development*, *10*, 475–497.

Radloff, L. S. (1977). The CES-D Scale: A self-report depression scale for research in the general population. *Applied Psychological Measurement*, *1*, 385–401.

Ramirez, M. (1989). A biocognitive-multicultural model for a pluralistic education. *Early Child Development and Care*, *51*, 129–136.

Rodriguez, M. V. (2006). Language and literacy practices in Dominican families in New York City. *Early Child Development and Care*, *176*, 171–182.

Roid, G. H., & Miller, L. J. (1997). *Examiners manual: Leiter International Performance Scale—Revised*. Chicago: Stoelting.

Rong, X. L., & Preissle, J. (1998). *Educating immigrant students*. Thousand Oaks, CA: Corwin Press.

Slavin, R. E., & Cheung, A. (2005). A synthesis of research on language or reading instruction for English language learners. *Review of Educational Research*, *75*, 247–284.

Springer, J. F., et al. (2003). *Starting Early Starting Smart final report: Summary of findings*. Washington, DC: Casey Family Programs and the U. S. Department of Health and Human Services, Substance Abuse and Mental Health Services Administration.

St. Pierre, R., Ricciutti, A., & Rimdziou, T. (2005). Effects of a family literacy program on low-literate children and their parents: Findings from an evaluation of the Even Start family literacy program. *Developmental Psychology*, *41*, 953–970.

St. Pierre, R., Ricciutti, A., Tao, F., Creps, C., Swartz, J., Lee, W., et al. (2003). *Third national Even Start evaluation: Program impacts and implications for improvement*. Cambridge, MA: Abt Associates Inc.

Takanishi, R. (2004). Leveling the playing field: Supporting immigrant children from birth to eight. *The Future of Children*, *14*, 61–79.

U.S. Department of Health and Human Services, Administration for Children and Families. (2005, May). *Head Start impact study: First year findings*. Washington, DC: Author.

West, M. M. (2001). Teaching the third culture child. *Young Children, 55*, 27–32.

Woodcock, R. W., & Mather, N. (1989, 1990). *WJ-R Tests of Achievement: Examiner's manual.* In R. W. Woodcock & M. B. Johnson, *Woodcock–Johnson Psycho-Educational Battery—Revised.* Chicago: Riverside.

Zill, N., Resenick, G., Kim, K., O'Donnell, K., Sorongon, A. McKey, R. H., et al. (2003). *Head Start FACES 2000: A whole-child perspective on program performance.* Washington, DC: U.S. Department of Health and Human Services, Administration on Child and Families.

CHAPTER 10

The Role of Preschool and After-School Policies in Improving the School Achievement of Children of Immigrants

Jane Waldfogel *and* Claudia Lahaie

Children of immigrants are the fastest growing group of children in the United States and now make up 20% of children in the United States (Hernandez, Denton, & Macartney, Chapter 1, this volume). During the last great wave of immigration in the late 1800s and early 1900s, most immigrants and their children were of European origin. Today, in contrast, Mexico is the single largest source country. Over a third of immigrant parents in the United States are from Mexico, with another sixth from other Latin American and Caribbean nations, and the remainder from a range of countries in Asia, Europe, Oceania, and Africa, as well as from Canada.

Although their source countries may have changed, immigrants today share some characteristics with their predecessors. Current immigrant populations, like immigrant groups of the past, continue to be very diverse, but on average are more likely than natives to be poor and less educated. For this reason, helping lower income and less educated immigrants to succeed in school and other domains has been an ongoing challenge (Hernandez, 2004; Portes & Rumbaut, 2001). A hundred years ago, policymakers responded to the challenge by expanding the K–12 education system, which was seen as key to helping immigrants succeed (Callahan, 1962). Yet public schools have not always been successful in equalizing achievement for immigrant populations. Although children of immigrants are very diverse, and some children of immigrants do extremely well, on average children of immigrants tend to be overrepresented among those who experience academic difficulties and failure in school (Hernandez, 1999; Kao & Tienda, 1995). Hispanic children, many of whose families have migrated from Mexico or other Latin American countries, are at particularly high risk of school failure and dropout (Fuligni & Hardway, 2004; Schneider, Martinez, & Owens, 2006; U.S. Department of Education, 2000).

A large body of work in education has considered what schools can do to help children of immigrants learn and progress (Fuligni & Hardway, 2004; Suarez-Orozco, 2001). There is also a fairly large body of research on families' role in the school achievement of children of immigrants (Fuligni & Fuligni, Chapter 13, this volume). However, less attention has been paid to out-of-school policies that might help boost the school achievement of children of immigrants.

This omission is all the more striking given what we know about the importance of out-of-school experiences for school achievement and the increasing attention such factors have been receiving from education researchers (see, e.g., Levin & Belfield, 2002). In particular, we know that large gaps in school readiness between more and less advantaged children are already present at the time of school entry and that preschool policies can effectively reduce those gaps (Magnuson & Waldfogel, 2005). We also know that how school-age children and youth spend their after-school time can have important consequences for school achievement and progression (Eccles & Gootman, 2000). Therefore, in this chapter, we consider the role that two major types of out-of-school programs—preschool programs and after-school programs—might play in promoting the school achievement of children of immigrants.

PRESCHOOL PROGRAMS AND SCHOOL READINESS FOR CHILDREN OF IMMIGRANTS

Although many children of immigrants start school with the skills and knowledge expected of entering kindergarteners, a considerable share enter school at a disadvantage. Children of immigrants often come from low-income families, who may have fewer resources to support children's learning. Half of the children of immigrants in elementary school are from low-income families (incomes below 185% of the poverty line), compared to only a third of children of native-born parents. Another common challenge is limited proficiency in English. Roughly half of the children of immigrants come from homes where a language other than English is spoken and are not able to speak English very well themselves. In addition, parents in some immigrant groups have attended less school than is customary for parents born in the United States. A third of the children of immigrants have parents with less than a high school education, compared to less than one-tenth of the children of native-born parents (Hernandez et al., Chapter 1, in this volume).

Each of these factors—low income, lack of English proficiency, and low parental education—places children at risk of lower levels of readiness for school (Levin & Belfield, 2002). Consequently, increased attention is focusing on the role that preschool might play in promoting children of immigrants' school readiness and later academic success (Brandon, 2004; Hernandez, 2004; Hernandez & Charney, 1998; Matthews & Ewen, 2006; Rumberger & Tran, 2006; Shonkoff & Phillips, 2000; Takanishi, 2004).

Preschool programs are of course very heterogeneous. The term "preschool" is used as a catch-all label for many different types of school- or center-based programs for children who have not yet begun school, including private programs based in daycare centers or nursery schools as well as the publicly funded Head Start and prekindergarten programs. Head Start, which serves low-income children and children with disabilities, is often analyzed separately from other types of preschool programs because its funding source and target population are so distinct. The Head Start program traditionally served 3- to 5-year-olds, but has recently been expanded to serve a small number of children under age 3 through the Early Head Start program. There is also a distinct Migrant Head Start program. Migrant Head Start agencies are designed to serve migrant farmworker families and therefore operate under special rules (e.g., they allow children as young as 6 weeks old, they may stay open extended hours to accommodate families' work schedules) (U.S. Department of Health and Human Services, 2006). Prekindergarten programs, funded and supervised by school departments and housed in local schools or community-based programs (depending on the state), are also often analyzed separately from other types of preschool programs due to their distinct character and funding source.

We consider two key questions with regard to preschool and the school readiness of children of immigrants (i.e., children with at least one foreign-born parent). The first concerns the enrollment of the children of immigrants in preschool programs. The second concerns the effect of that enrollment on their school readiness.

The Enrollment of Children of Immigrants in Preschool

It is well established that young children in immigrant families are more likely to be home with a parent, and less likely to participate in preschool, than children in native-born families (Brandon, 2004; Capps, Fix, Ost, Reardon-Anderson, & Passel, 2005; Crosnoe, 2004; Hernandez & Charney, 1998; Matthews & Ewen, 2006; Takanishi, 2004). Children whose parents do not speak English at home have particularly low rates of enrollment (Chiswick & DebBurman, 2006; Crosnoe, in press; Rumberger & Tran, 2006), and, if they are enrolled, are more likely to be enrolled in settings where the caregiver does not speak English (Ishizawa, 2006). In analyses of kindergarteners in the fall of 1998 (from the Early Childhood Longitudinal Study—Kindergarten Cohort [ECLS-K]), Magnuson, Lahaie, and Waldfogel (2006) found that children of immigrants were much less likely to be enrolled in a school- or center-based preschool program (46% vs. 63%) and more likely to be cared for by their parents (29% vs. 16%) than children of native-born parents.

Although it is not known why children of immigrants are less likely to be enrolled in preschool, there is some prior research on why Hispanic children, many of whom are children of immigrants, are less likely to be enrolled. Hispanic children are more likely than other children to live in low-income families and families where the mother does not work outside the home, both factors that are associated with lower rates of enrollment in school- or center-based care (Bainbridge, Meyers, Tanaka, & Waldfogel, 2005). However, even holding constant factors such as income and employment, Hispanic children are still less likely than non-Hispanic children to be enrolled in preschool (Capizzano, Adams, & Ost, 2006). One factor that may help explain these differential enrollment patterns is language. In analyses that control for factors such as family income and maternal employment, children whose families speak Spanish at home are less likely to be enrolled in preschool (Fuller, Holloway, & Liang, 1996; Liang, Fuller, & Singer, 2000; Rumberger & Tran, 2006).

Other factors that may deter the enrollment of children from immigrant families include concerns about legal status, knowledge about or availability of local programs, or cultural or linguistic preferences (Fuller et al., 1996; Matthews & Ewen, 2006). It may also be the case that selection of school- or center-based care is linked to U.S. middle-class norms about how to get children ready for school, norms that may not be shared by all immigrant groups (Liang et al., 2000).

However, it is worth noting that Hispanic children are at least as likely to attend prekindergarten programs in public schools as other children (Takanishi, 2004), a finding that suggests that when programs are explicitly labeled as school and provided free of charge, Hispanic families are likely to participate. It has also been found that language-minority children are as or more likely to attend Head Start as are children whose families speak only English at home, suggesting that when programs are publicly funded, language-minority families are as or more likely as others to participate (Ishizawa, 2006). These findings suggest that expansions in public programs might be effective in raising preschool participation rates among children of immigrants.

The Effects of Preschool on Children of Immigrants' School Readiness

Prior research on preschool (including Head Start, prekindergarten, and other types of preschool programs) suggests that it could play an important role in the school readiness of children of immigrants (see review in Magnuson et al., 2006). Although it is challenging to estimate the effects of preschool given the potential for families to select into preschool, evidence from experimental studies as well as rigorous observational studies has shown that preschool in the year or two prior to school entry improves reading and math skills, compared to the alternative of informal childcare or parental care (Shonkoff & Phillips, 2000). Gains from preschool are typically larger for economically disadvantaged children and those with lower levels of cognitive skills (Magnuson & Waldfogel, 2005; NICHD Early Child Care Research Network & Duncan, 2004). Several studies that have focused on prekindergarten programs have found them to be particularly effective in raising the reading and math readiness of children entering kindergarten (Barnett, Lamy, & Jung, 2005; Gormley & Gayer, 2005; Gormley, Gayer, Phillips, & Dawson, 2005; Magnuson, Meyers, Ruhm, & Waldfogel, 2004; Magnuson, Ruhm, & Waldfogel, 2005). Although the evidence on Head Start programs has been less conclusive, national random-assignment evaluations (Love et al., 2002; Puma, Bell, Cook, Heid, & Lopez, 2005) and econometric studies (Currie, 2001, 2005; Currie & Thomas, 1995, 1999, 2000; Garces, Thomas, & Currie, 2002) have found that Head Start also improves school readiness for the disadvantaged children it serves. Thus, there is now a large body of evidence linking preschool programs with improved academic skills.

Although children of immigrants have rarely been studied separately, prior research suggests that preschool should be at least as effective for them as for other children. For example, in studies using the ECLS-K, findings indicate that preschool programs have larger benefits for children whose parents speak a language other than English at home (a group almost entirely composed of children of immigrants) than for kindergarteners overall (Magnuson et al., 2004). Similarly, an evaluation of the Tulsa, Oklahoma, prekindergarten program found larger impacts of the program on language skills for Hispanic children (many of whom are children of immigrants) than for non-Hispanic white children (Gormley & Gayer, 2005; Gormley et al., 2005). Finally, Currie and Thomas (1999) found that Head Start significantly improved test scores and reduced grade repetition for Hispanic children (see also Lee & Burkam, 2002). In sum, it seems likely that children of immigrants should derive as much, if not more, benefit from preschool than other children (although see also some evidence reviewed in Bradley and McKelvey, Chapter 9, this volume, suggesting that children likely to come from immigrant groups [e.g., children who are Hispanic or who do not speak English as a native language] have not always benefited as much as other children from early intervention programs).

It is important to note that school readiness encompasses not just children's skill levels in academic subjects such as reading and math, but also their social and emotional functioning. A common finding in the early childhood care and education research is that children who have attended school- or center-based care, particularly if that care began at an early age and was for long hours, may enter school with higher levels of externalizing behavior problems such as aggression (see review in Belsky, 2001). The links between attending center-based care and later behavior problems tend to be more commonly found for boys than for girls, and may vary by other factors such as the child's temperament (Shonkoff & Phillips, 2000). Quality matters as well: elevated levels of behavior problems are not found for children attending model, high-quality early childhood interventions (such as Perry Preschool or Abecedarian) (Karoly et al., 1998; Karoly, Kilburn, & Cannon, 2005) but have been found for children attending more typical preschool programs (see, e.g., Loeb, Bridges, Bassok, Fuller, & Rumberger, in press; NICHD Early Child Care Research Network, 2003).

Thus, in considering the effects of preschool on school readiness, it is important to take into account possible effects on children's behavior as well as academic outcomes. If attending preschool is linked with more behavior problems for at least some children, while also being linked with better reading and math readiness for most children, then the effects of expanding the enrollment of children of immigrants could be mixed: improving school readiness in terms of reading and math skills but possibly worsening school readiness in terms of classroom behavior, particularly if that enrollment was in poor-quality care.

To date, two studies have examined the effect of preschool participation on children of immigrants' school readiness. Both take advantage of the data from the ECLS-K on a nationally representative sample of children in kindergarten in the fall of 1998. Crosnoe (in press) examined children of Mexican immigrants and found that children who had attended preschool entered school with higher levels of math skills, but children of Mexican immigrants were less likely than other children to have attended preschool. This finding suggests that increasing the preschool attendance of children of immigrants would help close the gap in math skills at school entry between children of immigrants and other children. However, Crosnoe also found that children of immigrants were advantaged by their lower levels of enrollment in preschool because children who had attended preschool entered school with higher levels of externalizing behaviors.

Magnuson and coauthors (2006) compared children who attended Head Start or other types of preschool to children who did not attend any program the year prior to kindergarten. Holding constant other child and family background characteristics, they found that attending Head Start improved the probability that children were English proficient (although the magnitude of the association was small), but did not affect reading or math scores (effect size = .02). In contrast, attending other types of preschool was not associated with English language proficiency but was associated with higher reading and math skills, even after controlling for child and family background characteristics (effect sizes = .17 for reading and .18 for math). Magnuson and colleagues looked at whether children of immigrants benefit from preschool enrollment more than other children. They found that preschool had a larger positive effect on English proficiency for children of immigrants than for other children, but attending preschool did not have significantly larger effects on reading and math for children of immigrants than for other children.

In further analyses in the Magnuson and colleagues (2006) paper, although the differences were not statistically significant, the patterns of results suggested that compared with kindergartners of native-born mothers, preschool's effects (and Head Start's effects) tended to be larger for children of immigrant mothers who spoke another language and smaller for children of immigrant mothers who spoke only English. Similarly, the effects of Head Start on English proficiency were significantly larger for children of immigrants whose mothers had less than a high school education than for children of more educated immigrant mothers. Moreover, although Head Start had no effect on math scores overall, it was associated with higher levels of math skills for children of immigrants whose mothers had less than a high school education (effect size = .23). These latter results indicate that Head Start may be particularly beneficial for children of immigrants with less educated mothers.

Magnuson and colleagues (2006) did not consider the effects of preschool on the behavioral adjustment of children of immigrants. In other work with the ECLS-K examining the overall student population, Magnuson and coauthors (2005) did find associations between attending preschool and higher levels of externalizing behavior problems at school entry. However, they also found that these effects depend on the type of preschool program attended. In particular, prekindergarten programs had larger effects on academic measures of school readiness than other types of preschool programs, and children who had attended prekindergarten in the same school as their kindergarten did not have elevated levels of behavior problems at school entry. These findings suggest that prekindergarten programs, which now serve about one in six children in the year before school entry, may be particularly good candidates for expansion.

Analyses of language-minority students, many of whom are children of immigrants, also shed some light on the role that preschool might play. Rumberger and Tran (2006) found that preschool promotes academic school readiness for all children, whether language minority or not, but, consistent with other research, they also found that attending preschool is associated with more externalizing behavior problems, for language-minority children as well as other children. (See also Bradley and McKelvey, Chapter 9, this volume, for other evidence on the effects of preschool on language-minority students.)

AFTER-SCHOOL PROGRAMS AND SCHOOL READINESS FOR CHILDREN OF IMMIGRANTS

The second major type of out-of-school program that we consider is after-school programs. As with preschool programs, after-school programs are quite varied. One point of difference is the location in which they are offered, with some programs located in schools and other programs sited elsewhere in the community. After-school programs also vary widely in their aim and focus. Although programs often have multiple objectives, some programs are focused mainly on helping children with their homework, others are more recreationally oriented, while still others may have a focus on promoting positive youth development or preventing teen pregnancy or substance abuse.

Historically, after-school programs have been heavily reliant on parent fees to cover their costs. We do not know what share of immigrant parents pay fees or how high those fees are, but we do know that about 75% of parents in the United States pay a fee when their children participate in after-school programs, and that these fees typically cover about 75% of program costs (Waldfogel, 2006). Although some subsidies or sliding-scale fee programs have been available, it has often been the case that low-income children, whose parents are less able to afford the fees, have been less likely to attend (Halpern, 1999; Vandell & Shumow, 1999). As foundations and public sources (localities, states, and the federal government) have increased their involvement in this sector, the fee structure is changing, and more low-income families are able to participate. Another recent trend is the increased share of schools offering such programs, whether they operate them directly or have them operated by community-based organizations. The share of public schools with programs that provide services to children before or after the school day increased from 16% in 1988 to nearly 50% in 2000 (Waldfogel, 2006). This trend too has increased the participation of low-income families.

In the following sections, we consider the evidence about the enrollment of children of immigrants in after-school programs, and the effects of such programs on their school achievement.

The Enrollment of Children of Immigrants in After-School Programs

Many studies have found that children from racial and ethnic minority groups are less likely to participate in after-school programs than non-Hispanic white children (Brown & Evans, 2005; Fuligni & Hardway, 2004; Little & Lauver, 2005), but relatively little is known about whether children of immigrants participate in after-school programs at the same rate as other children. In estimates from the ECLS-K for the spring of kindergarten, Lahaie (2006) found that children of immigrants were significantly less likely to attend a center-based after-school program than children of natives (their participation rates were 11.5% and 18.5%, respectively). They were also significantly less likely to participate in a host of after-school activities such as lessons, clubs, or athletics, although they were more likely to take music lessons. We were not able to locate a study using nationally representative data that compared the after-school arrangements of children of immigrants and children of natives among older school-age children. Studies of language-minority children, many of whom are likely to be children of immigrants, indicate that language-minority children in elementary and middle school are more likely to be in self-care (looking after themselves without adult supervision) after school than are non-language-minority children (Thurlow, Duran, Kato, & Albus, 2006).

As funding for after-school programs increases, gaps in participation between children of immigrants and children of natives may be narrowing. One of the largest funding streams for after-school programs is the 21st Century Community Learning Centers (21st CCLC) program, which began as a demonstration program with $1 million in funding from the U.S. Department of Education in 1997, had grown to $40 million by 1998, and was funded at a level of $1 billion in 2002 (Waldfogel, 2006). Located in elementary and middle schools, 21st CCLC programs are meant to be educational in focus and must include an educational component such as help with homework or the provision of tutoring. The evidence from the national evaluation of the 21st CCLC program (James-Burdumy et al., 2005), discussed in more detail below, suggests that school-based after-school programs have more impact on increasing the participation of Hispanic children than they do on increasing the participation of non-Hispanic white or black children. This evidence is consistent with what we saw in the preschool arena: when publicly funded and school-based programs are offered, Hispanic children are as likely, or more likely, than other children to take advantage of them. Thus, it seems likely that if this sector were expanded further, more Hispanic children would participate. Whether other children of immigrants would participate as well is unclear from the present research, and is a question that should be addressed in future research.

The Effects of After-School Programs on the School Achievement of Children of Immigrants

Although it is generally recognized that high-quality after-school programs can promote school achievement and other positive outcomes for children and youth (Eccles & Gootman, 2000; Fuligni & Hardway, 2004; Mahoney, Lord, & Carryl, 2005; Roth & Brooks-Gunn, 2003), the wide variety of after-school programs makes it difficult to generalize about the effects of such programs. A further challenge is that many studies of program effectiveness have been observational and thus have not been able to adequately address the possibility that their estimates of effectiveness may be biased by differences between children who attend and children who do not attend such programs (this is the well-known "selection bias" problem). In this regard, the results from some recent randomized evaluations, and other evaluation studies that have taken special steps to address selection bias, are particularly informative.

Kane (2004) reviews the results of four such studies: the national evaluation of the 21st Century Community Learning Centers; the evaluation of The After-School Corporation in New York City; the evaluation of extended-service schools in six cities; and the evaluation of the San

Francisco Beacons Initiative (see also Blau & Currie, 2006; Granger & Kane, 2004). In none of the four studies were there statistically significant effects on children's school achievement after 1 year of participation. Needless to say, this is a disappointing conclusion, although, as Kane points out, we need to be realistic as to how large we expect the effects of a part-time after-school intervention to be, particularly given the low attendance rates in many programs. Kane also found some positive findings related to school achievement: some of the programs examined were effective in promoting parental involvement, student engagement in school, or student commitment to homework.

Is there any evidence that after-school programs are more helpful in raising school achievement for children of immigrants than for other children? Unfortunately, prior studies of after-school programs have not directly addressed this question. Studies that have examined differences by other characteristics that may be related to immigrant status offer some indirect evidence. For instance, studies have found that low-income children benefit more than other children from attending well-implemented programs on a regular basis (Mahoney et al., 2005).

There is some evidence that Hispanic children may benefit more from after-school programs than other children. In the 21st CCLC evaluation, in results analyzing children separately by race–ethnicity, it emerges that the offer of the after-school program significantly increased the share of students spending time at an after-school program only among Hispanic children: compared to the control group who were not offered the chance to participate, the share of Hispanic children at school or some other place for activities at least 3 days a week increased by 14.5% (in contrast to no significant impact on non-Hispanic white or black children) (James-Burdumy et al., 2005, Table D 1b). Moreover, being in the treatment group increased Hispanic parents' involvement at school, raising the share of parents who attended a parent teacher organization meeting at least three times a year by 24%, and raising the share of parents attending an after-school event by 15%. Again, these positive impacts were seen only for families of Hispanic children, and not for non-Hispanic white or black children (James-Burdumy et al., 2005, Table D 4b). Also relevant to the question of differential impact is evidence from LA's BEST program. This long-running Los Angeles after-school program serves a diverse population of children, about a third of whom have limited English proficiency. Participation in the program has been linked to better academic achievement and better social functioning, with larger effects for limited English proficiency students than for other children (Huang et al., 2005).

Other evidence of possible differential effects for language-minority children comes from a study by Thurlow and coauthors (2006), who used the National Household Education Survey (NHES) to look at language-minority children's participation in before- and after-school programs and the effects of that participation on their school performance. Compared to non-language-minority children, they found that there were some significant differences in how participating in before- and after-school programs affected grades for language-minority children. Although participation was associated with better grades for both groups, this effect was slightly weaker for language-minority children than for non-language-minority children. At the same time, participating in an out-of-school program appeared to be less beneficial for language-minority children than for non-language-minority children in terms of its impact on behavior problems, with participation associated with slightly lower levels of problems for non-language-minority children versus slightly higher levels of problems for language-minority children. It is important to note that program quality was not controlled for in this study. Thus, it may be that language-minority children benefited less from their participation because they attended poorer quality programs than other children.

In conclusion, although the evidence base on after-school programs is relatively weak, the evidence we do have suggests that such programs may offer promise for raising school achievement, although it is not certain whether children of immigrants would benefit more (or less) from such programs than other children. An overriding concern is that such programs can only benefit children if they have access to them and attend them. Thus, an important priority for future research is to learn more about patterns of attendance in after-school programs, and specifically to learn whether children of immigrants are attending at rates similar to other children, and what types of programs they are attending.

CONCLUSIONS

What role do preschool and after-school programs play in boosting the school achievement of children of immigrants, and is there scope for them to play a greater role in the future? Although this question is hard to answer conclusively based on current evidence, the evidence we do have suggests that there is certainly an important role to be played by preschool programs in helping to narrow the gaps in school readiness between children of immigrants and other children. Whether children of immigrants might also benefit from expanded access to after-school programs is harder to determine. We do not know the extent to which children of immigrants are underenrolled at this point. Nor do we know with certainty how much they might benefit if they were enrolled. This uncertainty reflects both the limited state of knowledge about after-school programs and the lack of attention that children of immigrants have received in this area.

Thus, there are many fruitful directions for future research: further studies of the factors affecting the enrollment of children of immigrants in out-of-school programs, with particular attention to after-school programs, as well as further studies of the effects of out-of-school programs on children of immigrants, again with particular attention to after-school programs. But even the limited knowledge we have to date provides some direction for policy. There is clearly a case to be made for making preschool more widely available to children of immigrants. The research to date also suggests that if children of immigrants are to take up preschool places, they are most likely to do so if those places are in publicly provided programs such as Head Start and prekindergarten.

ACKNOWLEDGMENTS

We are grateful to Wen-Jui Han and Katherine Magnuson for many helpful conversations, and to the volume editors for helpful comments. We would also like to thank Jacquelynne Eccles, Andrew Fuligni, Joseph Mahoney, and Ed Seidman for their help in locating studies of after-school programs. Finally, we gratefully acknowledge funding support from the Russell Sage Foundation and the John D. and Catherine T. MacArthur Foundation.

REFERENCES

Bainbridge, J., Meyers, M., Tanaka, S., & Waldfogel, J. (2005). Who gets an early education?: Family income and the gaps in enrollment of 3–5 year olds from 1968–2000. *Social Science Quarterly, 86*, 724–745.

Barnett, W. S., Lamy, C., & Jung, K. (2005). *The effects of state prekindergarten programs on young children's school readiness in five states*. Available online from the National Institute for Early Education Research at *www.nieer.org*

Belsky, J. (2001). Developmental risk (still) associated with early child care. *Journal of Child Psychology and Psychiatry, 42*, 845–860.

Blau, D., & Currie, J. (2006). Pre-school, day care, and after-school care: Who's minding the kids? In E. Hanushek & F. Welch (Eds.), *Handbook on the economics of education*. Amsterdam: North-Holland.

Brandon, P. (2004). The child care arrangements of preschool age children in immigrant families in the United States. *International Migration Review, 42*, 65–88.

Brown, R., & Evans, W. (2005). Developing school connectedness in diverse youth through extracurricular programming. *Prevention Researcher, 12*, 14–17.

Callahan, R. (1962). *Education and the cult of efficiency.* Chicago: University of Chicago Press.

Capizzano, J., Adams, G., & Ost, J. (2006). *Caring for children of color: The child care patterns of white, black, and Hispanic children under 5* (Occasional Paper No. 72). Washington, DC: Urban Institute.

Capps, R., Fix, M., Ost, J., Reardon-Anderson, J., & Passel, J. (2005). *The health and well-being of young children of immigrants.* Washington, DC: Urban Institute.

Chiswick, B., & DebBurman, N. (2006). Preschool enrollment: An analysis by immigrant generation. *Social Science Research, 35,* 60–87.

Crosnoe, R. (in press). Child care and the early educational experiences of children from Mexican immigrant families. *International Migration Review.*

Currie, J. (2001). Early childhood education programs. *Journal of Economic Perspectives, 15,* 213–238.

Currie, J. (2005). Health disparities and gaps in school readiness. *The Future of Children, 15,* 117–138.

Currie, J., & Thomas, D. (1995). Does Head Start make a difference? *American Economic Review, 85,* 341–364.

Currie, J., & Thomas, D. (1999). Does Head Start help Hispanic children? *Journal of Public Economics, 74,* 235–262.

Currie, J., & Thomas, D. (2000). School quality and the long-term effects of Head Start. *Journal of Human Resources, 35,* 755–774.

Eccles, J., & Gootman, J. (Eds.). (2000). *Community programs to promote youth development.* Washington, DC: National Academy Press.

Fuligni, A., & Hardway, C. (2004). Preparing diverse adolescents for the transition to adulthood. *The Future of Children, 14,* 99–119.

Fuller, B., Holloway, S., & Liang, X. (1996). Family selection of child care centers: The influence of household support, ethnicity, and parental practices. *Child Development, 67,* 3320–3337.

Garces, E., Thomas, D., & Currie, J. (2002). Long-term effects of Head Start. *American Economic Review, 92,* 999–1012.

Gormley, W., & Gayer, T. (2005). Promoting school readiness in Oklahoma: An evaluation of Tulsa's pre-K program. *Journal of Human Resources, 40,* 533–558.

Gormley, W., Gayer, T., Phillips, D., & Dawson, B. (2005). The effects of universal pre-K on cognitive development. *Developmental Psychology, 41,* 872–884.

Granger, R., & Kane, T. (2004). *Improving the quality of after-school programs.* New York: William T. Grant Foundation.

Halpern, R. (1999). After-school programs for low-income children: Promise and challenges. *The Future of Children, 9,* 81–95.

Hernandez, D. (Ed.). (1999). *Children of immigrants: Health, adjustment, and public assistance.* Washington, DC: National Academy of Sciences Press.

Hernandez, D. (2004). Demographic change and the life circumstances of immigrant families. *The Future of Children, 14,* 17–48.

Hernandez, D., & Charney, E. (1998). Executive summary. In D. Hernandez & E. Charney (Eds.), *From generation to generation: The health and well-being of children in immigrant families* (pp. 1–16). Washington, DC: National Academy Press.

Huang, D., Kim, K. S., Marshall, A., & Perez, P. (2005). *Keeping kids in school: An LA's BEST example. A study examining the long-term impact of LA's Best on students' dropout rates.* Los Angeles: National Center for Research on Evaluation, Standards, and Student Testing, University of California at Los Angeles.

Ishizawa, H. (2006). *Child care arrangements of language-minority children: Care provider's language use.* Unpublished manuscript, Department of Sociology, University of Illinois at Urbana–Champaign.

James-Burdumy, S., Dynarski, M., Moore, M., Deke, J., Mansfield, W., & Pistorino, C. (2005). *When schools stay open late: The national evaluation of the 21st Century Community Learning Centers program: Final report.* Washington, DC: Institute of Education Sciences, U.S. Department of Education. Available online at *www.ed.gov/ies/ncee*

Kane, T. (2004). *The impact of after-school programs: Interpreting the results of four recent evaluations.* New York: William T. Grant Foundation.

Kao, G., & Tienda, M. (1995). Optimism and achievement: The educational performance of immigrant youth. *Social Science Quarterly, 76*, 1–19.

Karoly, L., Greenwood, P., Everingham, S., Hoube, J., Kilburn, R., Rydell, P., et al. (1998). *Investing in our children: What we know and don't know about the costs and benefits of early childhood interventions.* Santa Monica, CA: RAND Corporation.

Karoly, L., Kilburn, M. R., & Cannon, J. S. (2005). *Early childhood interventions: Proven results, future promise.* Santa Monica, CA: RAND Corporation.

Lahaie, C. (2006). *Parental involvement and the school achievement of children of immigrants.* Unpublished doctoral dissertation, Columbia University School of Social Work, New York.

Lee, V., & Burkam, T. (2002). *Inequality at the starting gate.* Washington, DC: Economic Policy Institute.

Levin, H., & Belfield, C. (2002). Families as contractual partners in education. *UCLA Law Review, 49*, 1799–1824.

Liang, X., Fuller, B., & Singer, J. (2000). Ethnic differences in child care selection: The influence of family structure, parental practices, and home language. *Early Childhood Research Quarterly, 15*, 357–384.

Little, P., & Lauver, S. (2005). Engaging adolescents in out-of-school time programs: Learning what works. *Prevention Researcher, 12*, 7–10.

Loeb, S., Bridges, M., Bassok, D., Fuller, B., & Rumberger, R. (in press). How much is too much?: The influence of preschool centers on children's social and cognitive development. *Economics of Education Review.*

Love, J., Eliason-Kisker, E., Ross, C., Schochet, P. Z., Brooks-Gunn, J., & Paulsell, D. (2002). *Making a difference in the lives of infants and toddlers and their families: The impacts of Early Head Start.* Washington, DC: Administration for Children and Families, U.S. Department of Health and Human Services.

Magnuson, K., Lahaie, C., & Waldfogel, J. (2006). Preschool and school readiness of children of immigrants. *Social Science Quarterly, 87*, 1241–1262.

Magnuson, K., Meyers, M., Ruhm, C., & Waldfogel, J. (2004). Inequality in preschool education and school readiness. *American Educational Research Journal, 41*, 115–157.

Magnuson, K., Ruhm, C., & Waldfogel, J. (2005). *Does prekindergarten improve school preparation and performance?* Mimeo, University of Wisconsin–Madison, University of North Carolina–Greensboro, and Columbia University, New York.

Magnuson, K., & Waldfogel, J. (2005). Early childhood care and education: Effects on ethnic and racial gaps in school readiness. *The Future of Children, 15*, 169–196.

Mahoney, J., Lord, H., & Carryl, E. (2005). An ecological analysis of after-school program participation and the development of academic performance and motivational attributes for disadvantaged children. *Child Development, 76*, 811–825.

Matthews, H., & Ewen, D. (2006). *Reaching all children?: Understanding early care and education participation among immigrant families.* Washington, DC: Center for Law and Social Policy.

NICHD Early Child Care Research Network. (2003). Does amount of time spent in child care predict socioemotional adjustment during the transition to kindergarten? *Child Development, 74*, 976–1005.

NICHD Early Child Care Research Network & Duncan, G. (2003). Modeling the impacts of child care quality on children's preschool cognitive development. *Child Development, 74*, 1454–1475.

Portes, A., & Rumbaut, R. (2001). *Legacies: The story of the immigrant second generation.* Berkeley: University of California Press.

Puma, M., Bell, S., Cook, R., Heid, C., & Lopez, M. (2005). *Head Start impact study: First year findings.* Washington, DC: Administration for Children and Families, U.S. Department of Health and Human Services.

Roth, J., & Brooks-Gunn, J. (2003). Youth development programs: Risk, prevention, and policy. *Journal of Adolescent Health, 32*, 170–182.

Rumberger, R., & Tran, L. (2006). *Preschool participation and the cognitive and social development of language minority students.* Unpublished manuscript, Center for the Study of Evaluation, University of California, Los Angeles.

Schneider, B., Martinez, S., & Owens, A. (2006). Barriers to educational opportunity for Hispanics in the U.S. In M. Tienda & F. Mitchell (Eds.), *Hispanics and the future of America* (pp. 179–227). Washington, DC: National Academy Press.

Shonkoff, J. P., & Phillips, D. A. (Eds.). (2000). *From neurons to neighborhoods: The science of early childhood development.* Washington, DC: National Academy Press.

Suarez-Orozco, C. (2001). Understanding and serving the children of immigrants. *Harvard Educational Review, 71*, 579–589.

Takanishi, R. (2004). Leveling the playing field: Supporting immigrant children from birth to eight. *The Future of Children, 14*, 61–80.

Thurlow, M. L., Duran, R. P., Kato, K., & Albus, D. (2006). *Before- and after-school care arrangements and activities of school-age language minority children.* Unpublished manuscript, National Center on Educational Outcomes and University of California, Santa Barbara.

U.S. Department of Education. (2000). *Status and trends in the education of Hispanics.* Available online at *http://nces.ed.gov*

U.S. Department of Health and Human Services, Administration for Children and Families. (2006). *Head Start fact sheet*. Available online at *http://www.acf.hhs.gov*

Vandell, D. L., & Shumow, L. (1999). After-school child care programs. *The Future of Children*, 9, 64–80.

Waldfogel, J. (2006). *What children need*. Cambridge, MA: Harvard University Press.

CHAPTER 11

Cultural and Religious Contexts of Parenting by Immigrant South Asian Muslim Mothers

Fariyal Ross-Sheriff, M. Taqi Tirmazi,
and Tasanee R. Walsh

Despite the increasing numbers and relative economic well-being and achievements of Muslim immigrant families in the United States, little is known about their culture, religious distinctiveness, and multigenerational acculturation processes. Even less is known about how Muslims socialize their children to integrate within U.S. society, which may discriminate against Muslims. Extant literature focusing on the socialization of Muslim girls by their mothers is limited. The present chapter addresses this gap in knowledge and assesses the socialization of daughters by South Asian immigrant Muslim mothers in the United States by employing a qualitative study.

As a backdrop for understanding the socialization of Muslim mothers, we first present a brief historical background, including religious and cultural contexts, and circumstances facing Muslim immigrant families in the United States. Second, we provide a literature review on South Asian Muslims, the target group for the chapter. Third, we discuss our recent qualitative research study on socialization practices of South Asian mothers. In our research we examined mothers' aspirations for their daughters, the challenges they face, and the strategies they employ to pass down their religious and cultural traditions. We end the chapter with a presentation of implications for social work practice and policy.

HISTORICAL BACKGROUND

Muslims in the United States come from all over the world and represent diverse ethnicities, nationalities, and cultures. Maloof and Ross-Sheriff (2003) note that Muslims have been part of the U.S. population since long before the country was founded. Indeed, there is evidence that suggests that Muslims were present in Spanish Colonial America before 1550. Through forced migration, a significant number of African Muslims were brought to the United States as slaves (Maloof & Ross-Sheriff, 2003; Smith, 1999).

Historically, Muslims have migrated to the United States in a series of distinguishable periods often referred to as "waves." The first wave of immigration occurred during the post–Civil War period; the second wave took place at the end of World War I; the third wave occurred from 1947 to 1960; and the fourth and most recent wave of Muslim immigration occurred after the 1965 immigration act (Smith, 1999). This last wave of Muslim migration has occurred due to several reasons including changes in the immigration act of 1965 that resulted in the abolition of race and ethnic quotas for immigration and refugee admissions post-1967. Scholars have estimated that more than half of the immigrants who came to the United States as a result of the changes in the 1965 immigration laws have been Muslims (Maloof & Ross-Sheriff, 2003; Smith, 1999).

DEMOGRAPHIC PROFILE, LOCATION, AND POPULATION CONCENTRATIONS

Numerous scholars believe that Islam is one of the fastest growing religions in the United States (Haddad, 1997; Maloof & Ross-Sheriff, 2003; Smith, 1999) and cite estimates of Muslims residing in the United States to be between 1.9 and 8 million (Bagby, Perl, & Froehle, 2001; Ba-Yunus & Siddiqui, 1998; Council on American-Islamic Relations [CAIR], 2001; Eck, 1997; Kosmin, Mayer, & Keysar, 2001; Power, 1998; Smith, 1999; Strum, 2003).

Muslims in America belong to over 75 different ethnicities and nationalities. Expressions of religious practices within Islam are diverse (Maloof & Ross-Sheriff, 2003). Like other religious groups, Muslim Americans practice and "express their faith through discourses that range the spectrum from liberal to conservative. Some of these discourses may stress outward visible dimensions of faith such as rituals and the law (shari'a) while others may stress spiritual and mystical aspects" (Maloof & Ross-Sheriff, 2003, p. 4). To understand Muslim immigrants in the

United States, the reader is cautioned to appreciate their diversity, and not to consider them as a homogenous, unidimensional group.

According to the Muslim in American Public Square (MAPS) project data, 36% of Muslims in the United States were born in the United States while 64% were foreign-born (Bukhari, 2001). These estimates are comparable to those reported by Haddad and Lummis (1987) who state that two-thirds of the Muslims in the United States are immigrants and their descendents. According to Denny (1995), most Muslims in the United States come from the Middle East, North Africa, and South and Southeast Asia where Islam is the predominant religion. Immigrant Muslims in the United States are divided among three major ethnic groups: 32–33% are South Asians, 25–26% are Arabs, and 20–30% are African Americans (Bukhari, 2001; CAIR, 2003). Immigration of a record number of South Asians since the early 1990s has increased the immigrant population that is the focus of this chapter. This group of Muslims is predominantly composed of first-generation immigrants.

Bukhari (2001) suggests that the Muslim community is fairly young, educated, and prosperous. According to the MAPS project, 75% of Muslims are younger than 50 years of age, 58% are college graduates in various professional fields, and 50% have an annual household income of over $50,000 (Bukhari, 2001). Most Muslims in the United States live in major cosmopolitan areas: 20% in California, 16% in New York, 8% in Illinois, 4% in New Jersey and Indiana, and 3% in other states such as Michigan, Virginia, Texas, and Ohio (American Muslim Council, 1992). According to the Arab American Institute (2003), the average household size of a Muslim family in the United States is 4.9 people. It is estimated that 5% of students in the public school system are Muslim (Carter & El Hindi, 1999).

South Asian Muslims are people from India, Pakistan, and Bangladesh (for historical background, refer to Ross-Sheriff & Husain, 2004, p. 164). South Asians are the largest group of Muslims in the United States, with over 30% of the total Muslim population (Strum, 2003); estimates of the South Asian Muslim population in the United States range from 1.4 to 2.4 million (Ba-Yunus & Siddiqui, 1998; Eck, 1997). South Asian Muslim immigration to the United States is a fairly new phenomenon. South Asian Muslims migrated in small numbers during the early 1900s but the majority of South Asian Muslims migrated after the immigration act of 1965 (Ahmed, Kaufman, & Naim, 1996).

Scholars explain that a significant number of the South Asian Muslims who migrated after 1965 were well-educated professionals with specialized skills (Ahmed et al., 1996; Haddad, 1997). In many cases the South Asian Muslim immigrants who arrived during the 1960s have sponsored their relatives, who comprise the most recent arrivals (Balgopal, 2000; Ross-Sheriff & Husain, 2001). This later group of sponsored immigrants is more diverse, and includes rural, somewhat less educated, and less affluent families (Ross-Sheriff & Husain, 2004).

LITERATURE REVIEW

While the body of literature on children of immigrants continues to grow (Alvarez, 1992; Portes & Rumbaut, 2001; Portes & Zhou, 1993; Ross-Sheriff, 2001; Rumbaut, 1995, 1996; Rumbaut & Cornelius, 1995; Suarez-Orozco & Suarez-Orozco, 2001), there is a paucity of literature on Muslim immigrant women or on socialization of immigrant children. Although there has been some research on Muslims in the United States, research that seeks to explore, describe, and explain the adaptation and experience of Muslims in the United States remains limited. Recent events such as the tragedy of September 11, 2001; protests in France; caricatures of the Prophet Mohammad appearing in international media sources; the wars in Iraq and Lebanon; as well as other incidents of victimization of Muslims in the United States and allegations of Muslims' perpetration of crime, have brought greater attention to this understudied U.S. immigrant population.

To date, a few studies have attempted to understand the adaptation experiences of Muslim youth. Barazangi (1996) found that Muslim youth in the United States participated in Western culture to a greater extent than their parents and faced the need to accommodate potentially conflicting points of view. Parents and youth have significantly different levels and natures of perception regarding their experience in the United States (Barazangi, 1996). In an illustrative case vignette related to ethics and values for social work practice, Ross-Sheriff and Husain (2001) discovered parent–child conflict due to Pakistani Muslim parents' misunderstanding of their adolescent daughters' behavior, which was age-appropriate in the United States. This confusion was further complicated by the misinterpretation of the parents' cultural values on the part of the social worker involved. Given the significant effects of socialization during the teenage years, many Muslim parents fear that their children will be socialized into Western secular values that will do little to advance their child's well-being in this world or the next (Smith, 1999).

Literature on Muslim youth in Australia suggests that they are less likely to assimilate than youth from other religious backgrounds (Cox, 1983). Ghuman (1997), in a study conducted in British public schools, found that Muslim adolescents were much more likely to retain their own values than Hindu or Sikh adolescents. Simmons and Allah (1994), in a study conducted in Britain, found that Saudi adolescents were more concerned with Islamic values in comparison to British adolescents, who were concerned with secular themes such as idolizing and meeting famous people. A study of primarily second-generation North American Muslim youth discovered that Muslim youth strongly desire to retain their Islamic values (Barazangi, 1991). Finally, another study conducted in the United States found that Muslims born or raised in the United States identify with the cultural heritage of their immigrant parents which, in turn, impacts the decisions they make in regard to marriage (Al-Johar, 2005).

Muslim youth face barriers in their educational settings in which, often times, there is a lack of cultural sensitivity on the part of mainstream service providers. A few scholars have described the challenges faced by Muslim youth in the public school system. Practicing Islam in the public school system, where secular discourse predominates, can lead to conflict for Muslim youth (Carter & El Hindi, 1999; Shaikh, 1995). Mahmoud (1996) explains that it is difficult for Muslim youth to pray and fast during the month of Ramadan if schools are not cooperative. Shaikh (1995) reports that young Muslim adolescent females prefer to wear sweat pants and long-sleeved T-shirts instead of shorts and tank tops in physical education classes. Mahmoud suggests that many adolescent Muslim females are ridiculed because they choose to wear a hijab, which covers their forehead and hair. In addition, many immigrant Muslim youth encounter conflicts because of differences in sexual values (Shaikh, 1995). U.S. secular dating habits are incompatible with Islamic values and many immigrant Muslim youths feel pressured to conform to secular practices. Sex education may conflict with Islamic beliefs regarding modesty (Hodge, 2002). Although behaviors such as dating and premarital sex may be viewed as normal from a Western lens, they are considered inappropriate in many Muslim and immigrant communities. The Arab American Institute (2003) reports that many Muslim youth have been harassed because of their religious beliefs and stereotypes that have been perpetuated by the media.

Livengood and Stodolska (2004) examined the treatment that U.S. Muslims were subjected to over a 12-month period following the events of September 11, 2001, its impact on their leisure behavior, their responses to discrimination, and their strategies used to overcome obstacles to their leisure participation. They found that Muslims experienced discrimination, and that most discrimination was of a nonviolent nature including bad looks, verbal abuse, and social isolation. They restricted their leisure activities and employed strategies such as being vigilant, being conscious of their surroundings, walking in groups, and and blending in.

While the above study and other anecdotal reports provide information about harassment of Muslim youth and strategies employed by them, especially females and their families, there is hardly any research on the socialization of Muslim girls by their mothers. Research studies on the socialization of South Asian youth in general and South Asian girls (who share cultural background with South Asian Muslims) in particular may provide some insights.

SOCIALIZATION OF SOUTH ASIAN GIRLS

Research on South Asians, regardless of religious affiliation, points toward the importance of the parent–child relationship. Most of the research is descriptive and focuses on acculturation and adaptation of immigrant South Asian families, parental expectations of children, and disparity in the rates of adaptation of parents and children. Baptiste (2005) and Farver, Narang, and Bhadha (2002) found that divergent acculturation modes between parents and children lead to unhealthy family cohesion. South Asian immigrant parents face difficulties in parenting their children in the United States because of the different filial and cultural expectations for children in the United States compared to South Asia. In addition, South Asian parenting is made more challenging by the disparity in the rates between the adaptation (Baptiste, 2005) and acculturation of parents and their children (Bhattacharya, 2002). South Asian parents express several common concerns such as loss of children to U.S. culture, loss of parental authority over children, loss of authority to discipline children according to native customs, loss of authority to select children's mates, and loss of face within the East Indian community because of children's "out of culture" behavior (Baptiste, 2005). In South Asian families parent–child relationships are commonly hierarchical, with parent authority at the top, flowing down to their children (Baptiste, 2005). Although deemed to be authoritative, South Asian parents' primary concern is in rearing their children toward a healthy adulthood.

Identity formation among South Asian immigrants is challenged and complicated when their cultural values and beliefs drastically differ from the U.S. host culture (Farver et al., 2002). Farver and colleagues (2002) discovered that parents who had separation and marginalized acculturation modes (restricting most interactions to those with individuals and families from their culture of origin or limiting interactions with any group) reported higher family conflict than did families that selected assimilation or integration modes (interacting with the host culture and adopting the values of the host culture totally or maintaining the culture of origin while still adopting the host culture).

In a qualitative study of socialization of South Asian children, Maiter and George (2003) found that character formation and identity formation are the key goals of parenting for South Asian mothers. The method for character formation was through teaching their children certain personal qualities that are a part of their "internalized cultural values system" and "contribute to the formation of character." The personal qualities instilled by the mothers included "respect for the elders, modesty, humility, hard work, perseverance and having a disciplined life, which, from their perspective, was most likely to be attained through adherence to religion" (p. 420). Though they had concerns about sex and health education in the curriculum of the schools their children attended and about the Canadian social behaviors which they found different and challenging, they were flexible about giving permission to their children to participate in classes and focused on teaching them about their own culture and values. They believed in the importance of providing knowledge about their culture and imparting cultural values, which would result in the development of identity. They achieved this through personal examples, providing guidelines, and setting boundaries, through participation in religious and cultural activities, and through intervention as well as "active participation in the lives of their children even into adulthood" (p. 424). Immigrant South Asian Muslim mothers in the United States are likely to have similar common concerns as those expressed by South Asian Canadian mothers in the study reported above. However, they are likely to have more serious challenges and concerns arising from the environmental and social stressors for Muslims post-9/11.

Information for this chapter was obtained through a qualitative study of socialization of adolescent daughters by first-generation immigrant South Asian Muslim mothers. The major objective of the research was to learn about the goals of mothers for their adolescent daughters, their hopes and aspirations, their fears, and strategies they planned to use to meet their goals for their daughters.

Data Source and Methods for Data Analysis

In-depth interviews were conducted with 10 middle-class Muslim mothers on socialization of their daughters between the ages of 16 and 23. The interviews were 2–3 hours long and based on thematically grouped open-ended questions. The interviews were conducted by the authors in English in combination with Gujarati or Urdu, the mother tongues of the women who were interviewed. Though findings of such studies as ours may be detailed and complete, they should be used with caution to generalize to other Muslim population or even to South Asian Muslim women. However, the findings can contribute toward knowledge and theory building, especially toward providing a highly nuanced understanding for social work professionals who are faced with providing services to this population.

Each case study was analyzed through open coding and the identification of themes (Denzin & Lincoln, 2003). Thematic analyses were conducted separately for each case study and then a comparison was made between cases studies to uncover like themes. The findings represent four major themes that were identified across most of the cases studies. Data were examined further to uncover subthemes within each of the four major themes.

Reliability checks were conducted with the participants to verify whether the findings reflected their understanding of their socialization process and methods. The participants indicated that the major themes captured their lived experiences.

Findings

Muslim women had come to the United States in an effort to improve the quality of life, their families' economic well-being, and their children's education. The mothers' level of education ranged from less than high school education to postbaccalaureate. Eight out of 10 were employed or involved in family businesses. However, except for two, all those who were employed at the time of the interview had stopped working at some point between the period their daughters were born and when they were in high school. All of them identified themselves as women living in two-parent families with adequate resources as well as support from their husbands, extended family, and friends in the socialization of their children.

The goals and aspiration for the daughters can be summarized in three categories: development of a positive identity as a Muslim, a south Asian, a female and future family member; high level of education and skills to achieve self-sufficiency, if needed; and capacity to navigate an uncertain environment. Related socialization strategies were (1) promoting a worldview and a lifestyle that reflects Islamic values, (2) promoting values reflecting high achievement, and (3) protecting daughters from negative forces in U.S. society including risky behaviors, fear about Islamophobia, and resultant harassment of Muslims. They all had challenges with their daughters and were aware of challenges their daughters faced as a result of conflicting expectations of family and peers. They expressed concerns and fears about the harassment of their daughters and discussed how they "protected" their daughters. While there were differences in the practices followed by their daughters such as choice of clothing (wearing a head scarf or not), selection of friends (all Muslims vs. friends from different religious and cultural groups), and selection of location of college environments (close to home vs. away from home), all expected their daughters to practice Islam and appropriate behaviors such as modesty in dressing, respect for self and others through personal behaviors and relationships, and discretion in decisions that would reflect the family "name" through their *adab* (code of behavior; see Metcalf, 1984).

The strategies they used to socialize their daughters included articulation of their expectations to their daughters, personal examples, involvement in their daughters' educational programs whenever possible, education and training, persistent vigilance, promotion of family rituals, family gatherings, and participation in activities and programs of their religious community as well as communities of countries of origin. They had to adapt their socialization strategies to reflect the U.S. culture and environment, which were in many cases different from the socialization strategies used by their mothers. They acknowledged that they listened to, or had to listen to, their daughters, kept open communication, and learned a lot from their daughters. The findings of the study are presented below under three themes reflecting the voices of the mothers.

Promoting a Worldview and a Lifestyle That Reflect Islamic Values

The mothers talked at length about developing an understanding about Islam, Islamic practices, lifestyle, and values. They were aware of and had faced challenges instilling and forming an Islamic worldview in an environment that does not have extended family support and, at times, denigrates Islam. They had to work hard at it. Salima[1] stated it as follows:

> "We had my mother's and my father's family and uncles, aunts, and cousins in the city where I grew up. In addition, in the community we grew up in, our neighbors, our friends, teachers, and workers respected Muslims or were Muslims. So, my parents did not have to worry about teaching me and my siblings about Islam. We lived Islam; we breathed Islam; we learned about Islam and were proud to be identified as Muslims. Here, we do not have close family where we live. Though we have good neighbors, they know little about Islam. My daughter's teachers, counselors, and friends in school are all non-Muslims and do not know much about Islam. So, I have to make special efforts to make sure that my children learn about Islam. How will they develop respect for their religion, pride about their religion, and a Muslim identity unless I make a special effort, and unless I counteract negative messages they are getting from TV and radio?"

All the mothers used conscious strategies to develop positive worldviews about Islam by participation in prayer and religious activities organized by the local mosques for young people. Six of the 10 mothers indicated that they had quit their jobs when their first child was born and did not work outside the home again until their children entered primary school. They socialized with coreligionists, promoted and facilitated participation of daughters in religious education classes where available, and developed religious education classes. They offered their services as religious education teachers or teacher assistants. When their daughters were in secondary school, they promoted the friendship and socialization of their daughters with their coreligionists, specifically female friends. Two mothers, on the other hand, promoted friendships across religious and national groups. All the women felt that the best way to teach about their practice of faith is through personal example, and so they prayed regularly with their children and took them to cultural celebrations and religious festivals. Both mothers and daughters enjoyed the shared experiences and grew closer. The importance of participation in religious practices and social functions was stated by Kamila:

> "When I was growing up, I did not fast or go to mosque regularly. However, since my children were born, I have started fasting, going for Friday prayers, and getting involved in social and religious activities at the mosque, including teaching children's religion classes. My daughter looks forward to Fridays and all the programs we enjoy together. She even likes to go to Sunday school at the mosque. Not only has she learned about Islam, but she also has made friends and feels good. She has learned other Islamic values such as respect for the elders in the community, modesty, *adab* [translated in English, appropriate behaviors toward different groups of people]. We both enjoy going to programs organized at our mosque. All this without arguing with her!"

Two of the mothers expressed serious concerns about their daughters adopting non-Muslim values and limited their interactions with non-Muslim peers. Khadija, a middle-age mother who originally migrated from Pakistan, candidly shared her anxiety about her daughters becoming "too Americanized." In attempting to protect her daughters from becoming "too Americanized" she discouraged her two daughters from attending college, despite the fact that she valued education and wanted her daughters to get higher education. Additionally, she successfully pressured them into getting married after graduation from high school. She feared that in college her daughters would be overly exposed to U.S.

culture, would socialize (dress, party, and date) in a similar manner as non-Muslim women, and marry non-Muslims.

All the mothers, including Khadija, who denied her daughters' entry into college, desired a good future for their daughters. They defined "good future" as the completion of a college degree, ability to earn a high income, a happy married life, and children who they would bring up as Muslims.

In addition to programs organized by their religious community, mothers also promoted participation in cultural programs such as festivities outside the places of worship, musical programs, and concerts. They also had regular dinner parties at their homes or were invited to parties by their conationals. These reflected attempts by mothers to teach their daughters about their cultural traditions, enjoy such traditions, and in the process socialize their daughters to develop their cultural and gender identities. Though all mothers promoted participation in cultural activities, they were not as conscious about the development of their daughters' multiple identities. For example, Salima stated:

> "I want my daughter to be not only a good Muslim, but also to enjoy her Indian culture, socialize with Indian friends, and learn to be a happy Indian woman. I have many American friends (meaning non-Muslim and non-Indian), but I have special Indian friends and I want my daughter to wear Indian clothes, not be embarrassed about being an Indian, and have special Indian friends in whose company she will enjoy our culture."

Thus mothers socialized their daughters to have multiple identities as Muslims, as women, and as members of cultural groups from their countries of origin, such as India, Pakistan, and Bangladesh. All saw the future of their daughters in the United States and considered themselves as U.S. Muslims, and as Indian/Pakistani/Bangladeshi American women.

Promoting High Achievement

All the mothers desired high education and achievement for their daughters. They had migrated to the United States to improve their economic and social well-being and for the future of their children. Opportunities for a high standard of living for their families and higher education for their children were two of the main reasons for their migration to the United States. They justified their emphasis on education by presenting pursuit of knowledge and education as Islamic and quoting from the Quran, history, and cultural background. They also felt that high levels of education would ensure a secure future for their daughters and future grandchildren in the United States.

Semina, who had come as a South Asian refugee from Uganda, described the emphasis on intellect and high value placed on education, as well as the sayings in South Asian culture such as "If you educate a son you educate one person; if you educate a daughter, you educate a family." She referred the interviewer to the scientific and philosophical achievements of Muslims, and quoted a hadith of Prophet Mohamed in Daftary's book entitled *Intellectual Traditions in Islam* (Leaman, 2000): "Seek knowledge even though it comes from China." She cautioned the interviewer to remember the context of the culture of the time of the hadith. She first quoted a religious poem from Kalame Mawla attributed to the first Imam Ali s.a.s., followed by a cultural saying as follows:

> *"Ilm martabaa dariyaa jaisaa, jis kaa vaar na paar*
> *"Bahot gaheraa hai behad undaa, us me(n) chizaa(n) anant apaar*
> *"Je koi us me(n) gothaa khaave, aur aap fanaa ho jaave*
> *"Sohi amulakh saahi apnaa, moti upar le aave."*

Translation:

> "Knowledge is like a vast ocean
> "With neither shore nor end
> "It is fathomless, profound and immeasurable
> "Containing infinite treasures
> "Those who dive into this ocean
> "And annihiliate their own existence
> "Will obtain a priceless treasure,
> "Bringing to the surface
> "A matchless pearl!"

Semina, who had entered as a refugee to the United States after 1972, quoted another South Asian cultural saying:

> "They can take away all the material possessions from you, but they cannot take away your *din* [interpreted Islamic way of life, religion] and your education."

In their stories and life experiences mothers described the efforts they had gone through to provide opportunities for higher education for their daughters, which is described in the story of Zehra, who took the risk of alienating her husband so that her daughter could enter college to get a "good" education.

Zehra, a Bangladeshi migrant with 10th-grade education and minimal English language proficiency, passionately explained how greatly she valued education. She shared how she had lied to her husband and secretly used her savings so that her oldest daughter could register for college to follow her desire for higher education. She explained that even though her husband valued education, he did not feel they had the money to send all of their seven children to college. Furthermore, her husband felt that it was more important for his daughters to be good Muslim women, wives, and mothers rather than be educated but poor Muslim women, unfit wives, and unfit mothers. However, once Zehra's husband discovered the joy his daughter felt in attending college and pursuing her dreams, he supported her as well as his other daughters. Subsequently, all four of Zehra's daughters graduated from college, got married, and now have successful careers. Zehra feels proud of herself. She told her story with great pride and explained that she was not worried that her daughters might make poor judgments since she has provided a good Islamic foundation for her daughters. She expressed that her daughters benefited from the college experience by becoming more knowledgeable about the world and broadening their perspective by meeting others. Consequently, they have become stronger in their own faith as well.

Shaheen, another mother, felt that high levels of education would increase options for marrying a well-educated man and, in turn, would secure a good future for her. This was in contrast to Khadija, whose story was presented earlier. She did not let her daughters enroll in college due to the fear of negative influences in college and the likelihood that her daughters would meet non-Muslim men and end up marrying them.

Protecting Daughters from Negative Forces in U.S. Society

All the mothers had experienced challenges with their daughters as a result of differences in behaviors and expectations of the family that were in contrast to socially acceptable behaviors in U.S. society. They had used diverse ways as described above to influence their daughters as well as protecting their daughters from the negative forces of society. Their methods were flexible and varied. None of the mothers took a laissez-faire approach to parenting. One of the mothers—who was relatively more Westernized, had a high level of education, and had friends from diverse groups—expressed concerns arising from the lack of knowledge about Islam and cultural nuances among most Americans she came in contact with. She noted that the situation of Muslims in the United

States and the Western world is very difficult. Before 9/11 she did not worry about her children at all. Now, she fears for herself and her daughter. The example below illustrates the source of her concern.

> "Last week, I wore my *Khameez* [long Indian tunic] over my pants. A well-educated friend at work joked and said: 'You are dressed for racial profiling.' When I was telling my husband about what my friend said, I became aware that even my friend does not make a distinction that a traditional Muslim usually wears a scarf with the long tunic and pants and I did not have the scarf. What I mean is that this brought to my attention that the climate in the United States is very anti-Muslim. Most Americans don't know the fine distinction in dressing. I am afraid what this means for my children, especially my daughter, who likes to wear Pakistani outfits."

Another mother stated:

> "Ten years ago, I always told anyone who asked me 'Where you are from?' that I am from Pakistan. Now, I am afraid and I generally wear shirts and pants rather than my Pakistani outfits to the store and I am afraid to tell a stranger that I am Pakistani. I caution my daughter about her dress and what she says. She is not as careful as I am. We have had good discussion about this at home."

The sentiments of the mothers for protecting their daughters were expressed by Parin as follows:

> "I love my daughter. I show my feelings. I listen to her and try different ways. I ask for her father's help, but I would rather err on the side of making a mistake by directly intervening, if she does not listen. During her teen ages, I did not like her to go to the mall just for wandering around. I know she was upset and sulked, but I feel responsible for my children. I still like for her as well as my son to let me know where they are. I want my children to succeed!"

Six of the 10 mothers expressed fear that their children might be harassed. They discussed the need to be vigilant, and cautioned their daughters about the attitudes of others. Sometimes they restricted their daughters' behaviors and only let their daughters go out in groups or with their brothers. Two of these 10 mothers had special concerns related to Islamophobia and increasing anti-Muslim sentiments since 9/11. They had to protect their daughters.

The daughter of one study participant had started wearing the *hijab* (head scarf and long dress) during the second year of college in the fall of 2003. This girl's mother did not wear the *hijab*. She had always worn modest Western clothes that covered her arms and knees. She was alarmed when her daughter informed her of her adoption of the *hijab* for fear that her daughter would be a target of harassment and even severe violent action. Her daughter felt she had the right to select clothing that was an expression of her identity. While the mother understood and appreciated that her daughter's day-to-day life and behaviors reflected an Islamic lifestyle that she valued, she wanted her daughter to discard the hijab for her safety and security. However, she was not able to convince her daughter and had to accept her choice of dressing. Only two women did not express fear. When asked about any concerns arising from anti-Muslim sentiments, they indicated that their daughters are cautious and do not present themselves in ways that would result in harassment.

CONCLUSION

Muslim immigrant mothers have migrated to the United States for their children's future. They feel responsible for their daughters' achievements, future life, and success or failure. They are vigilant and consciously work hard to assure that their daughters follow Islamic religious practices; gain the necessary education and life skills to enable them to lead a good quality of life; be self-sufficient in case of difficulties; and, most importantly, have the necessary skills to inculcate Islamic values in their grandchildren.

At times, the goals and aspirations of mothers for their daughters lead to decisions that are contradictory. Mothers struggle with competing goals, such as the development of an identity that reflects religious, cultural, social, and personal components. These are difficult to capture in surveys. The current research has identified areas of concern and struggles in the socialization processes of Muslim American mothers.

Through their own personal examples and sacrifices they promote a modest lifestyle and utilize their husbands, extended family members, *masjids* (places of worship), and coethnics as the major vehicles for socializing their daughters. They believe that whatever happens in their homes, their relationships with their daughters will determine the future of their daughters and the future of the next generation of Muslims in the United States.

NOTE

1. To protect the identity of participants, pseudonyms have been used.

REFERENCES

Ahmed, N., Kaufman, G., & Naim, S. (1996). South Asian families in the United States: Pakistani, Bangladeshi, and Indian Muslims. In B. C. Aswad & B. Bilge (Eds.), *Family and gender among American Muslims: Issues facing Middle Eastern Immigrants and their descendants* (pp. 155–172). Philadelphia: Temple University Press.

Al-Johar, D. (2005). Muslim marriages in America. *Muslim World, 95*, 557–574.

Alvarez, J. (1992). *How the Garcia girls lost their accents*. New York: Plume.

American Muslim Council. (1992). The Muslim population in the United States. Retrieved May 9, 2006, from *www.islam101.com/history/population2.usa.html*

Arab American Institute. (2003). *Healing the nation: The Arab American experience after September 11*. Washington, DC: Author.

Bagby, I., Perl, M. P., & Froehle, B. T. (2001). *The mosque in America: A national portrait*. Washington, DC: Council on American–Islamic Relations.

Balgopal, P. A. (2000). Social work practice with immigrants and refugees: An overview. In P. A. Balgopal (Ed.), *Social work practice with immigrant refugees* (pp. 1–29). New York: Columbia University Press.

Baptiste, D. A. (2005). Family therapy with East Indian immigrant parents rearing children in the United States: Parental concerns, therapeutic issues and recommendations. *Contemporary Family Therapy, 27*, 345–366.

Barazangi, N. H. (1991). Islamic education in the United States and Canada: Conception and practice of the Islamic belief system. In Y. Y. Hadad (Ed.), *The Muslims of America* (pp. 157–174). New York: Oxford University Press.

Barazangi, N. H. (1996). Parents and youth: Perceiving and practicing Islam in North America. In B. C. Aswad & B. Bilge (Eds.), *Family and gender among American Muslims: Issues facing Middle Eastern immigrants and their descendents* (pp. 129–142). Philadelphia: Temple University Press.

Ba-Yunus, B., & Siddiqui, M. M. (1998). *A report on the Muslim population in the United States of America*. New York: Center for American Muslim Research and Information.

Bhattacharya, G. (2002). Drug abuse risks for acculturating immigrant adolescents: Case study of Asian Indians in the United States. *Health and Social Work, 27*, 175–183.

Bukhari, Z. H. (2001). Demography, identity, space: Defining American Muslims. In P. Strum & D. Tarantolo (Eds.), *Muslims in the United States* (pp. 7–20). Washington, DC: Woodrow Wilson International Center for Scholars.

Carter, R. B., & El Hindi, A. E. (1999). Counseling Muslim children in school settings. *Professional School Counseling, 2*, 183–188.

Council on American–Islamic Relations. (2001). American Muslims: Population statistics. Retrieved June 5, 2006, from *www.cair.com/asp/populationstats.asp*

Cox, D. R. (1983). Religion and the welfare of immigrants. *Australian Social Work*, *36*, 3–10.

Denny, F. M. (1995). Islam in America. In J. L. Esposito (Ed.), *The Oxford encyclopedia of the modern Islamic world* (pp. 296–300). New York: Oxford University Press.

Denzin, N. K., & Lincoln, Y. S. (Eds.). (2003). *Collecting and interpreting qualitative materials* (2nd ed.). Thousand Oaks, CA: Sage.

Eck, D. L. (1997). *On common ground: World religions in America.* New York: Columbia University Press.

Farver, J. A., Narang, S. K., & Bhadha, B. R. (2002). East meets west: Ethnic identity, acculturation, and conflict in Asian Indian families. *Journal of Family Psychology*, *16*, 338–350.

Ghuman, P. A. (1997). Assimilation or integration?: A study of Asian adolescents. *Education Research*, *39*, 23–35.

Haddad, Y. Y. (1997). Make room for the Muslims? In W. H. Conser Jr. & S. B. Twiss (Eds.), *Religious diversity and American religious history* (pp. 218–261). Athens: University of Georgia Press.

Haddad, Y. Y., & Lummis, A. T. (1987). *Islamic values in the United States.* New York: Oxford University Press.

Hodge, D. R. (2002). Working with Muslim youths: Understanding the values and beliefs of Islamic discourse. *Children and Schools*, *24*, 6–20.

Kosmin, B. A., Mayer, E., & Keysar, A. (2001). American religious identification survey. The Graduate Center of the City University of New York. Retrieved June 5, 2006, from *http://www.gc.cuny.edu/faculty/researchstudies/aris.pdf*

Leaman, O. (2000). Scientific and philosophical enquiry: Achievements and reactions in Muslim history. In F. Daftary (Ed.), *Intellectual tradition in Islam* (pp. 31–43). London: I.B. Tauris in association with the Institute of Ismaili Studies.

Livengood, J. S., & Stodolska, M. (2004). The effects of discrimination and constraints negotiation on leisure behavior of American Muslims in post-September 11 America. *Journal of Leisure Research*, *36*, 183–208.

Mahmoud, V. (1996). African American Muslim families. In M. McGoldrick, J. Giordano, & J. K. Pearce (Eds.), *Ethnicity and family therapy* (pp. 122–128). New York: Guilford Press.

Maiter, S., & George, U. (2003). Understanding context and culture in the parenting approaches of immigrant South Asian mothers. *Affilia*, *18*, 411–428.

Maloof, P. S., & Ross-Sheriff, F. (2003). *Muslim refugees in the United States. A guide for service providers.* Washington, DC: Center for Applied Linguistics.

Metcalf, B. D. (1984). *Moral conduct and authority: The place of adab in South Asian Islam.* Berkeley: University of California Press.

Portes, A., & Rumbaut, R. G. (2001). *Legacies.* Berkeley: University of California Press.

Portes, A., & Zhou, M. (1993). The second generation: Segmented assimilation and its variants. *Annals of the American Academy of Political and Social Sciences*, *530*, 74–96.

Power, C. (1998, March 16). The new Islam. *Newsweek*, pp. 34–37.

Ross-Sheriff, F. (2001). Immigrant Muslim women in the United States: Adaptation to American society. *Journal of Social Work Research*, *2*, 283–294.

Ross-Sheriff, F., & Husain, A. (2001). Values and ethics in social work practice with Asian Americans: A South Asian Muslim case example. In R. Fong & S. Furuto (Eds.), *Culturally competent practice* (pp. 75–88). Boston: Allyn & Bacon.

Ross-Sheriff, F., & Husain, A. (2004). South Asian Muslim children and families. In R. Fong (Ed.), *Culturally competent practice with immigrant and refugee children and families* (pp. 163–182). New York: Guilford Press.

Rumbaut, R. G. (1995). The new Californians: Comparative research findings on the educational progress of immigrant children. In R. G. Rumbaut & W. A. Cornelius (Eds.), *California's immigrant children* (pp. 46–48). San Diego, CA: Center for U.S.–Mexican Studies.

Rumbaut, R. G. (1996). The crucible within: Ethnic identity, self-esteem, and segmented assimilation among children of immigrants. In A. Portes (Ed.), *The new second generation* (pp. 119–170). New York: Russell Sage Foundation.

Rumbaut, R. G., & Cornelius, W. A. (1995). *California immigrant children: Theory, research and implications for educational policy.* La Jolla: Center for U.S.–Mexican Studies, University of California–San Diego.

Shaikh, M. A. (1995). *Teaching about Islam and Muslims in the public school classroom* (3rd ed.). Mountain Valley, CA: Council on Islamic Education.

Simmons, C., & Allah, M. H. (1994). English, Israeli-Arab and Saudi Arabian adolescent values. *Educational Studies*, *20*, 69–86.

Smith, J. I. (1999). *Islam in America*. New York: Columbia University Press.

Strum, P. (2003). Executive summary. In P. Strum & D. Tarantolo (Eds.), *Muslims in the United States* (pp. 1–4). Washington, DC: Woodrow Wilson International Center for Scholars.

Suarez-Orozco, C., & Suarez-Orozco, M. (2001). *Children of immigration*. Cambridge, MA: Harvard University Press.

CHAPTER 12

Immigration, Globalization, and the Chinese American Family

Bernard P. Wong

Anthropological studies of Chinese immigrant families have been dominated by five perspectives: (1) continuity and change of the Chinese immigrant family from a national perspective, how Chinese families change according to the dominant society, or how Chinese immigrants continue the traditions of the Chinese society (Cheng, 1948; Hsu, 1971; Lee, 1960; Lin & Fu, 1990; Serrie, 1998; Wong, 1982, 1998); (2) conflicts of traditional versus new values (Hsu, 1985; Sung, 1967, 1979, 1998); (3) structure and functions of family and kinship organizations (Crissman, 1969;Weiss, 1974); (4) intrafamily relations (Hsu, 1971, 2001; Wong, 1985, 1998, 2001); and (5) class and assimilation processes (Serrie, 1998; Wong, 1978, 1979, 1998; Zhou, 1997). In anthropological studies of Chinese immigrant families, much attention has been paid to Chinese immigrants in ethnic enclaves but not enough research has been conducted on Chinese professionals who are linked with the global economy. Chinese family systems in the United States have often been labeled as homogeneous, laudatory cultural systems with "model families" that produce the so-called model minority without juvenile delinquent problems. This popular perception has obscured the social reality of Chinese American families. The focus of this chapter is on how transnational migration, economic opportunities, and globalization have created new family forms and social dynamics within the family and how family and kinship networks are used for decision-making activities.

Transnationalism refers to immigrants who maintain social, economic, and cultural contacts with both the sending and the receiving countries. This may involve constant movement across national boundaries, often in the process of economic globalization (Appadurai, 1996; Basch, Schiller, & Blanc, 1994; Lewellen, 2002; Wong, 2006). Participation in the global economy and transnational migration has had a great impact on the families of the transnational migrants, resulting in the following five new family arrangements: (1) the matrifocal family, (2) the patrifocal family, (3) the nonparented household, (4) the transnational extended family with members living in different parts of the world, and (5) the expatriate families of the ABC (American-born Chinese).

Modern transnationalism demands that immigrants develop and sustain multiple social relationships spanning different geographic, political, and cultural borders (Basch et al., 1995; Rosaldo, 1989, 1993). This concept of transnationalism differs significantly from the hitherto traditional concept of immigration. The concept of unidirectional immigration that proceeds one way from sending country to receiving country requires rethinking. During the period from 1940 to 1970, many scholars (Handlin, 1972; Gans, 1963; Gordon, 1964) believed that immigrants experience initial uprooting, make gradual adjustments to the receiving country, and eventually settle down and become members of the receiving society (i.e., they assimilate). However, current reality is much more complex. Transnational migrants experience more obstacles in adjusting and readjusting to both sending and receiving societies due to the fact that they are constantly crossing and recrossing borders. Transnational migrants have to negotiate, create, and maintain various social relationships in two or more communities or countries. Intrafamilial relationships that include husband–wife, sibling–sibling, father–child, and mother–child relationships are altered in the process.

TRANSNATIONALISM AS A NEW WAY OF LIFE

Chinese transnationals are called *tai kong ren* in Chinese. This has many meanings. One connotes an astronaut; another indicates an airline frequent flier. In Chinese there is also a colloquial usage of the term *tai kong ren* meaning a "wife without her husband" or vice versa. There are estimates that one out of four of the 20,000 Chinese engineers and high-tech personnel in Silicon Valley travels extensively between Silicon Valley and Asia on business (Murata, 2001). The home base of these "astronauts" is now the United States rather than Asia as was common in the 20th century. Due to the high proportion of male to female engineers, those who travel as astronauts are usually men. But in the case of a woman who does travel, her husband will stay in the United States with their children. And in some situations, both husband and wife travel as business partners, and have residences in different parts of the world. They sometimes call themselves "modern nomads." However, this is not common. By far the most common astronaut is a husband traveling back and forth between the United States and other parts of the world. The family patterns described below were gleaned from numerous stories of itinerant businesspeople traveling between the United States and Hong Kong, Taiwan, or China who found themselves entangled in new social relationships. For example, one of the informants is the wife of a Taiwan businessman. Another is a relocation expert who is familiar with the lives of the Chinese transnationals.

FAMILY PATTERNS OF THE TRANSNATIONALS

The phenomenon of returning to one's country of origin has recently caught on among immigrants to the United States. Major newspapers in the United States note that some of the country's most distinguished immigrant scientists and professionals (who have enriched the West with their talent and contributions) are returning to Asia. Although many young Chinese students and professionals continue to come to the United States for a university education and employment, more and more of them are returning to Asia where job opportunities are expanding. At the same time, their families often continue to live in the United States.

Their motives for returning home are complex. But these Chinese immigrants fear that the economic potential of the United States is limited. Its growth is inhibited by high costs, high wages, and low productivity. By contrast, China and Taiwan's economies are growing, and their proximity to the burgeoning Asian consumer market may hold greater promise. Furthermore, the U.S. recession of the early 1990s affected California more than many other states. The accompanying loss of consumer purchasing power affected many Chinese businesses. At the same time, the economies in Asia were experiencing unprecedented growth. These developments triggered a reverse immigrant exodus, especially during the period from 1990 to 1995 ("Skilled Asians," 1995; "Time of Opportunities," 1993). Then in the period from 1999 to 2001 we again saw a wave of return migration as a result of another recession, as well as other factors. Some Chinese felt that they were not treated equally by employers as they are often paid less for doing the same jobs as non-Chinese. Some believed that there was a "glass ceiling" blocking their social mobility because of their ethnic or racial status. They could see through the "glass" but could not go beyond the barrier of occupational mobility (Wong, 1994, 2006).

Among less-educated newcomers to the United States, returning to Asia or other parts of the world to seek employment during the recession of the early 1990s was an adaptive strategy. Many traveled to South Africa, Central America, Thailand, Nepal, Saudi Arabia, or China where they had social or economic connections. Among newly arrived immigrant families in the 1990s it was common to see one or both parents in a constant state of departure or arrival. This was, indeed, the life of an astronaut.

Matrifocal Families

A *matrifocal family* refers to a family made up of a mother and her children. Thus, it is a single-parent household. This family type is the result of migratory labor. Matrifocal families existed among the Chinese in the past when families were separated by the immigration exclusion laws of the United States (Wong, 1985). The U.S. Immigration Act of 1924 specifically prohibited the entry of Chinese wives. Chinese immigrants had to return to China to marry and sire children. They then returned to the United States. Their families in China continued to be tended by the wives they left behind. However, that situation has been reversed among today's Chinese transnational migrants. Chinese wage earners still leave their families behind, but now they leave them in the United States. In these matrifocal families, the men travel back and forth between the United States and other countries. In such cases, the fathers may return once or twice a year to visit the family. The resulting dominant dyadic relationship is not the father–child bond but that of mother–child. This is a change from the traditional Chinese kinship pattern, which emphasizes the father–child relationship in a patrilineal kinship system (Hsu, 2001). Among transnational Chinese families today, the communication between a father and his family is more often carried out via telephone and e-mail rather than by face-to-face interaction.

Another significant negative outcome of the transnational lifestyle is that some transnational migrants, on leaving their children and spouses behind, acquire a new sense of freedom. They suddenly become "bachelors" who are free and undisciplined in their daily regime. Then when they return to the United States, they find their families boring. Their children have become strangers to them and vice versa. Intrafamilial relationships can be devastated by this constant separation. The children are emotionally tied only to their mothers, and this bond persists even after the children's reunion with their father.

The decision to return to Asia is often initiated by the husband, but it is usually with the consent of his wife. After considering the financial advantages, the husband then departs with the reluctant blessing of his wife. Take Mr. Chung, for example. After graduating from National Taiwan University, Mr. Chung came to the United States for advanced study, getting an MA and a PhD in computer science at the University of Illinois. He then found employment in Silicon Valley. He purchased a car and met his future wife in San Jose where she was pursuing an MBA. They married, purchased a home in San Jose, and soon had two children. Thus far Mr. Chung had followed the ideal career path for a Taiwan engineer. In Silicon Valley, among the Taiwanese, it is called *wu zi dang ke* (five successful steps to be completed). After getting a job, the five steps are, in order: (1) earn money, (2) purchase a car, (3) get married, (4) purchase a house, and (5) have children. Chung did all these valued and desired things as a Taiwanese PhD graduate student in the United States. He then worked until 1997 in Silicon Valley as a project manager. With the semiconductor industry in Taiwan booming, he was given the opportunity to return to Taiwan to head a division at a company in Hsinchu. After discussing this with his wife, Chung decided that the opportunity was too good to pass up. He was offered stock, a company apartment, a travel allowance, and a salary comparable to what he was already receiving in the United States. An additional bonus was that the tax rate is much lower in Taiwan, while the responsibilities, being broader, provided an opportunity for Chang to eventually become vice president of the company.

His wife, on the other hand, felt that it was impossible for her to leave her job in America. After receiving her MBA from San Jose State University she had found a position of responsibility in a financial institution in Silicon Valley. The family home was situated in a desirable Los Alto neighborhood and their children were doing well in school. So she and Mr. Chung decided that the family would stay in the United States while he went to Taiwan. Mr. Chung commuted between Taiwan and the United States for 4 years. He has since returned to the United States, but other Chinese astronauts continue their frequent travel career. And nowadays, the commuting has become even more complicated. Some astronauts must travel to three or more destinations—the United States, Taiwan, Hong Kong, and mainland China, for example—all in one trip.

The lifestyle of the astronaut has become an established trend, especially during the last 10 years. Consider the experiences of the Tsenshau Yang and Samuel Liu families as reported by the *San Jose Mercury News* ("Time of Opportunities," 1993). Mr. Yang, an engineer in his late 30s, moved from Taiwan to the United States for study. After obtaining his

PhD in engineering at Stanford University, Yang stayed on to work in Silicon Valley. However, in 1993 he returned to Taiwan to work as vice president of a start-up company designing integrated circuits. His wife, Shyun, and their two children, still live in Cupertino. For Yang, Taiwan offers better opportunities in his field, but for his wife, an accountant, finding equivalent work in Taiwan is difficult. Yang returned to Taiwan with the blessing of his wife. She said, "I didn't want him to come to me in 10 years and tell me he regretted not starting his own business. . . . But now, I am beginning to regret it because he is not home most of the time." Yang comes back to visit his family several times a year.

This mode of adaptation is not without its perils. In some astronaut families, children go unsupervised and experience problems in school and at home. Other families experience emotional and marital problems. Indeed, new immigrants must pay a high price if they choose to lead this lifestyle.

Patrifocal Families

Patrifocal families are those headed by a male single parent—something relatively new and rare among Chinese immigrants, but it does exist. These families consist of a father and his children who live together as a social unit. Children in this kind of household derive their emotional support mainly from their father rather than from their absentee mother. The mother–child bond is replaced by the father–child bond, a departure from traditional childrearing practices. Both patrifocal and matrifocal households come about because of the need for economic betterment. Relatively speaking, matrifocal households are more numerous than patrifocal ones. This is probably due to the fact that men are the traditional wage earners in most families, especially in the high-tech industry. And in Chinese culture, it is more acceptable for a husband than a wife to travel overseas to seek employment (Hsu, 1983). However, with equality in education and greater economic opportunities for women, it is now possible to have patrifocal Chinese families with fathers as househusbands. This represents a change in traditional Chinese kinship because the husband has now assumed the wife's role. The women's liberation movement and the improved education and social capital of the Chinese woman have encouraged her to sometimes adopt a nontraditional sex role. Transnational migration can change the sex roles of its participants as well as the kinship system of the Chinese.

Among the new Chinese immigrants, there is another new breed of women and wives: *nu qiang ren* (in Mandarin) or *nuey keung yan* (in Cantonese). This phrase means "strong women [who are extremely talented].” At times these wives may have better *guanxi*, social capital, or professional training than their husbands. These wives may have had high-paying jobs in Asia prior to their migration to the United States. After their arrival here, however, they become impatient with the downward social mobility they are experiencing as the result of not being able to find suitable employment. So they return to China or Hong Kong to look for better economic opportunities. Here is the story of one such woman.

After much brainstorming and discussion, Mrs. A decided to leave Silicon Valley to go to Hainan Island to help with the development of a power plant. She left San Francisco and leased a hotel room in Hong Kong. From Hong Kong, she traveled to Hainan Island to conduct her business. Hong Kong was her business center; the United States was her home. Mrs. A returned twice a year to see her family. Her husband was an engineer and was in charge of raising their school-age children. Here was a reversal of the traditional gender role, with the man running the household, instead of his wife. He had to go to work daily, supervise the children’s schoolwork, and do household chores. He was the head of the family, the wage earner, and the homemaker all combined. Because of this, the children became more connected to their father than to their mother. However, the family was unhappy with this separation. After being gone for 3 years, Mrs. A successfully completed her business project and returned to the United States with much acquired wealth. The family then purchased a large house in the San Francisco Bay Area. Mrs. A believed they had suffered enough, and she vowed not to travel anymore.

This case of a temporarily separated patrifocal household had a happy ending. But it is a kind of separation that was almost unheard-of in traditional Chinese families of the past. Now it occurs often in modern Chinese immigrant families. While reliable statistics are not available, my informants estimated that at least 5% of the immigrants’ families are headed by fathers. Demonstrated talent and greater education on the women’s part and trust between a husband and wife are important factors in the success of such risky adaptive ventures. Both patrifocal and matrifocal households can disintegrate.

Nonparented Households and Parachute Children

Parachute children are children left in a foreign land with little or no adult supervision. According to the estimate of my informants, there are about 40,000 Chinese children in the United States who belong to this group. For the Chinese immigrant in the United States there are many reasons for treating one's children as parachute children. One is the perceived advantage of the education available in the United States. Due to stiff competition for limited space in Asian universities, many parents believe that their children will be able to attend a better university in the United States than in their country of origin. Curiously enough, there is the perception too that U.S. grade schools and high schools are better than those in Taiwan. Some parents feel that there are too many exams and too many hurdles for young students in Taiwan. Additionally, in order to go to universities, their children have to study day and night and complete extra *ngu pu* (cram courses). These cram sessions are in the evening and on Saturdays or Sundays after regular school hours, and they are intended to increase a student's chance of being admitted to a good university.

A second reason Chinese parents might employ this strategy is political and economic. Parents are worried about the political stability of Asia. Many believe that investing their savings in a U.S. property that their children can live in and watch over is a sound financial move. In the case of a disastrous political or economic change in Asia, they believe they can always fly back to the United States and live a comfortable life in a comfortable home. In other words, a home and legal residency in the United States are an "ace in the hole." "Plan before it rains," or "Don't wait to dig a well until you are dying of thirst"—these were the commonly quoted Chinese sayings given in response to my questions. Political instability between China and Taiwan is still a cause of great uncertainty. Many Taiwanese Chinese feel safer because their children and other assets are in the United States. Another reason for leaving one's children in the United States is avoidance of the mandatory military service imposed on Chinese males in Taiwan. All in all, educational opportunity, pursuit of wealth, and the perceived political instability of Asia are the major reasons that motivate parents to resort to this kind of adaptation.

The resulting nonparented household is another new phenomenon among Chinese transnational migrants. Some well-to-do Chinese immigrants from Hong Kong or Taiwan, after obtaining immigrant visas and green cards, set up a household for their children and then leave. The children remain behind in the United States to pursue their education. These parents will typically have purchased a house and found a school for their teenage children. Sometimes extracurricular activities are also arranged for them. Whenever possible, relatives or friends are instructed to visit or keep an eye on these children. In reality, the supervision is often nominal. After the arrangements are made, the parents return to their homes overseas. It can be expected that while some of these teenage children are doing well, others are not. Loneliness and a lack of parental supervision create problems. There is a certain amount of resentment against their parents. The traditional kinship warmth among Chinese families is now gone due to the absence of parents from their new household in America. Some educators in Southern California communities have had many truancy problems with parachute kids who were living alone. In 1991, the San Marino school board decided to address the issue by requiring legal guardians of students to be more distant than first cousins. Once the school finds out a student is living without adult supervision, the student is expelled and his or her parents are reported to immigrant officials and social services. Gangs bully some teenagers. For protection, some parachuted children form their own gangs. They did so also to show that they are "cool kids" but not "geeks." Some skip school and school work. Smoking, drinking, drugs, fighting, gambling, and sex are often considered to be "cool." Other children have problems with friends. Some juveniles contemplate committing suicide due to depression, loneliness, and feelings of hopelessness and frustration.

Not all of these parachute children are from astronaut families. Ranging in age from 8 to 18, some were sent here by affluent parents in Taiwan via arrangements with travel agencies (at a stiff price). Others came here on tourist visas or F1 student visas to stay in a boardinghouse or in the home of a relative. Some parachute children came to the United States with their parents on family reunion visas under a provision of the 1965 immigration law. Still others came to the United States with parents who had E2 investment visas (granted to a family that invests $1 million in the United States). In Silicon Valley, most of the parachute children are such for one of those reasons, but in general, parachute children come from relatively affluent families. No one really knows the exact number of parachute children in the United States but there are estimates that at least 30,000–40,000 such cases come from Taiwan alone.

Parachute children started to appear in the United States in the mid-1980s following the United States's recognition of the People's Republic of China. Parents of these children had great anxiety that Taiwan would be turned over to China. The second wave of parachute children came after 1987 when the U.S. Supreme Court ruled that public education could not be denied to illegal immigrants.

It is to be expected that not all the parachute children will do well under such circumstances. In fact, the majority have language problems when they first arrive, and consequently have difficulty getting along well with their U.S. peers. Homesickness is common. Frequently, these children and their parents cease to have anything in common. Often, on the occasion of family reunions, the children and their parents cannot even engage in ordinary conversation with one another. The children's ties to the family are weak and exist only in economic terms.

Transnational Extended Families

The *transnational extended family* refers to a large family headed by a patriarch. As a family it is a collection of many nuclear ones, with members who are often scattered across the United States and other parts of the world. Transnational extended families are not units of consumption, but rather units of economic activity. Extended families may coincide with family firms, and a transnational corporation may have several branches in different parts of the world administered by several children and their families. The headquarters of this corporation may be run by the founders and patriarchs of the family in Hong Kong, Taiwan, or Singapore. It is a traditional patriarchy running a nonresidential extended family and the family business around the world. This is an extension of the traditional Chinese family firm with modern modification.

Chinese family firms have been important for the economic activities of the Chinese in the Philippines (Amyot, 1993; Wong, 2001), China (Redding, 1990; Yang, 1994), Southeast Asia (Weidebaum & Hughes, 1996; Yeung, 1997, 2000), and the United States (Wong, 1987, 1988, 2001, 2005; Wong, McReynolds, & Wong, 1992). However, the development of transnational extended families among the Chinese is a relatively new phenomenon. A joint family venture, with various world branches run by family members and their spouses, is becoming a necessity in this global economy. In these ventures, strategic information is kept within the family. Decisions can be made quickly because of the centralization of authority and control. In certain circumstances, the chiefs of these family businesses can also delegate decision-making powers to family members in different local offices.

The movers and shakers of these big Chinese businesses and multinational corporations are small in number. They do not represent the majority of Chinese immigrants. Suffice it to say that class differences exist among the Chinese immigrant professionals. Some Chinese immigrant capitalists possess both the power and the money to pursue global business strategies which are otherwise available only to very wealthy Americans. There are only about two or three dozen Chinese families in the Bay Area who participate in such large-scale international business ventures. Most Chinese immigrants must return to Asia for similar employment opportunities.

There are positive and negative aspects to membership in an affluent transnational family. Some authors (Chan, 1997; Wong, 1997, 2006; Yeung & Olds, 1999) suggest that family members can facilitate the internationalization of their family businesses. As exemplified in these cases, rich, transnational, extended families have used adaptive responses to economic globalization. With trusted family members overseeing economic transactions in different parts of the world, these international family firms can achieve greater control over and more economic gain from their vast economic empires. However, some transnational family members are unhappy with their newly fashioned lifestyles. Some must travel constantly, thus creating a separation between themselves and their spouses and children. Some complain about their lack of "grounding." They comment that they are not tied closely to any nation or community. Some feel isolated from their parents and siblings in Hong Kong, Taiwan, and elsewhere. Discontentment and isolation may be part of the social cost of transnational migration.

Globalization and the ABC Families

The ABC (American-born Chinese) are highly Americanized. Families of ABC can be second-, third-, fourth-, or fifth-generation Americans. They tend to fare better economically as a group because of their training and education. They are raised in American-style nuclear families. Many are highly assimilated to U.S. culture. Some families are descendants of old immigrants, some descendants of first-generation professionals. The economic base of these families is no longer an ethnic niche. Some participate in the global economy. Many are engineers, computer scientists, accountants, lawyers, and business managers. Many values of the U.S. middle class have been absorbed by ABC. These include neolocal households, nuclear family living arrangements, equality between spouses, independence, privacy, the habits of purchasing appliances on credit, materialism, emphasis on success, and the like. Many choose schools and careers according to personal interests. However, some of them are still influenced by their parents' wishes, and these decide to become engineers or scientists. Here is a statement from one informant:

> "I told my two sons that they could do whatever they want to do. For practicality, I advised them to study engineering. I said to them that they can always make a living if they are engineers. Engineering should be their base. After they are done with engineering, they can pursue what they wanted to do. They did. One went to Stanford and the other went to Cornell. My older one is pursuing a graduate degree in computer science. My younger one is trying to transfer to another field from engineering. He said he was bored by engineering and is now trying to study psychology. It is OK with me." [personal interview]

Another parent told a similar story:

> "My children were born here and are much Americanized. I have a son and a daughter. When they were younger, I told them to do whatever they wanted to do. There is a future in every field. I told them to do something that will help them make a living. I did not tell my children to get an A in every subject. But I told them that they have to get at least one A just to feel how good it is. They followed my advice. They both did well in school. One chose to be a computer scientist. The other got an MFA in arts administration. They both did well and I am proud of them." [personal interview]

Some ABC high-tech engineers learned Mandarin and Chinese culture from home and from their Saturday Chinese schools. These children are seen by corporate headhunters as highly desirable bilingual professionals. Some have been recruited to work in China, Hong Kong, Taipei, and Singapore where they command six-figure salaries plus housing, travel, and dependent allowances. The ABC tend to travel with their families.

Not all of the ABC are happy with their transnational existence. They miss their homes in the United States. Their life in Hong Kong away from the United States is a transitory existence. They believe that it is good for them to have the opportunity to live overseas, but they plan to return to the United States permanently. Some of the ABC are no longer accustomed to the Chinese style of business. They do not feel comfortable with the business mentality in China and the emphasis on *guanxi* (connections). *Guanxi* includes kinship, friendship, colleague, and other personal relationships. There are also practical problems such as the education of their children and the maintenance of their properties in the United States. Some of my informants said that as soon as their children started school, they would like to transfer back to the United States so that their children would not experience any discontinuity or a disruption of their education. As for their houses in the United States, although the ABC may have rental agents or property managers to take care of their real estate, they are still concerned about this upkeep. The longer they are away, the more worried they become. They also feel homesickness for the United States where their parents have already established roots. This longing to return to the United States is common among ABC expatriates.

Young ABC have also started to look eastward. Some of these American Chinese professionals, who now have bilingual and bicultural backgrounds, are in demand. According to Heidrick & Struggles, an executive search company, there is a great deal of demand for talented people with multicultural backgrounds. This particular firm was at one point looking for high-tech engineers to serve as general managers for a number of Taiwanese companies, and after much effort they could locate only six candidates. Tony Scott of Trans-Pacific, a venture capital company, has said that bilingual skills and a bicultural background are absolute necessities in Asia-Pacific economic transactions ("Globalization," 2001).

The trend of the ABC going to Asia to look for jobs started in 1997. Miller (1998) noted that at this time many young Californian Chinese were going to Hong Kong, Taiwan, and China to look for employment. But their reason for going was not just the money. Some went to avoid the glass ceiling of discrimination. Miller found that many multinational corporations in Asia need managers who can understand the local environment.

It is this gap the United States–trained Asians are hoping to fill. This type of migration is nothing new; Asians in America journeyed across the Pacific throughout the past century. But there are several wrinkles today. As they search for economic opportunity, some younger people are also traveling to Asia to reconnect with their heritage or reunite with families. For others, it's a well-paid adventure. Many see it as a way to avoid the so-called glass ceiling they believe keeps them from competing for upper-management positions in the United States (Miller, 1998).

CONCLUSION

As the world gradually develops into a single production system, many Chinese businesspeople and educated professionals are deciding that they want to be players in the global economy. The center–periphery model of the global economy (Wallerstein, 1980) can no longer depict their boundary crossings and transnational economic activities. Their mode of operation involves the use of transnational social networks that are composed of family members using advanced technology, electronic media, and global capital (Appadurai, 1995, 1996; Braziel & Mannur, 2003). Some have built international social networks that respond successfully to the changing economy of the world.

Nuclear families, extended families, and nonresidential extended families continue to exist among the Chinese transnational migrants in the United States. Young or old, the first- and second-generation Chinese Americans still consider family important. However, among some immigrants, transnationalism has created new structural arrangements: nuclear families that have been transformed into patrifocal or matrifocal families, nonparented households, or transnational extended families. Overseas spousal employment has increased the number of single-parent households. Marital strain and problematic parent–child relationships are a frequent result of these structural changes. As a way of life, transnationalism has a high social cost, ranging through loneliness, alienation, juvenile delinquency, family separation, and divorce. Far from being a "model minority," some Chinese children experienced more family and social disorganization than the children of other minorities. Of all the different family types discussed in this chapter, it appears that ABC families are assimilated faster into U.S. society. However, the ABC are affected by the global economy as well. They have become expatriates. Some relocate their families to Asia and some develop patterns similar to other transnational migrant workers mentioned above.

Other trends are replacement of the father–son bond by the husband–wife bond, and the substitution of patrilocal, patrilineal kinship systems with neolocal-nuclear family systems. However, transnationalism often poses an obstacle for long periods of family reunion. Meanwhile, family life and experience are not comparable among all the Chinese in the United States, as they still live and are raised in a variety of households. The quality of family life and the evolution of the Chinese system in the United States will continue to depend on two forces that affected them in the past: immigration movements and economic opportunity.

We have seen thus far that extended families do not atrophy or disappear in contemporary societies. On the contrary, they are still used as tools by Chinese businesspeople and others to adapt to economic globalization. They use family and social connections to maximize profits. We have also seen that the relatively durable Chinese institution known as *family* is subject to change. As a social institution, the family has been shown to be diverse and fluid. But this fluidity means that the concept of the fixed, unitary, and bounded culture and its one-sided influence on that family is outmoded. The Chinese family can and has changed in our transnational world, because family types and relationships are being influenced by the cultural constraints and reinforcements of globalization.

REFERENCES

Allan, G. (1996). *Kinship and friendship in modern Britain.* New York: Oxford University Press.

Amyot, J. (1973). *The Manila Chinese.* Quezon City: Institute of Philippine Culture.

Appadurai, A. (1995). The production of locality. In R. Fardon (Ed.), *Counterworks: Managing the diversity of knowledge* (pp. 205–225). London: Routledge.

Appadurai, A. (1996). *Modernity at large: Cultural dimensions of globalization.* Minneapolis: University of Minnesota Press.

Asia influence comes of age. *San Francisco Examiner.* (1989, April 21).

Basch, L., Schiller, N. G., & Blanc, C. S. (Eds.). (1994). *Nations unbound: Transnational projects, postcolonial predicaments and deterritorialized nation-states.* Amsterdam: Gordon & Beach.

Braziel, J. E., & Mannur, A. (Eds.). (2003). *Theorizing diaspora.* Malden, MA: Blackwell.

Chan, K. (1997). A family affair: Migration, dispersal, and the emergent identity of Chinese metropolitan. *Diaspora, 6,* 195–213.

Cheng, D. T. (1948). *Acculturation of the Chinese in the U.S.: A Philadelphia study.* Fochow, China: Author.

Crissman, L. W. (1967). The segmentary structure of urban overseas Chinese communities. *Man, 2,* 185–204.

Gans, H. (1963). *Urban villagers: Group and class in the life of Italian-Americans.* New York: Free Press.

Globalization and bi-cultural advantage. (2001, December 8). *Sing Tao Daily.*

Gordon, M. (1964). *Assimilation of American life: The role of race, religion, and national origins.* New York: Oxford University Press.

Guldin, G. (1977). *Overseas at home: The Fujianese of Hong Kong.* Unpublished doctoral dissertation, University of Wisconsin, Madison.

Handlin, O. (1972). *Uprooted: The epic story of the great migrations that made the American people* (2nd ed.). Boston: Little, Brown.

Hsu, F. L. K. (1971). *The challenge of the American dream.* Belmont, CA: Wadsworth.

Hsu, F. L. K. (1983). *Americans and Chinese: Passage to differences.* Honolulu: University of Hawaii Press.

Hsu, F. L. K. (2001). The effect of the dominant kinship relationships on kin and non-kin behavior: A hypothesis. In B. Wong (Ed.), *Family, kin and community: A contemporary reader* (pp. 4–25). Dubuque, IA: Kendall-Hunt.

Hsu, J. (1985). The Chinese family: Relations, problems and therapy. In W. Tseng & D. Y. H. Wu (Eds.), *Chinese cultures and mental health* (pp. 95–112). Orlando, FL: Academic Press.

Lee, R. H. (1960). *The Chinese in the United States of America.* Hong Kong: Hong Kong University Press.

Lewellen, T. C. (2002). *The anthropology of globalization.* Westport, CT: Bergin & Garvey.

Lin, C. C., & Fu, V. R. (1990). A comparison of child-rearing practices among Chinese, immigrant Chinese, and Caucasian-American parents. *Child Development, 61,* 429–432.

Miller, M. (1998). New gold mountain. *Far Eastern Economic Review, 161(28), 76–77.*

Murata, L. (2001). *Transnationalism: The new kinship structure of Hong Kong Chinese.* San Francisco: Center for Urban Anthropology, San Francisco State University.

New money elite. *San Francisco Examiner.* (1989, April 20).

Redding, S. G. (1990). *The spirit of Chinese capitalism.* Berlin: Walter de Gruyter.

Rosaldo, R. (1989). *Culture and truth*. Boston: Beacon Press.

Rosaldo, R. (1993). *Borderlands of race and inequality*. Paper presented at the spring meeting of the Society for Cultural Anthropology, Washington, DC.

Serrie, H. (1998). Chinese around the world: The familial and the familiar. In F. L. K. Hsu & H. Serrie (Eds.), *The overseas Chinese* (pp. 189–217). Lanham, MD: University Press of America.

Skilled Asians leaving U.S. for high-tech jobs at home. *New York Times*. (1995, February 21).

Stack, C. B. (1974). *All our kin*. New York: Harper & Row.

Sung, B. L. (1967). *Mountain of gold*. New York: Macmillan.

Sung, B. L. (1979). *The adjustment experience of Chinese immigrant children*. Staten Island, NY: Center for Migration Studies.

Sung, B. L. (1998). Chinese immigrant children in New York City: Bicultural conflicts. In H. Serrie & F. Hsu (Eds.), *The overseas Chinese: Ethnicity in national context* (pp. 173–188). Lanham, MD: University Press of America.

Time of opportunities turns for Taiwanese engineers. *San Jose Mercury News*. (1993, August 22).

Wallerstein, I. (1980). *The world-system II*. New York: Academic Press.

Weidenbaum, M., & Hughes, S. (1996). *The bamboo network*. New York: Free Press.

Weiss, M. S. (1974). *Valley city: A Chinese community in America*. Cambridge, MA: Schenkman.

Wong, B. (1978). A comparative study of the assimilation of the Chinese in New York City and Lima, Peru. *Comparative Studies in Society and History*, *20*, 335–358.

Wong, B. (1979). *A Chinese American community: Ethnicity and survival strategies*. Singapore: Chopmen Enterprises.

Wong, B. (1982). *Chinatown*. New York: Holt, Rinehart & Winston.

Wong, B. (1985). Family, kinship and ethnic identity of the Chinese in New York City, with comparative remarks on the Chinese in Lima, Peru, and Manila, Philippines. *Journal of Comparative Family Studies*, *16*, 231–254.

Wong, B. (1987). The role of ethnicity in enclave enterprises: A study of the Chinese garment factories in New York City. *Human Organization*, *46*, 120–131.

Wong, B. (1988). *Patronage, brokerage, entrepreneurship and the Chinese community of New York*. New York: AMS Press.

Wong, B. (1988). Transnationalism and new Chinese: Immigrant families in the United States. In C. A. Mortland (Ed.), *Diasporic identity* (pp. 158–174). Arlington, VA: American Anthropological Association.

Wong, B. (1994). Hong Kong immigrants in San Francisco. In R. Skeldon (Ed.), *Reluctant exiles?* (pp. 235–254). Armonk, NY: Sharpe.

Wong, B. (1997). *Globalization, anthropology and the Chinese diaspora*. Keynote speech presented at the Second International Conference on Contemporary Diaspora, Tsukuba University, Tsukuba, Japan.

Wong, B. (1998). *Ethnicity and entrepreneurship: The new Chinese immigrants in the San Francisco Bay area*. Boston: Allyn & Bacon.

Wong, B. (Ed.). (2001). *Family, kin and community: A contemporary reader.* Dubuque, IA: Kendall/Hunt.

Wong, B. (2001). From enclave small businesses to high-tech industries: The Chinese in the San Francisco Bay area. In D. Haines & C. A. Mortland (Eds.), *Manifest destinies: Americanizing immigrants and internationalizing Americans* (pp. 111–130). Westport, CT: Praeger.

Wong, B. (2001). The role of kinship in the economic activities of the Chinese in the Philippines. In B. Wong (Ed.), *Family, kin and community: A contemporary reader* (Rev. ed., pp. 188–215). Dubuque, IA: Kendall/Hunt.

Wong, B. (2005). Chinese diasporas. In R. Hansen & M. Gibney (Eds.), *Immigration and asylum: From 1900 to the present* (pp. 80–86). Oxford, UK: ABC-Clio.

Wong, B. (2006). *The Chinese in Silicon Valley: Globalization, social networks, and ethnic identity.* Lanham, MD: Rowman & Littlefield.

Wong, B., McReynolds, B., & Wong, W. (1992). The Chinese family firms in the San Francisco Bay area. *Family Business Review, 5*, 355–372.

Yang, M. (1994). *Gifts, favors and banquets: The art of social relationships in China.* Ithaca, NY: Cornell University Press.

Yeung, H. W. (1997). Business networks and transnational corporations: A study of Hong Kong firms in the ASEAN region. *Economic Geography, 73*, 1–25.

Yeung, H. W. (2000). Economic globalization, crisis and the emergence of Chinese business communities in Southeast Asia. *International Sociology, 15*, 265–287.

Yeung, H. W., & Olds, K. (Eds.). (1999). *Globalization of Chinese business firms.* New York: St. Martin's Press.

Zhou, M. (1997). Growing up American: The challenge confronting immigrant children and children of immigrants. *Annual Review of Sociology, 23*, 63–69.

PART III

IMMIGRANT FAMILIES IN SOCIAL CONTEXTS

CHAPTER 13

Immigrant Families and the Educational Development of Their Children

Andrew J. Fuligni *and* Allison Sidle Fuligni

Children from immigrant families always have presented one of the most significant challenges to the U.S. educational system. Historically, both public and private schools in the United States have played critical roles in assisting the children of immigrants to adapt to this country. Today, the link between educational success and occupational attainment is stronger than it ever has been before, and high school completion and schooling beyond the 12th grade are now essential ingredients for a successful transition into adulthood in U.S. society. The difficulties facing both immigrant families and their schools go beyond simply the families being strangers in a new and different society, and include the challenges associated with the great cultural, linguistic, and economic diversity that characterizes the contemporary immigrant population in the United States. It is critical, therefore, to determine how immigrant families interact with the U.S. educational system in order to facilitate the successful adaptation of their children and, as a result, their future integration into U.S. society as adults.

In this chapter, we review research from a variety of disciplines that has focused on immigrant families and the educational adaptation of their children. In doing so, we address three key questions that we believe to be essential to understanding the educational issues facing this population: What are the socioeconomic features of immigrant families that are relevant to educational adjustment? What education-related beliefs and values do these families hold? How do socioeconomic resources, beliefs, and values shape the educational options and practices of the families at different stages in the children's educational trajectories? We conclude by briefly discussing the implications of the answers to these questions for educational policy and practice. Several of these issues have been discussed in detail in previous publications that focus on the general adaptation of immigrant families and their children (Fuligni & Hardway, 2004; Fuligni & Yoshikawa, 2003, 2004). Our intent in this chapter is to highlight key themes discussed in these previous publications as they relate specifically to the educational adjustment of children.

SOCIOECONOMIC RESOURCES

As with any group, an understanding of the impact of immigrant families on students' academic success must start with the nature of their socioeconomic resources. It is difficult to accurately describe these resources for the entire population of immigrant families because of their tremendous variability, which is greater than that of the American-born population. As a group, immigrant families are both less likely to have received a high school degree and equally likely to have received college degrees as compared to American-born families (see Hernandez, Denton, & Macartney, Chapter 1, this volume, for a detailed presentation of the demographic background of immigrant families). This bimodal distribution is due to the fact that factors such as parental education, occupation, and income differ dramatically across immigrant groups according to their country of origin. Overall, parents from Asian countries such as India, the Philippines, and Taiwan tend to have higher levels of education than do American-born parents. In contrast, families from Latin American countries such as Mexico and El Salvador have parents with less schooling. Variation exists even within these large sending regions. For example, only a minority of immigrants from Southeast Asian countries such as Cambodia and Laos has received a high school degree and foreign-born parents from some South American countries have levels of education comparable to those of American-born parents.

Variations in parental education such as these, particularly the very high and the low levels of education of certain groups, will play an important role in shaping the educational beliefs, practices, and outcomes of children from immigrant families. Yet this role may not be as clear as might be expected, because parental education among immigrant groups in the United States is highly constrained and selected by two key factors beyond their control: educational access in their native countries and the nature of U.S. immigration policies. In terms of educational access, most immigrant families originate in countries that have fewer opportunities for educational advancement as compared to the United States. For example, only approximately one-third of the populations in Mexico and China attend school beyond the primary school years (Fuligni & Yoshikawa, 2003). Although low levels of parental education will present challenges to immigrant children and their schools, it nevertheless is important to consider the parental education of immigrant families in light of these variations in access in order to avoid making erroneous assumptions. For example, parental education is often considered to be a key index of human capital, which is thought to represent values and motivation along with ability (Entwisle & Astone, 1994). Yet Mexican immigrants with high school degrees have gone further in their educational system than Americans with high school degrees, suggesting a potentially higher level of motivation and value of education among the immigrants than is captured by their educational levels. Indeed, as described in the next section, immigrant parents have higher aspirations for their children than would be predicted from their educational level (Fuligni, 1997).

U.S. immigration policies, which are highly selective, also shape the educational distribution of foreign-born parents. Immigrants are granted entrance into the United States under a variety of provisions, but the primary system involves a series of preference categories that determine which applicants from each country are given priority (Portes & Rumbaut, 1996). The top categories emphasize family reunification, such that applicants with close relatives already in the United States are given priority over others. After family reunification, the preference system gives priority to applicants who possess occupational skills that the United States deems to be needed and in short supply among the current U.S. population. On average, immigrants admitted under family reunification preferences tend to have lower levels of education as compared to those admitted under occupational preferences (Rumbaut & Portes, 1996).

The preference system was put into place with the passage of the Immigration Act of 1965, which also removed previous restrictions on immigration according to national origin. As a result, countries whose immigration had not been restricted prior to 1965 (e.g., Mexico) already had individuals living in the United States and were more likely to have immigrants admitted under family reunification preferences as compared to countries whose immigration had been severely restricted (e.g., China). This intersection of contemporary immigration policy with the history of exclusionary policies prior to 1965 helped to produce dramatic variations in educational level according to the national origin of immigrants. These trends have abated somewhat as more immigrants from Asian countries have been living in the United States for some time, but there remain other ways in which U.S. immigration policies can shape the nature of the populations. For example, special refugee and asylee designations can be used to allow entrance to individuals escaping political unrest and persecutions. These individuals are never random samples of their native countries, and it is important to determine from which social strata in their native countries they originate. For example, the Hmong and other Southeast Asian refugees were members of groups who had little formal schooling or contact with urban areas in their home countries. In contrast, the early refugees from Cuba after Castro came into power tended to be from the professional and business classes. The main point to derive from the role of U.S. immigration policies in shaping the variation in parental education is that most of these variations are preexisting, and do not necessarily reflect greater academic success in the United States on the part of their *parents*. Nevertheless, the differences can be quite profound and do result in children from some immigrant groups having a greater advantage over children from other immigrant groups by virtue of the manner by which their parents were admitted to this country.

Occupational and financial variations among immigrants tend to follow the differences in parental education, with more highly educated immigrant parents generally holding higher status and better paying jobs than those with lower levels of education. As a result, immigrant parents from countries such as India and Taiwan work in higher status occupations and have higher levels of income than the national average, whereas parents from many Latin American countries tend to work in low-wage jobs (Hernandez et al., Chapter 1, this volume). Parents' occupations and incomes clearly have implications for the financial resources available to support the educational progress of their children, but they should not be considered sufficient descriptors of the socioeconomic environment of the home. Immigrants often must work in jobs below the level of training that they received in their home countries because of their inability to transfer credentials to the United States (Waldinger, 2001). Many foreign-born parents in semiskilled and skilled occupations, therefore, actually may have educational levels that match those of American-born parents in semiprofessional and professional jobs. This is particularly true of newer immigrants, who need to work in lower status occupations in order to maintain a minimum level of economic stability before attempting to become established professionally in their new country (see Updegraff, Crouter, Umaña-Taylor, & Cansler, Chapter 14, this volume, for more discussion of the work lives of immigrant families).

Finally, English language ability and its use in immigrant families are critical factors that can shape the educational development of children. Foreign languages are spoken in the vast majority of immigrant families, but immigrant parents are highly variable in their ability to speak English well. For example, almost half of the parents in families from China, Mexico, and El Salvador report having a poor knowledge of English (Rumbaut, 1995). In contrast, approximately 90% of parents from India and the Philippines—former colonies of Britain and the United States—speak English fluently. English language ability is also highly confounded with socioeconomic status, with poorer, less well educated parents tending to have more difficulty speaking and understanding English. Children from immigrant parents generally have a much easier time learning English, particularly by the time that they are in middle and high school (Fuligni, 1998). Nevertheless, limited English proficiency is characteristic of certain groups of children, particularly during preschool and the early years of elementary school, and among adolescents who only recently entered the country. English difficulties can present challenges to both the students in their studies and the parents in their communication with schools, as described in a later section of this chapter.

In summary, the socioeconomic profiles of immigrant families are highly variable, both across different immigrant groups and across traditional demographic indicators such as parental education, occupation, and income. Although these variations among parents do have important implications for the adjustment of their children, it is important not to incorrectly estimate the educational values and resources available in the home by relying upon only a single indicator of socioeconomic status. The intersection of the families' socioeconomic status before coming to this country, the nature of U.S. immigration policy, and the potential difficulty for immigrants to obtain employment commensurate with their training creates the need to consider a broad range of demographic indicators when attempting to characterize the educational environments within immigrant families.

EDUCATION-RELATED BELIEFS AND VALUES

Given the cultural and socioeconomic diversity of contemporary immigrants, it is important to understand the beliefs and attitudes that the families bring to the educational development of their children as well as to their interactions with the U.S. school system. These attitudes derive from both their cultural backgrounds and their status as immigrants and ethnic minorities in U.S. society. Rather than survey a wide variety of beliefs and values that can shape education and learning, we instead focus on three key domains that should have the most relevance for educational behavior and practice: (1) the value and importance placed upon education, (2) the duties and obligations of children to their families, and (3) beliefs about learning and parental involvement.

Value of Education

Numerous studies employing different methods across a variety of disciplines have noted the strong value placed upon education among immigrant families. Regardless of their countries of origin, foreign-born parents believe in the importance of doing well in school and attempt to instill such an attitude in their children. These parents believe that the best way for their children to succeed in U.S. society is to receive good grades, complete high school, and attend college. The emphasis upon education is so strong among some foreign-born parents that the perceived cost of *not* doing well in school appears to be particularly high among many immigrant families. As newcomers, immigrant parents sometimes appear to be less secure about their status in the United States, thereby leading them to believe that more is riding upon the academic success of their children as compared to American-born parents (Fuligni & Yoshikawa, 2004). Some observers have noted that immigrant parents often contrast the educational opportunities in the United States with those in their home countries in order to help their children deal with the challenges that they may face to their academic success in this country (Gibson & Bhachu, 1991).

We have observed the high value of education among immigrant parents in our own research. In one study of adolescents from immigrant families with a variety of ethnic backgrounds, students with foreign-born parents consistently reported higher parental aspirations for college than did those with American-born parents (Fuligni, 1997). This generational difference existed within each ethnic group (e.g., first-generation Latino students vs. second- and third-generation Latino students) and could not be explained by differences in socioeconomic background. At each level of parental education, immigrant parents were reported by their adolescents to have significantly higher educational aspirations than were American-born parents. Among immigrant parents themselves, those from Asian countries such as China and India tend to have higher educational aspirations than those from countries such as Mexico and El Salvador. In contrast to the generational differences in educational aspirations *within* each ethnic group, the ethnic differences among immigrants themselves are attributable to the differences in parental education, occupation, and income that were discussed in the previous section.

Children from immigrant families appear to quickly internalize and endorse the value of education espoused by their parents. Like their parents, children whose families hail from countries as diverse as Vietnam, India, and the Caribbean place great importance on doing well in school and attending college (Caplan, Choy, & Whitmore, 1991; Gibson & Bhachu, 1991; Waters, 1999). As compared to their peers from American-born families, students from immigrant families spend more time studying, seeking extra help, and expending effort on their studies. One way that adolescents from immigrant families maintain such a strong emphasis on education, even during the teenage years when such values tend to decline in the United States, is through their peers. During the secondary school years, peer groups cleave such that foreign-born students tend not to be integrated into American-born peer groups, even if they are of the same ethnic background (Matute-Bianchi, 1991). As a result, students from immigrant families tend to have peers from similar backgrounds, and they report higher levels of encouragement and support for academic achievement from their friends (Fuligni, 1997). This is particularly true for high-achieving students from immigrant families, such as those from families with Asian and higher economic backgrounds.

Family Obligation

An important source of the academic motivation of children from immigrant families is their sense of duty and obligation to support, assist, and respect the authority of their families (Fuligni, 1998). A sense of family obligation exists within the cultural traditions of many immigrant families, most of whom originate from countries in Asia and Latin America. This tradition of the child contributing to the family becomes particularly salient once these families enter the United States. Foreign-born parents often know little about the official workings of U.S. society, from dealing with official government agencies to negotiating the bureaucracy of U.S. schools and colleges. The children's knowledge of English and generally greater exposure to U.S. institutions compel them to act as negotiators and "cultural brokers" for their parents. But in addition to providing daily assistance, children's obligations to the family include trying hard in school and attempting to get into college. Students from immigrant families are well aware of the sacrifices made by their parents to come to this country in order to provide them with better opportunities for their lives, and the desire to repay their parents combines with the traditional value placed upon the child assisting the family to fuel the motivations and efforts of the children to try hard in school.

Numerous studies in different disciplines have noted the link between family obligation and academic motivation among students from immigrant families. Themes of working hard for the sake of the family run through ethnographies of several immigrant groups. Gibson and Bhachu (1991) noted the importance of bringing honor and respect to the family among adolescents in Sikh families in the Central Valley of California, who lived in tight-knit ethnic communities where family reputation was an important motivator for both students and their parents. The parents had little formal education and earned limited incomes by working in the agricultural industry, and the children in these families often noted a desire to repay their parents for their hard work by doing well in school and going to college. Suárez-Orozco and Suárez-Orozco similarly noted frequent references to wanting to achieve in school in order to obtain good jobs to help the family among Central American and Mexican immigrant teenagers (Suárez-Orozco, 1991; Suárez-Orozco & Suárez-Orozco, 1995). As one parent from Central America said, "We came here for them so that they may become somebody tomorrow" (1991, p. 45). Their children, in turn, were well aware of their parents' motivation and often indicated high aspirations that stemmed from a desire to fulfill their parents' dreams.

The associations between family obligation and academic motivation also have been observed in more quantitative studies. When Caplan and colleagues (1991) asked Vietnamese adolescents to rank a set of values in terms of importance, the students listed "respect for family members," "educational achievement," "freedom," "family loyalty," and "hard work" as the top five values. Similarly, Zhou and Bankston (1998) found that Vietnamese adolescents in a different community rated "obedience" and "working hard" as the most important values in their families. In our own research, we have estimated the associations between adolescents' sense of obligation to the family, as measured by various attitudinal scales, and different aspects of their academic motivation. Consistently, adolescents who report a stronger sense of obligation to support, assist, and respect the family also indicate a stronger endorsement of the importance and usefulness of education for their future lives as adults (Fuligni & Tseng, 1999). This link is captured in a quote from an adolescent from a Mexican immigrant family who participated in one of our studies:

> " . . . they [his parents] did so much for us, especially my dad. They worked so hard just to get where we are and I really appreciate that. And, I mean . . . the way I can pay them back right now is to get good grades."

Yet the potential exists for family obligation to serve as a double-edged sword for the students' educational progress. Many children from immigrant families face the very real need to provide daily assistance to their families that could potentially interfere with their ability to complete their studies and pursue postsecondary degrees. On average, adolescents from immigrant families spend more time providing assistance to their families on a daily basis, including cleaning the house, preparing meals, and caring for siblings (Hardway & Fuligni, 2006). During young adulthood, those from immigrant families also are more likely to live with their families and provide financial assistance to their parents and siblings (Fuligni & Pedersen, 2002). As discussed in the next section, high levels of such family assistance potentially could take a toll on the educational trajectories of children over time, particularly those whose families face large economic and linguistic challenges in their adaptation to U.S. society.

Beliefs about Learning and Parental Involvement

Given the international variation in cultural beliefs about how children learn and the roles that parents play in that learning, it is reasonable to expect that some immigrant parents may have views that differ from those that are common in the United States. Less is known about the exact nature of these potential variations among diverse immigrant groups, but there has been some work that has focused on Latino parents that might inform variations in parenting behaviors. Cultural variation in beliefs about how children learn and the role of the parent in educating children may reduce the likelihood of immigrant parents engaging in activities that may be common among middle-income U.S. families of European background. For example, although it may be common in such nonimmigrant families to encourage toddlers' language development by pointing to and labeling objects in books or the environment or asking the child questions to which the adult clearly already knows the answer, these parental behaviors are less common among immigrant families. Cultural values may also be evident in the higher value some Latino groups place on children's compliance (Wasserman, Rauh, Brunelli, Garcia-Castro, & Necos, 1990), and lower levels of maternal verbalization to infants and toddlers among Latinos (Harkness & Super, 1995; Heath, 1982).

Latino parenting practices associated with early literacy and education are likely to be affected by levels of acculturation in immigrant families. Families who have been in the United States for longer periods of time are more likely to integrate practices typical of the mainstream culture into their parenting, such as direct teaching interactions, or asking young children questions about what they are doing or questions to which the answers are clearly known by the adult (Hammer & Miccio, 2004). In contrast, more traditional immigrant Latino parents emphasize parenting behaviors that model respect, politeness, and harmonious interactions with others (Roseberry-McKibben, 2002: Zuniga, 1988), and the value of individuals' dignity and respect of others (García-Coll, Meyer, & Brillon, 1995). The cultural views of more traditional Mexican American families are also expressed through maintaining what parents perceive as a respectful distance from the teacher, refraining from questioning the authority of the teacher, or presuming to do the teacher's job by providing academic instruction to children (Peña, 2000). A mismatch between immigrants' beliefs about education and the mainstream educational system in the United States may contribute to a lack of integration of immigrant parents into the educational experiences of their children (see Bradley & McKelvey, Chapter 9, this volume.)

Parental beliefs about the process of learning to read, for instance, are tied to their cultural background. In an ethnographic study of Mexican immigrant parents, Reese and Gallimore (2000) found that parents believed that learning to read involved the sequential learning of sounds, letters, syllables, and ultimately putting syllables together through repetitive practice typically occurring at school. This very traditional belief is inconsistent with current thinking in the United States, which considers early literacy development to be an "emergent" process, grounded in early experiences of shared book reading with parents, encouragement of oral language development, and exposure to print and literacy in the environment. In fact, the activity of reading stories to children at bedtime is not a traditional activity in less acculturated immigrant families, or may begin to occur at later ages for immigrant children, when parents believe the children are old enough to understand (often not until age 5). Therefore the immigrant parents in the study were likely to miss opportunities to elaborate on children's experiences and interactions with print in the home due to the fact that they typically did not view such interactions as supporting literacy development. However, when explicitly instructed to read with children as part of a school assignment, the immigrant parents began to engage in such activities (Reese & Gallimore, 2000).

In summary, although little research has been done specifically on the topic of cultural beliefs regarding children's learning and parental involvement, some studies of Latino families have suggested that immigrant parents may be less likely to endorse some middle-class U.S. values of parental instruction in academic matters and active involvement with the children's schools. These beliefs, in turn, may play a role in some of the patterns of educational behaviors and decision making among immigrant families that are explained in the next section.

EDUCATIONAL OPTIONS AND PRACTICES

The socioeconomic resources of immigrant families and their communities interact with the families' beliefs and values to shape the nature of the educational options available to them, as well as their educational practices and behaviors. In this section, we review research that has focused on three categories of educational options and practices that are both significant for the children's educational development and potentially amenable to intervention: (1) preschool program use, (2) parental involvement, and (3) postsecondary educational persistence. Overall, research suggests that economic resources, linguistic ability, and lack of information collectively constrain the options and practices of many immigrant families. Yet within the limits of their knowledge, ability, and comfort level, immigrant families attempt to do what they can to help fulfill their educational aspirations for their children.

Preschool Program Use

At the preschool level, the challenging socioeconomic conditions facing many immigrant families constrain both the availability and the use of early educational programs. Analyses of one national study, the National Household Education Survey (NHES), showed that the preschool-age children of immigrant parents are less likely to be enrolled in some type of early childhood program than children of American-born parents (Nord & Griffin, 1999). The same study indicated that usage of Head Start programs is lower among poor children of immigrants as compared to poor children of American-born parents. Due to many factors—long or nontraditional work hours, low education and income of Latino parents, and poor supply of available and affordable center-based care in heavily Latino neighborhoods—it has been noted that Latinos often utilize informal, unlicensed childcare arrangements which are more likely to be of poorer quality (see also Waldfogel & Lahaie, Chapter 10, this volume, for more discussion of preschool enrollment patterns of immigrant children). This pattern has led to the perception that Latinos are not interested in using formal childcare or that they prefer informal, unlicensed care. It is unclear, however, the extent to which ethnicity or immigrant status per se, rather than socioeconomic status and supply issues, actually account for these patterns of childcare usage (Fuller & Kubuyama, 2000). The problem with the lower rates of usage from a policy standpoint is that without showing patterns of usage, or demand, additional childcare slots are unlikely to be created (Fuller & Huang, 2003).

Within the state of California, the supply of center-based childcare and preschool programs is inversely related to the population of Latinos in each area: a full third of the variation by district in center-based child care availability is predicted by the proportional size of that district's Latino population (Fuller & Kubuyama, 2000). Low-income European American or African American communities in Los Angeles County have almost twice the supply of preschool spaces and three times the supply of spaces in licensed family childcare programs than communities that are primarily Latino (Malaske-Samu & Muranaka, 2000). Access to higher quality, center-based childcare and preschool has generally been found to be curvilinearly related to family income. Higher income families seek out and use center-based preschool programs which tend to be available in their neighborhoods. Among the lowest income families (those who qualify for childcare subsidies or government-run programs such as Head Start), rates of center-based childcare use among Latinos and African Americans is greater than usage of center-based care among low-income European American families or families with other income levels (Fuller, Holloway, & Liang, 1996).

Usage of childcare subsidies is often constrained by families' awareness of their availability, comfort navigating the bureaucratic requirements to obtain them, and language and cultural barriers. For instance, immigrant Latinos who are Spanish speaking have lower levels of awareness of the California welfare program's childcare subsidies than English speakers, resulting in a much lower rate of receipt of childcare support among Spanish speakers (38% versus 63% among English speakers; Hirshberg, Derbin, Robinson, Population Research Systems, & Freeman, Sullivan & Co., 2002). Overall, Latino families lack access to information about licensed childcare that is presented in their native language (Ball Cuthbertson, Burr, Fuller, & Hirshberg, 2000; Buriel & Hurtado-Ortiz, 1998; Malaske-Samu & Muranaka, 2000). A study by Buriel and Hurtado-Ortiz (1998) comparing childcare availability and preference among foreign-born and American-born Latinas in Southern California found that lack of availability of childcare in the preferred form near home or work is a bigger problem among foreign-born mothers than among either native-born Latinas or European descent mothers. One assessment of childcare supply and demand in Los Angeles County found that shortages existed (defined as families' reporting of unmet childcare needs) while at the same time there were licensed childcare spaces that were unfilled. The authors suggested that mismatches between families' linguistic needs and the programs' language might help explain this disparity (Ball Cuthbertson et al., 2000). Some reasons for the lower usage of licensed center-based childcare among Latino families may include lack of information about resources, lack of awareness of the importance of quality childcare, mismatch of linguistic cultural and educational backgrounds between families and childcare providers, and lack of affordable childcare options near parents' workplace (Howes & Zucker, 2003).

Parental Involvement

The linguistic abilities and relative lack of cultural knowledge of immigrant parents interact with their value of education to influence the nature of their parental involvement in their children's education by making them less likely to participate in activities that require such knowledge, and more likely participate in activities that do not require such knowledge (see also Gonzales, Dumka, Mauricio, & Germán, Chapter 15, this volume, for a discussion of parental involvement). Kao and Tienda (1995) observed that among eighth-grade students in the National Educational Longitudinal Study (NELS: 88), immigrant parents tended not to volunteer or to attend events at their children's school. As compared to American-born parents, however, immigrant parents were more likely to visit their child's classes and talk to their children's teachers, provide space for homework at home, and to attend parent–teacher meetings.

Similar patterns emerged among 3- to 8-year-old children in the NHES (Nord & Griffin, 1999). Like parents of adolescents, immigrant parents of these young children were less likely to attend school events and volunteer, but they were equally as likely as American-born parents to attend parent–teacher conferences. Immigrant parents also were similar to American-born parents in their rates of teaching their children letters, words, or numbers, and in telling or reading their children a story. But in terms of activities outside of the home, immigrant parents were less likely to take their children to the library or attend cultural events such as plays or concerts.

Within each of these two national studies, immigrant parents with higher levels of parental education and income are more likely to engage in learning activities such as teaching letters and numbers and reading to their children. These socioeconomic variations among immigrants themselves likely explain the tendency for Asian immigrant parents to engage in these activities more often than Latin American immigrant parents (Nord & Griffin, 1999). Even within the same immigrant group, differences in parental education, income, and English language skills also produce variations in these educational behaviors (Louie, 2001).

Postsecondary Educational Persistence

Adolescents from immigrant families tend to enroll in postsecondary school at rates equal to those of their American-born peers (Fuligni & Witkow, 2004; Glick & White, 2004). These enrollment rates are consistent with the high educational aspirations of immigrant families, which in turn likely enable them to overcome the many challenges to their educational success. Nevertheless, some segments of the population do not pursue college at very high rates. In particular, those from many Latin American immigrant families, particularly those from Mexico, attend college at lower rates than their peers from other immigrant families (Fuligni & Witkow, 2004).

Many of the variations in college enrollment among immigrant families follow the socioeconomic differences discussed earlier. Yet many immigrant families also are unaware of the complexities of the U.S. postsecondary system, and parents cannot advise their children on the proper steps to take toward enrollment in college. Minority and immigrant parents who have relatively little educational experience beyond primary school have less intimate experience with and knowledge about the secondary and postsecondary educational system, and the means by which students are accepted into and graduate from college. The knowledge necessary for a successful negotiation of U.S. schools is great, and includes whether and how parents can choose alternative public schools if their own school is undesirable, which secondary schools promise the highest chances of college acceptance, and the courses, achievement levels, standardized tests, financial aid forms, and entrance applications that must be completed in order to be eligible for college. Numerous studies have documented that many immigrant parents, particularly those with low levels of education themselves, have more difficulty obtaining appropriate information (Cooper et al., 1994; Tornatzky, Cutler, & Lee, 2002).

In their analyses of NELS: 88, Berkner, Chavez, and Carroll (1998) demonstrated how differences between Asian American and Latino students in 4-year college application and enrollment had a great deal to do with coursework and performance in high school. Yet even among those who were qualified for college on the basis of their high school coursework and academic performance, Latino students were less likely to take college entrance exams and submit applications to 4-year colleges. The importance of assisting students with taking the necessary steps to attend college, including exams, applications, and seeking financial aid, was demonstrated by the study finding that among those who were college-qualified, ethnic differences in 4-year college enrollment disappeared among those students who had taken the necessary exams and submitted applications. Differences between low-income and middle-income students also were eliminated.

The obligation to provide support and assistance to the family, which serves as an educational motivator for many students from immigrant families, can also present a challenge as they attempt to pursue postsecondary degrees. As a group, these students appear to meet the challenge. In one of our studies, students from immigrant families were just as likely to enroll and persist in postsecondary schools even though they also were more likely to provide financial assistance to their parents and siblings (Fuligni & Witkow, 2004). Yet among those from immigrant families themselves, those who had to provide more economic assistance to their families were less likely to persist in postsecondary school toward their degrees. It appears, then, that whereas a sense of family obligation provides more motivation for children from immigrant families to attend college, the very real need for the poorer segments of the population to provide actual assistance to their families could cut into their ability to complete their degrees.

IMPLICATIONS FOR POLICY AND PRACTICE

Policies and programs designed to assist the educational development of the children of immigrants must be tailored to specific ages, groups, and issues of concern. Yet the education-related strengths and needs of these families that were reviewed in this chapter point to a number of themes that efforts to improve the educational access and progress of the children from immigrant families should include. First, it is hard to imagine that the educational fortunes of the neediest segments of the immigrant population will be raised without improving access to quality educational programs at both the preschool and school levels. Second, it is clear from a number of studies that immigrant families often lack the necessary information about how to take advantage of educational resources that are indeed available to them, including availability of preschool programs, effective ways in which school teaching practices can be supported in the home, and their eligibility for college attendance and financial aid. Third, a key element of providing such information is to directly address the language difficulties of many immigrant parents by making publications, forms, and school events and meetings available in the parents' native languages. Finally, programs and policies should build on the cultural traditions and strengths of immigrant families (see

Bradley & McKelvey, Chapter 9, this volume, as well as Gonzales et al., Chapter 15, this volume, for additional discussion). In particular, the strong value of education that is buttressed by a strong sense of obligation to the family bodes well for the educational development of the children, as long as they are provided with the proper resources and means to fulfill their high aspirations to succeed in U.S. society.

REFERENCES

Ball Cuthbertson, B., Burr, E., Fuller, B., & Hirshberg, D. (2000). *Los Angeles County child care needs assessment* (PACE Report). Berkeley: University of California Press.

Berkner, L., Chavez, L., & Carroll, C. D. (1998). *Access to postsecondary education for the 1992 high school graduates* (NCES 98-105). Washington, DC: U.S. Department of Education, National Center for Education Statistics.

Buriel, R., & Hurtado-Ortiz, M. T. (1998). Child care practices and preferences of native- and foreign-born Latina mothers and Euro-American mothers. *Hispanic Journal of Behavioral Sciences*, *22*(3), 314–331.

Caplan, N., Choy, M. H., & Whitmore, J. K. (1991). *Children of the boat people: A study of educational success*. Ann Arbor: University of Michigan Press.

Cooper, C. R., Azmitia, M., Garcia, E. E., Ittel, A., Lopez, E., Rivera, L., et al. (2002). Aspirations of low-income Mexican American and European American parents for their children and adolescents. In F. Villarruel & R. M. Lerner (Eds.), *Community-based programs for socialization and learning: New directions in child development* (pp. 65–81). San Francisco: Jossey-Bass.

Entwisle, D. R., & Astone, N. M. (1994). Some practical guidelines for measuring youth's race–ethnicity and socioeconomic status. *Child Development*, *65*, 1521–1540.

Fuligni, A. J. (1997). The academic achievement of adolescents from immigrant families: The roles of family background, attitudes, and behavior. *Child Development*, *68*, 261–273.

Fuligni, A. J. (1998). Adolescents from immigrant families. In V. McLoyd & L. Steinberg (Eds.), *Research on minority adolescents: Conceptual, theoretical, and methodological issues* (pp. 127–143). Hillsdale, NJ: Erlbaum.

Fuligni, A. J., & Hardway, C. (2004). Preparing diverse adolescents for the transition to adulthood. *The Future of Children: Children from Immigrant Families*, *14*(2), 99–119.

Fuligni, A. J., & Pedersen, S. (2002). Family obligation and the transition to young adulthood. *Developmental Psychology*, *38*, 856–868.

Fuligni, A. J., & Tseng, V. (1999). Family obligations and the achievement motivation of children from immigrant and American-born families. In T. Urdan (Ed.), *Advances in motivation and achievement* (pp. 159–184). Stamford, CT: JAI Press.

Fuligni, A. J., & Witkow, M. (2004). The postsecondary educational progress of youth from immigrant families. *Journal of Research on Adolescence, 14*, 159–183.

Fuligni, A. J., & Yoshikawa, H. (2003). Socioeconomic resources, parenting, and child development among immigrant families. In M. Bornstein & R. Bradley (Eds.), *Socioeconomic status, parenting, and child development* (pp. 107–124). Mahwah, NJ: Erlbaum.

Fuligni, A. J., & Yoshikawa, H. (2004). Investments in children among immigrant families. In A. Kalil & T. DeLiere (Eds.), *Family investments in children's potential* (pp. 139–162). Mahwah, NJ: Erlbaum.

Fuller, B., Holloway, S. D., & Liang, X. (1996). Family selection of child-care centers: The influence of household support, ethnicity, and parental practices. *Child Development, 67*, 3320–3337.

Fuller, B., & Huang, S. (2003). *Targeting investments for universal preschool: Which families to serve first? Who will respond?* (PACE Working Paper No. 03-1). Berkeley: University of California.

Fuller, B., & Kubuyama, E. (2000, December). *Child care and early education: Policy problems and options* (PACE Policy Memo). [Memo presented to the California Legislature Latino Caucus Retreat.] Berkeley: University of California.

García-Coll, C., Meyer, E., & Brillon, L. (1995). Ethnic and minority parenting. In M. Bornstein (Ed.), *Handbook of parenting: Biology and ecology of parenting* (pp. 189–209). Mahwah, NJ: Erlbaum.

Gibson, M. A., & Bhachu, P. K. (1991). The dynamics of educational decision-making: A comparative study of Sikhs in Britain and the United States. In M. A. Gibson & J. U. Ogbu (Eds.), *Minority status and schooling: A comparative study of voluntary and involuntary minorities* (pp. 63–96). New York: Garland.

Glick, J. E., & White, M. J. (2004). Post-secondary school participation of immigrant and native youth: The role of familial resources and educational expectations. *Social Science Research, 33*, 272–299.

Hammer, C. S., & Miccio, A. W. (2004). Home literacy experiences of Latino families. In B. H. Wasik (Ed.), *Handbook of family literacy* (pp. 305–238). Mahwah, NJ: Erlbaum.

Hardway, C., & Fuligni, A. J. (2006). Dimensions of family connectedness among adolescents with Chinese, Mexican, and European backgrounds. *Developmental Psychology, 42*, 1246–1250.

Harkness, S., & Super, C. (1995). Culture and parenting. In M. Bornstein (Ed.), *Handbook of parenting: Vol. 2. Biology and ecology of parenting* (pp. 211–234). Hillsdale, NJ: Erlbaum.

Heath, S. B. (1982). What no bedtime story means: Narrative skills at home and school. *Language in Society, 11*, 49–76.

Hernandez, D. (2004). Demographic change and the life circumstances of immigrant families. *The Future of Children: Children from Immigrant Families, 14*(2), 17–47.

Hirshberg, D., Derbin, L., Robison, G., Population Research Systems, and Freeman, Sullivan & Co. (2002). *CDSS-PACE Child Care Planning Project: De-*

scriptive findings from the Child Care Subsidy Interview (PACE Working Paper No. 02-2). Berkeley: University of California.

Howes, C., & Zucker, E. (2003). *Relevant research on Latino families: Toward understanding preferences and use of early care and education* (Research policy report submitted to Los Angeles County First 5 L.A. Commission on Children and Families). Los Angeles: UCLA Graduate School of Education, UCLA Center for Improving Child Care Quality.

Kao, G., & Tienda, M. (1995). Optimism and achievement: The educational performance of immigrant youth. *Social Science Quarterly, 76*, 1–19.

Louie, V. (2001). Parental aspirations and investment: The role of social class in the educational experiences of 1.5- and second generation Chinese Americans. *Harvard Educational Review, 71*, 438–474.

Malaske-Samu, K., with Muranaka, A. (2000, August). *Child care counts: An analysis of the supply of and demand for early care and education service in Los Angeles County.* Los Angeles: Los Angeles County Child Care Planning Committee.

Matute-Bianchi, M. E. (1991). Situational ethnicity and patterns of school performance among immigrant and non-immigrant Mexican-descent students. In M. A. Gibson & J. U. Ogbu (Eds.), *Minority status and schooling: A comparative study of voluntary and involuntary minorities* (pp. 205–248). New York: Garland.

Nord, C. W., & Griffin, J. A. (1999). Educational profile of 3- to 8-year-old children of immigrants. In D. Hernandez (Ed.), *Children of immigrants: Health, adjustment, and public assistance* (pp. 348–409). Washington, DC: National Academy Press.

Peña, D. C. (2000). Parent involvement: Influencing factors and implications. *Journal of Educational Research, 94*, 42–54.

Portes, A., & Rumbaut, R. G. (1996). *Immigrant America: A portrait* (2nd ed.). Berkeley: University of California Press.

Reese, L., & Gallimore, R. (2000). Immigrant Latinos' cultural model of literacy development: An evolving perspective on home-school discontinuities. *American Journal of Education, 108*(2), 103–134.

Rumbaut, R. G. (1995). The new Californians: Comparative research findings on the educational progress of immigrant children. In R. G. Rumbaut & W. A. Cornelius (Eds.), *California's immigrant children: Theory, research, and implications for educational policy* (pp. 17–70). San Diego: University of California, San Diego.

Suárez-Orozco, C., & Suárez-Orozco, M. M. (1995). *Transformations: Immigration, family life, and achievement motivation among Latino adolescents.* Stanford, CA: Stanford University Press.

Suárez-Orozco, M. M. (1991). Immigrant adaptation to schooling: A Hispanic case. In M. A. Gibson & J. U. Ogbu (Eds.), *Minority status and schooling: A comparative study of immigrant and involuntary minorities* (pp. 37–62). New York: Garland.

Tornatzky, L. G., Cutler, R., & Lee, J. (2002). *College knowledge: What Latino parents need to know and why they don't know it.* Claremont, CA: Tomás Rivera Policy Institute.

Waldinger, R. (2001). Up from poverty?: "Race," immigration, and the fate of low-skilled workers. In R. Waldinger (Ed.), *Strangers at the gates: New immigrants in urban America* (pp. 80–116). Berkeley: University of California Press.

Wasserman, G. A., Rauh, V. A., Brunelli, S. A., Garcia-Castro, M., & Necos, B. (1990). Psychosocial attributes and life experiences of disadvantaged minority mothers: Age and ethnic variations. *Child Development*, *61*, 566–580.

Waters, M. (1999). *Black identities: West Indian immigrant dreams and American realities*. New York: Russell Sage Foundation.

Zhou, M., & Bankston, C. L. (1998). *Growing up American: How Vietnamese children adapt to life in the United States*. New York: Russell Sage Foundation.

Zuniga, M. (1988). Chicano self-concept: A proactive stance. In C. Jacobs & D. Bowles (Eds.), *Ethnicity and race: Critical concepts in social work* (pp. 71–83). Silver Spring, MD: National Association of Social Workers.

CHAPTER 14

Work–Family Linkages in the Lives of Families of Mexican Origin

Kimberly A. Updegraff, Ann C. Crouter,
Adriana J. Umaña-Taylor, *and* Emily Cansler

Immigrants have become an increasingly important part of the U.S. labor force in the last decade, accounting for almost half of the net growth (49%) in labor participation between 1996 and 2000 (Mosisa, 2002) and more than half (58%) between 2000 and 2003 (Sum, Khatiwada, Harrington, & Palma, 2003). A majority of immigrant workers are parents and have a strong commitment to paid employment to support their families (see Hernandez, Denton, & Macartney, Chapter 1, this volume). The growth of the immigrant workforce in the United States and the large percentage of working parents in this population underscore the importance of understanding how parents' work experiences serve as a context for family processes and individual development in immigrant families. Research on working- and middle-class families from predominantly European American backgrounds suggests that parents' work experiences have important and far-reaching implications for family relationship dynamics and youth and parent well-being (Parcel & Menaghan, 1994b; Perry-Jenkins, Repetti, & Crouter, 2000). Understanding work–family linkages in immigrant families serves as an important step for the development of prevention and intervention programs and policy initiatives to enhance the lives of youth and parents in a rapidly growing segment of the U.S. population and labor force (Mosisa, 2002; Sum et al., 2003).

We approach this set of issues from the field of human development, an interdisciplinary area of scholarship that is primarily concerned with how development across the life course is shaped by individual characteristics; close relationships; proximal processes in key settings such as family, school, and workplace; and larger contextual conditions (e.g., social stratification, cultural context). Because our field is interdisciplinary, we draw on literature from several fields, including family sociology, the sociology of work and occupations, developmental and clinical psychology, and anthropology.

The purpose of our chapter is to provide insights about the role of fathers' and mothers' work in the lives of immigrant families in the United States. We focus primarily on Latin American families, providing some empirical examples from an ongoing study of Mexican-origin families that pays equal attention to the experiences of fathers, mothers, and two adolescent offspring (McHale, Updegraff, Shanahan, Crouter, & Killoren, 2005; Updegraff, McHale, Whiteman, Thayer, & Delgado, 2005). In this chapter, we provide an overview of the literature on parental employment in Latino immigrant families, describe the salient dimensions of parents' work, and draw on our empirical findings to discuss how work experiences may be linked to family dynamics. Our final sections explore within-group variations in work–family linkages and discuss policy implications for Latino immigrant families.

PARENTAL EMPLOYMENT IN IMMIGRANT FAMILIES: WHAT DO WE KNOW?

To understand how immigrant parents' work experiences are linked to family dynamics, it is important to identify the dimensions of work that are salient for immigrant families and then to examine how these work processes are directly and indirectly related to family relationships and family members' well-being. Initial research on the work–family interface, however, has tended to focus on the correlates of parents' and primarily mothers' work *status* (i.e., employed vs. not employed) rather than on parents' work *experiences* or the nature and dynamics of their everyday lives at work. In the literature on working- and middle-class European American families, questions regarding parents' work status have largely been undertaken by developmental researchers interested in the implications of maternal employment for children's well-being (see review by Bronfenbrenner & Crouter, 1982). In this literature, there is a long history of research addressing whether there are problematic implications of maternal employment for children's social, emotional, and cognitive development (for an empirical example, see Brooks-Gunn, Han, & Waldvogel, 2002).

Although the literature on work and family connections in immigrant families has a similar goal of understanding the correlates of women's employment status, it has typically focused on questions about employed women themselves rather than their children. Specifically, research on maternal employment resulted from an initial interest in the impact of women's paid work on the traditional division of family roles (e.g., Baca Zinn, 1980; Ybarra, 1982) and on women's mental health in Latin American families (e.g., Krause & Markides, 1985; Roberts & Roberts, 1982). Early anecdotal writings described rigidly traditional gender roles of Mexican-origin parents involving male dominance and female subservience (e.g., Madsen, 1964; Peñalosa, 1968). Although the scant empirical evidence that followed revealed substantial variability in gender roles and ideology among Mexican-origin parents (e.g., Coltrane & Valdez, 1993; Williams, 1990), the initial emphasis on traditional marital roles set the stage for research questions about how maternal employment was related to the division of family responsibilities and marital relationship quality. Ybarra (1982), for example, interviewed 100 Mexican-origin individuals in California to explore the correlates of maternal employment. She found that maternal employment was an important predictor of an egalitarian role structure and egalitarian beliefs regarding housework and childcare, but not marital decision making (which most individuals indicated was a shared responsibility in their marriage). This line of work has also addressed the interrelations between maternal employment, marital relations, and women's well-being among Mexican Americans (Amaro, Russo, & Johnson, 1987; Roberts & Roberts, 1982; Saenz, Goudy, & Lorenz, 1989), with few differences noted in women's well-being as a function of work status. Consistent with earlier work, however, the division of household labor and marital satisfaction were related to maternal employment. Employed Mexican American women in one study, for example, received more help with housework, and this assistance was associated with higher levels of marital satisfaction (Saenz et al., 1989).

Additional insights about maternal employment in immigrant families comes from a perspective that draws on theories of international migration and focuses on the role of migration processes in parents' division of paid and unpaid work; this body of work has addressed the links between work and gender roles in immigrant couples of predominantly Latin American origin (Greenlees & Saenz, 1999; Menjívar, 2003; Parrado & Flippen, 2005; Parrado, Flippen, & McQuiston, 2005). Greenlees and Saenz (1999) provide an empirical illustration of the value of a contextually based approach to the study of Mexican immigrant women's employment status. In addition to identifying individual (e.g., age, English proficiency) and family (e.g., ages of children) predictors of maternal employment, this study showed that the larger community and the geographic context (e.g., female employment rates, proportion of Mexican-origin population) played an important role in predicting the likelihood of immigrant women being employed. Higher unemployment rates in the geographic region and a higher proportion of Mexican-origin females decreased the likelihood of immigrant women's employment, for example.

A number of scholars have drawn attention to immigrant women's employment as it relates to broader questions about the role of migration in shaping and reshaping gender role enactments and ideologies in immigrant families (Hondagneu-Sotelo, 2003; Parrado & Flippen, 2005; Parrado et al., 2005). Although there is consensus that migration to the United States typically offers greater opportunities for women, particularly Latina women, to seek employment, it is less clear how other aspects of parents' gender roles are altered by the migration process, and the extent to which female employment is associated with equalities in parents' division of family responsibilities remains an open question (Parrado & Flippen, 2005; Pressar, 2003). Parrado and Flippen addressed these issues in a comparative study of Mexican immigrants in North Carolina and nonmigrant women from four sending communities in Mexico using random sampling and a combination of quantitative and qualitative methods (Parrado & Flippen, 2005; Parrado et al., 2005). They examined the predictors of female labor force participation as well as the division of power in couples' relationships (e.g., the degree to which women assist with finances, men's involvement in housework) and also investigated whether and how patterns were similar or different for immigrant versus nonimmigrant Mexican-origin women. The findings of this study highlighted important differences in the correlates of maternal employment and the division of parents' gender roles for immigrant versus nonimmigrant women. Involvement in the labor force, for example, was more strongly associated with an egalitarian division of housework and women's assistance in finances for nonmigrant than for immigrant women. In contrast, social support from friends was associated with a more equal division of housework, but only for immigrant women. The findings of this study underscore the importance of attending to within-group variations in the links between migration and the division of parents' paid and unpaid roles and identifying the factors that give rise to these diverse responses.

Understanding how maternal employment is linked to parents' gender roles in the home and dimensions of marital quality represents an important step in building a foundation of study on the interconnections between work and family in immigrant families. There is important work to be done that moves beyond questions regarding employment status to examine the nature of both *mothers'* and *fathers' work experiences* and how these conditions relate to family dynamics (Bronfenbrenner & Crouter, 1982; Parcel & Menaghan, 1994b; Perry-Jenkins et al., 2000). Extending "social address" comparisons to consider the processes that mediate the relations between parents' everyday work experiences and their family relationships is consistent with the emphasis of an ecological orientation on parents' work conditions as an important extrafamilial context for parents' and children's development (Bronfenbrenner & Crouter, 1982; see also Bornstein & Cote, Chapter 7, this volume). The focus on maternal employment has resulted in limited attention to fathers' work in immigrant families and in a lacuna of research investigating the *combination* of mothers' and fathers' occupational circumstances. To address these questions, however, we must first identify the salient dimensions of immigrant parents' work.

DESCRIBING PARENTS' WORK IN IMMIGRANT FAMILIES

Individuals from immigrant backgrounds are overrepresented in the low-wage labor market (Hernandez et al., Chapter 1, this volume). In part because almost half of foreign-born workers have limited English skills and less than a high school education, these individuals comprise 75% of low educated individuals in the U.S. workforce (Nightingale & Fix, 2004). These trends highlight the importance of considering the salient dimensions of low-wage positions: *low pay, long hours, nonstandard hours (i.e., shift work)*, and, in many positions (e.g., farm laborer, construction positions), *high physical demands*. Experiences of *discrimination, underemployment*, and *chronic job stress* are also important dimensions of work to consider. In this section, we discuss each of these aspects of work for immigrant families and their implications for family life.

Low wages have important implications for family life. Earnings that are well below minimum wage describe almost half of immigrant workers' annual incomes (Nightingale & Fix, 2004) and result in many immigrant families living at or below the poverty level, jeopardizing families' living standards and contributing to feelings of economic strain and stress (Hernandez et al., Chapter 1, this volume). There is clear evidence that poverty places family members at risk for a variety of negative developmental outcomes, including problematic family interactions and poor psychosocial adjustment (e.g., Duncan & Brooks-Gunn, 1997;

Gonzales, Dumka, Mauricio, & Germán, Chapter 15, this volume). In our work with Mexican-origin families, we found that low paternal income was associated with high levels of depressive symptoms for mothers, fathers, and young adolescents. Mothers' acculturation moderated this association, however: when mothers were more strongly oriented toward Anglo culture, fathers' income was negatively associated with family members' depressive symptoms (Crouter, Davis, Updegraff, Delgado, & Fortner, 2006). It may be that when mothers and their families have strong ties to Anglo culture, they embrace more materialistic and individualistic values, making fathers' income particularly important for family members' well-being.

Parents who spend *long hours* on the job may be less available at home and, when physically present, may be fatigued and less engaged in family life. Although there are no published studies of the implications of parent' extensive work hours in immigrant families, Crouter, Bumpus, Head, and McHale (2001) found that long paternal work hours (i.e., over 60 hours per week), in combination with feelings of role overload, were associated with lower quality father–adolescent relationships in European American families. In our sample of Mexican-origin immigrant families living in the Southwest, we found that immigrant fathers' (but not mothers') work hours were associated with qualities of the marriage. When Mexican immigrant fathers worked more hours, they reported less positive feelings about the marriage and more conflict with their wives. Fathers were also less involved in housework and their wives were more involved in housework when they worked more hours at a paid job.

It is interesting to note, in contrast, that mothers' work hours were not associated with mothers' or fathers' involvement in housework. In other words, mothers did not receive additional help from fathers when mothers worked more hours for pay. We found some evidence that mothers may look to their children for assistance with housework, however. Consistent with other research showing that mothers may rely on daughters (Crouter, Head, Bumpus, & McHale, 2001; Manke, Seery, Crouter, & McHale, 1994), we found that teenage daughters were more involved in traditionally masculine household tasks (e.g., taking out the garbage, yard work) when their mothers worked more hours.

Although studies of European American families have focused on the implications of mothers', and to a lesser extent, fathers' work hours for the qualities of parent–child relationships, almost no research has examined these processes in immigrant families. We found, in our sample of Mexican immigrant families, that fathers' work hours were associated with qualities of the parent–adolescent relationship. Fathers perceived themselves as less warm and accepting toward their teenagers and also spent less time with them when they worked more hours. It will be important in future work to further explore the family conditions under which fathers' and mothers' work involvement has a positive versus a negative impact on mothers' and fathers' relationships with their offspring in immigrant families.

The transition of the U.S. workplace to a 24-hour/7-day-a-week economy means that increasing numbers of employees, particularly members of minority groups, have work schedules that involve *nonstandard hours* (Presser, 2003). Working nonstandard shifts also poses challenges for families because shift-working parents are often not at home during times of the day that are typically devoted to family life (Presser, 2003). Although there are no studies exploring connections between nonstandard hours and family life in immigrant families, this is an important direction of future research.

The *physical demands* that characterize many of the jobs that are typically assumed by immigrant males (e.g., farm labor, construction, meat packing) as well as some of the jobs assumed by immigrant females (e.g., factory work, hotel housekeeping) suggest that this is an important dimension of work to consider. The lifestyles of migrant farm workers, in particular, have been given some attention (e.g., Alderete, Vega, Kolody, & Aguilar-Gaxiola, 1999; Hovey & Magaña, 2002). Migrant farm labor positions have been described as physically demanding with dangerous work conditions; indeed, this occupation has one of the highest occurrences of workplace fatalities in the United States (Hovey & Magaña, 2002). The intense physical demands of immigrant males' work conditions may play a role in the division of responsibilities at home, as women may assume greater responsibilities for housework and childrearing even if they are also employed outside the home because of the daily physical demands that men face on the job (Parrado & Flippen, 2005). Physically demanding jobs may deplete men's energy and result in reduced interactions with family members and engagement in family activities.

Experiences of *discrimination* should be identified as an important correlate of children's and adults' mental health in minority populations (e.g., Finch, Kolody, & Vega, 2000; Kessler, Mickelson, & Williams, 1999); little research, however, has focused specifically on discrimination in the workplace. In an exception, Hughes and Dodge (1997) found that workplace discrimination was a more important predictor of African American mothers' perceptions of job quality than many more commonly studied work dimensions, such as task variety and supervision. Using an ethnic comparative design, Roberts, Swanson, and Murphy (2004) asked Latin American, African American, and European American employees to indicate by a "yes" or "no" response whether they had felt discrimination on the job because of their ethnic or racial background. They found that employees who said yes reported less job satisfaction. In addition, African American and Latin American employees reported more job stress when they perceived discrimination. Focusing only on Latin Americans, Sanchez and Brock (1996) found that workplace discrimination was related to job commitment, satisfaction, and tension, with different patterns emerging depending on employee's nativity, salary, and prior job experiences. Exploring how workplace discrimination is linked to individual well-being and family relationship experiences is uncharted territory. Crouter and colleagues (2006) took a first step by documenting positive associations between Mexican-origin fathers' experiences of job discrimination and family members' depressive symptoms and exploring the moderating role of parents' relative involvement in Anglo versus Mexican culture (i.e., a difference score subtracting parents' ratings of Mexican from Anglo cultural orientation). Their findings revealed that when families were more involved in Mexican culture (relative to Anglo culture) higher levels of racism were associated with family members' depressive symptoms (Crouter et al., 2006). It may be that in these families, racism targets the culture that families identify strongly with, making it especially detrimental to family members' well-being.

Underemployment, defined as working involuntarily less than full time or working for poverty-level wages (e.g., Dooley & Prause, 2004), is another aspect of immigrant workers' jobs that deserves consideration. This term has been expanded to include a variety of ways that individuals may be underemployed, including work hours, income, skill, and status (Friedland & Price, 2003). Mexican immigrant parents in our project described their underemployment in terms of benefits, income, job prestige, work autonomy, work hours, job security, and their overall perception of the job. Underemployment was a concern among parents in our sample, and it was related to parent well-being, marital quality, and qualities of the mother–adolescent relationship. Both mothers and fathers reported higher levels of depressive symptoms and mothers reported more marital conflict when they experienced more underemployment. In addition, we found that mothers, but not fathers, spent less dyadic time with adolescents when they experienced more underemployment. These findings suggest it will be important to explore in more depth the implications of underemployment for family dynamics in immigrant families.

A number of scholars have highlighted the implications of *chronic job stress* for family members' well-being when it results in conflicts between work and family roles or perceptions of role overload (for a review, see Perry-Jenkins et al., 2000). Crouter, Bumpus, Maguire, and McHale (1999) found, for example, that European American parents who described high levels of work pressure also reported feelings of role overload, which, in turn, were related to higher levels of conflict between parents and their adolescent offspring. Studies of job stress among minority individuals have typically focused on those in professional or university positions (Gutierres, Saenz, & Green, 1994; Rodriguez-Calcagno & Brewer, 2005) and have not specifically examined experiences of work stress among immigrant populations. Studying Latin American professionals and comparing the findings to national norms for European American professionals, Rodriguez-Calcagno and Brewer (2005) found that Latin Americans described higher levels of stress than did their European American counterparts and that Latin American women experienced greater stress than did Latin American men. It will be important to learn about the dimensions of immigrant workers' jobs that contribute to feelings of job stress and to explore the direct and indirect links between job stress and family dynamics and well-being. Research with European Americans suggest that job stressors tend to be indirectly linked to family dynamics and individual well-being through workers' internal responses of distress (Perry-Jenkins et al., 2000).

LINKING PARENTS' WORK EXPERIENCES TO FAMILY DYNAMICS

Studying the nature of parents' work as a context that provides socialization experiences that carry over to family life is an important direction of research on work–family connections in immigrant families. Over the last 15 years, the occupational socialization literature has directed considerable attention to understanding how the *complexity* of parents' work environments (i.e., the extent that work experiences offer autonomy and substantively complex tasks) is linked to parental attitudes and beliefs, parenting processes, and child well-being (Perry-Jenkins et al., 2000). In a national sample of women participating in the National Longitudinal Survey of Youth, for example, the complexity of mothers' work responsibilities was related to cognitive stimulation and emotional support in the mother–child relationship (Menaghan & Parcel, 1991; Parcel & Menaghan, 1994a, 1994b).

We have no information on the ways in which the characteristics and skills that Latino immigrant parents use in their jobs are related to parenting processes and to children's adjustment. Although immigrants are overrepresented in unskilled labor positions as compared to their native-born counterparts, there are equal proportions of foreign- and native-born minority individuals in skilled and professional positions (Nightingale & Fix, 2004). Understanding how work dimensions such as autonomy, problem solving, and complexity "spill over" to immigrant parents' lives outside of the work environment is an important avenue for future research. These dimensions of the job may be most applicable to immigrant parents in skilled and professional positions, however, suggesting that it is also important to identify the dimensions of unskilled positions that may have implications for specific parenting processes and children's social, emotional, and cognitive development (Lambert, 1999).

To begin to identify how unskilled versus skilled labor positions may provide different contexts for parents' work, we explored how mothers' and fathers' paid work experiences (i.e., self-direction, work pressure, underemployment, role overload, racism, income) were related to their education levels, their job prestige, and their language fluency using data from our Mexican immigrant sample. For fathers, we found that higher levels of education and more prestigious jobs were associated with greater self-direction, lower perceptions of underemployment, longer work hours, and higher annual incomes. Fathers' education and job prestige were not related to their perceptions of role overload, work pressure, or experiences of workplace racism. A slightly different pattern emerged for employed immigrant mothers. Mothers reported greater self-direction at work, higher incomes, and less racism when they had higher education levels and more prestigious jobs. Higher education also was associated with less work pressure, and a more prestigious job was associated with lower perceptions of underemployment.

Differences were also apparent based on parents' language fluency. English-speaking fathers reported more self-direction, longer work hours, and higher annual incomes than their Spanish-speaking counterparts. English-speaking mothers indicated that they had higher incomes, greater self-direction, and fewer experiences of racism and underemployment than Spanish-speaking mothers. Together, these findings highlight the importance of considering the correlates of unskilled versus skilled labor positions for *both* mothers *and* fathers. We found, for example, that there were consistent associations between language fluency, education level, occupational prestige, and experiences of discrimination only for mothers. More generally, we did not find differences as a function of education, job prestige, or language fluency in parents' perceptions of work pressure or in their feelings of role overload. These descriptive findings offer a first step in directing our attention to the dimensions of immigrant parents' skilled and unskilled jobs that may have implications for family life.

It is also important to consider how parents' work environments may serve as an opportunity for ethnic socialization experiences that have implications for family life. When parents work in environments where they are a numerical minority, and thus are exposed to majority culture in terms of language, values, and orientations on a daily basis, they may develop attitudes or skills that impact their role as a parent for better or worse. Some attention has been directed at the implications of being a numerical minority for individual work experiences and mental well-being (see Gutierres et al., 1994, for a review), although findings are inconsistent. Working in an environment that includes a majority of immigrants from similar cultural backgrounds may encourage the maintenance of strong ties to the ethnic culture. More research is needed on the ways in which parents' work environments are linked to parents' ethnic socialization of their offspring.

EXPLORING WITHIN-GROUP VARIABILITY IN THE CONNECTIONS BETWEEN WORK AND FAMILY

Another important part of exploring the connections between the dimensions of parents' work experiences and family relationship qualities and family members' well-being is identifying the *specific conditions* under which linkages emerge. We propose that it is important to use ethnic-homogeneous designs that illuminate the diversity of experiences within cultural groups and the cultural and ecological factors that give rise to within-group variations. Below, we highlight the role of parents' cultural orientations and values, socioeconomic resources, and migration experiences as important sources of within-group variability in the links between parents' work and family relationship dynamics.

Scholars interested in ethnic minority families have highlighted the importance of parents' *cultural orientations and values*. Early anecdotal writings emphasized traditional gender roles as a defining characteristic of Mexican-origin families (Madsen, 1964; Peñalosa, 1968). Although later researchers challenged this notion (e.g., Baca Zinn, 1982; Vega, 1990; Ybarra, 1982), arguing that early descriptions were not based on scientific evidence, the role of cultural beliefs and values in parents' gender roles cannot be ignored. Most researchers agree that gender is an important determinant of the division of household responsibilities in Mexican American families (Baca Zinn, 1980; Coltrane & Valdez, 1993; Williams, 1990). Extant research suggests that Mexican American couples are more traditional, on average, than other U.S. couples (e.g., Golding, 1990; Taylor, Tucker, & Michell-Kernan, 1999). In addition, within-group variability in cultural background and experiences is linked to variability in traditionality of gender role ideologies (Leaper & Valin, 1996; Phinney & Flores, 2002; Taylor et al., 1999). Men who have weaker ties to U.S. culture (defined by language fluency), for example, hold more traditional gender ideologies than men with stronger ties to U.S. culture (Taylor et al., 1999).

Consistent with a cultural–ecological perspective, theoretical and empirical work has hypothesized that Mexican-origin parents' gender roles (e.g., paid employment, decision making) are as closely tied to *social and economic conditions* as to individuals' cultural beliefs and values (Baca Zinn, 1980; Coltrane & Valdez, 1993; Williams, 1990; Ybarra, 1982). In support of this premise, studies have found that wives' paid employment, education level, and income are positively associated with patterns of shared decision making among Mexican American couples (e.g., Coltrane & Valdez, 1993; Williams, 1990). Findings from our project with Mexican immigrant families further highlight connections between parents' division of housework and paid work and economic resources. Mothers, for example, performed more household tasks when they earned less income, when fathers earned more income, and when there were greater differences in the two partners' incomes favoring fathers. Mothers also performed more housework when fathers worked more hours and when there was a greater difference in mothers' relative to fathers' work hours favoring fathers. Together, these studies provide support for the idea that the division of paid and unpaid work in Mexican-origin families results, in part, from "the social location of families . . . where they are situated in relation to societal institutions allocating resources" (Baca Zinn, 1990, p. 74).

Another important source of within-group variability is *parents' immigration history* (Hondagneu-Sotelo, 1992; Parrado & Flippen, 2005). Parrado and Flippen (2005) examined migration status (i.e., compared women who migrated from Mexico to the United States with women who remained in Mexico) as a moderator of the linkages between women's workforce participation and the division of marital roles. For women who migrated to the United States, social network involvement was related to a more equal division of marital roles and family ties were associated with a more traditional division of labor. The opposite was found for nonmigrant Mexican-origin women, with family ties linked to more egalitarian roles and involvement in paid labor resulting in a more equal division of labor for this group as compared to women who had migrated to the United States. These findings highlight important contextual differences in the factors that are associated with parents' division of paid and unpaid labor.

Hondagneu-Sotelo (1992) proposed that the migration process is important in defining parents' division of roles after settling in the United States. Using data from an in-depth qualitative study of 44 immigrant Mexican-origin individuals in California, Hondagneu-Sotelo examined family stage migration patterns before and after 1965. Those men who began the migration process prior to 1965 typically lived in all-male residences upon arriving in the United States and therefore learned and performed the domestic skills typically assumed by women in Mexico. Separations were typically long (averaging 6 years). During those years, women gained skills and acquired self-confidence that reflected their greater independence over time. Upon reunification, most couples established relatively egalitarian gender roles and decision-making patterns at home and dual-earner employment arrangements. In contrast, for families who began the migration process after 1965, the division of labor upon reunification was more traditional despite the fact that most women worked outside the home. Separations were shorter for this group of families. During the period of separation, men typically lived with extended kin or families rather than in all-male households. Hondagneu-Sotelo suggests that these differences in the migration process prior to and after 1965 had implications for the gender role enactments after reunification.

POLICY IMPLICATIONS

The overrepresentation of immigrant parents in low-wage, unskilled labor positions and the implications of these jobs for family life suggest the importance of addressing wages and underemployment through education and vocational training. Because many immigrant workers lack the basic occupational skills to obtain better paying positions, programs that provide resources or subsidies for training in skilled jobs may be an important avenue for addressing the limited earning potential of immigrant parents. Our findings also highlighted the advantages of parental education, revealing that education was associated with less underemployment, higher annual incomes, and higher prestige jobs. Providing greater support for this important step through high school completion programs will be important in increasing parents' earning potential. In addition, improving access to postsecondary education for immigrant parents and their offspring through financial support also will be beneficial for increasing the earning potential of immigrant workers. Expanding training for skilled employment and increasing support for postsecondary education among immigrants will be important in light of descriptions of the "hourglass economy—many good jobs at the top, many bad jobs at the bottom, few decent jobs between" (Perlmann & Waldinger, 1997, p. 910) in the United States as an important barrier to upward mobility for immigrants across generations and over time.

Despite the fact that immigrant parents in our sample had lived in the United States for an average of 12–15 years, the majority (90%) spoke primarily Spanish. Spanish-speaking parents had lower incomes, less autonomy in their jobs, and more limited work hours than their English-speaking counterparts. English-speaking mothers (but not fathers) also reported less underemployment and less discrimination than Spanish-speaking mothers. Providing access to programs to learn English may be an important first step in increasing immigrant parents' opportunities for education and advanced job training.

Our review also highlights the negative implications of workplace discrimination for families. Policy initiatives that focus on addressing workplace discrimination are an important step in improving the experiences of immigrant workers in all occupational fields. This not only includes fair hiring and promotion practices but supervisor training around creating and maintaining a work environment that values diversity. Developing and evaluating intervention programs that educate workers and supervisors on discrimination and address the elements of work environments that promote discrimination practices will be an important part of broader policy initiatives addressing discrimination. In conclusion, our review of research on the role of work in the lives of Latino immigrant families reveals there is much work to be done and that this work will have important implications for intervention, prevention, and policy initiatives addressing work–family linkages.

ACKNOWLEDGMENTS

We are grateful to the families and youth who participated in this project, and to the following schools and districts who collaborated: Osborn, Mesa, and Gilbert school districts, Willis Junior High School, Supai and Ingleside Middle Schools, St. Catherine of Sienna, St. Gregory, St. Francis Xavier, St. Mary-Basha, and St. John Bosco. We thank Mark Roosa, Nancy Gonzales, Roger Millsap, Jennifer Kennedy, Melissa Delgado, Lorey Wheeler, Devon Hageman, Lilly Shanahan, Shawna Thayer, and Sarah Killoren for their assistance in conducting this investigation. Funding was provided by National Institute of Child Health and Human Development Grant No. R01HD39666 (Kimberly Updegraff, principal investigator, and Susan M. McHale and Ann C. Crouter, coprincipal investigators, Mark Roosa, Nancy Gonzales, and Roger Millsap, coinvestigators) and the Cowden Fund to the Department of Family and Human Development at Arizona State University.

REFERENCES

Alderete, E., Vega, W. A., Kolody, B., & Aguilar-Gaxiola, S. (1999). Depressive symptomatology: Prevalence and psychosocial risk factors among Mexican migrant farmworkers in California. *Journal of Community Psychology, 27,* 457–471.

Amaro, H., Russo, N. F., & Johnson, J. (1987). Family and work predictors of psychological well-being among Hispanic women professionals. *Psychology of Women Quarterly, 11,* 505–521.

Baca Zinn, M. (1980). Employment and education of Mexican-American women. *Harvard Educational Review, 50*, 47–62.

Baca Zinn, M. (1982). Chicano men and masculinity. *Journal of Ethnic Studies, 10*, 29–44.

Baca Zinn, M. (1990). Family, feminism, and race in America. *Gender and Society, 4*, 68–82.

Bronfenbrenner, U., & Crouter, A. C. (1982). Work and family through time and space. In S. Kamerman & C. Hayes (Eds.), *Families that work: Children in a changing world* (pp. 39–83). Washington, DC: National Academy Press.

Brooks-Gunn, J., Han, W. J., & Waldfogel, J. (2002). Maternal employment and child cognitive outcomes in the first three years of life: The NICHD Study of Early Child Care. *Child Development, 73*, 1052–1072.

Coltrane, S., & Valdez, E. O. (1993). Reluctant compliance: Work–family role allocation in dual-earner Chicano families. In J. C. Hood (Ed.), *Men, work, and family* (pp. 151–175). Newbury Park, CA: Sage.

Crouter, A. C., Bumpus, M. F., Head, M. R., & McHale, S. M. (2001). Implications of overwork and overload for the quality of men's family relationships. *Journal of Marriage and Family, 63*, 404–416.

Crouter, A. C., Bumpus, M. F., Maguire, M. C., & McHale, S. M. (1999). Linking parents' work pressure and adolescents' well-being: Insights into dynamics in dual-earner families. *Developmental Psychology, 35*, 1453–1461.

Crouter, A. C., Davis, K. D., Updegraff, K. A., Delgado, M. Y., & Fortner, M. (2006). Mexican American fathers' occupational conditions: Links to family members' psychological adjustment. *Journal of Marriage and Family, 68*, 843–858.

Crouter, A. C., Head, M. R., Bumpus, M. F., & McHale, S. M. (2001). Household chores: Under what conditions do mothers lean on daughters? In A. Fuligni (Ed.), *Family assistance and obligation during adolescence: New Directions in Child Development* (pp. 23–41). San Francisco: Jossey-Bass.

Dooley, D., & Prause, J. (2004). *The social costs of underemployment: Inadequate employment as disguised unemployment*. New York: Cambridge University Press.

Duncan, G. J., & Brooks-Gunn, J. (Eds.). (1997). *Consequences of growing up poor.* New York: Russell Sage Foundation.

Finch, B. K., Kolody, B., & Vega, W. A. (2000). Perceived discrimination and depression among Mexican-origin adults in California. *Journal of Health and Social Behavior, 41*, 295–313.

Friedland, D. S., & Price, R. H. (2003). Underemployment: Consequences for the health and well-being of workers. *American Journal of Community Psychology, 32*, 33–45.

Golding, J. M. (1990). Division of household labor, strain, and depressive symptoms among Mexican Americans and non-Hispanic whites. *Psychology of Women Quarterly, 14*, 103–117.

Greenlees, C. S., & Saenz, R. (1999). Determinants of employment of recently arrived Mexican immigrant wives. *International Migration Review, 33*, 354–377.

Gutierres, S. E., Saenz, D. S., & Green, B. L. (1994). Job stress and health outcomes among white and Hispanic employees: A test of the person–environment fit model. In G. P. Keita & J. J. Hurrell, Jr. (Eds.), *Job stress in a changing workforce: Investigating gender, diversity, and family issues* (pp. 107–125). Washington, DC: American Psychological Association.

Hondagneu-Sotelo, P. (1992). Overcoming patriarchal constraints: The reconstruction of gender relations among Mexican immigrant women and men. *Gender and Society*, 6, 393–415.

Hondagneu-Sotelo, P. (Ed.). (2003). *Gender and U.S. immigration: Contemporary trends*. Berkeley: University of California Press.

Hovey, J. D., & Magaña, C. G. (2002). Exploring the mental health of Mexican farm workers in the Midwest: Psychosocial predictors of psychological distress and suggestions for prevention and treatment. *Journal of Psychology, 136*, 493–513.

Hughes, D., & Dodge, M. (1997). African American women in the workplace: Relationships between job conditions, sociocultural stress, and perceived job quality. *American Journal of Community Psychology, 25*, 581–599.

Kessler, R. C., Mickelson, K. D., & Williams, D. R. (1999). The prevalence, distribution, and mental health correlates of perceived discrimination in the United States. *Journal of Health and Social Behavior, 40*, 208–230.

Krause, N., & Markides, K. S. (1985). Employment and psychological well-being in Mexican American women. *Journal of Health and Social Behavior, 26*, 15–26.

Lambert, S. J. (1999). Lower-wage workers and the new realities of work and family. *Annals of the American Academy of Political and Social Science, 562*, 174–190.

Leaper, C., & Valin, D. (1996). Predictors of Mexican American mothers' and fathers' attitudes toward gender equality. *Hispanic Journal of Behavioral Sciences, 18*, 343–355.

Madsen, W. (1964). *The Mexican Americans of South Texas*. New York: Holt, Rinehart, & Winston.

Manke, B., Seery, B., Crouter, A. C., & McHale, S. M. (1994). The three corners of domestic labor: Mothers', fathers', and children's weekday and weekend housework. *Journal of Marriage and the Family, 56*, 657–668.

McHale, S. M., Updegraff, K. A., Shanahan, L. K., Crouter, A. C., & Killoren, S. E. (2005). Siblings' differential treatment in Mexican American families. *Journal of Marriage and Family, 67*, 1259–1274.

Menaghan, E. G., & Parcel, T. L. (1991). Determining children's home environments: The impact of maternal characteristics and current occupational and family conditions. *Journal of Marriage and the Family, 53*, 417–431.

Menjívar, C. (2003). The intersection of work and gender: Central American immigrant women and employment in California. In P. Hondagneu-Sotelo (Ed.), *Gender and U.S. immigration: Contemporary trends* (pp. 101–124). Berkeley: University of California Press.

Mosisa, A. T. (2002). The role of foreign-born workers in the U.S. economy. *Monthly Labor Review, 125*, 3–14.

Nightingale, D. M., & Fix, M. (2004). Economic and labor market trends. *The Future of Children, 14*(2), 49–59.

Parcel, T. L., & Menaghan, E. G. (1994a). Early parental work, family social capital, and early childhood outcomes. *American Journal of Sociology, 99*, 972–1009.

Parcel, T. L., & Menaghan, E. G. (1994b). *Parents' jobs and children's lives*. Hawthorne, NY: Aldine de Gruyter.

Parrado, E. A., & Flippen, C. A. (2005). Migration and gender among Mexican women. *American Sociological Review, 70*, 606–632.

Parrado, E. A., Flippen, C. A., & McQuiston, C. (2005). Migration and relationship power among Mexican women. *Demography, 42*, 347–372.

Peñalosa, P. (1968). Mexican family roles. *Journal of Marriage and the Family, 26*, 457–466.

Perlmann, J., & Waldinger, R. (1997). Second generation decline?: Children of immigrants, past and present—A reconsideration. *International Migration Review, 31*, 893–922.

Perry-Jenkins, M., Repetti, R. L., & Crouter, A. C. (2000). Work and family in the 1990s. *Journal of Marriage and the Family, 62*, 981–998.

Phinney, J. S., & Flores, J. (2002). "Unpackaging" acculturation: Aspects of acculturation as predictors of traditional sex role attitudes. *Journal of Cross-Cultural Psychology, 33*, 320–331.

Presser, H. B. (2003). *Working in a 24/7 economy: Challenges for American families*. New York: Russell Sage Foundation.

Roberts, R. E., & Roberts, C. R. (1982). Marriage, work, and depressive symptoms among Mexican Americans. *Hispanic Journal of Behavioral Sciences, 4*, 199–221.

Roberts, R. K., Swanson, N. G., & Murphy, L. R. (2004). Discrimination and occupational mental health. *Journal of Mental Health, 13*, 129–142.

Rodriguez-Calcagno, M., & Brewer, E. W. (2005). Job stress among Hispanic professionals. *Hispanic Journal of Behavioral Sciences, 27*, 504–516.

Saenz, R., Goudy, W. J., & Lorenz, F. O. (1989). The effects of employment and marital relations on depression among Mexican American women. *Journal of Marriage and the Family, 51*, 239–251.

Sanchez, J. I., & Brock, P. (1996). Outcomes of perceived discrimination among Hispanic employees: Is diversity management a luxury or a necessity? *Academy of Management Journal, 39*, 704–719.

Sum, A., Khatiwada, I., Harrington, P., & Palma, S. (2003). *New immigrants in the labor force and the number of employed new immigrants in the U.S. from 2000 through 2003: Continued growth amidst declining employment among the native born population*. Available online at *www.nupr.neu.edu/01-04/immigration_jan.pdf*

Taylor, P. L., Tucker, M. B., & Mitchell-Kernan, C. (1999). Ethnic variations in perceptions of men's provider role. *Psychology of Women Quarterly, 23*, 741–761.

Updegraff, K. A., McHale, S. M., Whiteman, S. D., Thayer, S. M., & Delgado, M. Y. (2005). Adolescent sibling relationships in Mexican American families: Exploring the role of familism. *Journal of Family Psychology, 19*, 512–522.

Vega, W. A. (1990). Hispanic families in the 1980s: A decade of research. *Journal of Marriage and the Family*, *52*, 1015–1024.
Williams, N. (1990). *The Mexican American family: Tradition and change*. Dix Hills, NY: General Hall.
Ybarra, L. (1982). When wives work: The impact on the Chicano family. *Journal of Marriage and the Family*, *44*, 169–178.

CHAPTER 15

Building Bridges

Strategies to Promote Academic and Psychological Resilience for Adolescents of Mexican Origin

Nancy A. Gonzales, Larry E. Dumka,
Anne Marie Mauricio, *and* Miguelina Germán

Children of Mexican national origin are one of the largest and fastest growing subpopulations in the United States, and a large proportion of this growth is due to immigration (Hernandez, Denton, & Macartney, Chapter 1, this volume). As described in several chapters in this volume, this burgeoning population is exposed to a number of challenging conditions that place them at increased risk for social, educational, and psychological difficulties. Children of Mexican origin must surmount significant disadvantages associated with high levels of poverty (Updegraff, Crouter, Umaña-Taylor, & Cansler, Chapter 14, this volume). In addition, these youth must simultaneously adapt to the expectations and values of the mainstream U.S. culture and their culture of origin (Berry, Chapter 4, this volume). And they must forge a positive self-concept and sustain motivation for the future within communities that often provide limited opportunities or expectations for them to succeed (Phinney & Ong, Chapter 3, this volume).

Many Mexican-origin youth develop optimally and enjoy positive psychosocial outcomes, despite these challenges. However, as a group, Mexican-origin youth are at elevated risk for a range of mental health and adjustment problems. Rates of depression, juvenile arrest, early initiation of substance use, and teenage pregnancy are higher for children of Mexican origin when compared to most other groups, including other Latinos (Gonzales, Knight, Morgan-Lopez, Saenz, & Sirolli, 2002; Jones & Krisberg, 1994; National Institute on Drug Abuse, 1998; Roberts & Chen, 1995). Among Mexican-origin youth that have enrolled in U.S. schools, almost a third drop out before graduation, far surpassing the 13% rate for African Americans and the 7% rate for white non-Hispanics (U.S. Department of Education, 2000).

Epidemiological studies show that immigrant youth from Mexico engage in fewer high-risk behaviors than Mexican-origin youth born in the United States (Mendoza, Javier, & Burgos, Chapter 2, this volume). They also have better outcomes on several key indicators of physical health, despite being substantially more disadvantaged economically. This "immigrant paradox" suggests that important cultural strengths may protect immigrant youth from poor physical and mental health. Understanding these strengths may be critical to inform prevention and treatment services and policies. On the other hand, data on educational attainment highlights a particular area of vulnerability for Mexican immigrant youth (Fuligni & Fuligni, Chapter 13, this volume). Despite having higher aspirations and greater belief in the importance of education, Mexican immigrants have more than twice the rate of school dropout compared to their American-born peers. Such a substantial lack of educational progress will subject a large number of these youth to economic hardship and unstable employment, conditions that ultimately increase risk for mental health problems in adulthood. Moreover, their children will become the vulnerable next generation that must cope with the legacy of poverty without the initial optimism that comes with recent immigration.

When combined with economic conditions that make it increasingly difficult for less educated families to earn living wages and access to health care, the demographic and epidemiological data presented in this volume highlight a pressing need for social programs and services to promote academic and psychological resilience for Mexican immigrant youth. We believe this need extends beyond the first generation to include United States-born children of immigrants as well as subsequent generations that continue to deal with the unique challenges associated with their ethnic minority status and cultural adaptation. However, despite a long history of prevention research and identification of evidence-based strategies for a variety of high-risk populations (Greenberg, Domitrovich, & Bumbarger, 1999), there is currently a lack of evidence-based interventions for Mexican-origin youth. This group has rarely been included in randomized trials focused on mental health outcomes besides substance use.

Focusing specifically on the U.S. Mexican-origin population, the current chapter explores how research in developmental, clinical, family, and cultural psychology can inform development of psychosocial interventions to promote positive adaptation of immigrant youth and families. The primary goals of this chapter are to identify empirically supported risk and protective processes that are viable targets for focused intervention efforts to promote academic and psychological resilience for Mexican-origin youth, and to describe intervention strategies that can impact these processes by drawing on existing interventions that have demonstrated efficacy with other high-risk populations. A secondary goal is to describe how these strategies were integrated in the design of the Bridges to High School Program/Puentes a la Secundária (Bridges/Puentes), an empirically based intervention that targets Mexican immigrant and Mexican American middle-school students attending low-income, urban schools. Bridges/Puentes is currently being evaluated in a randomized clinical trial to test its efficacy to prevent high school dropout, depression, and externalizing behavior problems.

In this chapter we discuss processes selected as targets for Bridges/Puentes because they potentially can be altered through individual- and family-level psychosocial interventions. The chapter is meant to illustrate rather than to exhaustively review the risk and protective factors or relevant prevention strategies for Mexican-origin youth. Although our discussion draws from educational research, we do not discuss interventions focused on school curriculum, structure, or climate, though we believe these approaches are critically important and should ultimately be included as part of a comprehensive prevention agenda. In the following section we describe the theoretical framework we used to identify the risk and protective processes we targeted. This is followed by a discussion of relevant intervention strategies and a description of those that we selected for inclusion in Bridges/Puentes. The final section discusses key issues that need to be addressed to ensure that the growing population of Mexican-origin and other immigrant youth will have access in the future to culturally sensitive and effective interventions.

BUILDING BRIDGES: A CULTURAL–ECOLOGICAL FRAMEWORK

We utilized a cultural–ecological framework to identify risk and protective processes presented in this chapter and targeted in Bridges/Puentes. The risk and protective factor framework attempts to identify conditions and processes that increase or decrease the probability of children and adolescents manifesting psychopathology or other forms of dysfunction (Sroufe & Rutter, 1984), with a particular interest in modifiable processes that can be altered through intervention (e.g., Hawkins, Catalano,

& Miller, 1992). Because we believe school dropout and poor mental health are equally serious, interrelated problems for Mexican-origin youth, we sought to identify processes that simultaneously impact both of these outcomes.

Building on Bronfenbrenner's (1979) theory of the social ecology of development and its subsequent extension to research with culturally distinct populations (e.g., Coatsworth, Pantin, & Szapocznik, 2002), a cultural–ecological framework recognizes the several layers of overlapping contextual and cultural influences that shape developmental processes. This approach attempts to understand how developing youth are influenced by and must adapt to multiple social contexts simultaneously, including their families, peers, neighborhoods, and schools, as well as macrolevel contexts that are shaped by local, state, and national attitudes and policies. This approach also recognizes the pervasive role of culture in shaping youth interactions and adaptation across contexts. For example, immigrant youth often encounter widely divergent cultural expectations and values as they navigate between home and peer contexts. Culture and context also intersect to expose Mexican-origin youth to unique challenges such as racism, acculturation, and discrimination that also shape their course of development.

Developmental considerations are also of critical importance within a cultural–ecological framework. Risk and protective processes vary in salience and impact as a function of children's cognitive, emotional, and social development, and with the specific developmental challenges and contexts that children and adolescent encounter across key developmental stages. Chase-Landsdale, D'Angelo, and Palacios (Chapter 8, this volume) describe multiple factors that contribute to academic risk early in life, and Bradley and McKelvey (Chapter 9, this volume) describe how these risks can be ameliorated through early interventions designed to increase academic readiness at school entry. Accumulating research also indicates that the transition to middle/junior high school represents a key turning point or "risky" transition for ethnic minority youth. Grades and attendance, documented predictors of dropping out, have been found to decline in the year following this transition and to represent permanent downward shifts, particularly for ethnic minority youth attending schools in low-income neighborhoods (Seidman, Aber, & French, 2004). Because the junior high transition is a time when trajectories of academic disengagement leading to high school dropout are set into motion, and adolescence is a time when rates of disorder such as depression and more serious delinquency begin to increase precipitously, Bridges/Puentes was designed to address this critical transition period.

Our goal in applying a cultural–ecological framework was to identify modifiable processes, based on our own research and the broader literature, that have cascading effects across overlapping contexts (e.g., family, school, peers) and to apply strategies for altering these processes drawing on a wide range of scientific knowledge and professional expertise to inform program practice. Cascading effects suggests that particular risk and protective processes can be strategically selected for intervention because of their potential to have a positive impact on youth development and adaptation across these contexts (Coatsworth et al., 1996).

BRIDGES/PUENTES: INTERVENTION TARGETS AND STRATEGIES

On the basis of the foregoing considerations, we developed an intervention to decrease risk and strengthen protective resources in four broad domains shown in prior research to be critical for Mexican-origin youth during the junior high/middle school transition: the quality of parenting and parent–child relations, youth coping competencies, family–school linkages, and culturally linked family interactions and traditions. In the following sections we discuss conditions and transactions within each of these domains that undermine or support academic and mental health outcomes and the intervention strategies that we used to target these processes.

Poverty Undermines Effective Parenting

Any attempt to explain academic or health disparities must start with recognition of the powerful role of poverty, perhaps the single greatest threat to the well-being of Mexican-origin youth and families. Immigrant families from Mexico settle in the United States with fewer socioeconomic resources than many other immigrant groups and the general American-born population (Hernandez et al., Chapter 1, this volume). Studies consistently find a strong link between family poverty and children's lowered cognitive development, academic failure, and poor mental health (e.g., Brooks-Gunn & Duncan, 1997). As discussed by Updegraff and colleagues (Chapter 14, this volume), the effects of poverty on child outcome are mediated by a series of factors but research has shown that the largest and most consistent effects occur within the family. As with the parents of other cultural groups in the United States, when Mexican-origin parents are unable to find stable jobs and a living wage, stress-related disruptions in the personal functioning and relationships of caregivers will have an adverse influence on their parenting practices (Barrera et al., 2002; Parke et al., 2004).

In addition, Mexican immigrant families often move into low-income areas characterized by poverty, transience, high crime rates, and schools with fewer resources, and these conditions exert added negative effects on family interactions, parenting, and youth outcomes (Barrera et al., 2002). Economically disadvantaged neighborhoods also have low levels of community resources, including an absence of youth-serving organizations to promote positive youth development, and a lack of community monitoring of youth activity (Sampson, Raudenbusch, & Earls, 1997). As a result, unsupervised and deviant peer groups emerge as serious threats in these neighborhoods (Tolan, Guerra, & Montaini-Klovdahl, 1997). These community conditions further compromise family functioning and parents' ability to guide and protect youth. Immigrant parents may have particular difficulties navigating these risks due to their unfamiliarity with local resources and decreased ability to monitor the activities of English-speaking peers.

Parenting interventions represent a potential source of support and guidance for Mexican immigrant parents coping with these challenges. Prior research has shown that parenting skills can be taught and can help parents improve parent–child relations and avoid specific practices that increase risk for maladjustment (Martinez & Eddy, 2005). Although rarely evaluated in clinical trials with Mexican-origin families, parenting interventions often are quite powerful at reducing and preventing symptomatology, even during adolescence (Greenberg et al., 1999). Indeed, of all possible interventions that might impact the course of children's development, parent skills training is one of the most promising because it can impact youth mental health directly and it has cascading effects across developmental contexts including school behavior and grades and problems within the peer context, such as delinquency, early sexual risk behavior, and substance use (Wolchik et al., 2002).

Given the central role of the family for Mexican-origin youth, we developed a parenting group intervention as a core component of Bridges/Puentes. Similar to other interventions that have been effective in preventing adolescent mental health problems (e.g., Irvine, Biglan, Smolkowski, Metzler, & Ary, 1999), the intervention was designed to impact parents' skills in three domains shown to be critical to adolescents' mental health and school engagement: support (involvement, responsiveness, and reinforcement for prosocial behavior), appropriate discipline (clear rules and consistent consequences), and adequate monitoring (to inhibit wandering and interaction with deviant peers). The parent intervention also sought to strengthen the coparenting alliance in two-parent households by actively seeking both parents' attendance and emphasizing interparental cooperation and consistency in parenting adolescents. In addition, the parenting intervention taught self-calming strategies to facilitate implementation of new parenting skills and reduce coercive interactions with adolescents. Skills were delivered in a group format in which parents could support one another and benefit from discussions with other parents encountering similar life circumstances and concerns.

Environmental Stressors Challenge Youth Coping Resources

Although we believe that bolstering parenting is a powerful strategy to counteract the negative effects of family and community poverty, prior research indicates that this approach alone may not provide sufficient protection for high-risk populations (Greenberg et al., 1999). Adolescents living in low-income communities, particularly those in central urban areas, are at high risk for experiencing a number of pervasive and chronic stressors outside the family context, such as exposure to crime, gang activity, drugs, and violence (Tolan et al., 1997). These youth also are exposed to a higher rate of serious problems within the family, including drug and mental health problems, domestic violence, and legal difficulties (Lynch & Cicchetti, 1998). There is overwhelming evidence that the multiple stressors endemic to low-income communities place a large number of ethnic minority youth at greatly increased risk for emotional, behavioral, and related disorders (Brooks-Gunn & Duncan, 1997).

Early adolescent declines in academic engagement also have been linked to an increase in the number of stressors that youth encounter in their daily lives (Simmons & Blyth, 1997). Transition to junior high or middle school typically corresponds with a new school structure in which youth must interact with a different teacher and a different group of peers several times throughout the day. As a result, students have fewer opportunities to develop strong connections at a time when peer relations and the need to "fit in" are becoming increasingly important. The loss of a stable attachment to a single teacher and group of peers can be especially difficult for Mexican-origin youth socialized to value connection and interdependence. At the same time, many adolescents are experiencing changes associated with puberty and are seeking greater distance from family members, which can further limit their access to support during this difficult transition.

The term "resilience" has been used as a label for processes or mechanisms that help individuals cope with stress and overcome significant adversity in their lives. Masten (2001) notes that a small set of individual characteristics have repeatedly been related to demonstrations of resilience. These psychological qualities include "cognitive and self-regulation skills, positive views of self, and motivation to be effective in the environment" (p. 234). Interventions that can build these competencies represent another potentially powerful strategy to impact risk and promote positive adaptation across contexts. Programs have been developed to target these competencies directly through group-based, classroom-based, and individual interventions that teach specific skills such as problem solving, emotion regulation, and support seeking (Greenberg et al., 1999). Competencies also can be fostered through participation in out-of-school activities that positively influence behavioral, emotional, and academic adjustment (Mahoney, 2000).

Mexican-origin youth also may need additional coping resources to counter culturally linked threats to their academic identity and motivation. For example, many Mexican-origin youth must seek out and sustain a sense of positive future possibilities within a stark social context of unemployment, low-wage jobs, and low educational attainment (Oyserman & Markus, 1990). These youth are likely to experience social contexts that do not afford construction of plausible futures in which school success leads to occupational success in adulthood. This bounding process tends to involve a diminished belief in one's ability to succeed in school and a parallel decline in interest and involvement in school. Identity negotiation may also involve the dual task of assembling a positive sense of self while discrediting negative academic stereotypes and reduced expectations directed at Mexican-origin youth (Okagaki, Frensch, & Dodson, 1996). Academic persistence in the face of these obstacles may be especially difficult for immigrant youth because family members often are unable to provide education role models or much active guidance on schoolwork or other behaviors associated with academic achievement.

A number of community and school-based programs have been developed to protect Latina/Latino youth against these risks. Examples include programs to enable youth to construct and pursue future-oriented goals (e.g., Oyserman, Terry, & Bybee, 2002), programs that provide successful mentors to counteract cultural stereotypes (e.g., Portwood, Ayer, Kinnison, Waris, & Wise, 2005), and programs that use peer mentoring to increase academic self-concept and success (Cardenas, Montecel, Supik, & Harria, 2001; Mehan, Villanueva, Hubbard, & Lintz, 1996).

Bridges/Puentes included an adolescent group intervention to run concurrently with the parent group to promote resilience by teaching coping strategies shown to protect youth from the negative effects of stress (Compas, Malcarne, & Fondacaro, 1988). The Bridges/Puentes adolescent group intervention provided direct instruction and practice in behavioral and cognitive strategies shown by our research and that of others to predict better mental health outcomes for low-income youth and provide some protection against the negative effects of stress in an inner-city context (Gonzales, Tein, Sandler, & Friedman, 2001). Adolescents received instruction, practice, and group support to use problem-solving strategies (e.g., generating solutions, means–ends thinking) and to manage interpersonal situations (with parents, teachers, peers) utilizing techniques that have demonstrated efficacy to reduce externalizing problems (e.g., Kazdin, Siegel, & Bass, 1992). Bridges/Puentes also taught distraction (e.g., engaging in pleasing activities to take one's mind off the problem) and cognitive reframing techniques that function as secondary control strategies shown to be effective in reducing depressive symptoms (Rothbaum, Weisz, & Snyder, 1982). Bridges/Puentes also emphasized support seeking as a coping skill and taught strategies to enlist support from family, prosocial peers, and teachers.

Development of the Bridges/Puentes adolescent intervention was guided by the hypothesis that strengthening adolescents' repertoire of specific coping techniques would provide them with some measure of immunity or resistance to the cumulative stressors and downward spiral initiated for many inner-city youths following the middle/junior high school transition. By encouraging more adaptive coping choices, such as extracurricular activity involvement, we also sought to increase opportunities for adolescents to satisfy their needs for competence, autonomy, and connectedness, three fundamental psychological needs that must be met to promote academic engagement and motivation (e.g., Connell & Wellborn, 1991). The group itself was designed to satisfy these needs and provide a supportive peer context in the midst of their transition to middle or junior high school. However, we also recognized that many youth may not be motivated to use coping strategies to make choices that would optimize future outcomes (e.g., study, resist deviant peer pressure) if these choices were not tied to self-relevant goals and future possibilities. Thus, we incorporated strategies used in other interventions to facilitate adolescents' exploration of possible selves (Oyserman et al., 2002) and to teach skills to identify and achieve desired personal goals (O'Hearn & Gatz, 2002).

Barriers to Involvement in Children's Education

Urban school districts are faced with the substantial challenge of educating the most diverse and underprivileged student population with limited resources and increasing public scrutiny. Pressures have intensified in schools across the country, particularly those deemed to be underperforming, resulting in an abundance of blame directed at school districts, state governments, teachers, students, and families. Unfortunately, these rising tensions serve to exacerbate the underlying reality that many Mexican-origin students do not feel supported in their schools (Gibson & Bejinez, 2002), their parents do not feel welcome (Valdés, 1996), and teachers do not feel efficacious in fulfilling their educational mission (Jussim & Eccles, 1995).

The concept of "cultural capital" is a useful organizing construct for understanding the cultural divide between Mexican-origin families and schools. Bourdieu (1977) argues that schools utilize particular cultural and social resources, and that children from higher socioeconomic classes enter schools already familiar with these social arrangements. Parental involvement in school is important for families to obtain access to these resources (i.e., one's cultural capital) and to support youth school engagement and success. However, as discussed by Fuligni and Fuligni (Chapter 13, this volume), Mexican-origin parents face significant barriers to involvement in their children's schooling. Immigrant parents, in particular, may have a poor understanding of U.S. schools and are ill-prepared to monitor their children's progress or to intervene when they have academic difficulties (Suárez-Orozco & Suárez-Orozco, 1995). Also, immigrant parents may not share the view that direct parental involvement with school is needed and may experience a "power-distance" phenomenon (Hofstedte, 1980) in which the large school system is seen as an institution that deserves great respect and reverence and something that parent should not interfere with; this is likely even more the case with undocumented parents. Teachers may fail to develop relationships with parents because they cannot speak Spanish, do not understand parents' lack of involvement, and may view Mexican-origin parents as part of the problem in educating their children, rather than as a resource (Epstein, 1986).

Ethnographic research indicates it is not a lack of value for education but a lack of information that prevents many Mexican-origin parents from being involved and supportive of education (Delgado-Gaitan, 1992). Research also has shown that these parents can benefit from specific direction, such as educating them about the U.S. school system and helping them establish working relationships with teachers and other school personnel (Gallimore, Goldenberg, & Weisner, 1993). Thus, an additional goal of our work with parents was to provide them with knowledge and skills to successfully support their children's education and navigate within their schools. Our focus on strengthening parent–youth–school linkages is reflected in our decision to structure Bridges/Puentes as a school-based intervention that brings parents and youth together with other families to increase their sense of belonging and trust within the school context. In addition, the parent group intervention sought to increase parents' understanding of teachers' expectations regarding student engagement, enhance parent–teacher communication through modeling and role play of skills, and increase parental behaviors associated with greater success in helping at-risk students (e.g., monitoring academic performance).

We also developed a school liaison intervention component to facilitate families' problem solving and parent–school communication related to their adolescents' school adjustment. The school liaison (SL) was consulted by families wanting additional help with a specific school-related difficulty (e.g., class grades, discipline, bullying). The SL's goal was not to intervene for families, but rather to increase parents' and adolescents' efficacy by coaching them to use the skills taught in the intervention (e.g., communication skills), to obtain needed resources (e.g., after school activities), or alleviate their particular school-related problem. Additionally, the SL encouraged and coached parents to communicate concerns, needs, and questions to teachers and school administrators, empowering parents to seize opportunities to build cultural capital.

Acculturation Has the Potential to Undermine or Promote Resilience

As discussed in greater detail by Berry (Chapter 4, this volume), Mexican-origin youth and their families must adapt to the culture of their new country through the process of *acculturation*, while simultaneously maintaining some connection and sense of identification with their culture of origin (i.e., *enculturation*). This dual cultural adaptation process can present increased opportunities to develop competencies or increase risk and distress, depending on the social contexts in which these processes unfold and the degree to which adolescents are exposed to culturally linked stressors within these contexts.

The process of learning English may be difficult for some immigrant youth, particularly when they attend schools that provide inadequate learning environments for students with limited English proficiency. Language barriers and feelings of marginalization are typically even more pronounced for immigrant parents, particularly those that have limited opportunities to interact within English-dominant settings. These parents will experience the greatest difficulty linking to their children's schools and accessing other needed services for family members, and their children may be placed in the stressful position of being responsible for negotiating important family matters on their behalf (Cooper, Denner, & Lopez, 1999).

The dual processes of acculturation and enculturation also may increase risk for disorder if they produce incompatibilities in cultural values or differing cultural proscriptions across contexts (e.g., family vs. school, family vs. peers) or between family members. For example, strained family interactions can arise when family members follow divergent paths of cultural adaptation (e.g., children acculturating faster than their parents). As they experience greater pressures to adopt U.S. cultural values and norms (e.g., have more freedom like their U.S. peers), some youths may reject their culture of origin, giving rise to conflict with family members, parent–child alienation, and loss of emotional bonds within the family (Szapocznik & Kurtines, 1993). The combination of intergenerational and intercultural conflicts may exacerbate normative family struggles and disrupt the traditional structure of the family.

However, research has shown that when acculturating Mexican-origin youth and families are able to maintain ties to competence-producing aspects of Mexican cultural values and traditions, family relations are less likely to deteriorate and adolescents may derive protective benefits against cultural conflicts and negative influences they encounter outside the family. Traditional family values are of particular importance because they maintain family unity and motivate family members to make choices that are centered on the good of the family (Vega, 1995). Cultural socialization practices aimed at instilling traditional values can also provide youth with a strong sense of ethnic identity and bicultural competence that enhances their coping abilities (Phinney & Ong, Chapter 3, this volume). Bicultural competence enables an individual to navigate successfully within whichever cultural context that person finds him- or herself, and thus experiences less stress that could result from conflicting cultures (LaFromboise, Coleman, & Gerton, 1993).

In an effort to build on these important cultural strengths, intervention strategies have been developed to increase ethnic pride, ethnic identity, and bicultural competence. For example, Cuento therapy (Malgady, Rogler, & Constantino, 1990) used biographical stories of prominent Puerto Ricans in order to expose adolescents to role models of achievement, thereby promoting ethnic pride, a strong sense of ethnic identity, and adaptive ways of coping with poverty and discrimination. Family effectiveness training (FET) was designed specifically for Latin American families (primarily of Cuban origin) with acting-out adolescents in which the effects of immigration and acculturation were exacerbating family conflict (Szapocznik et al., 1988). This program aimed to restore intergenerational communication, reconstruct traditional hierarchical structures in the family, and help parents and adolescents to forge bicultural identities. FET has demonstrated positive effects on family relations and reduction in adolescent antisocial behavior and substance use.

An important goal of Bridges/Puentes was to mobilize Mexican-origin families to use the strengths of their traditional culture to guide and support youth as they transition through middle/junior high and high school. Bridges/Puentes was structured as a family-centered intervention in which all activities were organized around strengthening the family and placing the family in charge of enhancing protective processes and decreasing risk within and across social contexts. The value of the family also was used to motivate family members to try new skills. For example, the parent component encouraged parents to use the strengths of their family to act as a bridge to help their children overcome barriers to school success and adolescents were encouraged to view their effort and success in school as one way to help the family stay strong during stressful times. We also developed a combined parent–child family strengthening intervention component to accompany the separate adolescent and parent groups. Drawing on family-based intervention strategies with demonstrated efficacy to strengthen family processes and decrease risk for problem behaviors (Molgaard, Kumpfer, & Fleming, 1997), our family sessions aimed to strengthen family relations and cohesion by providing structured opportunities for positive parent–child interactions. Activities such as constructing a family tree together, sharing family stories, and reflecting on familial and cultural strengths aimed to enhance family pride and bicultural understanding. We also employed a bicultural empowerment framework as a guiding program philosophy. In line with previous conceptions of empowerment (Zimmerman, 1995), we trained intervention staff to support families of Mexican origin to obtain new resources (skills, knowledge), while also acknowledging and building on their existing cultural strengths to direct their own lives.

FUTURE CONSIDERATIONS TO PROMOTE EFFECTIVE AND SUSTAINABLE INTERVENTIONS

In designing Bridges/Puentes, we identified modifiable processes associated with Mexican-origin adolescents' social ecologies described above and selected empirically supported strategies that could be integrated to form a coherent, multicomponent intervention. The integrated program included (1) a parent skills training group intervention, (2) an adolescent group intervention focused on social/cognitive coping skills, (3) a combined (parent–adolescent) family-strengthening intervention, and (4) a school liaison that worked with individual families to strengthen home–school linkages. This program is currently being evaluated in a multicohort randomized trial with 515 families recruited from four centrally located middle schools in Phoenix, Arizona. The parent training, adolescent coping, and family strengthening components were delivered through nine weekly group-based sessions and two home visitations.

Bridges/Puentes was based on a long-standing research program with Mexican-origin families living in low-income neighborhoods and with the school districts that were involved in the randomized trial. Input was solicited throughout program development from key cultural informants, including school personnel, targeted families, and service providers, to ensure cultural sensitivity to the needs, preferences, goals, experiences, and values of participants and schools. Our experience thus far shows that targeted families find the program to be culturally compatible and appealing such that they are willing to invest time in the program to promote their children's education. One critically important question that the outcome analyses will address is whether a family-focused, school-based intervention can reduce school dropout and mental health disorders for Mexican-origin youth. We also can evaluate which of our targeted risk and protective factors mediate program effects and whether effects vary as a function of individual (e.g., gender) and cultural (e.g., language of program delivery) factors. Answers to these questions will be critical to inform theory as well as future program refinements.

As the U.S. Mexican-origin population continues to grow, the psychological, physical, and educational health of this population must be matters of national priority. Although we believe that culturally sensitive preventive interventions can provide an important resource to increase resilience for future generation, we also believe that there are a number of critical considerations that need to be addressed to ensure that Mexican-origin families and other immigrant groups have fair access to the potential benefits of interventions.

First, despite an abundance of community-based strategies and grassroots efforts to develop culturally sensitive interventions for Mexican-origin families, very few of these promising programs have been evaluated in rigorous experimental trials. Clinical trials with culturally diverse populations are needed to provide a clearer foundation for identifying programs that work within and across groups. Thus, efforts should be intensified to ensure that culturally sensitive interventions are developed to reflect the needs of our diverse nation and that these interventions can meet the standards of evidence-based practice.

Cultural adaptation of existing interventions also must be a matter of priority. Empirically tested youth interventions have prevented and treated youth dysfunction for decades (Weisz, Sandler, Durlak, & Anton, 2005), and yet still very little is known about whether available strategies can ameliorate risk or treat dysfunction for culturally diverse families. Some degree of cultural adaptation (e.g., language translation) is undoubtedly necessary for all interventions (Dumka, Lopez, & JacobsCarter, 2000). Cultural adaptation is especially critical to increase recruitment and engagement of culturally diverse populations (Kumpfer, Alvarado, Smith, & Bellamy, 2002). However, it is possible that some existing programs may work with only modest cultural modifications while others may be fundamentally incompatible for specific segments of the U.S. population. In order for the next generation of intervention research to meet the challenge of our nation's changing demographics, there is a need to explore conditions that justify cultural adaptations to evidence-based interventions and to provide guidelines as to how those adaptations might be developed (Castro, Barrera, & Martinez, 2004).

Our final discussion point relates to concerns that have been raised about the lack of fit between research-based prevention programs and the organizational capabilities and preferences of provider agencies (e.g., schools) and stakeholders' (e.g., parents, community advocates) (Wandersman, 2003). Doubts also have been raised about the applicability of findings on program effectiveness to any particular community given that the clients and organizational context are likely to differ from those in the original evaluation of the program. For these reasons, and because most scientifically validated preventive interventions have not been widely adopted in communities, scholars have argued that prevention science should increase collaboration with key community stakeholders and policymakers, practitioners, and the agencies or institutions ultimately responsible for sustaining interventions (Spoth & Greenberg, 2005). We believe such linkages across stakeholder systems are especially critical when designing comprehensive efforts to promote resilience and successful integration of immigrant youth and families. Although psychosocial interventions represent an important tool to decrease academic disengagement and poor mental health of Mexican immigrant youth, they ultimately will be limited without local community support and broader systemic efforts to simultaneously address cultural–ecological conditions (within schools, classrooms, and communities) and policies that undermine cultural adaptation and optimal development for this population.

ACKNOWLEDGMENTS

This research was supported by National Institute of Mental Health Grant Nos. 5-P30-MH39246-13 (to fund a Preventive Intervention Research Center at Arizona State University) and 1-R01-MH64707.

REFERENCES

Barrera, M. J., Prelow, H. M., Dumka, L. E., Gonzales, N. A., Knight, G. K., Michaels, M. L., et al. (2002). Pathways from family economic conditions to adolescents' distress: Supportive parenting, stressors outside the family, and deviant peers. *Journal of Community Psychology, 30*, 135–152.

Bourdieu, P. (1977). Cultural reproduction and social reproduction. In J. Karabel & A. H. Halsey (Eds.), *Power and ideology in education* (pp. 487–511). New York: Oxford University Press.

Bronbenbrenner, U. (1979). *The ecology of human development: Experiments by nature and design.* Cambridge, MA: Harvard University Press.

Brooks-Gunn, J., & Duncan, G. (1997). The effects of poverty on children. *The Future of Children, 7*(2), 55–71.

Cardenas, J., Montecel, M., Supik, J., & Harria, R. (2001). The Coca-Cola Valued Youth Program: Dropout prevention strategies for at-risk students. *Texas Researcher, 3*, 11–130.

Castro, F. G., Barrera, M., Jr., & Martinez, C. R. (2004). The cultural adaptation of preventive interventions: Resolving tensions between fidelity and fit. *Prevention Science, 5*, 41–45.

Coatsworth, J. D., Pantin, H., & Szapocznik, J. (2002). Familias Unidas: A family-centered ecodevelopmental intervention to reduce risk for problem behavior among Hispanic adolescents. *Clinical Child and Family Psychology Review, 5*(2), 113–132.

Compas, B. E., Malcarne, V. L., & Fondacaro, R. M. (1988). Coping with stressful events in older children and young adolescents. *Journal of Consulting and Clinical Psychology, 56*, 405–411.

Connell, J. P., & Wellborn, J. G. (1991). Competence, autonomy, and relatedness: A motivational analysis of self-system processes. In M. Gunnar & A. Sroufe (Eds.), *The Minnesota Symposia on Child Psychology* (Vol. 23, pp. 43–78). Hillsdale, NJ: Erlbaum.

Cooper, C. R., Denner, J., & Lopez, E. M. (1999). Cultural brokers: Helping Latino children on pathways toward success. *The Future of Children, 9*, 51–57.

Delgado-Gaitan, C. (1992). School matters in the Mexican-American home: Socializing children to education. *American Educational Research Journal, 29*, 495–513.

Dumas, J. E., Rollock, D., Prinz, R. J., Hops, H., & Blechman, E. A. (1999). Cultural sensitivity: Problems and solutions in applied and preventive intervention. *Applied and Preventive Psychology, 8*(3), 175–196.

Dumka, L. E., Lopez, V., & JacobsCarter, S. (2000). Parenting interventions adapted for Latino families: Progress and prospects. In J. M. Contreras, K. A. Kerns, & A. M. Neal-Barnett (Eds.), *Latino children and families in the United States* (pp. 203–231). Westport, CT: Greenwood Press.

Epstein, J. L. (1986). Parents' reactions to teachers' practices of parent involvement. *Elementary School Journal, 86*, 277–294.

Gallimore, R., Goldenberg, C. N., & Weisner, T. S. (1993). The social construction of subjective reality in activity settings: Implications for community psychology. *American Journal of Community Psychology, 21*, 537–559.

Gibson, M. A., & Bejinez, L. F. (2002). Dropout prevention: How migrant education supports Mexican youth. *Journal of Latinos and Education, 1*, 155–175.

Gonzales, N. A., Knight, G. P., Morgan-Lopez, A., Saenz, D., & Sirolli, A. (2002). Acculturation and the mental health of Latino youths: An integration and critique of the literature. In J. Contreras, A. Neal-Barnett, & K. Kerns (Eds.), *Latino children and families in the United States: Current research and future directions* (pp. 45–74). Westport, CT: Praeger.

Gonzales, N. A., Tein, J., Sandler, I. N., & Friedman, R. J. (2001). On the limits of coping: Interactions between stress and coping for inner-city adolescents. *Journal of Adolescent Research, 16*, 372–395.

Greenberg, M. T., Domitrovich, C., & Bumbarger, B. (1999). *Preventing mental disorders in school-age children: A review of the effectiveness of prevention programs.* Washington, DC: U.S. Department of Health and Human Services, Center for Mental Health Services.

Hawkins, J. D., Catalano, R. F., & Miller, J. Y. (1992). Risk and protective factors for alcohol and other drug problems in adolescent and early childhood: Implications for substance abuse prevention. *Psychological Bulletin, 112*, 64–105.

Hofstedte, G. (1980). *Cultural consequences: International differences in work related values.* Beverly Hills, CA: Sage.

Irvine, A. B., Biglan, A., Smolkowski, K., Metzler, C. W., & Ary, D. V. (1999). The effectiveness of a parenting skills program for parents of middle school students in small communities. *Journal of Consulting and Clinical Psychology, 67*, 811–825.

Jones, M. A., & Krisberg, B. (1994). *Images and reality: Juvenile crime, youth violence and public policy.* San Francisco: National Council on Crime and Delinquency.

Jussim, L. J., & Eccles, J. (1995). Are teacher expectations biased by students' gender, social class, or ethnicity? In Y. Lee, L. J. Jussim, & C. R. McCauley (Eds.), *Stereotype accuracy: Toward appreciating group differences* (pp. 245–271). Washington, DC: American Psychological Association.

Kazdin, A. E., Siegel, T. C., & Bass, D. (1992). Cognitive problem-solving skills training and parent management training in the treatment of antisocial behavior in children. *Journal of Consulting and Clinical Psychology, 60*, 733–747.

Kumpfer, K. L., Alvarado, R., Smith, P., & Bellamy, N. (2002). Cultural sensitivity and adaptation in family-based prevention interventions. *Prevention Science, 3*, 241–246.

LaFromboise, T., Coleman, H. L. K., & Gerton, J. (1993). Psychological impact of biculturalism: Evidence and theory. *Psychological Bulletin, 114*, 395–412.

Lynch, M., & Cicchetti, D. (1998). An ecological–transactional analysis of children and contexts: The longitudinal interplay among child maltreatment, community violence, and children's symptomatology. *Development and Psychopathology, 10*, 235–257.

Mahoney, J. L. (2000). School extracurricular activity participation as a moderator in the development of antisocial patterns. *Child Development, 71*, 502–516.

Malgady, R., Rogler, L., & Costantino, G. (1990). Culturally sensitive psychotherapy for Puerto Rican children and adolescents: A program of treatment outcome research. *Journal of Consulting and Clinical Psychology, 58*, 704–712.

Martinez, C. R., Jr., & Eddy, J. M. (2005). Effects of culturally adapted parent management training on Latino youth behavioral health outcomes. *Journal of Consulting and Clinical Psychology, 73*, 841–851.

Masten, A. S. (2001). Ordinary magic: Resilience processes in development. *American Psychologist, 56*, 227–238.

Mehan, H., Villanueva, I., Hubbard, L., & Lintz, A. (1996). *Constructing school success: The consequences of untracking low-achieving students*. New York: Cambridge University Press.

Molgaard, V. K., Kumpfer, K. L., & Fleming, E. (1997). *The Strengthening Families Program: For parents and Iowa youth 10–14 leader guide.* Ames: Iowa State University Extension.

National Institute on Drug Abuse. (1998). *Drug use among racial/ethnic minorities*. Washington, DC: U.S. Department of Health and Human Services, National Institutes of Health.

O'Hearn, T. C., & Gatz, M. (2002). Going for the goal: Improving youth's problem-solving skills through a school-based intervention. *Journal of Community Psychology, 30*(3), 281–303.

Okagaki, L., Frensch, P. A., & Dodson, N. E. (1996). Mexican American children's perceptions of self and school achievement. *Hispanic Journal of Behavioral Sciences, 18*, 469–484.

Oyserman, D., & Markus, H. (1990). Possible selves in balance: Implications for delinquency. *Journal of Social Issues, 46*(2), 141–157.

Oyserman, D., Terry, K., & Bybee, D. (2002). A possible selves intervention to enhance school involvement. *Journal of Adolescence, 25*, 313–326.

Parke, R. D., Coltrane, S., Duffy, S., Buriel, R., Dennis, J., Power, J., et al. (2004). Economic stress, parenting, and child adjustment in Mexican American and European American families. *Child Development, 75*, 1632–1656.

Portwood, S., Ayer, P., Kinnison, R., Waris, R., & Wise, D. (2005). Youth friends: Outcomes from a school-based mentoring program. *Journal of Primary Prevention, 26*(2), 129–145.

Roberts, R. E., & Chen, Y. W. (1995). Depressive symptoms and suicidal ideation among Mexican-origin and Anglo adolescents. *Journal of the American Academy of Child and Adolescent Psychiatry, 34*, 81–90.

Roosa, M. W., Jones, S., Tein, J., & Cree, W. (2003). Prevention science and neighborhood influences on low-income children's development: Theoretical and methodological issues. *American Journal of Community Psychology, 31*, 55–72.

Rothbaum, F., Weisz, J. R., & Snyder, S. S. (1982). Changing the world and changing the self: A two-process model of perceived control. *Journal of Personality and Social Psychology, 42*, 5–37.

Sampson, R. J., Raudenbush, S. W., & Earls, F. (1997). Neighborhoods and violent crime: A multilevel study of collective efficacy. *Science*, *277*, 918–924.

Seidman, E., Aber, J. L., & French, S. E. (2004). The organization of schooling and adolescent development. In K. I. Maton, C. J. Schellenbach, B. J. Leadbeater, & A. L. Solarz (Eds.), *Investing in children, youth, families, and communities: Strengths-based research and policy* (pp. 233–250). Washington, DC: American Psychological Association

Simmons, R. G., & Blyth, D. A. (1987). *Moving into adolescence: The impact of pubertal change and school context*. Hawthorne, NY: Aldine de Gruyter.

Spoth, R. L., & Greenberg, M. T. (2005). Toward a comprehensive strategy for effective practitioner–scientist partnerships and larger-scale community health and well-being. *American Journal of Community Psychology*, *35*, 107–126.

Sroufe, L. A., & Rutter, M. (1984). The domain of developmental psychopathology. *Child Development*, *55*(1), 17–29.

Suárez-Orozco, C., & Suárez-Orozco, M. (1995). *Transformations: Immigration, family life, and achievement motivation among Latino adolescents*. Stanford, CA: Stanford University Press.

Szapocznik, J., & Kurtines, W. M. (1993). Family psychology and cultural diversity: Opportunities for theory, research and application. *American Psychologist*, *48*, 400–407.

Szapocznik, J., Perez-Vidal, A., Brickman, A. L., Foote, F. H., Santisteban, D., Hervis, O., et al. (1988). Engaging adolescent drug abusers and their families in treatment: A strategic structural systems approach. *Journal of Consulting and Clinical Psychology*, *56*, 552–557.

Tolan, P. H., Guerra, N. G., & Montaini-Klovdahl, L. R. (1997). Staying out of harm's way: Coping and the development of inner-city children. In I. N. Sandler & S. A. Wolchik (Eds.), *Handbook of children's coping: Linking theory and intervention* (pp. 453–479). New York: Plenum Press.

U.S. Department of Education. (2000). *Dropout rates in the United States: 1998* (NCES 2000-022). Washington, DC: U.S. Government Printing Office.

Valdés, G. (1996). *Con Respecto: Bridging the distance between culturally diverse families and schools*. New York: Teachers College Press.

Vega, W. A. (1995). The study of Latino families: A point of departure. In R. E. Zambrana (Ed.), *Understanding Latino families: Scholarship, policy, and practice* (pp. 3–17). Thousand Oaks, CA: Sage.

Wandersman, A. (2003). Community science: Bridging the gap between science and practice with community-centered models. *American Journal of Community Psychology*, *31*, 227–242.

Weisz, J. R., Sandler, I. N., Durlak, J. A., & Anton, B. S. (2005). Promoting and protecting youth mental health through evidence-based prevention and treatment. *American Psychologist*, *60*, 628–648.

Wolchik, S. A., Sandler, I. N., Millsap, R. E., Plummer, B. A., Greene, S. M., Anderson, E. R., et al. (2002). Six-year follow-up of a randomized controlled trial of preventive interventions for children of divorce. *Journal of the American Medical Association*, *288*, 1874–1881.

Zimmerman, M. A. (1995). Psychological empowerment: Issues and illustrations. *American Journal of Community Psychology*, *23*(5), 581–599.

CHAPTER 16

The Role of the Law in Relationships within Immigrant Families

Traditional Parenting Practices in Conflict with American Concepts of Maltreatment

Doriane Lambelet Coleman

The law plays an important role in immigrant families because (among other things) it describes maltreatment according to majoritarian norms. This means that traditional parenting practices that conflict or appear to conflict with those norms are subject to designation as "abusive" or "neglectful." The parent–child relationship within these immigrant families is thus at increased risk of official intervention, disruption, and even termination depending on the circumstances.

This chapter begins with a description of the legal doctrine that establishes majoritarian norms as the basis for evaluating the harmfulness of parental behavior toward children, and details the ways in which this doctrine creates problems for families with different traditions. It then summarizes the legal literature with respect to the propriety of imposing majoritarian norms on nonconforming immigrant families. Predictably, the views expressed by legal (and other) academics on the subject range from "absolutist" to "relativist" and include a number of intermediate positions. Finally, this chapter identifies modest reforms to child protective services (CPS) policies and protocols that would begin to make meaningful existing admonitions to consider cultural differences as immigrant families are engaged by the child welfare system.

"Cultural competence" has become a mainstream value within the social work profession. Nevertheless, there remains quite some work to be done to operationalize this value, particularly in the *gateway phases* of the system, that is, the reporting, screening, and investigation phases, where cultural conflicts concerning the definition of abuse and neglect first come to the fore. While it is certainly important to be culturally competent throughout all phases of the child maltreatment process, assuring that the state's initial interventions in the family reflect this value will go far toward its ultimate objective of safeguarding the health and welfare of all children and families.

THE ROLE OF THE LAW IN RELATIONSHIPS WITHIN THE IMMIGRANT FAMILY

The Constitution of the United States protects the right of all parents to raise their children as they see fit. The Supreme Court has read the Fourteenth Amendment's due process clause to provide parents with wide latitude in this regard, both because they are presumed by law to be the children's first and best caretakers and thus generally to act in the best interests of their children, and to protect the diversity of parenting practices in this ideologically, religiously, culturally, and ethnically heterogeneous society. The emerging rule, known as *the doctrine of parental autonomy*, trumps the right of individual states and their localities to define "the reasonable parent" in a way that would seek to standardize those practices—for example, according to native, white, middle-class traditions. At bottom what this means is that the states cannot generally intervene in the family to force particular parenting decisions or practices, or otherwise to govern the details of the parent–child relationship (*Troxel v. Granville*, 2000).

Like other fundamental constitutional rights, however, the right of parental autonomy is limited. In particular, the Supreme Court has been clear that the Fourteenth Amendment does not immunize parents from intervention when they abuse or neglect their children. Indeed, in both Supreme Court doctrine and practice, the boundaries of parental authority are generally established by the states' maltreatment laws: Parenting decisions and practices are "legal" so long as they cannot be described as "abusive" or "neglectful." Or they are "illegal" where they can be described as such. In this context, the law's presumption that parents act in their children's best interests is reversed, and the state is entitled to intervene in the family to check on or protect a victimized child (*Santosky v. Kramer*, 1982). There are narrow exceptions to this doctrine. For example, under the First Amendment, parents are entitled to refuse orthodox

(Western) medical treatment for their ill children on religious grounds so long as their refusal does not seriously jeopardize the health or life of those children (Child Welfare Information Gateway, 2005). Notably, however, there is no constitutional exception for traditional practices that are merely culturally based; the doctrine of parental autonomy protects (among other things) the right of parents to raise their children according to their culture so long as that culture does not dictate behavior or inaction that amounts to maltreatment.

At the same time, because parental autonomy as a federal constitutional principle trumps conflicting state laws, the states cannot describe parental decisions or practices as maltreatment unless they are likely to cause real harm. To use a classic illustration, parents cannot choose *not* to send their children to elementary and junior high school—or to send *only* their male children, for example—because this choice meets the states' definition of neglect *and* because the states' definition has been accepted by the Supreme Court as necessary to protect the opportunity of all children to develop into fully functioning citizens. On the other hand, the states are not entitled to set mandatory education requirements or to define "educational neglect" in such a way as to exclude parents' choice to send their children to private schools that assure a minimum core curriculum because such a definition is not necessary either to protect children or society from harm (*Meyer v. Nebraska*, 1923; *Pierce v. Society of Sisters*, 1925).

This check was most recently illustrated by a decision of the North Carolina Supreme Court denying CPS officials the right to define as a "neglected juvenile" a young child who had been seen naked and apparently unsupervised in her family's driveway. According to the court, "a single report" of such an event "does not trigger the investigative requirements" of the state's neglect provisions. What was reported in this case "does not in and of itself constitute 'neglect' " (*In the Matter of Joanie Stumbo, et al.*, 2003). While this decision was reached under state rather than federal constitutional law, it reinforces the point that while citizen reporters and CPS officials have quite a lot of leeway to initiate interventions in the parent–child relationship, their operating definitions of abuse and neglect are subject to supervision and eventually to override by the courts, whose job it is to assure that these definitions do not unduly trample upon the right of parents to raise their children as they see fit. Whether or not particular parental conduct or inaction causes or risks harm that amounts to maltreatment is thus initially and generally a question for the states and their designated local agents, with the possibility of a federal constitutional override or refinement in cases where the courts disagree with a particular designation.

The states arrive at their definitions of abuse and neglect in the same way that they develop other values-based legislation and policy: They apply prevailing (majoritarian) norms and sometimes also the recommendations of experts in the field about what is needed to achieve public policy goals. In the child welfare context, these definitions tend to be quite broad and even vague. For example, California "defines 'physical abuse' all-inclusively, as 'nonaccidental bodily injury that has been or is being inflicted on a child' " (State of California, *Manual of Policies and Procedures: Child Welfare Services*, § 31-002[9][B], 2002). North Carolina "defines a 'neglected juvenile' most broadly to include the child 'who does not receive proper care, supervision, or discipline . . . or who is not provided necessary medical . . . or . . . remedial care; or who lives in an environment injurious to [his or her] welfare . . ." (State of North Carolina, *General Statutes* § 7B-101, 2004). As I have written elsewhere, "This [breadth] is to assure that the state can exercise wide discretion in treating targeted parental conduct as maltreatment; and it ensures that the state is not precluded from addressing such conduct by the failure of the legislature or administrative officials to include all conceivable forms of abuse or neglect in its laws" (Coleman, 2005, pp. 428–429). While the U.S. Supreme Court will strike as unconstitutional statutes that are overly vague because they fail to give sufficient notice of their proscriptions, even the broadest child maltreatment definitions consistently survive this scrutiny (Coleman, 2005, p. 428 and note 33).

The states, through their officials and their process, take full advantage of the flexibility these definitions provide to target apparently nonconforming parental conduct or inaction as maltreatment. At the outset, this flexibility is exercised by child maltreatment reporters; these reporters can be state officials or private individuals who call child abuse hotlines when they have seen what appears to them to be abuse or neglect. Subsequently, it is exercised by those who screen reports, caseworkers who investigate them, their supervisors who oversee the decision whether or not to substantiate maltreatment allegations, and the judges who are ultimately responsible for evaluating the validity of individual substantiated claims.

Immigrant families are subject to official intervention under this paradigm in three different situations. First, the law may intervene in the family when a parent is in fact abusing or neglecting a child without regard to tradition or religion. Incest is an example of conduct that fits in this category because no culture (at least of which I am aware) condones this parental behavior. Second, the law may intervene when a parent is engaging in a childrearing practice that is acceptable according to his or her culture or religion of origin, but which in fact constitutes maltreatment as defined by the locality in which the conduct takes place. Traditional forms of female circumcision are an example that fits in this category. Third, the law may intervene when a parent is engaging in a traditional or religiously based parenting practice that only appears to constitute maltreatment. Oral contact with a child's genitalia either to cleanse or to show respect for the child according to religious or traditional custom (particularly of some Jews and Muslims) is an example of conduct that fits in this category.

This chapter does not address the first situation, in which parents are maltreating their children without regard to tradition, because these immigrant families are not different from other families. Rather, the remainder of the discussion focuses on the second and third situations, in which parents engage in traditional practices that violate or else only appear to violate maltreatment law. It begins by providing examples of these two categories of cases. The relevance of the distinction between the categories is then discussed below, in the context of my recommendations for reform of CPS protocols as these relate to the engagement of immigrant families.

There are many recorded instances in which immigrant parents have in fact contravened child maltreatment laws in connection with traditional parenting practices. Parents in this context typically are not aware that their traditions are inconsistent with local proscriptions. Sometimes, however, they know that they are violating the law, but believe that they should be permitted nevertheless to engage in those traditional practices because they came to the United States at least in part if not entirely on the assumption that we are a free, nondiscriminatory society. For example:

Somali and other African immigrant parents have had their daughters circumcised according to religious and/or cultural tradition that requires the surgery for the girls to be marriageable and otherwise acceptable members of the group. Depending on the tradition, the circumcision involves the cutting and removal of all or parts of a young girl's external genitalia, including the clitoris; in its most extreme form all of the genitalia is removed and the resulting wound is stitched together leaving only a small opening for urine to pass. This practice constitutes battery and is prohibited by state child abuse and criminal laws as well as by a federal law that specifically targets the procedure (Coleman, 1998).

Iraqi Kurdish immigrants have forced their teenaged daughters into arranged marriages with adult men. These adult men have subsequently consummated those marriages, also forcibly, and again according to custom. Both practices constitute sexual abuse of a child and are punishable under state maltreatment laws and, depending on the parties and the facts, also under state criminal law (Talbot, 1997).

And Laotian Hmong immigrants have been reluctant to treat their epileptic children according to standard (Western) medical protocols based on the traditional view that children exhibiting the symptoms of epilepsy are blessed. According to Fadiman (1997), "Their seizures are thought to be evidence that they have the power to perceive things other people cannot see, as well as facilitating their entry into trances, a prerequisite for their journeys into the realm of the unseen" (p. 21). This reluctance amounts to medical neglect, which is prohibited by state maltreatment law as well as by corresponding state criminal laws depending on the severity of the consequences.

A more complicated category of cases involves traditional parenting practices that only appear to contravene U.S. concepts of maltreatment. Recently, the facts in these cases have tended to involve allegations of sexual abuse. In the past, however, the majority of cases in this category involved simple neglect charges and mostly indigenous rather than immigrant minority groups. Parents in these cases are differently concerned (if they know enough to be concerned at all) because their apparently nonconforming traditions are driven by the same child welfare norms that undergird the maltreatment laws they are accused of violating. For example:

An Afghani immigrant living in Maine was accused, charged, and convicted of criminal sexual assault on a child as a result of having engulfed his infant son's penis in his mouth in front of witnesses according to a religious and cultural tradition that called for this conduct—which was described as putting the dirtiest part of the human body into the cleanest part—as a showing of ultimate love and respect for the child. The witnesses were his camera-wielding wife, his mother to whom the photographs of the event were sent as proof of his goodness as a father, and the neighboring babysitter and her mother who reported the conduct to local authorities after having seen the family's photo album. This practice appeared to the uninitiated U.S. witnesses and triers of fact as "sexual" in nature, despite that it was anything but that from the perspective of the defendant, his family, and his tradition. Indeed, in that tradition, the use of a child for sexual gratification is punishable by death. The Maine Supreme Court ultimately designated his offense "de minimis" based on his lack of sexual intent, which allowed him to be freed from prison and reunited with his wife and child (*Maine v. Kargar*, 1996).

Navajo parents were frequently charged with child neglect and their children removed from their custody for keeping a dirty house and for leaving their children unattended. These charges were based on findings by white officials that the families' traditional hogans had only dirt floors—hence they were, by definition, "dirty"—and that extended family kinship groups, either instead of or in addition to parents, often defined themselves as responsible for the children's day-to-day care and upbringing (Atwood, 2000; Indian Child Welfare Program, 1974). The officials' motivation is today understood to have been part of a policy to destroy the tribes by forcing assimilation of the children into white society. Contemporaneously, the sense of many was that the officials did not appreciate, or else refused to accept, that a bare floor could be a clean one, and that Navajo extended family kinship groups assured children a permanent home and continuity of care, neither of which could be assumed to exist in the majority culture. Ultimately, the United States intervened to force official acceptance of Native American, including these Navajo, parenting traditions, on the bases that the children were not at risk, and that prior official intervention had not only been misguided, but had in fact destroyed generations of families and the bonds that otherwise would have held them together in the best interests of the children (Indian Child Welfare Act, 1978).

In all of these cases, the state intervened in the family to protect children who were the subjects of traditional parenting practices on the basis that, from the outside and according to majoritarian norms, these practices looked like maltreatment. Again, the law supports such interventions because it defines maltreatment according to those norms. In the following section of this chapter, I discuss legal scholars' views concerning the propriety of such a role for the law in relationships within immigrant families.

LEGAL SCHOLARS' VIEWS ON THE PROPER ROLE OF THE LAW IN RELATIONSHIPS WITHIN IMMIGRANT FAMILIES

Legal academics from multiple subdisciplines have shown keen interest in the inevitable collisions that have surfaced over time between U.S. norms and the nonconforming traditional practices of mostly non-European immigrants and refugees. Central to their interest is how the law should respond to these collisions. Among others, this issue has been tackled by scholars of the criminal law, feminist jurisprudence, immigration, political science and law, culture and law, and families and children. Only a very few of the resulting works have concentrated specifically on traditional practices that violate maltreatment rules (Levesque, 2000; Renteln,

1994; Taylor, 1997). Nevertheless, the basic theoretical positions that have been adopted in the larger context are easily applied to this narrower setting.

The first of these theoretical positions has been characterized as "absolutist" in that its adherents hold the absolute view that, whatever the legal issue, U.S. law applies to the conduct of all individuals including immigrants in the United States (Renteln, 1994). Depending on the scholar, this view is variously based in a sense that the rule of law would be compromised by exceptions based in immigrant culture; on the basis that when immigrants are given the privilege of residence in the United States, they ought to adhere to U.S. norms as ensconced in the law, as in "when in Rome, do as the Romans do"; and on the belief that U.S. law in any event reflects the best normative choices. As applied to the child welfare context, this absolutist view provides that immigrant families are properly subjected to existing abuse and neglect definitions notwithstanding the fact that these might discriminate against non-native traditional parenting practices.

The second and opposing position has been characterized as "relativist" because its adherents hold the view that all cultures are equally valid and thus worthy of respect in the law (Renteln, 1994). This view is premised on the notion that the United States is an intentionally pluralistic society in which individual (and, by derivation, subgroup) liberty is a preeminent principle that denies the legitimacy of discrimination among its members' diverse values and norms. While it may be understood that immigrants from nonconforming traditions test the strength of this principle in ways that those from relatively consistent traditions do not, still it is assumed that the law must provide equal protection even to these traditions. Indeed, the United States's racist legal history is sometimes invoked by scholars associated with this position as separate justification for the country's obligation to remedy this history in part by taking affirmative steps to include and even embrace minority population subgroups' diverse traditions (Sing, 1999). As applied to the child welfare context, the relativist view provides that abuse and neglect may not be defined in ways that would preclude or penalize immigrant parents from engaging in their own traditional childrearing practices.

The third theoretical position on the question of how the law should respond to collisions between U.S. norms and nonconforming traditional practices reflects a range of intermediate views. The most important of these have been articulated by Alison Dundes Renteln and Leti Volpp.

Renteln has suggested that "the legal system should sanction intervention when the parental action will lead to irreparable physical injury" but not otherwise. Thus, for example, she would permit intervention in the family "to prevent scarification, female circumcision, and some types of corporal punishment, but not necessarily for the practice of folk medicine" (Renteln, 1994, p. 57). In Renteln's view, nonconforming traditional practices deserve respect within our constitutional framework, perhaps particularly when these are designed to reinforce the child's membership in his or her cultural or religious community. Nevertheless, because irreparable physical injuries such as scarification and circumcision can affect the ability of an immigrant child to assimilate into the majority culture should he or she eventually desire this outcome, the state should prevent his or her parents from foreclosing his or her options. Within this scheme, parents would be free to use folk remedies such as coining and cupping—which can be painful and cause bruising, but which do not have permanent consequences—despite the fact that their effects might otherwise meet abuse standards.

Volpp has suggested that patriarchal traditions should be devalued in U.S. law when they are invoked by traditional oppressors but valued when they are invoked by traditional victims as a way to equalize the relationship among the two groups as they move to this country. According to this "antisubordination" approach, a woman who engages in the traditional practice of mother–child suicide ought to be permitted to rely upon the acceptability of the practice in Japan as a court in the United States considers the nature and degree of her culpability for the murder of her child because the practice itself is based in a patriarchal tradition that condemns women to shame and then suicide when their husbands have been unfaithful. On the other hand, a man who kills his wife because she has been unfaithful ought not to be permitted to rely upon the acceptability of this conduct in China as a court in this country assesses his culpability for her murder because he is merely a patriarch engaged in a nonreciprocal traditional practice (Volpp, 1994, 1996).

In my own previous work, I have taken an absolutist position on the applicability of U.S. legal norms to the evaluation of the culpability of immigrants whose traditional practices transgress those norms. Unlike some others who hold this view, I do not find that U.S. law and cultural norms are always best; indeed, particularly as it relates to societal policies toward children, U.S. law is often severely lacking. On the other hand, I do believe in the overriding importance of maintaining the rule of law, and of privileging the antidiscrimination principle over pluralism, especially where women and children can be characterized as the victims of immigrant traditional practices. As I have written elsewhere:

> Respect for [immigrants] requires that we view multiculturalism as a positive and even necessary factor in the debate about how to resolve

> [cultural] conflicts. Without the sensitivity that multiculturalism injects into the debate, we have little hope of understanding the obstacles immigrants face, or of ensuring their successful integration into American society. Indeed, multiculturalism's twin caveats—that we recognize our natural tendency toward ethnocentrism, and that we tread gently if at all upon that which is at the core of immigrant culture—are essential to the attainment of these objectives. Nevertheless, multiculturalism should not be permitted either intentionally or incidentally to erode the progress we have made as a culture in protecting the rights of minorities, women, and children, or to reverse our relative success in elevating the rights of these groups to the level traditionally enjoyed by propertied men of European descent. (Coleman, 1996, p. 1166)

With respect to the relationship between immigrants and U.S. legal norms in particular, I have taken the position that

> For whatever reason or reasons immigrants come to this country, their coming is very much a "deal" (one that Americans are presumed to have accepted) whose terms include the adoption of American political culture's vision of liberty *and* their acceptance of its limitations. At bottom, this means two things. First, . . . this culture is entitled to define the harmful deviations that it accepts and those that it rejects, and it will enforce the lines thus drawn uniformly. Second, every individual who is a part of the social compact—including the native born and immigrant alike—is responsible for his or her own conformance with the law and, equally important, is entitled to its full protection. (Coleman, 2001, pp. 998–999)

Examining cultural collisions according to this view, I have, for example, rejected the claim that traditional forms of female circumcision are appropriately practiced in the United States, even when the proposal involves so-called medicalized circumcisions, because the practice on its face constitutes a serious physical injury whose rationale is fundamentally incompatible with progressive legal norms concerning the treatment of women and female children (Coleman, 1996, 1998). On the other hand, I have argued in favor of the legality of symbolic forms of female circumcision that involve a " 'simple, symbolic cut' amounting to a mere 'nick'—enough to draw blood, with no tissue removal or subsequent scarring"—because equal protection doctrine does not permit state child abuse laws simultaneously to define physical abuse to include such circumcisions and to exclude more damaging male circumcisions unless the latter can be characterized as medically required (Coleman, 1998).

In my support for the uniform application of the laws to all families residing in the United States, I do not deny that cultural differences should matter in the way the child maltreatment system engages immigrant families. Indeed, culturally insensitive interventions risk causing harm to the very children they are designed to protect. As I argue in the final section of this chapter, this is perhaps particularly true in the gateway phases of the system.

A VIEW TOWARD AMELIORATING THE CHILD PROTECTIVE SERVICES RESPONSE TO IMMIGRANT FAMILIES

Parents are their children's first and best caretakers. This is true even in many families where parents are maltreating their children. Neither the state nor other private citizens (e.g., foster parents) are obviously equipped to do a better job of ensuring the children's emotional and developmental well-being than their parents, with whom they share "natural bonds of affection" as well as an environment, experiences, and the knowledge and sensitivity that necessarily result from those sources (*Parham v. J. R.*, 1979). These presumptions are deeply ensconced in U.S. law as well as in the majority culture.

These presumptions are also particularly relevant to the development of CPS responses to reports that immigrant parents may be maltreating their children. Traditional parenting practices that conflict with U.S. concepts of maltreatment are likely to affect the parent–child relationship (and thus the child's emotional and developmental welfare) differently than would such practices engaged outside of their natural cultural context. Thus, for example, Asian children who are the subjects of physical bruising caused by the practice of folk medicine are likely to respond differently to these bruises and to their parents than are U.S. children who are the victims of the same degree of harm caused by a maliciously motivated parent. The proposition that parental motivation may affect the child's response to parentally inflicted physical harm is supported by studies tending to show that while frequent physical discipline is generally related to more child aggression, anxiety, and depression, in cultures where the use of physical discipline is normative, there is only a weak link between these factors (Lansford et al., 2005). While intervention in both families is appropriate given that bruising a child constitutes abuse, an uneducated CPS response to the immigrant family that represents an inappropriate or overreaction to the circumstances is likely to fail the child and his or her family in important respects. And certainly, a system that is predicated on the child's welfare and which otherwise values nonessential cultural differences should have a way to ensure that traditional parenting practices that only appear to conflict with U.S. concepts of maltreatment do not become the basis for a full-fledged adversarial intervention in the family, as such interventions can only result in harm to the child.

Cultural competence has become a central feature of the social work profession. As defined in the National Association of Social Workers (NASW) Standards for Cultural Competence in Social Work Practice, cultural competence "refers to the process by which individuals and systems respond respectfully and effectively to people of all cultures, languages, classes, races, ethnic backgrounds, religions, and other diversity factors in a manner that recognizes, affirms, and values the worth of individuals, families, and communities and protects and preserves the dignity of each" (NASW, 2001). As part of its goal of cultural competence, the NASW " 'supports and encourages the development of standards for culturally competent social work practice, a definition of expertise, and the advancement of practice models that have relevance for the range of needs and services represented by diverse client populations' " (NASW, 2000, p. 61). In part as a result of the NASW's efforts, "the concept of cultural competence has moved through a progression of ideas and theoretical constructs favoring cultural pluralism, cultural sensitivity, multiculturalism, and a transcultural orientation to social work practice" (Jackson, 2005, p. 5).

This movement from theory to practice has been slow, however, to the point where the NASW itself recently acknowledged that "efforts are required at the micro, mezzo and macro practice levels to affect direct practice and supervision, program administration, and social policy to achieve meaningful outcomes as defined by consumers, families and communities" (Jackson, 2005, p. 7). In other words, despite an apparently sincere desire within the social work community to bridge the theory–practice gap—a desire that is clearly in evidence in the organization's most recent policy statement announcing its intent "to promote the advancement of practice models that have relevance for the range of needs and services represented by diverse client populations" (Jackson, 2005, p. 12)—there remains a real dearth of such models. Of course, states and localities with important immigrant populations are likely to note the relevance of cultural competence in their maltreatment statutes and/or policies and protocols. And in general, formal admonitions to take culture into account when processing reports, conducting investigations, and intervening otherwise in the family are no longer rare (Levesque, 2000). What remains rare is the provision of appropriately sophisticated instruction for social workers, law enforcement officers, judges, and lawyers about how to operationalize those admonitions.

This state of affairs is particularly stark with respect to the gateway phases of the maltreatment reporting process—the reporting, screening, and investigation phases—which tend to receive the least attention from policymakers and researchers. Indeed, to the extent that the NASW's pronouncements describe the contexts in which cultural competence is most relevant, they tend to exclude these gateway phases, focusing instead on later aspects of the process that feature the delivery of social work services to families who are presumed properly to be within the system. While it is clearly important to develop culturally sensitive models for later phases of the process that also tend to be highly intrusive and thus impacting on the parent–child relationship, the significance of the gateway phases should not be ignored. As Howze (1996) has noted, it is essential "to recognize that the initial approach to parents or children by . . . social workers is often the first step in developing the walls of mistrust and anger that are part of" this process (p. 2). Most importantly, though, the gateway phases are the locus of the state's first interventions in the family, and thus the first opportunity the state has to get it right.

Getting it right at this stage requires the development of a model that is designed to achieve two goals. First, it must be designed so that cases that involve parenting practices that are abusive or neglectful are accurately and quickly separated from those that only appear to involve maltreatment because of the unusual nature of the parents' conduct. Successful triage along these lines will minimize overinclusiveness in subsequent phases of the process, which is good for children and for the overall effectiveness of the system. Second, in either case, the model must be designed so that the state's intervention is the least detrimental to the family and the child it seeks to protect. While this should always be a principal goal of the child welfare system, that system has had a tendency to be blind to the fact that its well-intentioned interventions often can cause quite a lot of harm (Coleman, 2005). Again, depending on the traditional practice, this risk may be amplified in the immigrant context where children, particularly young children who have not yet been exposed to the majority culture, are likelier than their native peers to experience the state's intervention as more harmful than their parents' conduct.

Given these goals, any model that would make meaningful existing admonitions to consider cultural differences in the gateway phases of the maltreatment process requires the following:

1. Prophylactic educational measures that target both the affected immigrant communities and those who staff the locality's child welfare agency. In communities with substantial immigrant populations, it is essential that CPS and immigrant community leaders work together to assure, in advance of cultural conflicts, that CPS gains relevant cultural

competence, including about nonconforming traditional practices that are likely to be perceived as maltreatment, and about culturally based sensitivities to interventions in the family to safeguard the welfare of its children. At the same time, immigrant leaders must be assured the means to educate their communities about U.S. legal norms so that immigrants who wish to assimilate are given a real opportunity, again in advance of conflicts, to conform their practices to those norms.

2. Amendment of the locality's screening procedures to include culturally relevant queries and data collection. The maltreatment reports screening stage is the locus of the state's first opportunity to develop relevant information about a child's situation. In the immigrant context, this is also its first opportunity to establish culturally relevant details about the family, and specifically to sort cases according to whether they are or only appear to constitute maltreatment—for example, to determine whether they actually represent an allegation of sexual abuse, or whether they only appear as such to the uneducated eye. To achieve these ends, personnel responsible for screening must receive training in the demographics of their territory, and must be provided with an appropriately sophisticated interview instrument that reflects the salient features of any demographic differences.

3. Investigative strategies that reflect (a) an understanding that any disruption of the family can have harmful consequences for the child, and that this risk is particularly high in the context of immigrant families; (b) the knowledge that there will be unusual parenting practices that only appear to be maltreatment; and (c) the judgment that immigrant families ought to be approached and treated throughout this stage with particular attention to cultural nuance so that the state does not engage in unnecessary or unnecessarily aggressive interventions.

CONCLUSION

The law plays an important role in relationships within immigrant families that engage in traditional practices that conflict or appear to conflict with U.S. concepts of maltreatment. While the Constitution allows all parents including immigrant parents quite a lot of liberty in the ways they choose to raise their children—the states cannot "standardize" the parent–child relationship according to majoritarian ideals—this liberty is very much bounded by the limits of the majority's tolerance for harm. In other words, "abuse" and "neglect" are not culturally relative terms in U.S. law.

Scholars differ on whether the law ought to play such an important role in the lives of immigrant families. Some are committed to a vision of this country as multicultural in all of its institutions; they hold the view that the law ought to respect immigrant traditions absolutely, even when these cause what we would otherwise view as impermissible harm to children. Also out of a respect for immigrant traditions and the multicultural ideal, others would tolerate most nonconforming practices, but would draw the line at more severe forms of physical harm, or else at their use to perpetuate discriminatory hierarchies. Yet others support the imposition of majoritarian legal norms on nonconforming immigrant families, on the view that those norms are "best" and/or that the society's commitment to pluralism does not deny it the right (or else the inevitability) of a predominant legal culture.

However these theoretical debates are ultimately resolved, children are clearly better off when the state intervenes in the family only when it is necessary to protect them from greater harm, and then only in the least detrimental way possible. In the case of immigrant children, meeting these goals requires cultural competence in all phases of the child maltreatment system. To date, the social work community has focused on developing practice models to incorporate cultural competence in the latter phases of that system. It is equally important to develop cultural competence models for the earlier gateway phases, because this is the first opportunity the state has to assure a correct and appropriately tailored intervention. To be most effective in these respects, practice models for the gateway phases must include prophylactic educational measures that target both the affected immigrant communities and those who staff the locality's child welfare agency; screening procedures that include culturally relevant queries and data collection; and investigative approaches that reflect an appropriately sophisticated understanding of relevant cultural differences and their implications for the state's role in relationships within the immigrant family.

REFERENCES

Atwood, B. A. (2000). Tribal jurisprudence and cultural meanings of the family. *Nebraska Law Review, 79*, 577–656.

Child Welfare Information Gateway. (2005). *Definitions of abuse and neglect.* Retrieved September 7, 2006, from *www.childwelfare.gov/systemwise/laws_policies/statutes/define.cfm*

Coleman, D. L. (1996). Individualizing justice through multiculturalism: The liberals' dilemma. *Columbia Law Review, 96*, 1093–1167.

Coleman, D. L. (1998). The Seattle compromise: Multicultural sensitivity and Americanization. *Duke Law Journal, 47*, 717–783.

Coleman, D. L. (2001). Culture, cloaked in mens rea. *South Atlantic Quarterly, 100*, 981–1004.

Coleman, D. L. (2005). Storming the castle to save the children: The ironic costs of a child welfare exception to the Fourth Amendment. *William and Mary Law Review*, *47*, 413–540.

Fadiman, A. (1997). *The spirit catches you and you fall down*. New York: Farrar, Straus & Giroux.

Howze, K. A. (1996). *Cultural context in abuse and neglect practice for judges and attorneys*. Washington, DC: American Bar Association.

In the Matter of Joanie Stumbo, et al., 582 S.E.2d 255 (N.C. 2003).

Indian Child Welfare Act. (1978). 25 U.S.C. §1901 et seq. Retrieved September 7, 2006, from *www4.law.cornell.edu/uscode/uscode25/usc_sup_01_25_10_21.html*

Indian Child Welfare Program. (1974, April 8–9). *Hearings Before the Subcommittee of Indian Affairs of the Committee on Interior and Insular Affairs, Unites States Senate, 99th Cong., 2nd Sess., On Problems that American Indian Families Face in Raising their Children and how these Problems are Affected by Federal Action or Inaction*. Retrieved September 7, 2006, from *www.liftingtheveil.org/byler.htm*

Jackson, V. (2005). *Draft NASW Policy on Cultural and Linguistic Competence in the Social Work Profession, Proposed Revisions for Consideration at the 2005 NASW Delegate Assembly*. Unpublished manuscript.

Lansford, J. E., Chang, L., Dodge, K. A., Malone, P. S., Oburu, P., Palmerus, K., et al. (2005). Physical discipline and children's adjustment: Cultural normativeness as a moderator. *Child Development*, *76*, 1234–1246.

Levesque, R. J. R. (2000). Cultural evidence, child maltreatment, and the law. *Child Maltreatment*, *5*, 146–160.

Maine v. Kargar, 679 A.2d 81 (1996).

Meyer v. Nebraska, 262 U.S. 390 (1923).

National Association of Social Workers. (2000). Cultural competence in the social work profession. In *Social work speaks: NASW policy statements* (pp. 59–62). Washington, DC: NASW Press.

National Association of Social Workers. (2001). *Standards for cultural competence in social work practice*. Retrieved September 7, 2006, from *www.socialworkers.org/sections/credentials/cultural_comp.asp*

Parham v. JR, 442 U.S. 584, 602 (1979).

Pierce v. Society of Sisters, 268 U.S. 510 (1925).

Renteln, A. D. (1994). Is the cultural defense detrimental to the health of children? In R. Kuppe & R. Potz (Eds.), *Law and anthropology: International yearbook for legal anthropology* (Vol. 7., pp. 27–106). Dordrecht, The Netherlands: Kluwer Academic.

Santosky v. Kramer, 455 U.S. 745 (1982).

Sing, J. J. (1999). Culture as sameness: Toward a synthetic view of provocation and culture in the criminal law. *Yale Law Journal*, *108*, 1845–1884.

Talbot, M. (August 11, 1997). Baghdad on the Plains. *The New Republic*. Retrieved September 7, 2006, from *members.tripod.com/jummahcrew/baghdad.htm*

Taylor, T. (1997). The cultural defense and its irrelevancy in child protection law. *Boston College Third World Law Journal*, *17*, 331–344.

Troxel v. Granville, 530 U.S. 57 (2000).

Volpp, L. (1994). (Mis)Identifying culture: Asian women and the "cultural defense." *Harvard Women's Law Journal*, *17*, 57–77.

Volpp, L. (1996). Talking "culture": Gender, race, nation, and the politics of multiculturalism. *Columbia Law Review*, *96*, 1573–1617.

Closing Thoughts

Kirby Deater-Deckard, Marc H. Bornstein,
and Jennifer E. Lansford

Why do some groups of foreign-born families—and particular individuals within those groups—show better "outcomes" than others? And what can we do, as social scientists, policymakers, practitioners, and engaged citizens, to use the answer to that question to improve the lives and communities of the children, parents, and grandparents for all families? For those who work with, advocate for, and study individuals and families in immigrant groups, these are the ultimate questions to answer.

In the afterword to this volume, Suárez-Orozco outlines the state of the science on immigrant families and describes directions that would be fruitful for additional attention. The work represented in this volume goes far in supplementing our scientific and policy fields' growing databases on immigrant families. However, this work is a snapshot of the current state of affairs. This realization, when coupled with the fact that the social and psychological processes that are operating in the real world are inordinately complex, can lead quickly to pessimism if one focuses on the barriers to knowledge and translation into social policy. However, there are also grounds for optimism about the opportunities that lie before us for making progress in research and practice that informs social policy in ways that benefit families in need. As these chapters attest, there is reasonable cause for drawing both conclusions (we suspect that all of the authors would agree that "the more you learn, the more you realize how little you know"). That conundrum aside, it is clear that what we are left with is more knowledge and a deeper appreciation of the complexities in the lives of immigrant families and our communities.

The cross-cultural research that is so well represented in this volume will continue to be conducted and will continue to transform our knowledge. This is because the study of immigrant families affords many opportunities from a basic social and behavioral science perspective. The study of populations of individuals as they enter and evolve within a new nation and culture is a unique quasi-experimental method that has the potential to answer many questions about the impact of cultural and biological factors on healthy and maladaptive outcomes. Today, many social and behavioral scientists understand that the study of diverse populations is necessary in its own right and at the same time constitutes a rigorous foundation for more basic empirical inquiry.

This field of research is not only moving, it is maturing. There already are, and will be in the future, opportunities for drawing solid conclusions about ways to alter social policy and practice to improve the lives of immigrant families. To this end, a "twin track" approach will be necessary. On the one hand, we need to be practical and seek out the most parsimonious explanations for the differences that we see in the outcomes of individuals in immigrant families or the differences between whole immigrant groups. On the other hand, we also should learn as much as we can about the intricacies and complexities of the lives of these individuals and groups.

Based on our reading of these chapters, it is clear that one of the most important factors is education. Bradley and McKelvey (Chapter 9), Waldfogel and Lahaie (Chapter 10), and Fuligni and Fuligni (Chapter 13) all point out in various ways a puzzle to be solved: that there is a need for more opportunities for education, though at the same time there remain barriers to immigrant families' utilization of educational opportunities that already exist. Although there is uncertainty about the extent to which immigrant families are underrepresented in early childhood and after-school education programs, there is evidence that access to childcare and formal schooling at all levels is impeded for foreign-born youth. This situation arises in part from parents not having information about educational opportunities and supports that are available to them (due to language or other communication barriers), and in part from society's tendency to overlook the strongly held beliefs about the value of education (not to mention many other strengths) among immigrant family members.

Physical and mental health care are also critically important. When it comes to such services, even the highest quality prevention and intervention programs—whether they target physical, mental, behavioral, or social outcomes—will fail if there is not careful consideration of the needs of the multiple constituencies involved (parents, children, practitioners, communities, and researchers). But the needs may be even more basic. Mendoza, Javier, and Burgos (Chapter 2) emphasize the importance of establishing stable systems of medical data gathering and reporting that are inclusive, as well as lowering barriers to access to existing physical and mental health care while also improving the cultural sensitivity of that care. Gonzales, Dumka, Mauricio, and Germán (Chapter 15) observe that there exists little in the way of rigorous empirical trials examining clinical psychosocial interventions for immigrant youth and families. Underrepresentation of immigrants in clinical trials remains a critical concern, as does the lack of methodical testing of culture-specific adaptations of current state-of-the-art programs. Bornstein and Cote (Chapter 7) underscore in comparative analyses of two immigrant groups the importance of parents' understanding parenting and child development. Similarly, Chase-Lansdale, D'Angelo, and Palacios (Chapter 8) urge scientists to do research that more adequately captures the processes underlying the health and development of the very youngest of immigrant children. Their model for moving the agenda forward has clear implications regarding the need for growing our knowledge about contextual and biological influences on the development of immigrant children.

The breadth of contexts and systems outside of the family that in fluence, and are influenced by, immigrant families is extensive. Updegraff, Crouter, Umaña-Taylor, and Cansler (Chapter 14) focus on one of these contexts: the world of work. They note that a disproportionate number of immigrant parents work in low-paying and sometimes dangerous jobs. What is needed are relatively inexpensive and widely available opportunities for technical skills and English language training, as well as more formalized education including the completion of high school—not to mention improving access to college, as well as continued vigilance against workplace discrimination. At the other end of the socioeconomic spectrum are the highly educated and sought-after Chinese professionals described by Wong (Chapter 12). These are individuals who have adapted their family lives to work within their transient, transnational employment situations. Family adaptations for wealthy immigrants have both positive and negative effects for parents and children alike. In one sense, Wong's chapter may warn researchers and policymakers not to delude themselves about education and well-paying work as "the solution" to the difficulties faced by immigrant families. In our rapidly changing global economy, having access to these resources surely resolves many impediments to successful outcomes, but also creates new challenges and problems that impinge on the family in ways that can be detrimental to children and adults alike.

The role of economics in immigration cannot be overstated. After all, families are economic units as well as social and psychological entities. Kaushal and Reimers (Chapter 6) show that in spite of the importance of economic realities to the lives of immigrant families, the data regarding the effects of economic changes on the outcomes of immigrant youth are surprisingly scant (surprising in light of the plethora of economic data that are otherwise collected). Coupled with this lack of basic information is an even larger gap in our knowledge about the shorter and longer term effects of legal status. It stands to reason that we probably know the least about the most vulnerable group of people who are both economically and legally at risk: undocumented immigrant workers and their children. Unfortunately, it also stands to reason that this population is the group of immigrants that social scientists are least likely to be able to study.

Families also are legal entities. Coleman's (Chapter 16) work reminds us that immigrant families are more likely to be exposed to legal risks arising from being from different cultures that use childrearing practices that may come into direct conflict with prevailing views regarding abuse and neglect. One of the bigger problems is the lack of knowledge or application of existing knowledge to the decision making surrounding the removal of children from the homes of immigrant parents whose behavior does not conform to interpreted standards of appropriate caregiving.

Differences between cultures have implications far beyond legal issues. Conflicts between the values of the majority and those of the immigrant's native culture play out in profound ways in the lives of foreign-born parents and children. An intricate tapestry of different values and beliefs shows many challenges to immigrant youth as they seek out their identities in multiethnic and multicultural societies. As Berry (Chapter 4) emphasizes, the processes of acculturation are complex and varied (both between distinct immigrant groups and within those groups), and the traditional view of a shared goal to assimilate simply does not explain what immigrant families and youth are doing. In addition, acculturation is operating not only at the level of the individual, but also at the levels of the family, the community, and the entire cultural group.

The intersection of these different levels of analysis and conflicts in values is apparent in the lives of the families described by Ross-Sheriff, Tirmazi, and Walsh (Chapter 11). They show the various ways that Muslim mothers utilize and contribute to their Muslim American community as they strive to rear devout daughters and grandchildren. This striving occurs against a backdrop of a prevailing culture that values individuality and materialism over spirituality and communalism. More generally, Phinney and Ong (Chapter 3) describe the developing ethnic identities of youth in immigrant families. The development of children's ethnic identities has far-reaching and long-lasting effects, not only on their own and their families' adaptation and well-being but on their views of other foreign-born and native-born individuals and groups. Accordingly, it is in everyone's best interest to support ethnic identity development and expression of ethnic and cultural values and practices among immigrant youth and their families.

Unfortunately, the conflicts in values that exist between the beliefs of the larger society and those of each distinct immigrant group are instantiated in the tendency of some social scientists and policymakers to apply "deficit models" to nonmajority immigrant groups. As Tyyskä (Chapter 5) emphasizes from the field of sociology, numerous research literatures continue to contrast the majority and the immigrant cultures of the family as though each group was homogeneous. She proposes that this way of thinking plays out in many aspects of our social, economic, educational, legal, and political worlds as well, with the result being stable discriminatory policies and practices—one of the broadest barriers to accessing resources, as pointed out by a number of authors in this volume.

When it comes to applying the implications of all of the research embodied here, some humbling pragmatic concerns come to the fore. First, it is clear given the demographic situation described by Hernandez, Denton, and Macartney (Chapter 1) that understanding how best to meet the needs of immigrant families is of vital importance given their large and increasing presence in U.S. society. However, to be of any use to policymakers and practitioners, empirical inquiries into the lives of immigrant families ultimately should identify a handful of key factors that are both powerful (in the statistical sense) and modifiable—all the while being identified in research that still captures as much of the breadth and depth of the immigrant family experience as possible. But like the diversity of the research represented by the chapters in this volume, the broader literature on immigrant family health and development has not yet converged on what these key factors are or should be. However, there are some contenders that deserve emphasis, including access to education and vocational training, stable and safe employment, adequate physical and mental health care, and legal protection and services. One theme that runs through this volume is that the more problematic outcomes observed for immigrant children and their families arise from barriers to *access* to these very resources.

The key factors that are identified and emphasized in social policy and practice should first stand up to rigorous scrutiny in the field and in the laboratory. To be of broad utility, these factors must not only survive this scrutiny but also emerge as influences that can be generalized to large populations of immigrant parents and youth. Candidate factors that are statistically powerful in predicting outcomes and that lend themselves to being altered through good social policy and clinical practice are, nevertheless, curtailed severely if they operate only for a particular subgroup of people under certain circumstances. At the same time, these factors have to be considered within the political, social, and economic contexts that surround immigrant families, and how these contexts alter the effects of these key factors in the lives of parents and youth.

The models for how these factors operate must not ignore the agency of the individual. Regardless of nation of birth or generation, people differ widely from each other in their competencies and weaknesses, goals and motivations, beliefs, appraisals, and interpretations of their experiences. A number of the chapters in this volume help us get "inside the heads" of immigrant parents and youth. They also address the inherent heterogeneity of families *within* every immigrant and ethnic group being studied. Understanding what it is that explains differences in experiences and outcomes within, as well as between, identifiable national and ethnic immigrant groups will certainly improve our understanding of the processes that promote the best outcomes—and this certainly will require the examination of external and internal psychological and social factors.

With so much emphasis on the need to examine differences between immigrant groups and people more generally, it is easy to forget that nearly all parents—regardless of sex, age, race, ethnicity, or nationality—seek to lead happy, healthy lives and to have happy, healthy children, grandchildren, and great-grandchildren. This is why parents make great sacrifices for their partners and children, including moving to other regions, nations, and continents—sometimes at great legal, economic, and physical peril. The debates about our knowledge and social policies that stem from the examination of differences between people will be well served if we all strive to remember this universal goal held by family members around the world.

Afterword

Reflections on Research with Immigrant Families

Carola Suárez-Orozco

The forces of globalization are transforming economies, cultures, societies, and families. International flows of trade and capital along with large-scale political, religious, and ethnic upheavals have led to unprecedented levels of worldwide migration. As a result, at the beginning of the new millennium, there are nearly 200 million immigrants and refugees worldwide (United Nations, 2005). New immigrants to America, for example, are extraordinarily diverse, and their experiences resist facile generalizations. Nearly 80% come from Latin America, Asia, and the Caribbean. They bring with them an astonishingly wide array of languages, religions, cultural beliefs, and practices. Some come from highly educated professional backgrounds, others are illiterate and low skilled, struggling in the lowest paid sectors of the service economy (Suárez-Orozco, 2000). Some are escaping political, religious, or ethnic persecution; others are lured by the promise of better jobs and the hope for better educational opportunities. Some families have officially documented legal status, some do not, and still others have families with mixed documentation—some siblings are documented and others are not. Some come to settle permanently, some come as sojourners with the intent to return to their homeland after a specified period of time, and others move from one migrant work camp to another. Some engage in transnational strategies, living both "here and there"—shuttling between their country of birth and their country of choice (Levitt, 2001). The immigrant journey today follows complex paths bifurcating into divergent experiences and varied outcomes—some thrive with immigration, whereas others struggle, all too quickly joining the "rainbow underclasses" (Portes & Zhou, 1993).

Migration is fundamentally a family affair. Young men take the migratory voyage to earn enough money to purchase a home so that they can start a family. Older daughters and sons leave home to send back remittances to support their parents and younger siblings. Young fathers leave home to support their wives and children when the economy in their region does not provide jobs with living wages. Widows leave their children to feed them. Children join their parents who went ahead some years before. More often than not, family obligations and family ties are the very foundation of the arduous immigrant voyage.

The process of migration, however, asserts a tremendous stress on family members in myriad ways. Families often must be apart for long periods of time before they can come together (see Wong, Chapter 12, this volume). The losses and stresses of immigration often lead to parents who report feeling depressed. The pressures to survive economically in the new land while sending back remittances to the family in the country of origin lead parents to work multiple jobs and long hours. Children acculturate more quickly than their parents, turning family roles on their heads. These myriad pressures serve as both centripetal and centrifugal forces in immigrant families (Falicov, 1980, 1998; Suárez-Orozco & Suárez-Orozco, 2001).[1] Yet the family as a unit of analysis has been understudied by scholars of migration. In part, this state of affairs may be linked to the challenge of conducting sound research with immigrant families given the magnitude, diversity, and complexity of the migratory phenomenon as well as the dearth of cross-culturally effective and meaningful research strategies. This volume goes far in addressing this gap in the literature by taking a family perspective on immigration.

At the eve of the 21st century, the scholarship of migration was dominated by demographers (focusing on where the new immigrants were from and where they were settling; see Hernandez, Denton, & Macartney, Chapter 1, this volume), economists (concerned with understanding the economic forces that push migrants from their homes and lure them to new destinations as well as establishing the fiscal and wage implications of immigrants' economies in their society of destination; see Kaushal & Reimers, Chapter 6, this volume), sociologists (investigating how immigrants were adapting to the new society; see Tyyskä, Chapter 5, this volume), and anthropologists (inquiring into what cultural practices the new immigrants brought with them and how those in the society of destination responded to them; see Berry, Chapter 4, this volume). However, past disciplinary gazes for the most part took a telescopic view.

The more family- and person-centered aspects of migration—a logical purview of the discipline of psychology—have only recently begun to fall within the gaze of this discipline (see Bornstein & Cote, Chapter 7, this volume). Each of these disciplines represents an important point of view and, when taken together, provide an even more complete and complex understanding of immigrant families. In this Afterword, I briefly review gaps in the literature, how this volume addresses some of those lacunae, and I make recommendations for further research on the migratory experience—a growing issue encountered in nearly every postindustrial nation.

SIGNIFICANT GAPS IN MIGRATION RESEARCH

Neglected Populations

Research on immigrant origin groups tends to focus on so-called "problem" populations. Research abounds around why Latinos are not doing better as a group in the educational system or how particular groups are overrepresented in the penal system or in gangs. Conversely, researchers also look toward the other end of the continuum—the so-called "model minority" (Lee, 1996). Asian immigrants are often held up as the gold standard—why can't children of other groups do as well as Asian students? This stereotype, while on the surface flattering, politically pits groups against one another and ignores the fact that many Asian-origin Americans also struggle with structural barriers (Lee, 1996). Furthermore, groups that tend neither to overachieve nor to dramatically underachieve are often underresearched. Filipinos are an example—there is little research in this group, although they were until recently the second largest country of origin group in the United States. Ross-Sheriff, Tirmazi, and Walsh (Chapter 11, this volume) contribute to the study of neglected populations by focusing on South Asian Muslim mothers, and Bornstein and Cote (Chapter 7, this volume) add to the literature by studying immigrants from Japan, Korea, and South America.

Pan-Ethnic Confabulation

Much of the research that could shed light on the immigrant family experience tends to examine pan-ethnic categories (such as Latinos, Asians, and African Americans). This kind of work, while important, tends to lose sight of the wide variety of incoming resources and generational patterns that exist within these larger designations. Chapters in this volume pay careful attention to how experiences may differ for first, second, and later generations of immigrants and how factors such as socioeconomic resources shape immigrants' experiences.

At over 43 million individuals, the complex category of Latinos represents well over half of all immigrants to the United States (U.S. Census Bureau, 2006). Latinos are extraordinarily diverse—some have ancestors who were established on what is now U.S. territory long before the current borders were set through conquest and land purchases. On the other hand, 40% of Latinos are born abroad. Mexican Americans, Puerto Ricans, and Cubans have historically been the most represented groups in the aggregated Latino category. In recent decades, however, large numbers of Latinos have been immigrating from dozens of countries (such as Ecuador, Colombia, and Brazil), which fuel this burgeoning population. Today, an estimated two-thirds of Latinos are either immigrants or the children of immigrants (Suárez-Orozco & Paez, 2002). Latinos tend to share Spanish as the common language of origin (with the exception of the Brazilians and indigenous speakers), but language loss is very rapid across generations and it is rare to encounter a completely fluent Spanish speaker by the third generation (Portes & Rumbaut, 2001). The sending countries, areas of settlement, historical timing of migration, political climate, and economic circumstances vary considerably for Latinos from different countries of origin. This array of backgrounds and experiences challenges any semblance of Latino homogeneity.

The Asian and Pacific Islander population in the United States has grown rapidly since the 1990s. Currently, this population is estimated to include 12.5 million, totaling 4.3% of the U.S. population. This broad category includes individuals from a wide array of countries including China, the Philippines, Japan, Korea, Vietnam, Thailand, Laos, India, Pakistan, Bangladesh, and others. These countries represent a range of cultural traditions, religious practices, and languages. Some are amongst the most educated (Indians on average have higher levels of educational attainment than native-born U.S. citizens), but others have low levels of literacy (e.g., Laotians, Hmong, and individuals from the Fujian province of China). More than two-thirds of Asian and Pacific Islanders in the United States are born abroad, but some have been here for many generations and have high rates of intermarriage with native-born U.S. citizens (U.S. Census Bureau, 2006; see Hernandez et al., Chapter 1, this volume).

From the earliest inception of U.S. history, Africans were brought as involuntary migrants. The descendants of slavery made up approximately 10% of the population at the turn of the 20th century—currently African Americans compose 12.8% of the total U.S. population. At that time, only .02% of the black population were of voluntary immigrant origin; today, this has changed considerably as African and West Indian/

Caribbean immigrants account for over 6% of the black population (Tormala & Deaux, 2006.) In New York, one-third of the black population is of immigrant origin from such diverse sending countries as Ghana, Jamaica, Guyana, and Haiti. Again, within this population there is tremendous diversity. On one end of the spectrum, a high proportion of Ghanaian doctors are practicing in New York rather than in their country where they were trained (Mullan, 2005); at another end, many of the newest wave of Haitian immigrants have limited literacy and interrupted schooling. Some arrive with elite experiences, but others have encountered tremendous violence and arrive suffering from posttraumatic stress disorder. These experiences have implications for family life and adaptation to the new society.

Immigrant Youth

Research in the field of migration has focused on immigrant adults. The immigrant child and youth experience has largely been neglected (García-Coll & Magnuson, 1997; Suárez-Orozco & Suárez-Orozco, 2001). This is quite puzzling given that, at the turn of the century, one in five children growing up in the United States is a child of immigrants and that proportion is projected to increase to one in three by 2030 (Rong & Preissle, 1998). Migration certainly presents a variety of challenges to the development of immigrant youth (Phinney & Ong, Chapter 3, this volume; Suárez-Orozco & Suárez-Orozco, 2001) including disrupted networks or relations and family separations (Suárez-Orozco, Todorova, & Louie, 2002),[2] parents who are unavailable because they work long hours or are depressed (Ahearn & Athey, 1991), a hostile ethos of reception (Suárez-Orozco, 2000), neighborhood and school segregation (Orfield & Yun, 1999), and challenges to identity formation (Suárez-Orozco, 2004). It is notable, therefore, that several chapters in this volume are devoted to the experiences of immigrant children and adolescents (Bradley & McKelvey, Chapter 9; Chase-Lansdale, D'Angelo, & Palacios, Chapter 8; Coleman, Chapter 16; Gonzales, Dumka, Mauricio, & Germán, Chapter 15; Ross-Sheriff et al., Chapter 11; Updegraff, Crouter, Umaña-Taylor, & Cansler, Chapter 14; Waldfogel & Lahaie, Chapter 10).

Academic adaptations are a particular area of importance for research because for newcomer children schools are the primary entry point into the society of destination as well as the first setting of sustained contact with the new culture. Furthermore, academic outcomes are a powerful barometer of current as well as future psychosocial functioning (Mandel & Marcus, 1988; Steinberg, Brown, & Dornbusch, 1996). Much of the research literature on immigrant youth has focused on questions related to second-language acquisition. The immigrant family research in this area all too often tends to fall into a "blame the family" paradigm (e.g., Why don't immigrant families participate in school activities more?, Why do some groups of origin "value" education more than others?). Given the numbers of youth involved, clearly how these children adapt and the educational pathways they take will have profound implications for society. This is a fertile area for important future research. Chapters in this volume by Bradley and McKelvey (Chapter 9), Waldfogel and Lahaie (Chapter 10), and Fuligni and Fuligni (Chapter 13) move the field in exciting new directions in terms of understanding the educational needs of immigrant children.

Gendered Patterns of Adaptation

Gendered migratory experiences are another domain of significant neglect within the immigration research community. Scholars too often fail to consider whether or not women are motivated by the same forces as men as well as how women's experiences within the new context may or may not differ from that of their male counterparts. There is ample evidence to suggest that there are many dimensions of experience that differ for males and females (Hongdagneu-Sotelo, 1999; Mahler, 1999; Pessar, 1989). Females seem to do better within academic contexts, for example, and young men tend to contend with a more unforgiving, hostile reception within the new county (Suárez-Orozco & Qin-Hilliard, 2004). However, assuming that gender always leads to different experiences is a mistake. Although there are certainly differences between immigrant males and females there are also many similarities (Cornell, 2000; Suárez-Orozco & Qin-Hilliard, 2004, 2006). Many of the dimensions we have examined over the years have revealed *no* gender differences, including attitudes toward teachers, perceptions of school safety, attitudes toward Americans, self-reports of somatization, and hostility (Suárez-Orozco & Qin-Hilliard, 2004; Suárez-Orozco & Suárez-Orozco, 1995). We have also found that often country of origin trumps gender—that is to say being from a particular country of origin has more salience (or is more predictive) than being a particular gender. Although it is important to consider gender, it is also important to recognize that nonfindings of overlap in attitudes, behaviors, and experiences are in some ways as interesting as findings of differences. Future research should consider *how, when* and *why* it makes a difference to be an immigrant or to be from a particular country or to be female rather than male (Eckes & Trautner, 2000; see Tyyskä, Chapter 5, this volume).

Focus on Pathology

Psychologists in particular, but social scientists in general, have focused excessively on pathology. Much research has searched for links between the stresses of the migratory experience and expected negative fallout (depression, marital conflict, crises of identity, incarceration rates, and the like) resulting from that experience (Ainslie, 1998; Arredondo-Dowd, 1980; Grinberg & Grinberg, 1990; Sluzki, 1979; Suárez-Orozco, 2000).[3] When sampling from a nonclinical population, the data that have emerged have demonstrated little relation between migration and psychopathology, however (Suárez-Orozco & Qin-Hilliard, 2006). Though few studies examine mental health issues in the country of origin, there is some evidence that there is not a significant difference between nonmigrants in their country of origin and migrants in a new setting. Furthermore, when comparing immigrants to nonimmigrants, it appears that immigrants do not demonstrate significantly higher rates of psychopathology than do nonimmigrants (Arorian, 1990; Noh, Speechley, Kaspar, & Wu, 1992).

This general finding that the link between migration and negative mental health outcomes is relatively weak is consistent with growing, if counterintuitive, evidence that the first generation in fact seems to do better on a variety of indicators of well-being when compared to second-generation as well as native-born peers (Davies & McKelvey, 1998; Hernández & Charney, 1998). Several international large-scale studies have replicated this epidemiological paradox in Canada (e.g., Beiser, Hou, Dion, Gotowiec, Hyman, & Vu, 1995), in New Zealand (e.g., Davies & McKelvey, 1998), as well as in Europe. First-generation immigrants seem to do considerably better on a number of mental and physical health indicators in spite of their higher poverty levels (see Mendoza, Javier, & Burgos, Chapter 2, this volume).

The underlying explanation for this phenomenon has yet to be proven, but a number of potential explanations could be considered. There may be a selective pattern of migration—individuals with greater psychological and physical robustness may be more likely to embark on the immigrant journey. First-generation immigrants may also engage in healthier cultural practices. The longer they are in the country of destination, the more likely they are to assimilate to less healthy habits—greater dependence on processed, high-fat, low-fiber fast food; employment in work sectors that require less physical exertion; greater likelihood to abuse substances; and the like. Those in the first generation may be more likely to draw on the inoculating effects of the dual frame of reference between the country of origin and the new setting ("My lot is in substantive ways better here than there") (Suárez-Orozco & Suárez-Orozco,

1995) as well as hope (Suárez-Orozco & Suárez-Orozco, 2001). Furthermore, the 1.5 generation and beyond may be made more vulnerable as a result of developing in the face of a negative social mirror that reflects back a distorted negative image of their worth and potential (Suárez-Orozco, 2000). The chapters in this volume consider not simply pathological outcomes but also the particular strengths and resiliencies that may emerge through migration.

BEST PRACTICES IN FUTURE IMMIGRANT FAMILY RESEARCH

Cross-cultural research on immigrants forces us to reexamine the traditional social science assumptions around validity and reliability (McLoyd & Steinberg, 1998; Suárez-Orozco & Suárez-Orozco, 1995). Questions and prompts that are valid for one group may not be so for another (Bornstein, 1995). Hence, it is a challenge to develop single instruments or approaches that capture the experiences of individuals from a variety of backgrounds (for real-world examples in the legal system, see Coleman, Chapter 16, this volume). There is a growing consensus in the field of cross-cultural research that mixed-method designs, linking emic (insider) and etic (outsider) approaches, triangulating data, and embedding emerging findings into an ecological framework, are essential to this kind of endeavor (Branch, 1999; Bronfenbrenner, 1979; Doucette-Gates, Brooks-Gunn, & Chase-Lansdale, 1998; Hughes, Seidman, & Edwards, 1993; Sue & Sue, 1987).

The goal of research should be to capture the migratory experience in all of its subtleties—understanding that there are many common denominators of experience between the groups of origin while recognizing the specificity of experience of particular groups as well as individuals. To paraphrase Clyde Kluckhohn (1949), every immigrant is like all other immigrants, like some other immigrants, and like no other immigrants. The accomplished researcher should strive to capture that reality. The complex model presented by Chase-Lansdale and colleagues (Chapter 8, this volume) is an admirable framework within which to understand many of these subtleties.

Briefly, I now turn to some broad recommendations for researchers of migration.

Interdisciplinary Collaborations

Migrations are complex and outcomes are multiply determined. We must recognize that this domain requires interdisciplinary, mixed-method strategies to achieve any depth. Psychologists need the perspective of the sociological understanding of social forces (such as power inequities) as well as the cultural insights that anthropologists can provide. Interdisciplinary teams whose members are "bicultural" in one another's methodologies lead to more robust research contributions. The works in this volume reflect a significant contribution in this direction.

Etic and Emic Perspectives

Combining "outsider" (etic) and "insider"(emic) approaches to diverse populations is important in the phases of both data collection and analysis (Cooper, Jackson, Azmitia, & Lopez, 1998). Bicultural and bilingual researchers are better able to establish rapport and trust within their communities and gain entry into immigrant populations that might otherwise be difficult to access. Furthermore, insiders are essential for appropriate linguistic and cultural translations of protocols. Their perspective is also essential to accurate and culturally relevant interpretations. If the research is not conducted by members of the immigrant community, it is essential that cultural experts be consulted in the development of instruments as well as the interpretation of findings. Outsiders provide a fresh interpretive perspective and may lend specific disciplinary expertise. Interpretive communities of "insiders" and "outsiders" as well as individuals representing a range of disciplinary expertise are strongly recommended.

Culturally Sensitive Tools

Research protocols should always be provided in the dominant language of the informant. Measures developed with mainstream English-speaking populations (as are many standardized instruments) are often culturally and linguistically biased (Doucette-Gates et al., 1998). New tools, either adapting preexisting instruments or developing entirely new approaches, often must be developed for research with immigrants. The process of development should be dynamic and inductive involving theoretically based formulations along with themes emerging from the field. As culturally informed questionnaires are developed, they must be carefully translated and piloted.

Triangulated Data

Using triangulated data in multiple settings and taking multiple perspectives is crucial when faced with the challenges of validity in conducting research with groups of diverse backgrounds. A variety of approaches and sources of data instills greater confidence that the data accurately capture the phenomenon under consideration. Researchers should consider various levels of analysis in their research including the individual, interpersonal relationships, context-specific social groups (e.g., workforce peers, church members), as well as cultural dimensions. Triangulated data serve to counteract the inherent limitations of self-report data—a problem that may be exaggerated among immigrant youth. By sifting through a variety of perspectives—self-reports, parent reports, teacher reports (in the case of youth), or other community members (in the case of adults) as well as researcher observations—concurrence and disconnections can be established between what informants say they do, what others say they do, and what the researcher sees them do.

Sending and Host Contexts Perspectives

Researchers should consider the historical, political, and cultural forces at work, not simply within the country of destination but also that of sending countries. Within the sending context, for example, the circumstances surrounding the migration, the socioeconomic background of the immigrants, whether or not there has been a rural to urban shift, as well as how cohesive the family is and whether or not they were separated as a result of the migration, can greatly affect postmigratory adjustment. Within the receiving context, the available networks of social relationships, whether or not immigrants are documented, neighborhood segregation, the availability of work for adults, and the quality of schools for youth as well as the ethos of reception toward the particular immigrant group and the disparagement and social mirroring they may encounter all will contribute to variable pathways of adjustment (see, e.g., Updegraff et al., Chapter 14, this volume).

Longitudinal Perspectives

Cross-sectional data are necessarily limited because they limit the ability to detect change over time. Though time consuming and expensive, longitudinal research has much to offer and should be pursued when possible (Fuligni, 2001; Suárez-Orozco & Suárez-Orozco, 2001; Suárez-Orozco, Suárez-Orozco, & Todorova, in press).

Comparison Samples

Whenever possible, it is important to incorporate nonimmigrants within the country of destination as well as nonimmigrants in the sending culture into the study design. Are immigrants different from peers who have not migrated in their country of origin or from native-born peers in the host country? These comparison groups provide "baselines" to contextualize findings (see Suárez-Orozco & Suárez-Orozco, 1995).

Considering Understudied Groups

The majority of work in the United States has focused on Latinos and most especially those of Mexican, Puerto Rican, Cuban, and Central American origins. We need to expand research to consider South Americans, Caribbeans, and other ethnic groups from a variety of Asian, Eastern European, and African origins (in this volume, see Bornstein & Cote, Chapter 7; Ross-Sheriff et al., Chapter 11; Wong, Chapter 12).

Immigrant Generations

Researchers should recognize the differences between the first, the 1.5 generation, and the second generation and beyond in their analyses. This is a frequently ignored dimension of analyses. Much of the work on Latinos in particular simply ignores generational dimensions altogether. Identity research (see Phinney & Ong, Chapter 3, this volume) is an example of where generation is extremely relevant; while grappling to establish an ethnic, racial, and country identity is a central task of the 1.5, second, and third generation, this task is of little consequence for newly arrived immigrants (whose identity tends to stay quite linked to their country of origin).

Developmental Perspectives

Sociologists and anthropologists have provided great insight into the experience of migration for adults but have neglected youth. Developmental scientists have much to offer in providing a nuanced developmental perspective about immigrants across a range of developmental stages including early childhood, latency, adolescence, and adulthood.

Racial Awareness

Overlooking the racialized experiences of immigrants is a serious oversight. Immigrants encounter very different receptions depending on whether or not they are "racially marked" by phenotype (Bailey, 2001; López, 2002; Waters, 1999). Given the color spectrum represented by new immigrants, keeping this perspective in mind is essential while conducting research into the adaptation of new immigrants in a racially conscious society.

Strategic Sampling

The settings from which informants and participants are drawn are likely to influence the kinds of conclusions at which we arrive. If we sample from a clinical context, we are likely to find more pathological outcomes. Drawing representative samples is critical, though challenging, in static group comparisons (Campbell & Stanley, 1963). In our analyses, and as we draw conclusions, we must always ask ourselves if and how our sample may or may not be representative.

Theory Building

Researchers should willingly engage in theory building as part of the process of doing research. When observations of differences are made, theories of why and under what circumstances those differences occur should be developed. The next stage of research should then involve testing hypotheses that emerge from those theories.

Focus on Resilience

Research should consider sources of resilience that arise from the migratory experience. For example, are such inoculating traits as hope, perseverance, and capacity to delay gratification more often found among immigrants than their native-born peers? Immigrant families bring with them many strengths (e.g., the centrality of the family unit, the value of educational pursuits, a sense of family purpose) as well as challenges (e.g., frequent and long family separations as a result of migration, poverty, acculturative tensions; Suárez-Orozco et al., in press). This shift to a consideration of both challenges and strengths has the potential to deepen our understanding considerably.

In this Afterword, I have outlined what have historically been the most glaring oversights in past immigrant research, shown how this volume addresses some of them, and made a number of recommendations for future research. Meaningful understanding requires insights provided by parallel fields of the social sciences. Interdisciplinary, triangulated research is essential to begin to unpackage the nuanced effects of migration on families and youth, considering its particular challenges as well as its protective characteristics. This volume presents a rich collection of studies that exemplify the coming state-of-the-art research on immigrant families.

NOTES

1. Research on the migratory experience done by psychologists has tended to examine four broad domains: (1) acculturative stress and migration morbidity, (2) relational strains in family dynamics, (3) the challenges in identity formation, and (4) educational outcomes.
2. Immigrant youth often immigrate not just to new homes but also to new family structures. In our study of 400 immigrant youth to the United States coming from a variety of sending origins including Central America, China, the Dominican Republic, Mexico, and Haiti, we found that fully 85% of the youth had been separated from one or both parents for periods of several months to several years.
3. It should be noted that these outcomes would most likely more pronounced among refugees.

REFERENCES

Ahearn, F. L., & Athey, J. L. (1991). *Refugee children: Theory, research and services*. Baltimore: Johns Hopkins University Press.

Ainslie, R. (1998). Cultural mourning, immigration, and engagement: Vignettes from the Mexican experience. In M. M. Suárez-Orozco (Ed.), *Crossings: Mexican immigration in interdisciplinary perspectives* (pp. 283–300). Cambridge, MA: David Rockefeller Center for Latin American Studies/Harvard University Press.

Aroian, K. J. (1990). A model of psychological adaptation to immigration and resettlement. *Nursing Research, 39*, 5–10.

Arredondo-Dowd, P. (1980). *The development process in the bilingual immigrant adolescent's identity search*. Unpublished manuscript.

Bailey, B. H. (2001). Dominican-American ethnic/racial identities and United States social categories. *International Migration Review, 35*, 677–708.

Beiser, M., Dion, R., Gotowiec, A., Hyman, I., & Vu, N. (1995). Immigrant and refugee children in Canada. *Canadian Journal of Psychiatry, 40*, 67–72.

Bornstein, M. H. (1995), Form and function: Implications for studies of culture and human development. *Culture and Psychology, 1*, 123–137.

Branch, C. W. (1999). Race and human development. In R. H. Sheets & E. R. Hollins (Eds.), *Racial and ethnic identity in school practices: Aspects of human development* (pp. 7–28). Mahwah, NJ: Erlbaum.

Bronfenbrenner, U. (1979). *The ecology of human development*. Cambridge, MA: Harvard University Press.

Campbell, D. T., & Stanley, J. C. (1963). *Experimental and quasi-experimental designs for research*. Chicago: Rand-McNally.

Cooper, C. R., Jackson, J. F., Azmitia, M., & Lopez, E. M. (1998). Multiple selves, multiple worlds: Three useful strategies for research with ethnic minority youth on identity, relationship and opportunity structures. In V. McLoyd & L. Steinberg (Eds.), *Studying minority adolescents: Conceptual, methodological, and theoretical issues* (pp. 111–125). Mahwah, NJ: Erlbaum.

Cornell, R. W. (2000). *Men and boys*. Berkeley: University of California Press.

Darvies, L. G., & McKelvey, R. S. (1998). Emotional and behavioural problems and competencies among immigrant and non-immigrant adolescents. *Australian and New Zealand Journal of Psychiatry, 35*(5), 658–665.

Doucette-Gates, A., Brooks-Gunn, J., & Chase-Lansdale, L. P. (1998). The role of bias and equivalence in the study of race, class, and ethnicity. In V. C. McLoyd & L. Steinberg (Eds.), *Studying minority adolescents: Conceptual, methodological, and theoretical issues* (pp. 211–236). Mahwah, NJ: Erlbaum.

Eckes, T., & Trautner, H. M. (Eds.). (2000). *The developmental social psychology of gender.* Mahwah, NJ: Erlbaum.

Falicov, C. J. (1980). Cultural variations in the family life cycle: The Mexican American family. In M. McGoldrick (Ed.), *The family life cycle: A framework for family therapy.* New York: Gardner Press.

Falicov, C. J. (1998). *Latino families in therapy: A guide to multicultural practice.* New York: Guilford Press.

Fuligni, A. (2001). A comparative longitudinal approach to acculturation among children from immigrant families. *Harvard Educational Review, 71,* 566–578.

García-Coll, C., & Magnuson, K. (1997). The psychological experience of immigration: A developmental perspective. In A. Booth, A. C. Crouter, & N. Landale (Eds.), *Immigration and the family: Research and policy on U.S. immigrants* (pp. 91–131). Mahwah, NJ: Erlbaum.

Grinberg, L., & Grinberg, R. (1990). *Psychoanalytic perspectives on migration and exile.* New Haven, CT: Yale University Press.

Hernández, D., & Charney, E. (Eds.). (1998). *From generation to generation: The health and well-being of children of immigrant families.* Washington, DC: National Academy Press.

Hongdagneu-Sotelo, P. (1999). Gender and contemporary U.S. immigration. *American Behavioral Scientist, 42,* 565–576.

Hughes, D., Seidman, E., & Edwards, D. (1993). Cultural phenomena and the research enterprise: Toward a culturally anchored methodology. *American Journal of Community Psychology, 21,* 687–703.

Kluckhohn, C. (1949). *Mirror for man: The relation of anthropology to modern life.* New York: Whitssley House.

Lee, S. (1996). *Unraveling the "model minority" stereotype: Listening to Asian American youth.* New York: Teachers College Press.

Levitt, P. (2001). *The transnational villagers.* Berkeley: University of California Press.

López, N. (2002). *Hopeful girls, troubled boys: Race and gender disparity in urban education.* New York: Routledge.

Mahler, S. J. (1999). Engendering transnational migration: A case study of Salvadorans. *American Behavioral Scientist, 42,* 690–719.

Mandel, H. P., & Marcus, S. I. (1988). *The psychology of underachievement: Differential diagnosis and differential treatment.* New York: Wiley.

McLoyd, V., & Steinberg, L. (Eds.). (1998). *Studying minority adolescents: Conceptual, methodological, and theoretical issues.* Mahwah, NJ: Erlbaum.

Mullan, F. (2005). The metrics of the physician brain drain. *New England Journal of Medicine, 353,* 1810–1818.

Noh, S., Speechley, M., Kasper, V., & Wu, Z. (1992). Depression in Korean immigrants in Canada. I. Method of the study and prevalence of depression. *Journal of Nervous and Mental Disease, 180*, 573–577.

Orfield, G., & Yun, J. T. (1999). *Resegregation in American schools*. Cambridge, MA: The Civil Rights Project, Harvard University.

Pessar, P. R. (1989). *The Dominicans: Women in the household and the garment industry* (N. Foner, Ed.). Santa Fe, NM: School for American Research.

Portes, A., & Rumbaut, R. G. (2001). *Legacies: The story of the second generation*. Berkeley: University of California Press.

Portes, A., & Zhou, M. (1993). The new second generation: Segmented assimilation and its variants. *The Annals of the American Academy of Political and Social Science, 530*, 74–96.

Rong, X. L., & Preissle, J. (1998). *Educating immigrant students: What we need to know to meet the challenges*. Thousand Oaks, CA: Corwin Press.

Sluzki, C. (1979). Migration and family conflict. *Family Process, 18*, 379–390.

Steinberg, S., Brown, B. B., & Dornbusch, S. M. (1996). *Beyond the classroom*. New York: Simon & Schuster.

Suárez-Orozco, C. (2000). Identities under siege: Immigration stress and social mirroring among the children of immigrants. In A. Robben & M. Suárez-Orozco (Eds.), *Cultures under siege: Social violence and trauma* (pp. 194–226). Cambridge, UK: Cambridge University Press.

Suárez-Orozco, C. (2004). Formulating identity in a globalized world. In M. Suárez-Orozco & D. B. Qin-Hilliard (Eds.), *Globalization: Culture and education in the new millennium* (pp. 173–202). Berkeley: University of California Press & Ross Institute.

Suárez-Orozco, C., & Qin-Hilliard, D. B. (2004). The cultural psychology of academic engagement: Immigrant boys' experiences in U.S. schools. In N. Way & J. Chu (Eds.), *Adolescent boys: Exploring diverse cultures of boyhood* (pp. 295–316). New York: New York University Press.

Suárez-Orozco, C., & Qin-Hilliard, D. B. (2006). Gendered perspectives in psychology: Immigrant origin youth. *International Migration Review, 40*(1), 165–198.

Suárez-Orozco, C., & Suárez-Orozco, M. (1995). *Transformations: Immigration, family life, and achievement motivation among Latino adolescents*. Stanford, CA: Stanford University Press.

Suárez-Orozco, C., & Suárez-Orozco, M. (2001). *Children of immigration* (4th ed.). Cambridge, MA: Harvard University Press.

Suárez-Orozco, C., Suárez-Orozco, M., & Todorova, I. (in press). *Learning in a new land: Immigrant students in American society*. Cambridge, MA: Harvard University Press.

Suárez-Orozco, C., Todorova, I., & Louie, J. (2002). Making up for lost time: The experience of separations and reunifications among immigrant families. *Family Process, 41*, 625–643.

Suárez-Orozco, M., & Paez, M. (2002). *Latinos: Remaking America*. Berkeley: University of California Press.

Sue, D., & Sue, S. (1987). Cultural factors in the clinical assessment of Asian Americans. *Journal of Consulting and Clinical Psychology, 55*, 579–487.

Tormala, T. T., & Deaux, K. (2006). Black immigrants to the United States: Confronting and constructing ethnicity and race. In R. Mahalingam (Ed.), *Cultural psychology of immigrants* (pp. 131–150). Mahwah, NJ: Erlbaum.

United Nations. (2005). *Trends in the total migrant stock*. Department of Economic and Social Affairs, Population Division. Available at *www.un.org/esa/population/publications/migration/UN_Migrant_Stock_Documentation_2005.pdf*

U.S. Census Bureau. (2006). *The 2005 American community survey.* Washington, DC: Author.

Waters, M. (1999). *Black identities: West Indian dreams and American realities.* Cambridge, MA: Harvard University Press.

Index

Page numbers followed by an *f* indicate figure, *t* indicate table

N

S

T

U

V

W